D0897593

The Relationship of Verbal
and Nonverbal Communication

Contributions to the Sociology of Language

25

Joshua A. Fishman
Editor

MOUTON PUBLISHERS · THE HAGUE · PARIS · NEW YORK

The Relationship of Verbal and Nonverbal Communication

Edited by
Mary Ritchie Key

MOUTON PUBLISHERS · THE HAGUE · PARIS · NEW YORK

ISBN: 90–279–7878–6 (casebound)
90–279–7637–6 (paperback)
Jacket design by Jurriaan Schrofer
© 1980, Mouton Publishers, The Hague, The Netherlands
Printed in Great Britain

Washington, February 16, 1977—President Carter paid a visit Wednesday to the Department of Health, Education and Welfare and spoke briefly to employees there. Here, as he speaks, HEW Secretary Joseph Califano, left, seems to be trying to emulate his boss.

Ap Wirephoto

Preface

This book has grown out of Wondering How People Communicate and Interact. It is the result of contact and correspondence between the authors who participated in this Wonderment. None of us feels that our statements are the last word on the subject; in a very large sense these contributions are the beginnings of research that consider the inextricable relationship of language and the movements that initiate and accompany it. Our beginning premise is that when human beings interact, language, in a linguistic sense, may or may not occur, but extralinguistic correlates *always* occur. Such correlates may be seen or heard — they may be movements of any part of the body or they may be noises produced by the vocal mechanisms. This study shows that the main channel of communication between human beings very often is not language. For some purposes, of course, such as where the communication is principally informative, language is the conveyor. But for other purposes in human interaction, such as expressive and directive communication, nonverbal correlates carry the heavy load in the dialogue.

But beyond our common goal, we authors don't always agree. In fact, one contributor hesitated about participating since his research differed sharply from another's. As editor, I encouraged differing points of view. I would recall the legend about the blind men and the elephant. In the early stages of discovery, we don't know why our hunches/ methods/descriptions differ so sharply. Academic cliques are an insidious enemy to the search for knowledge. Strange bedfellows are needed. In looking at the list of contributors, one will note a wide range of disciplines and backgrounds, as well as cross-cultural experiences.

My own background is linguistics, and at this stage in the research in nonverbal communicative behavior, few linguists are involved. This is seen in the scarcity of contributions by linguists to the bibliographies on nonverbal behavior. I believe this will change in time, for reasons made obvious in this volume. Sapir and Bloomfield, renowned linguists of the first half of this century, anticipated the notion that linguistic methodology would be useful to other disciplines in studies of human behavior. Subsequently the emic/etic concepts were set forth as useful ways to analyze other behaviors. These concepts are still not fully grasped; they still have not been given a fair trial. The interpretive power of these concepts needs to be exploited in order to approach universal theories.

Since this book is intended to foster and encourage research, the references at the end of the book have been thoughtfully and selectively chosen. I am not of the school of thought that says a bibliography can be compiled by a computer. We hope this list will provide a working guide for research in the topics of this book. It is not a comprehensive bibliography on nonverbal behavior. My two previous books on nonverbal behavior were intended to fulfill that purpose, and might have been titled, 'All You Ever Wanted to Know About Nonverbal Behavior'.

One of the problems of research is that theory often changes faster than it can be published. By the time researchers begin to find the answers, the questions have been changed! This is as it should be; this distinguishes between investigative sciences and dogmatism. We realize (and my previous bibliographies have demonstrated) that we stand on the shoulders of our predecessors. In our acknowledgement to the past, however, we do not want the future to be blinded by previous misconceptions. In my introductory comments I have tried to be respectfully aware of and appreciative of past findings, and at the same time sprightly imaginative and adventurous in creating and setting up explorations for the future. I do not believe that we will ever find the quarks by doing 'safe' research.

Lake Forest, Illinois   Mary Ritchie Key
September 1977

Contents

Contents

List of Contributors

Heidelise Als, Research Associate, Children's Hospital, Boston. Has done observational studies of normal and abnormal development in human infants.

Donald M. Bahr is Associate Professor of Anthropology at Arizona State University, Tempe, and a long-time student of Pima–Papago culture. His current interest in this people's songs follows previous studies of their theory of sickness, mythology, and ritual oratory. The latter study resulted in a book, *Pima–Papago Ritual Oratory*, published by the Indian Historian Press.

Dwight Bolinger, Professor Emeritus of Romance Languages and Literatures, Harvard University. Spanish teacher and dabbler in linguistics, especially meaning and intonation. Most recent book: *Meaning and Form* (Longman, 1977).

T. Berry Brazelton, Associate Professor of Pediatrics, Harvard Medical School, Boston. Has performed numerous studies on the development of individual differences in human infants and has developed a major infant assessment technique.

Thomas J. Bruneau, Chairman and Coordinator of the Center for Communication Studies, University of Guam. His major interests are in the areas of time and silence as communication variables, with particular interest in multi-ethnic/cultural contexts of interaction.

F. T. Cloak, Jr., lives in Albuquerque, New Mexico. He was formerly Assistant Professor of Anthropology at S.U.N.Y. College, Oswego, New York. He has written extensively in the area of human, especially cultural, ecology, ethology, and evolution.

William S. Condon is presently at the Department of Psychiatry of the Boston University School of Medicine. His Ph.D. was obtained in philosophy but he has spent the past fifteen years studying human communication using sound films. His area of specialization is the micro (frame-by-frame) analysis of the organization of speaker and listener behaviors, both normal and pathological.

Shannon Devoe, Research Associate in the Department of Psychology at Clark University. Concerns have been with problems of nonverbal communication and other nonverbal behaviors.

Starkey Duncan, Jr., Associate Professor on the Committee on

Cognition and Communication in the Department of Behavioral Sciences, University of Chicago, where he received his degree. With Donald Fiske he published *Face-to-face Interaction: Research, Methods, and Theory* (Erlbaum, 1977).

Professor Dr. Irenäus Eibl-Eibesfeldt, Forschungsstelle für Humanethologie am Max-Planck-Institut für Verhaltensphysiologie, 8131 Seewiesen, West Germany. Main scientific interest is human ethology: observation of unstaged social interactions by film and tape in numerous cultures (Africa, South America, New Guinea, for example); exploration of the ontogeny and phylogeny of human behavior, cultural ritualisation, aggression, control of aggression. Study of the behavior of children born deaf and blind. Recent book, *Ethology, The Biology of Behavior*, 1975.

Ivan Fónagy, *maître de recherche* at the Centre National de Recherches Scientifiques (CNRS). Doctoral work at the University of Budapest and the University of Paris in Romance linguistics and prosodic feature analysis. Latest book: *The Voice of the Poet: Acoustic and Functional Analysis of Vocal Creation*, Budapest, 1975.

Ruth Fridman, musicologist, studied at the State Municipal Conservatory of Buenos Aires. Has taught and composed music; Fulbright lecturer in the U.S.A. At present is an invited researcher at the Centro de Investigaciones Filosóficas, Department of Psychology. Among her publications, *Los Comienzos de la Conducta Musical*.

Margaret Hancks (M.A., University of Kansas, 1977) currently is Intergroup Activities Intern for The Advisory Committee on Mexican-American Affairs, associated with the Kansas Department of Human Resources.

Dr. phil. Volker Heeschen, Lecturer in the Department of Romance Languages, Ruhr-Universität Bochum, and co-worker of the Projektgruppe für Psycholinguistik, Max-Planck-Gesellschaft, Nijmegen, The Netherlands. Fieldwork in Irian Jaya (West New Guinea) during 1974–1976. Actually engaged in working on the findings of fieldwork from various standpoints (linguistics, human ethology, ethnology). *Die Sprachphilosophie Wilhelm von Humboldts*, Phil. diss., Bochum, Ruhr-Universität, 1972.

Willett Main Kempton received his Ph.D. in anthropology in 1977 from the University of Texas in Austin, and is currently a postdoctoral fellow in the Program in Quantitative Anthropology with Public Policy Emphasis at the University of California, Berkeley. His dissertation topic was 'Grading of Category Membership in the Folk Classification of Ceramics', based on fieldwork in Tlaxcala, Mexico. His interests include folk classification systematics, micro–kinesic synchrony, and computer applications in anthropology.

Adam Kendon's *Studies in the Behavior of Face-to-Face Interaction* was published recently by Peter de Ridder, Lisse, The Netherlands. He has been associated with Oxford University (where he took his D.Phil.), with the University of Pittsburgh, Cornell University, Bronx State Hospital in New York City and Australian National University.

Mary Ritchie Key, University of California at Irvine, has published linguistic studies in comparative American Indian, socio-linguistics, phonology, and nonverbal behavior. Latest book, *Nonverbal Communication: A Research Guide and Bibliography*, 1977.

Carolyn Leonard-Dolan, Rosary College, Illinois, is an anthropologist. She developed the methodology for film analysis of nonverbal communication at the University of Illinois and completed this phase of the work while on leave, as research associate at Harvard University.

Ana María Martirena, Ph.D. in linguistics, is now at the Centro de Investigaciones en Ciencias de la Educación, Instituto Torcuato Di Tella, Buenos Aires. She does conversational analysis in the Spanish language.

Charles E. Osgood, Professor of Communications and Psychology, and Professor in the Center for Advanced Study, at the University of Illinois. Professional life has had three foci (in roughly time-devoted order): Psycholinguistic Theory and Research generally; Cross-cultural Research on Human Affective Meaning Systems (near 20 years and now involving 30 language–culture communities around the world); Psychological Dynamics in International Relations. Author of forthcoming *Toward an Abstract Performance Grammar*, Springer, 1979.

Howard M. Rosenfeld (Ph.D., University of Michigan, 1961) is Professor in the Department of Psychology and the Department of Human Development at the University of Kansas. He has published over a dozen articles on nonverbal communication in social inter-action, with particular emphasis on the regulation of intimacy and information exchange.

Dr. Wulf Schiefenhövel, Forschungsstelle für Humanethologie am Max-Planck-Institut, Seewiesen, West Germany. Research in ethno-medicine and human ethology. Three-and-a-half years of fieldwork in Papua New Guinea and Irian Jaya (West New Guinea), in last area as field director of the priority program 'Man, Culture, and Environment in the Central Highlands of Irian Jaya', of the German Research Foundation. Among several publications: *Ethnomedizin* with G. Rudnitzki and E. Schröder.

Robert Shilkret, Assistant Professor of Psychology, Mount Holyoke College. Concerns have been with tonal features in language and verbal language and development.

Albert Szent-Györgyi, biochemist, Marine Biological Laboratory, Woods Hole, Massachusetts. Recipient of Nobel prizes in medicine in 1937 and 1955.

Edward C. Tronick, Associate Professor of Developmental Psychology, University of Massachusetts, Amherst, Massachusetts. Has carried out studies of perceptual development and social development in infants and has done fieldwork in Africa and Latin America on child development.

D. Jean Umiker-Sebeok (Ph.D., 1976, Indiana University, Bloomington) is concerned with problems at the intersection of anthropology and semiotics. Her recent publications include: *Speech Surrogates: Drum and Whistle Systems* (with T. A. Sebeok, 1976); *Aboriginal Sign Languages of North America and Australia* (with T. A. Sebeok, 1978).

Morton Wiener, Professor of Psychology, Clark University. Concerns have been with the ubiquitous area called communication, verbal and nonverbal, as well as with other socially patterned forms of behaviors as predictors of personality patterns or as a source of inference about status of the 'person' or 'situation'. (*Language Within Language: Immediacy as a Channel of Communication* with Albert Mehrabian, Appleton-Century-Crofts.)

Arnold M. Zwicky, Ohio State University, Linguistics. Interested in linguistic universals, speech acts, casual speech, analysis of linguists' argumentation.

PART I

Language and Nonverbal Behavior as Organizers of Social Systems

MARY RITCHIE KEY

Language and Nonverbal Behavior as Organizers of Social Systems

A. BEHAVIORAL ASPECTS OF INTERACTION[1]

Human beings, fully aware of mirages, optical illusions, and hallucinations, still are unable to describe or understand their own communicative behavior. They operate in a continuum of myths, clichés, misperceptions, and an ingenuous array of irrational behavior, at least by their own definitions of 'meaning' and 'logic'. Could it be that such behavior will be seen to be 'rational' if approached from another system of organization? Meaning is exceedingly variable, as was Proteus, who had the power of taking on various aspects or characteristics. Because of the protean nature of meaning, perhaps we will never arrive at a theory of linguistics or a theory of meaning in the traditional ways.

The variability of communicative behavior is well illustrated in sociolinguistics, a subdiscipline of linguistics that looks at the varieties of language. Even with the givens of the seemingly infinite variety of human expressions, linguists are committed to the idea that all of these varieties follow sets of rules. In order to grasp how complicated, but still orderly, this is, we might use the analogy of a chess game. Steiner has noted the possible variants in a game of chess (quoted in Carpenter 1972: 157):

The number of possible legitimate ways of playing the first four moves on each side comes to 318,979,584,000. Playing one game a minute and never repeating it, the entire population of the globe would need two hundred and sixteen billion years to exhaust all conceivable ways of playing the first ten moves.

Perhaps we may come to realize that it is impossible to define communication from the point of view of linguists who have been struggling with the definitions of language and meaning. From another point of view we may come to recognize that language is primarily a system of accommodation, to get from one point in time to another point in time, and to get from one relationship or situation to another. As walking is a system to get from one place to another — in *space* — so language is a system to get from one place to another — in *time* (Key 1977a:21). A biologist says, '. . . a name or a sentence functions as a tool to produce an appropriate reaction in another person' (Young 1960:91). The study of language, then, would go beyond the study of sounds and syntax. The focus, or orientation, would be concerned with how the organism survives and maneuvers in its universe.

Human beings can be viewed as certain organisms in a particular environment. All organisms are in an interactional situation — with each other and with the environment. As Jacob von Uexküll skillfully analogized, no organism is a mere spectator. It is a reactor and an actor in a dramatic and dynamic world. According to Von Uexküll (in Bertalanffy 1955), an organism:

. . . cuts out . . . a small number of characteristics to which it reacts and whose ensemble forms its "ambient" (*Umwelt*). All the rest is nonexistent for that particular organism. Every animal is surrounded, as by a soap-bubble, by its specific ambient, replenished by those characteristics which are amenable to it. If, reconstructing an animal's ambient, we enter this soap-bubble, the world is profoundly changed: Many characteristics disappear, others arise, and a completely new world is found (248).

This organism has a limited number of possibilities of behavior, such as in a chess game — possibilities that are unique to each particular organism — in a world which other organisms cannot identify, nor approach. Any stimulus (or behavioral event, if we may) is experienced not as it is, but as the organism reacts to it. If we look at language as the expressive behavior of this acting and reacting organism, we might see it as more ritualistic and symbolic than we have heretofore realized. In this sense, verbal and nonverbal expressions are a means of establishing and maintaining contact or interaction between people and the environment, as well as rejecting and breaking relationships. Communication can be seen as a means of integrating self and developing a self-image in order to cope with relationships. One has to validate oneself before one can relate to others in the social paradigm. Thus one chooses one's own inventory of speech acts and nonverbal acts from the vast array of possibilities in the varieties of language.

The use of language as a system of accommodation, to get from one point in time to another point in time, is illustrated in Edward Hall's most recent book (1977), where he describes the continuous conversational behavior of a group of Spanish-American workers. The speaking behavior of the participants did not cease even though the content was not relevant to the work.

They were talking to be talking. If the conversation lagged, the work lagged. Two or three men could work in a very small area without ever seeming to interfere with each other, and they worked very close together. Whether adobe bricks were being laid, plaster was being applied to the walls, or cement was being smoothed, the whole operation was like a ballet, with the rhythm of the conversation providing the unconscious score that strengthened the group bond and kept them from interfering with each other (78).

The symbolic or conventional use of language has been readily identified in such acts as greetings, leave takings, introductions, memorized rituals, and Rites of Passage. Etiquette books are concerned with conventional expressions and polite phrases. Austin (1962: 81) points out differences between phrases which express real emotion and conventional phrases such as 'I have pleasure in . . . I am sorry . . . I am grateful. . . .'

Conventional phrases and gestures are used freely in all of our institutions. It would appear that written communications have reached a saturation point in the use of polysyllabic jargon today. Observers of the human scene are commenting on the proliferation of verbal pomposity and vogue words (e.g. Ferris 1977). The following game, which is a parody of gobbledygook, is a reminder that human beings glide through life on cliché-ridden conversations and writings. This was composed in jest, but I think it has important implications for the idea that language and nonverbal behavior are organizers of social actions.

Construct phrases from the following words. Choose any word from each of the columns to combine into a three-constituent phrase:

A	B	C
optimal	digital	projection
systemized	third-generation	options
balanced	organizational	concept
integrated	reciprocal	programming
parallel	incremental	contingency
synchronized	management	mobility
functional	logistical	hardware
compatible	organizational	time-phrase
responsive	transitional	capability

The universality of symbolic speech acts and nonverbal acts is yet to be explored. There are suggestions that palm presentation is universal among humans and some other primates. This was ritualized in outer space in 1975 when Russian and American scientists memorized each other's greetings and shook hands in a breathless moment of human interaction. Other possibilities of universal symbolic acts are hand raising and eye avoidance. The hand raising has been ritualized in the classroom as an attention-getter. Eye avoidance has been ritualized in parliamentary proceedings when a chairman does not want to give the floor to a member of the assembly. The occurrence of a particular nonverbal act may be universal; *how it is done* is conventional.

Status categories are signaled by symbolic acts, as noted in etiquette books that list phrases and gestures that can or cannot be used in certain social situations. Status categories have to do with the 'haves' and the 'have nots'. One is reminded of Lévi-Strauss's comparison of language exchange with exchange of goods. Lévi-Strauss (1944–1957) saw a 'Copernican revolution' in his theory of communication which interpreted society as a whole:

This endeavour is possible on three levels, since the rules of kinship and marriage serve to insure the circulation of women between groups, just as economic rules serve to insure the circulation of goods and services, and linguistic rules the circulation of messages. . . . Therefore, kinship studies, economics, and linguistics approach the same kinds of problems on different strategic levels and really pertain to the same field. . . . The next advantage of this increasing consolidation of social anthropology, economics, and linguistics into one great field, that of communication, is to make clear that they consist exclusively of the study of *rules* and have little concern with the nature of the partners (either individuals or groups) whose play is being patterned after these rules (86, 296–299).

Jakobson (1970) further expanded on the 'centuries-old history of economics and linguistics', though he updated the discussion somewhat by referring to 'exchange of mates' rather than 'exchange of women'. He noted that questions uniting both economics and linguistics have arisen repeatedly:

One may recall that economists of the Enlightenment Period used to attack linguistic problems, as, for example, Anne-Robert-Jacques Turgot, who compiled a study on etymology for the *Encyclopédie*, or Adam Smith, who wrote on the origin of language. G. Tarde's influence on Saussure's doctrine in such matters as circuit, exchange, value, output/input, producer/consumer is well known. Many common topics, as, for instance, 'dynamic synchrony', contradictions within the system, and its continual motion, undergo similar developments in both fields. Fundamental economic concepts were repeatedly subjected to tentative semiotic interpretation. In the early eighteenth century, the Russian economist Ivan Pososkov coined the catchphrase 'a ruble is not silver, a ruble is the ruler's word,' and John Law taught that money has only the wealth of a sign based on the prince's signature. At present, Talcott Parsons . . . systematically treats money as 'a very highly specialized language', economic transactions as 'certain types of conversations', the circulation of money as 'the sending of messages', and the monetary system as 'a code in the grammatical-syntactical sense.' He avowedly applies to the economic interchange the theory of code and message developed in linguistics. Or, according to the formulation of Ferruccio Rossi-Landi, *'l'economia in senso proprio è studio di quel settore del segnico non-verbale, che consiste nella circolazione di un particolar tipo di messaggi solitamente chiamati "merci." Più in breve, e con una formula*: l'economia è studio dei messaggi-merci'. . . . In order to avoid a metaphorical extension of the term 'language', it is, perhaps, preferable to interpret money as a semiotic system with a particular destination. A semiotic interpretation of the processes and concepts involved is necessary for the exact scrutiny of this medium of communication. Since, however, 'the most general matrix' of symbolic systems, as Parsons rightly points out, 'is language', linguistics actually appears to offer the most helpful model for such an analysis. Yet there are further reasons for connecting economics with linguistic studies: the exchange of utilities 'converted' into words, . . . the direct concomitant role of language in all monetary transactions, and the translatability of money into purely verbal messages, such as checks or other obligations. . . . Indeed, the symbolic verbal aspect of the economic transactions deserves a systematic interdisciplinary investigation as one of the most beneficial tasks of *applied* semiotics (425–428).

Money (or lack of it) binds people together in a kind of way that language does. As Jakobson said, this concept has been recognized since early times. Aphra Behn (1640–1689) expressed it, 'Money speaks sense in a language all nations understand.' And in classical times, Publius Syrus observed that, 'Money alone sets all the world in motion.' The relationship of linguistics and economics continues to fascinate people, as seen by continued studies on the relationship (Benveniste 1973; Rossi-Landi 1975). Money, like language, organizes the members of a society into the social system which prevails. McLuhan analogizes (1962):

Language is metaphor in the sense that it not only stores but translates experience from one mode into another. Money is metaphor in the sense that it stores skill and labour and also translates one skill into another (5).

I propose that verbal and nonverbal expressions of status (reflecting the economic system) and male/female differences are the most important features of differentiation in the dynamics of human interaction. But, N.B., in proportion to their significance, they are the least studied in linguistics. Are we all embarrassed by such stark realities? (See Fónagy and Fónagy 1976; Key 1975a, 1977a; Ounsted and Taylor 1972; Thorne and Henley 1975, for sex differences in nonverbal behavior.)

Very intense emotions are usually dealt with euphemistically by means of symbolic acts. Direct speech is not the modality for such communications as 'I hate you'. Even 'I love you', said in so many words, can be meaningless. Insulting and obscene gestures replace speech as a means of rejecting and repelling in the interactional behavior. In warfare, gestures bind and make communities cohesive, inciting behavior that could not take place otherwise. Military salutes symbolize profound beliefs and values.

People who are too intense in their strong convictions are often rejected in conversations, because the topic, or the subject matter, is not the real reason for talking anyhow. I believe there are grave fallacies in many contemporary discussions of interpersonal relationships, when claims are made that communication would be enhanced by 'talking it out'. Even though language is a possible modality to convey information, there are times when it is impossible or ill-advised to use it. Information which is overwhelming and too powerful cannot be conveyed by verbal means. Havelock Ellis comments on the use of language in marriage proposals (in Turner 1954): 'The recognition that direct speech is out of place in courtship must not be regarded as a refinement of civilization. . . . Among so-called primitive peoples everywhere it is well recognized that the offer of love, and its acceptance or refusal, must be made by action symbolically, and not by the crude method of question and answer' (219).

The symbolic use of language and nonverbal communication goes much further than the readily identifiable symbolic acts. Talking about the weather, or sports, or the news of the day links human beings together. Television sports programs in the United States provide a common link between males and enable any male to carry on intense conversations with any other (Tiger 1969: 121). Surely what goes on in sports year after year couldn't possibly be as interesting to highly intelligent males as the amount of conversation and intensity of dialogue would make it seem to be.

If language as a tool is used then, not so much for information, but for establishing relationships, then verbal skills become more important for survival (see Hewes 1973a). In a hunting society, relationships were/are based on the ability to hunt. In a technological society, verbal skills replace hunting skills. As Bolinger said (1975: 295), 'Gabby people get ahead in a gabby world.' Verbal skills vary with the culture and may include such acts as bluffing, the put down, one upmanship, satire, irony, sarcasm, the white lie, debating techniques, gossip, ability to write a letter well, ability to think on one's feet, verbal dueling, the review or evaluation, skillful questioning, joking, large vocabulary, and many others. The language of reviews could easily be reconstituted in a parody such as the illustration above. Some reviews are obviously a kind of verbal strategy used to maneuver in the academic community and the world of the Fine Arts. This explains the undeserved 'good' and 'bad' reviews that continue to be published in highly respected newspapers and academic journals that usually maintain a high level of integrity.

The survival of the fittest is seen at its best in verbal dueling and in the debate. The content of the words spoken is not as important as the skill that the participants command in the use of the language-tool. It is probably not a coincidence that many of the women who have attained prominent public positions today have had a background in debating techniques. The Lincoln–Douglas type of debate was possible in a small community. Television makes the debate possible even in an enormously large population. The most recent presidential election in the United States restored the debate as a means of choosing leadership for the tribe.

> O what a tangled web we weave,
> When first we practise to deceive!
> *Sir Walter Scott*

> Fabulla swears the hair she buys is hers;
> Does that place her among the perjurers?
> *Marcus Valerius Martialis*

> 'Honey, you know I would never lie to you!'

Keen observers of human communication have painfully concluded that people are prone to be deceitful or to lie. Sturtevant (1947: 48) said that, 'Language must have been invented for the purpose of lying.' Leonardo da Vinci was troubled by man's deceit (Critchley 1961):

Man has great power of speech, but the greater part thereof is empty and deceitful. The animals have little, but that little is useful and true; and better is a small and certain thing than a great falsehood (252).

Westerners have long poked fun at other cultures which make use of the 'lie' to 'save face', at the same time recognizing that their own politicians are careful about their public utterances, which are 'somewhere between a cliché and a falsehood', as someone has said. The late Harvey Sacks (1975) wryly — and poignantly — observed that 'Everyone has to lie.' Leo Strauss (1952) discusses truth/falsehood and the resultant phenomenon of persecution, from the most cruel type to a mild social ostracism. See also Weinrich (1966) for a linguistic study of the 'lie'.

We can observe the organism and how it reacts to a behavioral event, i.e. a speech act or a nonverbal act, in terms of the organization of social relationships rather than the act being a conveyor of information which is either a 'truth' or a 'falsehood'. In this sense one can note that it is just as impossible to define a 'lie' as it is to define 'truth'. In fact, the concept of Truth may be one of the greatest deceptions that humans have devised.

The following hypothetical situation illustrates how the concept of the falsehood/truth is useless for semantic analysis. Further, it can contribute to human misery. A youngster comes to the door to sell me a subscription to a newspaper. He is a finalist in a contest — intense and panicky in his determination to win that trip to a resort lake for the summer. I neither want nor need another newspaper. What do I tell him?
1. I don't want it;
2. I don't have enough money;
3. I don't have time to read any more publications;
4. The head of the household is not at home;
5. I have just subscribed from my neighbor's son . . .
If I tell him (1), which is True from my point of view, he goes away in anger. And after he has lost the contest, he may lash back with vandalic retaliation when he passes my house in disgust. Would the interaction have resolved itself and his anger be dissipated if I had given another kind of answer, such as (2) or (5)? After all, are they not all 'lies' in a pedantic sense? The concept of truth/falsehood turns the end result into a complete breakdown in my relationship to self and to the youngster, as he and I wallow in guilt, misguided intention, and counterfeit motivation.

The concept of lie/truth is particularly useless when motivation is considered. Thomas Hobbes (1588–1679) eloquently brings this to our attention in *Leviathan* (1651). He noted the varying interpretation of the 'simple passions' from differing points of view:

. . . appetite, with an opinion of attaining, is called *hope* . . . without such opinion, *despair*.

'Desire', Hobbes noted, could result in any number of meanings: benevolence, covetousness, ambition, revengefulness, curiosity, and so on.

The extraction of meaning from a verbal or a nonverbal act has to do with discovering the motivation for that act. Imagine, for example, a situation in the rain forest of the Amazon jungle. A woman goes into the jungle, without stating her reason for doing so. There are various realistic possibilities, such as: to get food or firewood; to escape an enemy; to eliminate; to meet a lover; to avoid having to share the cooking chores; and others. Or, to bring it closer home, the man turned abruptly and entered the department store because he: saw a business partner approaching whom he disliked; just remembered that he had to buy film for the weekend outing; noticed the window display which reminded him of his wife's birthday; needed to use the restroom before his next conference; his son just got a new job in the shoe department and he wanted to encourage him.

So far, in the analysis of human behavior, we have not had the tools to deal with motivation. Perhaps if we could eliminate the dead end of trying to define truths/falsehoods, we could come closer to dealing with motivation. Langer (1971) treats motivation in the relationship of cause and effect. Another avenue of approach is through animal studies. The ideas of 'selfish' and 'altruistic' behavior are now being studied; these would seem to be useful for identifying similar behaviors in humans (e.g. see Hamilton 1971).

Ambiguity is another concept which must be considered in the realm of information that is false/true. The computer pointed up the prevalence of ambiguity in natural language as attempts were made to do machine translation. (Here it should be noted that annotating paralinguistic and intonational features would have eliminated much of the ambiguity.) Successful human interaction is fraught with ambiguity. It paves the way toward continued relationships, when the false/true concept would cut off and destroy human relationships. For an insightful synthesis of ambiguity in linguistic constructions, see Zwicky and Sadock (1975). Black (1973) discusses ambiguity in the framework of etiquette among the Ojibwa Indians.

Falsehoods often fall into the realm of gossip, and here the result can be just as effective as though facts had been reiterated — again showing how futile is the concept of truth/untruth. Gossip itself manipulates, whether or not it is true. Even when it is retracted and apologized for, it has fulfilled its purpose: it has organized the behavior that was desired. When gossiping, the participant may articulate the lie with paralinguistic effects — a lowered voice or a whisper. Is this an attempt at lessening the guilt felt?

Purposeful leaks of information seem to be the order of the day in management. Recently a journalist (Ostrow 1977) outlined the techniques in an article, 'Leaks and retaliation'. In an interview, a government official detailed 'seven basic techniques or "principles" . . . the bureaucrats use in their efforts to control . . .' These are: retaliation; flooding [too many papers to read]; burying [submerge the topic deep within a long report]; leaking; crying politics [to incite inquiry]; avoiding decision-making [further study]; expanding [add another agency or administrator].

Gossip can also be useful in passing information (e.g. Handelman 1973). As we document and describe the social use of verbal and non-verbal encounters we begin to see patterns that give us a picture of the nature of the human being. Until we can recognize our nature — our power and our weakness both individually and collectively — we will be at the mercy of the Unknown, or worse, of the manipulators who do understand our nature.

Articulations of falsehoods, contradictions, and ambiguities are noted in the interface of language and nonverbal acts. A simple statement may be innocuous with a neutral tone of voice, but with paralinguistic overtones the statement may take on other meanings, such as satire, irony, or sarcasm, in the great repertoire of verbal skills. See Fónagy (1971c) for an instrumental analysis of irony. Thus the speech act (verbal act) may be in accordance with the nonverbal act, or it may be in contradiction to it (Key 1975b: 32–35). These nonverbal components, of course, appeal to the auditory channels, and therefore in written language they have to be expressed in other ways.

There are also conversations in which the verbal (or language) and the nonverbal acts are simply incongruent with each other. This may occur when one of the participants is thinking of something else. It may also occur when there are actually two conversations going on simultaneously. The second conversation may include a third person, such as the waiter in a restaurant, or an interrupting child. The second conversation may also be an aside about certain artifacts in the environment: 'Gad, this hamburger tastes awful! . . .' interspersed in a dialogue about a recent tennis match. The paralinguistic elements correlate with these conversational intrusions.

Do humans communicate . . . or do they organize? Consider the kind of communication/organization that went into the feat of landing people on the moon. How much of interaction is physiologically based response? When does a learned response become irreversible — can human beings relearn imprinted patterns? The physiological aspects of human interaction are being explored now in various areas of scholarly endeavor. See, for example, such works as Chapple (1970), Chomsky (1976, in press), Delgado (1969), Dewey and Mandino (1971), Eibl-Eibesfeldt (1970a), Eisenberg and Dillon (1971), Hamilton (1971), Lashley (1951), Lenneberg (1967), Marshall, John (1970a,1970b), Morton (1970), Ott (1973), Ounsted and Taylor (1972), Palmer (1976), Uexküll (1934), Wilson (1975). For other references to physiology and their function in communicative behavior, see Key (1977a: 12–18) and references in the index. Osgood (Part III) has revised the Little Black Box to read, the Little Black Egg, in order to be more appropriate for understanding biological entities. The importance of facial behavior and hand gestures in human interaction is seen dramatically in studies of the brain. Figure 1 emphasizes the relevance of extralinguistic correlates as it sketches the origins of nonverbal articulations. See Key (1977a: 15–18) for suggestions of the origin of nonverbal behavior in the brain, and observations on right–left incidence.

Perhaps the difficulties that scholars have in understanding *meaning* can be traced to the wrong focus in looking at the use of language. The proportion of people who read and write books compared with the number of people who do not use language in this informative way is vastly unbalanced. This fact perhaps has distorted our understanding of what language is and has led us in academia to believe that language is first of all a vehicle to convey ideas — a propositional artifact. It is possible that much of language has little 'meaning' as such, but is rather a 'programed' way of getting from here to there in time.

B. THE SUPRASEGMENTALS OF INTERACTION

The articles of the first group in this volume have to do with elements that make up rhythm. Perhaps it is in the rhythms or cycles of human behavior that we see illustrated most clearly the inexorable forces in human interaction. Here we can observe predictability in human behavior. The recurring patterns that make up the structure of behavioral events can be seen in two types: those that are cyclic in nature and those that are rhythmic in nature. A cyclic phase is that in which an event returns upon itself as in a circle. A rhythmic phase moves in measured recurrence with uniform timing. See Dewey (1971) for a lucid explanation.

The term *patterns of behavior* implies a cyclic nature in the interaction of human beings with the environment or with other human beings. Linguistic and nonverbal signals have been called 'regulators' and 'control mechanisms'. Scholars have referred to the synchrony of inter-actional events — 'self-synchrony' (inner rhythms of an idosyncratic nature) and 'interactional synchrony' (conversational rhythms). 'Sync-ing' or 'being in sync' are common terms now among people studying interactional behavior, as well as among professionals in the film industry.

It is of interest to note how other cultures describe the stumbling when

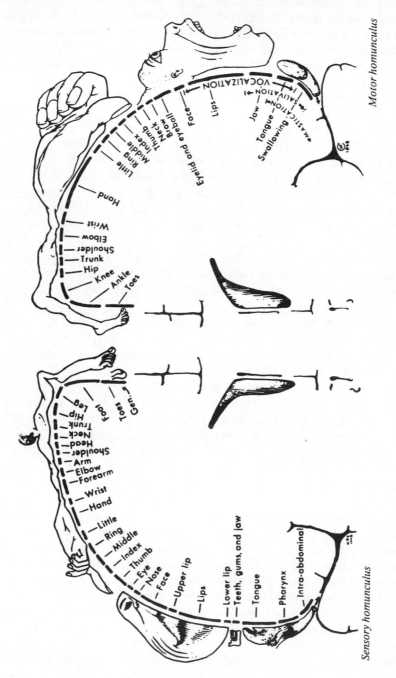

Figure 1. *Cerebral representation of the human body. Left side: sensory representation. Right side: motor representation (Penfield and Rasmussen 1950)*

rhythm patterns go awry, or 'out of sync'. People in West Africa, according to Herzog (1976: 572–573), refer to this as 'spilling', an expression for getting out of rhythm or for causing someone to get out of rhythm in music, signaling, or dancing. Stumbling rhythms may occur between cultures who haven't yet learned acculturation. In a film study of greeting behavior between Black, Polish, and American participants, body movement was charted from the film frames (Leonard-Dolan, Part II). Symmetric and asymmetric patterns resulted from cross-cultural differences. The symmetric patterns had an 'even gait'; asymmetric patterns would either 'stumble' — and subsequently recover — or 'fall', when the out-of-phase interaction persisted.

It is fairly easy to identify rhythmic units that correlate with observable natural phenomena, such as the light and darkness of day and night patterns, or the monthly units which correspond to the movement of heavenly bodies. In general, culturally learned rhythms involve a more subtle timing cycle of symmetric and asymmetric patterns which may be extremely difficult to identify. The number of really good studies on intonation, for example, is minuscule, and studies of rhythm in body movement are rare indeed, except in the ritualized and codified form of dance.

The rhythmic units of natural phenomena — light and darkness, the change of the moon, the blossoming of springtime — have long been mentioned by poets and comedians, as affecting human behavior. More recently serious scientific studies are speaking to the relationship between human behavior and biological/physical phenomena. See Ott (1973), for example, on the effect of light on human activity.

Repetition in behavior is another aspect of human activity that deserves attention. In linguistics the term *reduplication* is used when a morpheme is repeated (see Bolinger, Part II). Repetition can be seen at all levels of behavior and throughout the developmental stages, from infant acquisition of communication to Shakespeare's 'Tomorrow, and tomorrow, and tomorrow'. It is not unusual for children to repeat an expression half a dozen times or more. Repetition occurs in conversational behavior to an astonishing degree. Young people have a remarkable tolerance to repetition in Rock and Roll music. Yet again, some people cannot tolerate the repetition in Ravel's *Boléro*. In trauma, people are known to repeat a phrase or a particular movement. Some activities may be repetitious, and helpful in their monotony, because, by following habits, the brain can be freed to other creative productivity. But when the repetitious activity is important, a person may balance novelty with repetition. I heard an actor talk about how he took a different route to the theater every night, to keep from being bored. In the theater, he spoke the same lines — followed the same routine.

The suprasegmental features of language are among the most important of the linguistic subsystems. The prosodic components may be referred to as *intonation*, or the melody of language, or emotional expression. It is generally agreed that infants learn intonation patterns before speech; intonation is fundamentally basic, and inseparable from speech. Intonation is made up of the stress and timing elements of rhythm, plus pitch. Intonation can be identified as having a range of *pitch,* a range of *stress* (or force of articulation), and *length* (the timing or rate of speech). These intonational features can be correlated to movement in gestural communication. Thus pitch correlates with range of movement, stress correlates with intensity or force of movement, and length correlates with the duration or timing of the movement (Key 1975b:77).

Bolinger's contribution in Part II treats intensity or force of articulation, which I have called *stress*, and how it reflects the expressiveness of speech. Bolinger makes a distinction between *stress* and *accent* — a distinction that has to be made to understand the affective function articulated by the intonational system.

The timing elements of suprasegmental features are observed in synchronous and isochronal behavior. Stress and timing are delicately balanced in the rhythmic organization of speech and gestural movement. Condon (e.g. 1963b) recognized the synchronous nature of body movement and interactional behavior long ago, and he has spent many dedicated years laboriously documenting the intricate detail by instrumental measure. A small sample of one of his transcriptions is included in his article in Part II. Kempton follows with a discussion and comparison of interactional research. It is a commonplace now that interactional activities are structured by timing elements, among other things.

Timing elements have been studied in isolated speech for some time now, but it wasn't until the advent of instrumental technology that scholars could analyze these features with real precision. In 1939 Classe did instrumental studies of the stress patterns of English. The term 'isochrony' has since been used to refer to the phenomenon that in a stress-timed language, such as English, stressed syllables follow each other at approximately equal time intervals (e.g. Pike 1945). Some 40 years later Lehiste (1977) reports on experimental research that appears to have extraordinary implications. An important finding pertains to the integration of isochrony in the grammar of English at the syntactic level. The rhythmic organization of speech is related to syntactic boundaries and elements of length may be manipulated to achieve isochrony. Another important contribution from Lehiste is the information gained on perception. This is a matter of interpretation — how the listener perceives, and the likelihood of the listener imposing a rhythmic structure on sequences heard. (See Lehiste for a summary of previous work on these aspects.) The implications of this carefully devised and reliable experimentation are of interest to those working with larger behaviors and interactional sequences. External stimulations may interfere with the rhythmic organization of small units, as well as larger units. Apparently human beings have learned to calibrate their rhythms as they maneuver in the interactional ambient. How is this done? Is it done out-of-awareness? Can behavior be modified by others? Young (1960) hypothesizes biological organization:

. . . meanwhile the world does not stand still. The mother becomes gradually less co-operative and the child has to learn to get what it needs by ways other than crying. The eye movements are used to discriminate between faces, cups, and other objects, so that the output of the brain leads to the making of appropriate noises, the giving of names that produce satisfactory actions by others — that establish communication. The effect of stimulations, external or internal, is to break up the unison of action of some part or the whole of the brain. A speculative suggestion is that the disturbance in some way breaks the unity of the actual pattern that has been previously built up in the brain. The brain then selects those features from the input that tend to repair the model and to return the cells to their regular synchronous beating. I cannot pretend to be able to develop this area of models in our brain in detail, but it has great possibilities in showing how we tend to fit ourselves to the world and the world to ourselves. . . . In some way the brain initiates sequences of actions that tend to return it to its rhythmic pattern, this return being the act of consummation, or completion. If the first action performed fails to do this, fails that is to stop the original disturbance, then other sequences may be tried. The brain runs through its rules one after another, matching the input with its various models until somehow unison is achieved. This may perhaps only be after strenuous, varied, and prolonged searching. During this random activity further connexions and action patterns are formed and they in turn will determine future sequences (67–68).

Synchronous movement can also be studied on a group level. A significant illustration of a group of children playing informally was filmed by one of Hall's students (Edward Hall 1977: 76–77). From a hidden position in an abandoned car the student photographed the children dancing and skipping in a school playground during their lunch hour. After viewing the film repeatedly at different speeds, the researchers gradually became aware that the whole group was moving in synchrony to a definite rhythm. They also noticed that one little girl was moving more than the rest. She covered the entire playground, moving in and out among the other children. They came to realize that this most active child was the director, the orchestrator of the playground rhythm! In further collaboration with an expert in rock music they found a tune which could be synchronized with the film. The result was that the four and a half minutes of the film clip showed an orchestrated group activity which was successfully synchronized with recorded music that fit the rhythm of the children moving.

When are the suprasegmentals of interaction learned? Are they innate? Or both? Fridman (Part II) calls the early forerunners of supra-segmentals 'proto-rhythms'. She has transcribed the cries of newborn infants and followed their cry/intonational development for a year following birth. A small phonograph record accompanies her (1974b) publication, and in this, one can hear an infant of nine months singing a tune along with the author! Studies such as these are essential before it can be determined how much of the rhythmic behavior is physiological and how much is cultural.

Bruneau's studies on *time* (in this volume and elsewhere) focus on an important element of rhythm. But Bruneau is also looking at time in a much larger sense with far-reaching implications. The study of time is called *chronemics*, a term introduced by Poyatos (1972). Bruneau, however, is defining chronemics somewhat differently (Bruneau, 1977). He brings to our attention this feature of human behavior, which can be analogized to the studies of *proxemics* which Hall brought to our attention in the 1950s.

The concept of biological/circadian rhythms is generally accepted today, especially among those who have experienced the disorientation of being jet-propelled from one time zone to another! The concept was little understood, and less accepted when Dewey started his quantitative research some 40 years ago. Since then the Foundation for the Study of Cycles has documented and published on these phenomena through its journal, *Cycles*. Now the concept is an established fact. Fraisse (1973) has studied activity rhythms and their relationship to the social orga-nization of life by experiments in isolation. He reports on two individuals isolated in caves for 58 days and 174 days, respectively. Unable to ob-serve sun/moon cycles and other natural and social events, the men underestimated their stays by about one-half.

Before leaving the topic of *chronemics* I want to comment on the emic/etic concept. Scholars would no doubt agree that people all over the world see and hear and smell with equal ability. But it is also generally accepted that perception is the learned organization of what is perceived to be 'same' or 'different'. A musician 'hears' more distinctions in pitch differences; an interior decorator 'sees' more distinctions in color differences; a tobacco buyer 'feels' more leaf qualities with his fingers; a wine taster 'smells' more fragrances in the bouquet. The emic/etic concepts are tools which reduce the complexities and great variety of differences and abstract the features that are distinctive. To take an example from linguistics, there are many different ways to pronounce a 't'. It may be aspirated or unaspirated; it may be released or unreleased; it may be articulated with the tongue between the teeth or at any degree in the palatal arch; it may be flapped; it may be retroflexed; it may have lateral or glottal involvement; etc. (see Key 1975b, 164–167). For some purposes it is useful to be able to distinguish all the phonetic varieties, using brackets [t^h] to illustrate the etic level. But for other purposes it is less confusing simply to refer to the 't's as a single event — a phonemic unit — /t/, using slant lines (virgules) to signify the emic level. The traditional notational system is extremely useful in understanding the relationship of the varieties. For example, in one language 't' and 't^h' may be interpreted as one emic unit with two etic varieties: /t/ [t] [t^h]; and in another language as two emic units with their respective articulations: /t/ [t] and /t^h/ [t^h].

In the 1950s Pike explicated these emic/etic notions now familiar to linguists, and further, extrapolated the usefulness of this analytical tool to larger units of behavior, i.e. behavioremes (see Pike 1966). The advantages of dealing with a smaller number of units are obvious, particularly as these concepts are used for analyzing kinesic behavior. Film and spectrograms furnish enormous amounts of information; the fine detail provides more than is desired or needed. By applying emic analysis fine differences can be filtered out and the investigator is left with manageable units. These procedures may be used at any level. For further application of the emic concept, see Osgood (Part III).

The perceiving of space and time is dependent on the organization of the organism. Proxemic and chronemic research is now available. The next step is to study the interaction of *time* and *space* and their effect on human behavior. The comparison between cultures of the use of time and space provides some insight. It is curious that in dreams one encounters the anachronism of scenes where persons from different periods of one's life are interacting.

The term 'culture space' is used in a study of the Japanese language to define the physiotemporal spaces in which individuals are experiencing their daily life. The Voegelins and the Yamamotos (1977) have analyzed a culture space as a:

. . . dynamic, composite and particular physical space where an "actual" activity takes place at a given time. Persons who can enter such a culture space will acquire (or already have acquired) kinds of knowledge about the culture space. That knowledge or assumptions or presuppositions about the culture space imposes on those persons, in this case, what and how they can speak to a particular category of persons in that culture space. Presuppositions about a culture space include:

A. Any physical space which can potentially form a discrete and significant entity in daily life;

B. A social time which may be signalled by the clock, seasonal changes, presence or absence of a particular person, or some other kind of clue in the physical space, and which specifies the meaning of the physical space by identifying the discreteness and significance of it, and which furthermore narrows down the range of the activities (to usually one) that persons can carry out in it;

C. Person(s) to whom the culture space belongs;

D. Person(s) permitted into and now present in the culture space;

E. Person(s) not allowed to enter the culture space; and

F. Person(s) who may be allowed to enter but not permitted to participate in the on-going activity or who may be permitted to carry out some peripheral subactivity which is essentially a service (or support) to the on-going activity (334–335).

The consideration of *time* calls for communicating the concept of 'yesterday' and 'tomorrow'. In some languages the same term is used for both of these English words, though assuredly the people also have a way of dealing with past and future actions. For example, in Chama (Tacanan) *mekawaxe* means both 'yesterday' and 'tomorrow'. It is of interest that this same language group deals with space in a similar way. Thus, in Chama *šani* means both 'left' and 'right'; in Alacaluf *a'san-tərəq* 'left/right'. In these languages still a third kind of ecological and linguistic arrangement is seen in the matter of relationships. In the Chacobo (Panoan) language the word *ïbaba* 'grandchild' is cognate with the related Tacanan **-baba*, which means 'grandfather'. A similar reciprocal relationship occurs in Mapuche kinship terms, where the same word is used for father-in-law and son-in-law. The distinctive feature is distance from Ego. One can sense a kind of equilibrium — a rhythm and a balance in the organization of ecological arrangements.

The larger units in the rhythms of life have changed dramatically with faster communications and instantaneous media. Note, for example, the difference of dates on wills made today compared with wills written two hundred years ago. In those days when death came in natural ways — by disease or old age, people had some idea when they were going to die, and accordingly made their wills at the crucial times. Nowadays with accidents taking lives in unscheduled moments the will has to be made beforehand. In many ways, 'civilized' people have not changed their schedules of transactions in rhythm with the technological changes; they are out of kilter — out of sync. Today we live in an 'instant' society — with instant-friendships; instant-experts; instant-millionaires; instant-news coverage; and instant-publishing. We have eliminated the apprenticeship stage of learning or adapting. Darwin made observations for more than 30 years before publishing *The Expression of the Emotions in Man and Animals*. Lorenz (1973) has related this loss of time to savor, to the numbing of consciousness, the dulling of people's feelings and perceptions. He argues that the ability to experience joy, achievement or enthusiasm has been all but destroyed and says that the great joys in life 'seldom come to pass without some labor pains. Instant coffee is a bit like instant-copulation — you save time, but you lose something else.' The effects of the physiological rhythms of life have their resultant effects on the communicative interaction between human beings.

The final paper in Part II, by Bahr, is a study of rhythm in a non-Western culture. Rhythm probably is best known as ritualized in song and dance. Rhythms might well be studied by observing the music of the culture in relationship to movement. Edward Hall (1977: 78) reports that another anthropologist observed the Tiv of Nigeria and found that they have four drums, one for each part of the body. During the dancing each drummer beats out a different rhythm, and talented dancers can move to all four. Still another anthropologist reports on a relationship between the movement of household duties and the music of the culture (Ashley Montagu 1971):

. . . it is of great interest to learn that Colin McPhee, the leading authority on Balinese music, found that the basic tempo of Balinese music is the same as the tempo of the women's rice pounding (119).

Other cross-cultural studies which are concerned with rhythm have been done on the preaching style of black ministers. Rosenberg (1970) and Titon (1975, etc.) have recorded, transcribed, and analyzed the sermons of several black preachers. Toward the end of the sermon, the prose moves into a chantlike rhythmic structure, with patterned audience participation. It is a commonplace that rhythm occurs in these ritualistic forms. What is being discovered nowadays is the rhythmic or cyclic nature of conversation and other everyday interactions.

C. ORGANIZATION OF LANGUAGE AND NONVERBAL BEHAVIOR

People 'live by the rules' and the articles in Part III of this volume are concerned with the rule behavior involved in interaction. Few things are certain to investigators in the study of conversation, at the present state-of-the-art. The certainties, however, are a good place to start. That the rules are going to change throughout time and place is a commonplace that linguists have lived with for some time: 'Voiced stops became voiceless at a later stage . . .' In other aspects of behavior, the rules change as the organism needs to maneuver and to survive in a changing ambient.

Another certainty is that many, if not most, of the behaviors are articulated *out-of-awareness*. Some of these can be brought to awareness, but it is not at all clear how much the human being is capable of perceiving. In fact, a good case could be made for the human being or a family, group, or institution, becoming dysfunctional if too much is brought to awareness. Some of the most intriguing examples of out-of-awareness are observed in the expert use of linguistic structures by masters of the language who may be poets, comedians, writers, preachers, or politicians, and who know nothing of linguistics. Even the oral use of language, by particularly gifted speakers, may reflect rule-governed structures. The following example shows the use of vowel sounds according to the distinctive features of vowel production. John M. Jasper, a slave who became a famous preacher in post-Civil-War times, was known for his sermon 'De Sun Do Move'.[3] In his own phrasing, he lists the great peoples of the earth:

        /a/ /a/   /u/   /a/
    The Hottentots, the Huguenots,

     /æ/   /I/ /ε/   /I/   /ε/
    The Abyssinians, and the Virginians.

On the stressed syllables, the first line contains back vowels; the second line contains front vowels, according to the vowel chart of English phonemes.

	front	*back*
high	i	u
	I	U
	e	o
	ε	
low	æ	
	a	

Another illustration from a Black speaker is even more sophisticated in the use of vowel quality. The syllables represent the vowel chart, starting from high vowels and moving down the chart, again on the stressed syllables.

/i/ /I/   /e/   /a/   /u/   /u/

Whitey has beat, kicked, raped, and robbed, used, abused, and made a

/U/   /U/   /o/

tool and a fool of niggas for four hundred years.

Order is another certainty that linguists have dealt with for some time, and investigators of human behavior are increasingly recognizing its importance. The ordering of events can be illustrated on many levels. One might speak of the order of phonemes: the sequence pl- may occur (as in 'play'), but lp- never occurs in English at the beginning of a word. The order is crucial in syntax: 'dog-house' is not the same as 'house-dog'. The meaning that is involved in compounds such as these is of a different kind than the meaning that is changed by the differing order of the word 'only' in the sequence: 'He kissed her once; 'Only he kissed her once; He only kissed her once; He kissed only her, once; He kissed her only once; He kissed her once only.'

Another dimension of order is seen in the acquisition of language, where children are observed to introduce constructions in their language in a certain order. Or in *language change*, a certain rule is seen to change, 'only after another rule has taken its place'. Linguists are studying 'cyclical rules' and their recursive behavior, where the ordering of events is crucial to the structure of language. Order in conversational behavior is receiving attention these days (e.g. Schegloff 1968).

The matter of order in sequences of behavior has its effect on perception. Birdwhistell (1970a: 159) found, in his study of courtship behavior of American teenagers, that the partner would be considered 'fast' or 'slow' according to the ordering of the steps of the interaction, not according to the actual time of events.

Some disturbances of order in linguistic structures are known as *slips of the tongue*, or *lapses*, as Edgar H. Sturtevant called them (1917, 1947). Scholars have commented on these 'Spoonerisms' for at least a century. A recent linguistic study was done by Fromkin (1971), who showed that the analysis of speech errors could provide evidence for the psychological reality of certain linguistic concepts. Lashley (1951) was concerned with 'The Problem of Serial Order in Behavior'. He kept records of mistakes made in typing. Lapses in nonverbal behavior, such as putting the newspaper instead of the milk into the refrigerator, have never been studied as far as I know. Wondering if they would show insight into human behavior, I began to collect examples from colleagues and students. Here are two examples. Item 1: 'I began to make a cup of instant coffee, and as I took the bottle out of the cupboard, I looked over at the bottle of vitamins and thought to myself that I should take one with the coffee. As I opened the instant coffee jar, while looking at the vitamin bottle, I dumped the instant coffee into my hand as one would dump out a pill into one's hand.' Item 2: 'I began to make a cup of instant coffee. I turned to get a teaspoon out of the drawer. But I turned to the right instead of the left, where the drawers are located. The reason was that I had been away for the summer, in a house where the teaspoon drawer was on the right. Directional habit had pulled me in the wrong direction.' What can slips/lapses such as these have to say about non-verbal behavior?

When dialogues and exchanges are studied in human interaction, how does one determine the beginnings and the ends? The answer seems easy enough, until one starts to transcribe spoken language, when even determining the beginning and end of a sentence is unsolvable at times. I recall one exchange that took twenty-four hours to complete, though the actual expressions amounted to just a couple of sentences. In one of our midwestern capitals the sons of the out-going governor and the in-coming governor were attending the same high school. After the new governor had moved into the governor's mansion, the sons passed in the hall between classes, and the former governor's son said something to the effect, 'How do you like that big house?' In the fast-moving traffic, they moved on, but the next day, during the same interval between classes, his classmate answered, 'It's kinda big!'

John Ciardi relates an anecdote where the exchange took place over a year's time.[4] In a meeting with Robert Frost one time, Frost asked Ciardi what he thought of a film that had been made about himself. Ciardi disliked it and said so, adding 'As nearly as I can put it, because Robert Frost is no lollipop.' Frost's response was to grunt and turn away. A year later they met again, and Frost said simply, 'It's as you say — I'm no lollipop.' How do we segment dialogues? How do we know when they are finished?

Interactions or conversations are often thought of as exchanges between two parties — a face-to-face encounter. But a delicate or sensitive transaction or relationship may better be handled by a third-party 'advocate' that precludes direct confrontation.

Third-party
advocate

The third party may take many forms. The marriage broker is a classic illustration. A friend or family member may be used for person A to get a message over to person B. The third party may take the form of a joke. Even a dog may be used as the third party: A talks to the dog in the presence of B, conveying a message that is meant for B. The third party may be in the form of a written message, obviating the nonverbal concomitants which carry the emotional and attitudinal messages. A Japanese novelist wrote a poignant account of a marriage, during which the husband and wife communicated their intimate messages to each other by their diaries (Tanizaki 1961).

In Part II we are concerned with the suprasegmentals of interaction — roughly, intonation for speech, and space–time for movement behavior. In Part III, where conversational behavior is in particular focus, we can speak of style or sociolinguistic (sociononverbal?) aspects of expression. It might be well to remember Joos's classic study of usage-scales in *The Five Clocks*: age, style, breadth, and responsibility. His scale of style has five levels: intimate, casual, consultative, formal, frozen. These might be approximately correlated with Edward Hall's distances (1966: 110–120): intimate, personal, social, and public.

The contributions in Part III are particularly rich in cross-cultural perspectives, with observations from New Guinea, Europe, Latin America, and the American Indian. Of considerable value these days is the use of film — the technological advance that in turn increased our ability to analyze human behavior. Several studies in this volume are the result of painstaking viewing of film over and over again.

One of the important advances made in the last generation of research is the bringing together of sound and movement in the analysis. Neonates first exemplify the pattern of these inseparable concomitants. Throughout one's life interaction is a symphony of vocalization and a melodic line of movement, at times punctuated by speech segments, at times punctuated by silence — perhaps to dance — or to think.

D. ACQUISITION OF COMMUNICATIVE BEHAVIOR

Out of the mouths of babes — in New Guinea — reported by an anthropologist, about Samantha, her six-year-old daughter:[5]

At a premarriage ritual for women only, in a dim, crowded hut, I worked hour after hour with my lantern, tape recorder, and note pad, feeling painfully hot and thirsty. At last sugarcane was passed around. I could hardly wait. But I was passed by. I was hurt, and said so later to [my husband] and Samantha.

She said, "Mommy, were you smiling?" I said yes, of course, in anticipation of the refreshing sugarcane.

"Well, that's why you didn't get any. Nobody has to give you anything to please you when you are already pleased. When I want something, I frown and look away. Then I always get a lot, so I won't be angry."

It is now recognized that children learn social/linguistic constructs at a very early age. A principal question is: How early? Studying child language, or acquisition of language with no consideration of motor activity (gesture and facial expression) has perhaps been a deterrent in understanding not only language, but other aspects of infant development. Motor-acoustic correlates are inseparable in the developmental/maturational process. Recent studies show a positive tendency toward studying the whole 'communicative behavior' rather than just the syntax of linguistic items. The great surge of studies during the last decade or so is having a beneficial effect on linguistic theory.

The learning of grammatical categories and all that is entailed in classifying other humans and artifacts of the environment begins with the infant in the prelinguistic stages (Key 1977a: 29–35). As an organism learning to maneuver in its ambient, the infant relates to categories and concepts in nonverbal ways — using all the sensory phenomena available before speech. One of the first distinctions learned is the classification of animate and inanimate — essential linguistic categories. Brazelton et al. (1975: 144–145) observe the responses of infants to objects and humans, and indicate that the infant is able to differentiate inanimate and animate experiences at as early as two or three weeks of age. The infant soon learns which things are dangerous and which are benign; it soon learns what is edible and what is inedible. In play behavior babies experiment with imaginative and 'pretend' categories. They pretend to pick things out of the air, or pretend to eat, or pretend to be Mommy or Daddy. Babies spend a good deal of time inserting or removing objects from containers: toy box, clothes hamper, purse, suitcase, wastepaper basket, dishwasher, drawers. They exchange things within these containers and 'tease' Mommy by surprising her with these pack-rat exchanges. Before they learn language, infants gain control over such factors as: affirmation/negation; deictic processes; complaints/demands/requests/ commands; alternative (if, and, or); cause/effect (pushing, dropping, hitting); rejection/denial; question types: Who? Where? What? Why?

Infants can, at times, get along for a long developmental period without speaking, or using language in the sense that an adult does. All of us know exceptional children who 'didn't talk' until some time after the normal talking stage. Nevertheless, these children function well and interact constantly with their peers and caretakers and others in the environment, by using nonverbal means — both receiving information as well as expressing themselves.

Intonational features (suprasegmentals) appear to start at birth, and even before perhaps, if rhythm is considered. The neonate's cry can be described in terms of pitch range, intensity, timing, intervals, and rhythm — all elements of intonation. Before the age of one year infants are babbling and vocalizing learned differences of intonation (see Key 1977a). Bolinger (1978) has brought together several recent references in a discussion of the innate features of intonation. Halliday (1975b: 61) has isolated five elements of a system of meaning that his infant had acquired at about nine months. Two of these were vocalizations with a certain intonational pattern, and three of the elements were manifested as gestures.

The analysis of interactional behavior between infant and caretaker has been a major concern in studies of proto-rhythms (as Fridman calls them, in Part II). Condon and the following discussion by Kempton (Part II) also speak to these issues. Kirk and Burton (1977) treat the mother–child dyad with attention to the cognitive development. White (1977) treats the acquisition devices as socialization systems.

The analysis of conversational behavior is very much a part of linguistic studies today. See e.g. Black (1973), Blount and Padgug (1977), Chapple (1971), Cicourel (1973), Duncan (1972–1977), Ervin-Tripp (1970–1977), Fónagy (1956–1976), Garvey (1977b), Gelman and Shatz (1977), Halliday (1975a), Handelman (1973), Jefferson (1973), Lakoff (1973), Lewis and Rosenblum (1977), McCormack and Wurm (1976), Mathiot (1979), Sacks (1975), Sacks, Scheqloff and Jefferson (1974), Sanches and Blount (1975), Scheqloff (1968), Umiker-Sebeok (1976–1977), Voegelin, Voegelin, Yamamoto and Yamamoto (1977). Increasingly, nonverbal articulations (eye movement, posture change, hand gesture) are seen to be markers of units and major cues to meaning in the interactional exchanges. Umiker-Sebeok (Part IV) takes the analysis of conversation to the pre-school level (see her references for other studies of children's conversation).

E. THEORETICAL APPROACHES TO HUMAN INTERACTION

Alas, there simply is no viable theory of human behavior. The variability of human interaction encompasses far too much for one single person to comprehend. If something as relatively simple as a chess game has 318,979,584,000 possibilities in the first four moves, human interaction would surely have more, with its subtleties from various cultures, age, sex, status, and occupational differences. The only way that theoretical explanations could be constructed would be to have a network of resources and research personnel such as it took to get to the moon. No one person knew what was going on everywhere; not even a handful understood the work of all the units which were contributing to the task. If we ever are to understand human interaction, it will take a similar operation.

In the past, researchers have used one science to explain another. The two-time Nobel Prize winner, Linus Pauling, used physics to understand chemistry. Hayek (1960) also understood this dynamic. Quite independently from each other, several scholars recently have set forth ideas about explaining human communicative behavior by analogies to physics, or chemistry, or some of the hard sciences. For example Ashby (1960), Bertalanffy (1968), Cloak (Part V), Noyes (1974b), Russett (1966), Stewart (1976), Thom (1975), Norbert Wiener (1948), and Zwicky (Part V). In these works are tantalizing and challenging extrapolations which cannot be dismissed lightly.

According to Russett, the attempt to explain social behavior by scientific principles has a long tradition. In the seventeenth century they spoke of 'social physics' (1966: 11–12): 'Man was regarded as a physical object, and society was thought to obey the same laws of attraction and repulsion as the celestial system.' Later, in an atmosphere that was sensitive to the discoveries in thermodynamics, scholars were intrigued by the possibility of using thermodynamic principles to interpret the universe as a whole (57). Russett reviews the work of these scholars, including one who felt that some of these ideas could be used 'for the interpretation of a wide range of phenomena, whenever and wherever men act and react upon one another'. Russett goes on to say:

Now within the confines of a physicochemical system it is quite clear that all the factors involved are in a condition of mutual dependence which defies explanation by means of a cause-and-effect relationship. . . . Similarly, the social system does not operate in terms of cause and effect; social conditions, like physicochemical conditions, are the resultant of simultaneous variations in mutually dependent variables (114–115).

Could it be that a theory of human behavior will come from the hard sciences — not from the disciplines that study human beings?

Most of the discussions mentioned above deal with the social behavior of people; Stewart (1976) and Zwicky (Part V) deal with language, and none that I know of treats the nonverbal aspects of human interaction. It could be that nonverbal behavior is where physiology and psychology or linguistics meet; nonverbal behavior is the interface where body and language blend.

We are ready for a new paradigm; we must move into a new era in our attempts at finding a viable theory of communicative meaning. In saying this, may I quickly add that I do not think we should stop all our research and writings until a new paradigm is found. Indeed not, there is still much to be learned and appropriated through the methodology available to us now. But we should keep it in perspective and not take ourselves too seriously in frenetic efforts to produce theory. In recent times many young scholars have plunged toward oblivion by operating in the rarified atmosphere — thinking they were producing 'theory'. Much of the heady stuff that claims to be theoretically important is simply another kind of explanatory reasoning or a new notational system. We must distinguish between those explanations that describe 'how it works' and the theory that explains 'why it works'. It is like someone explaining how the new copying machine works, i.e. which of the twenty buttons to push, with instructions to push the green button before you push the grey one. Though it does explain the rules of operation, it is not a theory of how the symbols are transferred to a blank sheet of paper.

In order to find the unifying scheme in which all the forces inherent in language and nonverbal exchanges are connected we might try another point of view. As I have suggested at the beginning of this chapter, we can look at language and nonverbal behavior as organizers of social systems. Physicists can explain much about the universe in relatively simple ways, by reducing the interaction to four basic forces. We can find easily applied analogies in human interaction by thinking of such terms as: attract–repel; affiliate–withdraw. Scholars speak of 'making and breaking of human boundaries' (Ashcraft and Scheflen 1976).

It is tempting to follow the advances in physics today, which suggest many analogies to the mysteries we struggle with in language behavior and human interaction. Large teams of physicists are working with constituents known as *quarks*. Apparently there are various kinds of quarks which have been labeled: up, down, strange, and charm. It is not easy (if even possible) to isolate these quarks, if, indeed they exist at all! It may be that they appear only in bound combination (countless illustrations come to mind, from language and nonverbal behavior!). It is hypothesized that the quarks 'change color', so to speak, with every new combination. In human behavior, the very thing we are looking at changes appearance as we are looking. Heisenberg's uncertainty principle is operating everywhere around us.

One linguist suggests an illustration of how Newton's 'first law of physics' might be seen in language change (Robert Hall 1964):

The principle of regular phonemic change is an assumption of the same type . . . that every body remains in a state of rest or of uniform motion in a straight line unless it is compelled to change that state by force acting upon it. This 'law', like the principle of absolutely regular phonemic change, is something we never see in nature, because there are always other factors entering in; but it is, nevertheless, the assumption of regularity that enables us to sort out the various factors that cause irregularity (305).

Einstein recognized that gravity could distort *time* and *space*, and we find instances in human attractions where 'Time stands still'.

In illustrating inventory and arrangement of linguistic items, I have used sketches of the chemical compounds ethyl alcohol and dimethyl ether. They both contain the same number of elements, but the arrangement is distinct:

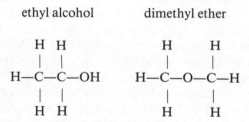

The words 'pit' and 'tip' both contain the same inventory of elements, but the differing arrangements result in two different items. The same application can be made in other areas. The musical comedy, *The Music Man*, contains two tunes that are made up of the same elements, but with a different beat and rhythm they result in two distinct songs:

The helix is another structure known to scientists that might be seen to illustrate human behavior. Here can be seen the principle of equilibrium, where social scientists might speak of the pendulum swinging. Zipf (1935) referred to the concept of equilibrium, as well as the underlying forces of the mind. Several scholars have used the term 'homeostasis', in discussing the self-regulating properties of living processes, borrowing and extending the word which Walter B. Cannon introduced in 1939 to explain the oxygen concentration in the blood. But Grinker (1956: 162, 226) warns not to treat stability in homeostasis 'as an absolute stability, but as dynamic and relative', and notes the paradox: it is stable, and yet it cannot be rigid. Linguists, like physicists, are increasingly concerned with the processes, not the bits and pieces. It is a world of relations of ongoing movements. It is not a linear world, but a world of many things going on at once (multilinear?). All these separate systems are successfully integrated in a progressive continuum of human interactions (see Condon, Part II). Several dimensions are overlapping, intermingling, intertwining. This is seen in linguistics in the way that suprasegmentals weave through language, changing its color, varying its impact, and disguising its purpose. Perhaps *intonation* is one of the quarks reflecting an underlying force of the mind. It exists only in bound combination; it cannot occur in isolation — it cannot occur without language.

With such technological aids as film and tape, it would appear that we are on the edge of discovery in the areas of human interaction. The bibliographies suggest that much is known and much work has been done. Still, for all that has been studied and written about human communication and language, there are huge lacunae in the data. We lack information on the basic characteristics and properties of the human being, especially from cross-cultural perspectives. For example, what things *embarrass* people? What is the dynamic of the *unforgiving* nature that endures throughout a lifetime? Why are some *rebellious* people heroes, and other criminals? Why is *conformity* at one time plastic, uninteresting, and disgusting, and at another time peacemaking and stabilizing? Who can explain the *sense of justice* which wells up in humans in some circumstances and the apathy that occurs at other times, sending fellow-beings into oblivion — or prison?

In order to understand language and nonverbal behavior as organizers of social systems we need a sophisticated combination of fieldwork in distinctly differing cultures of the world along with a wildly imaginative field theory that will explain the attraction and repulsion between human beings and their environment. We need various kinds of thinking — the Apollonian and the Dionysian, as Szent-Györgyi has so charmingly outlined (in Part V). A discovery, Szent-Györgyi reminds us, must necessarily be at variance with existing knowledge. This hazard complicates the life of the researcher, who is dependent on grants, promotions, and fundings. It forces scholars into doing what is acceptable; it intimidates scholars from undertaking an investigation that might turn out to be a mistake. We forget that Babe Ruth struck out 1,330 times. Roman Jakobson (1972) commented on the evaluation of the current scene in linguistics, and his comment can be applied to other areas of research:

. . . success or failure may be stated only at the conclusion and not at the start of a new set of assays and experiments. Any working hypothesis is "of promise" to be corroborated or discarded by subsequent experimentation. Presumptive dogmas which prohibit any linkage between the principles of autonomy and integration and which replace autonomy by isolationism, alias "apartheid", or integration by heteronomy, alias, "colonialism", obviously prove to be devastating both in life and in science (14).

We need to stretch our minds with other kinds of thinking that we may not be comfortable with. We need to imagine, as Edwin Abbott (1884 [1963]) imagined in his Romance of Many Dimensions, wherein his characters maneuvered in a *Flatland*. We need to study how other people look at the world and navigate as Gladwin (1964, 1970) has described the logic of the Trukese. We need to learn how to make and read maps (Robinson and Petchenik 1976) in order to see where we have been and where we might be going. We need to study past models, such as Stewart (1976) has done, bringing together the philosophy of science and the principles of modern design, in order to dream up new models. See also Hayek (1955), Hesse (1966), and Lévi-Strauss (1966). Other disciplines can suggest improvements on our own models, as architecture has provided the *torus* for explaining phonological space (Stewart 1976: 159–163). We need to watch a mobile spin and twist in space to reflect on how human beings approach and drift in their interaction. We need to fold pieces of paper over against each other and bend and curve the edges and centers as is suggested in catastrophe theory (Thom 1975; Thom and Zeeman 1975). And to put it all together, we need to take on the delusions of Walter Mitty and work toward a unified research plan, the type of which actually landed people on the moon. (See Bertalanffy (1968) for a general system theory.) With mind-stretching activities, scholars, journalists, poets, advertisers, politicians — all who are interested in what-makes-people-tick — will add to the stream of thinking that contributes to a unified theory.

NOTES

1. Some of the ideas in this chapter were presented at the University of Chicago, April 1977, in a paper, 'Nonverbal behavior in spoken and written language'.
2. The references in this first chapter are of two kinds. References to authors in this book are cited as (Bolinger, Part II). Other authors that are included in the bibliography at the end of the book are cited as: (Bertalanffy 1955).
3. Joseph C. Robert, *The Story of Tobacco in America*. New York, Alfred A. Knopf, 1949: 91.
4. John Ciardi, 'Manner of speaking', *Saturday Review* (September 1977): 48.
5. Gillian Gillison, 'Fertility rites and sorcery in a New Guinea village', *National Geographic* 152(1): 128.

PART II

The Suprasegmentals of Interaction

DWIGHT BOLINGER

Accents that Determine Stress

Why is it that among languages with demarcative stress (stress that occurs on a predictable syllable of a word counting from right or left) there are very few with stress later than the second syllable counting rightward or the third counting left? (I use the statistics from Hyman [1975].) One reason might be that a position deeper within the word would presuppose the regularity of fairly long words. But that would not explain the heavy preference that is found, even within this narrow range of possibilities, for stress on the first, the last, and the next-to-last syllables. A word could just as easily be identified as a word by having its stress on the second syllable as on the first, yet stress on the second syllable is comparatively rare. Alternatively, one might suppose that the best place to signal a word division would be right at the point where it starts or ends. That would explain the relatively great popularity of stress on the initial syllable, but not the equally popular stress on the next-to-last. There must be other reasons besides demarcation for the favored stress positions in words. For the readers of this volume, the most interesting possibility is that elements in some nonverbal channel may be affecting that part of the physical shape of words that we call stress.

First, some definitions. I use *stress* to refer to the syllable marked to receive an *accent* or intonational prominence. In the sentences:

    al   always behave like that?

He

      ways behaves like that. Does he

        Does he

            always behave like that ?

the word *always*, which is lexically marked with stress on the first syllable, receives the sentence accent, manifested in the pitch jumps that obtrude the syllable *al-*. The word *behave*, which is stressed on the second syllable, is not accented, and the syllable -*have* is accordingly merged without prominence in the general intonational drift. The same stressed syllable -*have* would be the one to receive an accent, however, if the speaker conferred one at that point:

You shouldn't be^{have} like that.

Here, the syllables *should-* and -*have* are both accented, and this particular intonational shape is a very common one.

The failure to distinguish stress and accent results from the reliance on citation forms as a means of identifying which syllable or syllables in a word are stressed. Unless a word is accented it is pretty difficult to tell where it is stressed. The word *trombone* is handled differently by different speakers, but if we hear

In^{stead} of just ^{look}ing _{at} it, _I ^{wish} _{you'd} ^{play} that trombone for a change.

there is no way to tell whether to mark *trómbone* or *trombóne*. So we query the speaker and he gives us one of the following:

Trom
   bone.

Trom^{bo}n_{e.}

A citation form is not an abstract word, but a word converted to a sentence and bearing a sentence accent.

If the function of stress is to tell us which syllable to accent when an accent is called for, the interdependence of the two is obvious. A child will learn which syllable of a word is stressed by hearing that syllable accented — when it is accented, which is often enough to create the necessary memory trace. And if stress exists to serve intonation (to tell us what syllables within a sentence are allowed to receive an accent), then whatever position serves intonation best is bound to be favored as the position of stress. There are of course other factors. At times (and in varying degrees from language to language) stress performs other functions. It may be distinctive (increasing the lexicon by acting as a phoneme, e.g. *úndertaking* 'funeral directing' and *undertáking* 'enterprise'), morphological (assisting in the paradigmatic identity of a group of related words, say an inflected verb that is always stressed on the same syllable), grammatical (distinguishing function words from content words by the lack of stress on the former), and, as noted earlier, demarcative (helping to segment the stream of speech). If stress did not have to serve a variety of purposes, we might expect it to be quite regular in its placement. As matters stand, the location of a stress may not always be ideal for the intonation, but is always within tolerable limits; and intonation will override the opposition if necessary.

The effect of accent on stress placement is best viewed in terms of a theme–rheme function and an affective function. Accent is one of the means of expressing the thematic and rhematic relations in a sentence. In general a sentence contains two main accents, one for the rheme, the part of the sentence that 'answers the question', so to speak (or, in a question, the part that asks the question), the other for the theme, which is the principal qualifier of the rheme. I put this somewhat differently from the usual theme–rheme or topic–comment explanation, because a broader view is needed. The principal qualifier, as I have called it, *includes* the topic if there is one, but the topic is only one type of principal qualifier. Suppose we look at three possible answers to the question *Who talks the most?*:

```
     Hen                        Hen                      Hen
                      talk                       ho
1.                2.      The              3.       At  me,
     r                        er is   r                     r
      y.                              y.                     y.
```

In (1), we have a bare answer to the question — rheme alone. In (2), the topic is added; obviously it is not needed for identification, since (1) gets along without it, so it must be added for some other purpose, perhaps to imply 'If you want to know about the talker', suggesting that other topics might be under discussion instead of this one — it is a qualification on the mentioning of Henry. In (3), we have something that is clearly new information — a restrictive modifier on Henry as the talker. Yet (2) and (3) are seen to have the same intonation. And the same thing happens to the intonation of (2) and (3) if the two main divisions of the sentence are reversed: they carry their intonation along with them (still in answer to the question *Who talks the most?*):

```
      Hen                        Hen
2'.            talk          3'.          ho
      ry's the     er.            ry, at     me.
```

— the incomplete fall at the end of the qualifying element is now transferred to final position. In other words, the way the accents are distributed still tells us which part answers the question and which part does the qualifying.

The counterpoise of theme and rheme not only accounts for the tendency of sentences to have two main accents, but also helps to explain why longer words, when given in citation form, tend to take this same shape — the favored sentence pattern becomes generalized, and we have what is usually termed a 'secondary stress'. It is not as reliably located as the primary, and permits itself sometimes to be influenced by what a speaker fancies to be an underlying theme — the two pronunciations *ácademícian* and *acádemícian* reflect *ácadémic* and *acádemy*. But the important thing for this discussion is simply the fact that the typical shape of a sentence is that of the double prominence (a 'hat pattern' as Cohen and 't Hart [1970] call it, or a 'suspension bridge', as I prefer to view it). I give one more example with a different intonation on the qualifying element to show how the two accents remain despite the change from a falling accent to a rising one (the answer is still to *Who talks the most?*):

2″. $\text{Un}^{\text{fortun}\text{ately,}}$ Hen $_{\text{r}_{\text{y.}}}$ 3″. ^{Hen} ry, $\text{un}^{\text{fortun}\text{ately.}}$

Now while the two accents occur *toward* the beginning and *toward* the end, nothing said thus far compels them to be *at* a particular syllable in either vicinity. If the only condition were that one syllable in each of the two main constituents of the sentence had to be highlighted, the two might occur directly on either side of the dividing line, and well toward the center of the sentence as a whole. Or the rhematic accent could be predominantly on the last syllable, whereas the next-to-last is slightly favored. There must be other factors at work besides theme and rheme.

Given that an accent is a pitch prominence, what are the best conditions for it to be realized? First, there must be something for it to predominate *over*. This is clearly best accomplished when there are flanking syllables that are not accented. The avoidance of contiguous accents is carried out, no doubt universally, in 'rhythm rules'. In English it even affects the syntax of certain words, for example *too, not,* and *so* — we say *so good a person*, not *a só góod pérson* (though *a só unnérving expérience* may get by, when we are not avoiding the whole problem by substituting *such a*). So to the extent that the accent in the second constituent tends to occur as late as possible (reasons for this in a moment), and given that there must be an intonational fade at the end which needs some phonetic bulk of its own, the most convenient arrangement is for the last accent to occur on the next-to-last syllable —

the final syllable then serves both as a foil to the accent and as a carrier
for the terminal fade:

$$\text{The } ^{\text{wind}} \text{ was } ^{\text{fright}}$$
$$\text{ful.}$$

If accent depended for its realization on this ideal stress pattern,
penultimate stress would be the rule rather than just the best option.
Actually the accent will simply override any difficulty posed by a terminal stress — in effect, it geminates the vowel, splitting the syllable and
forcing the second half to behave as an unstressed syllable:

$$\text{She } ^{\text{looks}} \text{ so } ^{\text{sa:}}$$
$$\text{d!}$$

The disadvantage of this — and one reason for preferring a penultimate
stress — can be seen in the difficulty of geminating a very short vowel,
such as the one in *I have to spit*: much of the intonational downturn goes
by the board. A second line of defense, when the syntax permits it, is to
prefer an arrangement whereby such recalcitrant syllables as *spit* are
moved away from the end, so that the end is occupied either by a
relatively more sonorous syllable or by an unstressed syllable. We see this
in the reduplications and binomials that are so common in English and
other Western languages: *tick-tock, mishmash, flimflam, seesaw; spick
and span, hearth and home, weak and weary, from head to toe* (Spanish
de pies a cabeza reverses the direction but the prosody remains the same).

As for stress on the second-to-last syllable, or even farther back — say
on the first — there may be some waste of syllabic bulk but no problem
in the clear realization of the accent:

$$\text{He } ^{\text{stood}} \text{ there } ^{\text{sniv}} \qquad\qquad \text{It's be}^{\text{cause}} \text{ of the } ^{\text{tem}}$$
$$\text{eling.} \qquad\qquad\qquad\qquad\qquad \text{perature.}$$

$$\text{I'm ap}^{\text{palled}} \text{ at its } ^{\text{for}}$$
$$\text{midableness.}$$

The reason these stress patterns are less favored brings us to the factor
that disposes stress as far to the right as possible (and meets its match
only in the need of the final accent to display itself clearly). This factor is
an affective one.

The phenomena described thus far relating to accent on the second constituent are generally true for all languages that use accent. The affective phenomenon that I am about to describe likewise seems to be some sort of universal, and is found in tonal as well as nontonal languages. I refer to it as *climax*. It is a device — probably reflecting the psychological principle of *recency* — for emphasizing the utterance as a whole by putting the biggest bang at the end. The effect can be seen by comparing a verb such as *recover* with one such as *get back* (and this tells us something about the tremendous vitality of phrasal verbs, which permit the end-shifting of the stressed particle):

```
              cov                        ba
   could                   could
I        n't re         I        n't get it
          er it.                         ck.
```

The second is more forceful, other things being equal.

Climax is a productive process. If the other elements of a sentence — the syntax and the normal stress positions — do not permit an accent at or very close to the end, speakers quite easily achieve extra emphasis by putting one there anyway. The following are all attested examples, with the accent occurring before a full stop or a comma:

```
                                        tis
            cen              sa
... that      ter around the    crament of bap
                                        m.[1]

                     me
   think
I      it could be tor
                    nt.[2]

                  lations                        shi
... rules and regu        governing teaching fellow
                                          ps.[3]

                                                    be
         wondering        being  lo     all         up
I've been           whether    in  ve is   it's cracked   to
                                                      .[4]
```

It helps, when the speaker has this urge, to have a syllable with a full vowel to put the shifted accent on, and the accent then may proceed no farther to the right:

... students may resist their apparent arbitráriness.[5]
I'm tired of being a closet secretáry.[6]

But if the urge is strong enough, the shift will go onto a reduced vowel, usually making it full. We would expect the urge to be strong in exclamations, and a common pronunciation of *gólly* is *góllée*. *Máybe* is similarly converted to *máybé*, and I have caught myself saying *hárdlée* for *hárdly*. Similarly

. . . was the enormous and the enormitý of . . .[7]

As several of the examples already quoted have shown, the effect is not necessarily one of a shift of accent but of an *added* accent at the end. Thus *Beliéve me* becomes *Beliéve mé*, where the accent on *me* is clearly climactic and not contrastive. Climax frequently distorts the normal stress on compounds and similar collocations. Thus for one speaker, *Cárroll and Company* became *Cárroll and Cómpany*; for another, a *Tréasury official* became a *Tréasury offícial*. Similarly it may happen that a popular saying, which a speaker tends to be didactic about, comes to shift the accent away from where, in view of presuppositions, it ought to go: *Half a loaf is better than no bread* should logically have the final accent on *no*, but we put it on *bread*. Some words in English have a hovering stress occasioned by the frequent play of climax on them (*almost, maybe, cannot*), and others, for some speakers, have undergone a permanent shift: *justifíable, inflúence, ordinárily, necessárily*.

Climactic accent has been reported in some form or other for at least the following languages: Cayuvava, Chichewa, Chontal, Chuave, German, Javanese, Kunimaipa, Mantjiltjara, Marinahua, Mixtec, Otomí, Persian, Seri, Spanish, Sundanese, Tagalog, Telugu, Waltmanjari, Western Desert, and Yurok (Bolinger 1978). The most frequent association that observers have noted is with the imperative, in languages as widely separated as Southern Italian and Cayuvava. In Buenos Aires Spanish it probably accounts for the reaction to the *vos* form of the imperative, with its terminal stress, as more emphatic than the *tú* form. In Chichewa it is found in the 'radical descriptive' words (e.g. English *kersplash*). In Tagalog, climactic shift is claimed to be a regular morphological process.

While we become aware of climax mostly when it distorts the expected stress on a word, it is present to some degree at all times, cooperating with the rhematic accent to lend emphasis to the utterance. That is to say, the rhematic accent is required under normal circumstances to assume the function of climax as well. That explains the syntactic adjustments that are needed to get the rhematic focus as close as possible to the end — passive voice, 'left dislocation', chiasmus, etc.; for example:

Jóhn did it → It was done by Jóhn.
I háte spinach → Spinach I háte.
He's OK as a writer but he's a bóre as a talker → He's OK as a writer but as a talker he's a bóre.

The gradience of climax can be seen in its opposite, anticlimax, which is the tendency in unemphatic discourse to move the accent leftward (but never onto an unstressed syllable), leaving a certain number of syllables (usually two or more) dangling without accent at the end. The velvet glove is obvious in the second of the following, spoken as a warning:

If I were you, I'd be cáreful.
I'd be cáreful, if I were you.

The spinach example above shows, to the left, what might be said good-humoredly to a host with whom one is on familiar terms; its climactic partner to the right would be serious and probably rude. A word may be thrown in as a way of avoiding a terminal accent, in a situation where such an accent might seem discourteous. Thus in accosting someone we sense a simple *Yóu!* or a *Héy, yóu!* to be rude, but *Yóu there!*, with a *there* that adds nothing logically, is less insistent.

We now have what we need to appreciate the relatively greater popularity of penultimate stress. A language, say, has no determinate stress on any particular syllable of any word (a condition still true of some languages). That word occurs, as most words may at one time or another, directly before a pause. The speaker wants to make an impression, and maneuvers the main final accent close to the end. He may move it all the way, but that interferes with marking the accent clearly — an intonational prominence is set off best when there are non-prominences to either side. So he settles for the next-to-last syllable. Penultimate position is the best compromise between climax and clarity. If it is used often enough and other advantages accrue (such as having a fixed intonational shape with which to teach words to young children), the penultimate accent may be regularized for all words and produce a penultimate-stress system. But since all stress systems are the result of compromise, no one system imposes itself universally.

This is an oversimplification, and looks at stress only from the standpoint of intonation. There are other factors, including syllabic weight, suffixation and eventual loss of unstressed suffixes, regularization of paradigms, etc.; but to the extent that stress reflects the expressiveness of speech, it behaves more or less as we have seen.

As for the accent on the principal qualifier, the thematic accent, which provides the first pillar of the suspension-bridge pattern, it probably has less effect in determining the main stress of words, but undoubtedly is the basis for the secondary in long words. One of the principles mentioned earlier is again applicable: for the efficient display of an accent, it is best to have unaccented syllables on either side. This calls for delaying the initial accent to some point after the first syllable. In addition, hesitation sounds (or makeweight words) are most apt to occur at the beginning of an utterance, as the speaker organizes what he is going to say: *Mmm . . . yes; Oh, . . . ten I suppose.* But the most important thing is for the speaker to get the hearer's attention; and for that, an accent well to the left is desirable. The result is the double peak of the suspension bridge, which is manifested most strikingly in the citation form of longer words:

```
     ca           bil        sa            ti
 rad         pen        con          re
e   i       im   etra        ver         cita
     tion            ity           tion         ve
```

If for extra emphasis the speaker desires to add more accents to an utterance, he is free to use the secondary:

```
        not         sa
              con
That was      a    ver
              tion!
```

The secondary also replaces the primary at times to avoid successive accents, especially in the sequence modifier + noun, as in the second of the following:

```
            he                  si
   sign                  ov
The      is over      An   erhead
          ad.                   gn.
```

Elsewhere the secondary has little opportunity to manifest itself.

It is a common practice to regard as secondarily stressed all syllables containing full vowels and separated from the primary stress by at least one syllable containing a reduced vowel. This results in words with 'secondaries' not only to the left of the main stress, as in the examples cited previously, but to the right as well; the latter, however, are treated quite differently by the intonation: they do not normally receive an accent. Compare *dìsenchánt* and *dúplicàte* — the former readily accents the secondary for extra emphasis, the latter not:

```
                              have
Some
        will    dis   chant
   one I     not   en      if I don't
                              to.
```

                                        have
Some
        will   du
    thing I   not   plicate if I don't
                                        to.

— an accent on *-cate* would not be normal. On the other hand, if *duplicate* is in final position, climax may move the main accent to that last full vowel: *You know very well that I didn't duplicate anything because there was nothing to duplicáte!* The failure of a full vowel after the main stress to be a true secondary again reflects the behavior of the utterance as a whole. Accentual prominences are infrequent after the rhematic accent; when they do occur they are parenthetical, e.g.:

              late
It's too
                for that,   mut   sol
                    he   tered   emnly.

— and parentheses do not occur within words.

Too little is known about the influence of intonation on secondary stress to try to generalize these few remarks beyond English.

There remains one other type of affective accent with a potential effect on stress placement, for which I have evidence only from Hungarian. The accentual phenomenon may well be universal: it is an *emotive* accent manifested in a striking prominence well before the end of the utterance (usually on a very early syllable) and followed by a low level with no prominences at all. It is common on epithets. For example, *Jesus Christ!* normally has an accent on *Christ*, but may be spoken:

Je::
    sus Christ!

as if the speaker were simulating complete collapse after his initial outburst. But it is not confined to epithets; it conveys irrepressible emotion in everything from apologies to protests:

        aw::   ter::
I'm   He was
        fully sorry!   ribly tactless!

As might be expected and as these last two examples show, the emotive accent is readily adopted by intensifiers. In Hungarian adverb-adjective phrases, adverbs that express 'completeness' regularly backshift their stress; other adverbs do not (Varga 1975: 35–36). In English this is optional with intensifiers but impossible with other adverbs. Compare the following:

        god::   slight::
It was so   *It was
                awfully bad!   ly worn!

The latter would have to be contrastive for *slightly* to carry the accent.

In all this interplay we see the often-remarked competition for *Lebensraum*. Speech is perforce linear, and the stress system of a language represents its best effort to harmonize the interaction of accent with the other manifestations of linearity.

NOTES

1. Prof. Lawrence Kiddle, Univ. of Michigan, Dec. 29, 1964.
2. Prof. James Redfern, Harvard Univ., Feb. 21, 1967.
3. Graduate Dean Peter Elder, Harvard Univ., Oct. 8, 1968.
4. Cary Grant in film 'Monkey Business', c. 1962.
5. D. Bolinger, Apr. 5, 1966.
6. NBC radio ad, heard El Paso, Texas, Aug. 25, 1976, 7:02 A.M.
7. Overheard May 1964, from speaker trying to be very emphatic at that point.

WILLIAM S. CONDON[1]

The Relation of Interactional Synchrony to Cognitive and Emotional Processes

In reflecting on the 15 years which I have spent in the frame-by-frame microanalysis of sound films of human behavior and communication, the most perplexing and persistent theoretical and observational issue, for me at least, has been that of the dichotomy of the discretelike and the continuous. This also involves, at a wider level, the question of the segmentation (analysis) and organization (synthesis) of man's study of Nature and himself. How we cognitively dissect and structure the universe, including our human position and destiny within it, has a profound and far-reaching effect upon how existence will be lived and felt. Perhaps much of human life is lived in terms of categorizations about nature and human existence which are mythological, yet these exert a force in the form of quasi-real entities which dominate human life. Man is a naturally evolved animal who constructs pictures: of the nature of the universe, of himself, and of his destiny; and of all the things included under those categories.

A basic issue in the study of human communication, then, centers around the analysis and synthesis of behavior; behaviors that extend across many domains and take many forms. Indeed, the nature of the relationship between levels itself requires examination. It is the problem of whether or not it is possible to analyze organization into segments or units which are subelements of organization or whether organization can only be analyzed into discrete or atomistic parts of which it is then said to be composed. While this issue has emerged particularly sharply in the microanalysis of human behavior and interaction, it extends to many other domains.

This paper will be primarily theoretical and seek to present a perspective which includes both the discretelike and the continuous — without contradiction. The microanalysis of sound films is a very limited dimension, but it has provided me with a model of how organization might be analyzed as organization. It led to the elaboration of 'forms-of-order' which appear to be segments or units of organization. Some of the background of how this began is presented briefly below. Frieda Fromm-Reichmann, a noted psychoanalyst, was deeply interested in what she referred to as human intuition. She had many subtle, quasi-informed hunches or feelings about her patients but did not know the source of them. She felt that they might be the result of subtle clues she was picking up during interactions with her patients. In 1956, while she was at the Institute for Advanced Studies in the Behavioral Sciences at Palo Alto, she prevailed upon several behavioral scientists to begin a naturalistic and wholistic study of the human communicational process (McQuown et al. 1971). It was an attempt to put the human being and his natural processes of communication back together again. The human animal had been split apart and studied by separate disciplines, each carving out its own private domain. An attempt was thus initiated to study the natural behavior of interactants within their own culture and to try to integrate the diverse segmental analyses of the separate disciplines. This would require an effort to clarify the relationship between the segmental schemas of these separate disciplines as well. Much of the work in this area since has been implicitly involved with questions concerning the nature of the segmentation and organization of human behavior across multiple dimensions. Following in this tradition, in 1962 I began to study human behavior and communication at the micro level using sound film and frame-by-frame analytic techniques. There is a need to reemphasize the great complexity of human interaction before attempting to present observations from the analysis of it. Such an interaction might be as commonplace and familiar as two friends sitting and talking together. We often forget the nature or context of the situation with which we began and, ultimately, it is the nature of that situation we are trying to comprehend. Human interaction brings together multiple dimensions of ordered involvement simultaneously. They are all there, all at once, and they do not appear to have any difficulty in occupying the same behavioral 'space'. It would require a long list with clarifying commentaries to even begin to encompass all these simultaneous involvements: the physical, the biological, the neurophysiological, the social, the psychological, the cultural, the historical, the personal; and less tangible things like the hopeful, the fearful, the lovable, the hateful, etc. This would also need to include all of the complex dimensions and interconnections of all the items which might be contained in such a list. The past, too, is there with its powerful molding force and the future with its aspirations. In dealing with behavior we are dealing with multiple, on-going events and their intertwining histories. Behavior is so integrated across all these dimensions that it is difficult to determine where the boundary of one ends and another begins. The nature of units (including their boundaries) and the organization of units constitute the observational aspect of the theoretical issue of the discretelike and the continuous.

When the investigator first begins to study the on-going flow of behavior at the micro level he is confronted by many things seemingly occurring all at once. As the speaker talks several.parts of his body may be moving in different directions and at differing speeds. The listener may also be moving at the same time. What items or distinguishable boundary points or events could one select *a priori* to posit as units? The essential point is that at this level there did not appear to be any events or things which might serve as a basis for units. It would seem that one of the logical requirements for the basic units of organized behavior would be an on-going continuity of existence. We cannot explain the continuous (the organized) by reducing the size and increasing the number of discrete bits. This is the ultimate dilemma of the experimentalist who slavishly follows a physicalistic Newtonian model in the study of behavior.

I will describe some of the major findings which have emerged from the frame-by-frame analysis of normal and pathological behavior in order to illustrate the organizational model. Using frame-numbered sound film it is possible to describe the points of change of movement of the body parts, using the joints as the descriptive points of change. The frame-numbered sound film serves somewhat like a clock but with the features to be timed embedded on it. For example the right forearm of a speaker may begin to extend at the elbow at frame number 106. It may continue extending for five frames or through frame number 111 and then begin to flex starting at frame number 112. Any other body parts also moving at the same time can be similarly described. After many months of such analysis and comparison of the movements of the body parts in relation to each other, I little by little began to be aware of a synchronicity or order in their relationships. The order did not reside in an individual body part by itself but in the relationship of the changes of the body parts in relation to each other. A relationship is sustained or maintained between the body parts for a brief duration, usually lasting two or three frames at 24 frames per second (f.p.s.). The body parts may be moving in different directions and with different speeds but they sustain these together.

The organizing or integrating of these synchronous change patterns was not (and could not have been) a function of the individual body parts as discrete or isolated entities. In other words, these ordered patterns of change were the expression of the wholistic behavioral unity of the organism and as such were still forms of organization although emerging as on-going movement bundles or quanta (Condon 1963b, 1964). This would clearly imply that behavioral organization cannot be derived from any exogenous combination of discrete segments or bits. This applies to interactional behavior as well. A unit of organized behavior at this minimal level was not 'thinglike' but was a form-of-order running through behavior. These forms of on-going order in the relationships of changes of the body parts in relation to each other in speaker behavior were isomorphic (both dimensionally and intensively) with the emergent flow of the units of his speech. Speech and body motion are behaviorally unified. The emergence of a new way to conceptualize the familiar requires hundreds of hours of laborious observations. This seems to be methodologically necessary in order to break through one's *a priori* assumptions about the nature of the material which only tend to permit things to be observed which are compatible with the structural framework imposed by those assumptions. This 'organizational' way of viewing processes has relevance for the analysis of the wider dimensions of both individual and interactional behavior.

As a speaker talks in normal everyday conversation there are very few times when he is absolutely still. He may be still during a pause in his speech or when he is listening. When no movement can be detected no statement can be made about the structure of the movement. (The person is, at these moments, however, sustaining a relationship between the resting body parts, i.e. a posture.) I am referring to the nature of the organization of behavior when the body is continuously moving across several sentences. The sustained relationship or movement bundle creates a momentary unity-of-form during the on-going movement of these body parts which can be contrasted with succeeding and following sustained relationships. One unity transforms into another as new relationships emerge and are sustained between the body parts. It is a continuous and on-going process: behavior is genuinely continuous yet discretelike. These units are the characteristic forms-of-order between the moving body parts. They are a wholistic description of the movement of the organism at this level. A boundary occurs at the point where one sustained pattern changes into another. A boundary is not defined in terms of a 'content enclosing surface' which separates units into isolated entities. When units are conceived in this fashion an external 'glue' or force is needed to combine them together. Behavior is of the organism as a wholistic unity and cannot be composed of isolated units combined in some fashion. Isolated parts could not provide the synchronous timing of movement changes in relation to each other which is basic to organized behavior. This also applies to the wider integration of behavior. The generalization of this pattern of serially emergent forms of momentary 'sustained relationships' in the flow of movement led to the hypothesis that these constituted the 'units' of behavior as organized. This form-of-order can be predicted to occur in normal movement structure no matter what body parts are moving. It occurs in animal behavior as well. I have studied baboon behavior and the behavior of a lion walking and it occurs in a similarly organized fashion. It appears to be a feature of the basic structural logic of the organized processing of nervous systems in general, at least at the mammalian level. How and where one body part is moving at a given moment and where it will be moments later is not separate from where the other body parts are and where they will be moments later. Such precise organization occurs between movements and speech in a normal speaker's behavior. I have called these movement bundles 'process units' to emphasize this organizational nature. These process units are felt to represent the basic nature of behavioral organization at the minimal level. They are the naturalistic units in terms of which organized behavior occurs and by which it must be described, at least at this micro level. As indicated, speaker behavior was discovered to be self-synchronous. This integration of speech and body motion extends across multiple dimensions. In essence, human speaker behavior is continuous and rhythmic both serially and hierarchically. This has been referred to as a 'rhythm hierarchy'. Figure 1 ('Keeping') illustrates the continuous nature of the relationship between levels. This wider organization within behavior will be discussed here.

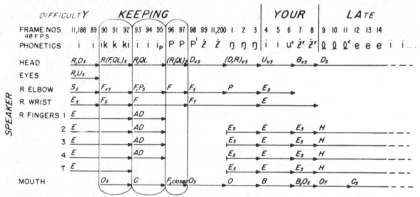

Figure 1.   *'Keeping'*

R = right; QL = incline left; D = down; U = up; B = back; S = supinate; P = pronate; F = flex.

E = extend; O = open (mouth); AD = adduct; C = close (mouth); H = hold of no movement.

Subscripts: s = slight; f = fast; vs = very slight, etc.

Figure I is a section from an actual transcription of a dyadic interaction. Two male friends are discussing their work and the speaker, at
the top, is saying, 'I was gonna ask you . . . why do you
. . . um . . . have difficulty with your late appointments?' The sustained body motion pattern across /iii/, frame numbers 93, 94, 95,
illustrates a process unit. The fingers had been extending but they
adduct (AD) precisely across the emission of /iii/ and isomorphic with it.
That which demarcates the three encircled process units is their contrast
with each other as three different and distinguishable forms where
separate relationships are being sustained. There is an on-going flow of
movements where a relationship is sustained to be followed by another.
These relational sustainings or pulses in the movement are isomorphic
with the emergent features of speech. Thus the 'keeping' behavior has
five speech features and five concomitant body motion quanta (five
process units) at this minimal level. The closed mouth precisely across the
stop consonant /pp/ at frame number 96, 97 indicates the precision
attainable in microanalysis.

Behavior is both serially and hierarchically continuous. Organization is
not just serial but occurs across multiple dimensions. The transcription
in Figure 1 was actually made prior to the hypothesis of hierarchic
continuity (the continuity between levels). In reviewing this material,
seeking an appropriate segment to illustrate that continuity, I became
aware of the following example. This had been done blind so to speak.
The illustration reveals how this hierarchic unity is organizationally
'hidden' in the behavior. Across /kkkiiipp/ the head moves right and
inclines left. This contrasts with a preceding right and down slight
movement and a following down very slight. That which gave rise to the
observation of this body motion isomorphism at this syllabic level was
the contrast indicated above. This item (the head sustaining a right and
incline left movement) was discovered to be a form of order by being
observed to sustain a unity of form in contrast with other similarly
sustained forms within the total behavior. It is not observed or
demarcated as such by putting together the three minimal units. This
wider unit does not exist as such in a sense until the wider forms are
available. We do not know that R,QL ends until the following movement
occurs: which did in fact end it precisely at that point. That which makes
the three minimal units to be such is their contrast as relational
sustainings at that level. In this sense they constitute the level. That
which makes the body motion across /kkkiiipp/ to be a unit is its contrast with forms at its level. It is a different form of order and arrived at
differently, but is integrated with the more minimal forms. The concept
that minimal forms of behavior are combined to form wider forms is
therefore not logically correct.

Body motion also precisely accompanies the emission of the total word 'keeping'. The right wrist had been extending. It begins to flex at the onset of the word and continues flexing until the end of the word where it then changes to extension. This organized integration of speech and body motion also characteristically exists across phrasal and sentence levels as well. There seems to be a marked one-second rhythm form in human speaker behavior (Condon 1977). That body motion should precisely accompany the emission of speech across multiple dimensions in this unitary fashion ties the motoric and the verbal together.

There appear to be different suborganizations of this rhythm hierarchy in different cultures. The rhythms are formed in complicated ways which involve the timing of change and speed of movement of the body parts in relation to each other. American Black speaker movement exhibits a syncopated rhythm in contrast to American White movement. Each language group will probably manifest its own body motion rhythms. Such differences may affect the interaction. Micro sound-film analysis is only just beginning to provide information about this complex dimension of behavior.

Analysis begins with processes which were organized to begin with (the speaker's total behavior, for example) and discovers contrastive sub-forms of organization of many kinds existing all at the same time within that unified behavior. The motion picture stores the sequential flow of an interaction (its history) so that it can be re-viewed hundreds of times with special slow-motion projection equipment in the search for these various suborganizations. One is able to shift one's focus flexibly and review over and over the varying dimensions of relationships that had occurred during the behavior. It must be remembered that these wider relationships, as in the case of the process units, are the integrated product of the total, unified organism.

The integration of human behavior does not stop with the individual however. There are many different forms and degrees of involvement in natural order. The human being participates simultaneously in many diverse systems of order. Just as the subforms of organization within an individual speaker's behavior can be detected so can a person's organizational relationship to the world in which he or she evolved. These seem to be no less legitimate organizational relationships than those within individual behavior. The human is as much a part of Nature as anything else. Man's involvement in wider human organizations, to use the previous analogy, cannot be reduced to an exogenous combination of human individuals. That which regulates or integrates these complex relationships between humans and the surround, including fellow human beings, can be discovered in the interpenetrating wider forms-of-order discernable in those relationships. The individuals do not create that order but participate in it. They 'live into' the forms and experiences which surround them and these forms become part of their very being.

The intensive, frame-by-frame microanalysis of listener behavior led to the development of a view of a person's relationship 'to' the surround as one of a living, participant involvement. This analysis revealed that the listener moves synchronously with the articulatory structure of the speaker's speech. Since listener behavior had never been intensively, organizationally analyzed at this microlevel, this phenomenon had remained unnoticed. I called this process 'interactional synchrony'. It reflects a complicated form of organizational relationship with the surround: this relationship seems to be both perceptual and emotional. The listener moves in organizations-of-change (process units) which parallel the articulatory patterning and intensity of the speaker's speech. There is a physical continuity in the flow of sound between interactants. The sound waves from the speaker's voice are propagated through the air. Assemblies of cells in the listener's auditory system convey the order of the sound which is being received. Millions of years were required to achieve this ability. The listener appears to precisely modulate this in-coming auditory signal in on-going fashion and such modulation is wholistically reflected in the organizations-of-change of his or her body motion. This modulation occurs within a latency time of 50 msec. The listener moves in synchrony with the speaker's speech almost as well as the speaker himself does. There is an unbroken continuity in the propagation of ordered patterns through the various media linking the speaker and the listener. We speak of communication occurring 'between' people and sometimes overlook the fact that this distinction does not create a vacuum in the intervening space between them. The media may differ: the brain, vocal cords and mouth of the speaker — the compression and rarefaction of the intervening air — the auditory receptive system of the listener. But that which flows through them is a similar order; so that what is sent and what is received are understood and shared by both speaker and listener. What all aspects of this process have in common is the propagation and reception of order. There is no 'between' in the continuum of order.

There can be a relatively continuous yet constantly varying stream of speech from the speaker which is being almost simultaneously and organizationally tracked as expressed in the varying body motion configurations of the listener. The body of the normal listener moves in organized bundles-of-change which emerge in on-going, serial, parallel fashion (entrain) with the emergent structure of the speaker's speech.

The precision and speed with which the listener's body moves in synchronized organization with the speaker's speech led to the postulation of a primary, short-latency entrainment component in the human responding process (Condon 1977). We are organizationally interfaced with and are part of the world which surrounds us: the organization of change of the listener's body reflects such perceptual involvement. The postulated, primary entrainment phase also probably simultaneously involves an incipient discrimination process. That the listener's body motion patterns reflect the structure of the incoming signal indicates that the brain is also tracking the incoming structure of that signal. Since such incoming structures contain the segmental units of speech, such tracking provides a basis for discriminating these units. It also provides a concomitant basis for the reception and discrimination of larger syntactic forms. The speaker provides the listener with the speech elements already organized into larger integrated forms. The listener does not have to assemble the incoming words into meaningful sentences since this is done for him by the speaker. Pitch and stress function importantly in this syntactic organizing. It is quite possible and probable that the listener processes speech across several levels simultaneously. The view being presented here (and it reflects the basic view espoused in the paper) is that the listener processes incoming speech at both discretelike and continuous levels simultaneously without contradiction.

The view that wholes are made up of parts and must be analyzed into parts dominates our thought and culture so extensively that we find it difficult to imagine how an alternative perspective could even be conceived. But an intensive analysis of behavior reveals that it is, in fact, both discretelike and continuous. Nature itself, however, is neither discretelike nor continuous, but is such that these distinctions arise when its eventfulness is subjected to inquiry. All of our categories and distinctions arise within Nature and do not apply to Nature as a totality. Nature is not in space or in time, but space and time are categories within Nature. Nature is neither fast nor slow, or sometimes in the light and sometimes in the dark. We need to examine how we categorize existence, where these categories come from, and how we might be clearer about them.

Interactional synchrony or entrainment begins very early in human life. Sound films were obtained of 16 normal neonates, one to four days old. Audio tape records of human voices, including spoken Chinese from learning tapes, and live human voices were presented during the filming. All of the infants exhibited a marked synchronization of body movement with both tape-recorded and live human voices (Condon and Sander 1974a, 1974b). It has been observed in a sound film of an infant as early as 20 minutes after birth, and may exist *in utero*. The infant lives itself into language and culture: into the forms which surround and support it. It does not 'acquire' them as if from a separate system existing apart.

The microanalysis of behavior has led me to a deep conviction of the profound interweaving of Nature's processes. Interactional synchrony or entrainment, particularly, emphasizes the role of the brain as the mediating organ of perception and reason. It reflects the order of events and a consciousness of them so that there is a shared world expanded before us. The order pervading the universe is perceptually and cognitively available to man in precise detail. To the persistently inquiring mind it reveals lawful and predictable patterns across multiple dimensions. Nature's own materials cooperate in the attainment of greater understanding: clocks and yardsticks are as much a part of Nature as anything else and obey the laws which they help us discover. The sharpness and clarity of this participation can diminish when damage to the brain interferes with its ability to adequately convey the order of events or when it conveys them in distorted form. The study of pathology accentuates the regularities of the normal perceptual and cognitive response relationship with the surround. The knowledge relationship depends on a far deeper intimacy with Nature than can be comprehended by the juxtaposition of an isolated organism in relation to an equally separate surround. Knowing is a form of communication with the surround and that communication was developed within and is continually supported by natural processes. Human communication also ultimately depends upon and is derived from this basic per-ceptual/cognitive continuity.

Normal response exhibits temporal regularities which can be observed in the timing of the eye movements, the turn of the head, the verbal acknowledgement, and the motion and rhythms of the listener's body in relation to sounds, particularly human speech. A listener provides the speaker with almost constant feedback that he is attending, including information about the level of that attending. The body of the listener moves in time and intensity with the speech of the speaker. The speaker is probably aware at some level of the listener's responsive entrainment and the many subtle variations in it. We, as normals, participate across many levels and in many ways in all the subtle timings and complexities of this responsive process. The microanalytic, sound-film analysis of autisticlike children, however, reveals response configurations which differ markedly from those of normal subjects. When the organizational linkage of the brain with the surround is disturbed, the familiar world, as revealed in our responses to it, appears to be lost. The brain is organizationally and functionally linked to the surround through sharing in a common order: it is as if the order of Nature and the order of the brain were one. It is this order that provides the continuity in the brain–surround relationship. That the form of the order propagated by aspects of Nature (light, sound, etc.) is the order receivable by the sensory/brain-system (another aspect of Nature) can be accounted for by the hypothesis that this reciprocity was evolved over countless millenia: and that both are integrated aspects of still wider, natural processes. The following material on the auditory response of autisticlike children is presented to heighten the awareness of this dependency of normal perception and cognition on the orderly processing of the order of the surround by the brain.

Some autisticlike children do not seem to be in full contact with the world. These children appear as if they are not responding to many of the events (particularly auditory events) in *our* world. These children do not respond to sounds with the timing structures or patterns we are accustomed to expect of people in relation to the sounds in the world about them. The post-sound-stimulus body movement behavior of autisticlike children was studied using the frame-by-frame, microanalytic approach. The concept of entrainment to sound, served as the criterion of response. These children exhibited three major behavioral differences from normal controls.

1. *Asynchrony.* The body motion of these children was asynchronous in contrast to the precise self-synchrony of normal children. For example, one side of the face might pull markedly to the side, one eyelid might move faster than the other, or one eye might move faster. One side of the face would look different than the other side. In general, one half of the body appeared to be asynchronous or out-of-phase with the other half as if one half of the brain were out of phase with the other. All of this suggests some degree of neurological impairment.

2. *Multiple entrainment to sound.* These children appear to respond to the same sound as if the sound were echoing or reverberating. They have marked, post-sound-stimulus, body motion perturbations. Their bodies jump and jerk at various intervals (latencies) following a sound. When one steps on the accelerator of a finely tuned automobile it moves ahead smoothly and evenly. This would be a crude analogy of how a normal child processes sound stimuli. However, when one steps on the accelerator of a badly tuned auto it moves forward haltingly, with starts and jerks. This would be analogous to the way sound stimuli seem to pass through the neurological processes of dysfunctional children. This post-sound-stimulus perturbation seems to take the form of a multiple entrainment to the sound. It is as if the short-latency entrainment phase, instead of occurring just once as in normal behavior, were repeated several times and at specific delay intervals. Each sound input seems to

follow a particular neurological pattern of damage for a given child. Most of these children probably do not actually hear sound multiple times but some aspect of the nervous system consistently acts as if the same sound were recurring and this recurrence is manifested in observable body motion entrainments.

3. *Multiple orienting response.* The more severely autisticlike children exhibit a multiple *orienting* response as well. These seem to be directly related to (as if they were in response to) the postulated multiple entrainments to sound. An orienting response is the response of orienting oneself toward perceived stimuli, such as looking around in response to hearing one's name called. In daily life such looking around (within a certain time limit) provides the speaker with evidence that the person has heard him. Autisticlike children, however, look around several times (usually late) following most of the sound stimuli around them, even inanimate sounds. A single sound is oriented to as if it were occurring several times and each time from a different location. The systematic timing of these orienting responses in relation to the postulated repeating sound inputs gives an impression that these children are not in 'contact' with the world. It is as if these children were receiving a distorted version of natural stimulus patterns due to neurological malfunction and their 'response' reflected the structure of that distortion. We may get some idea of their world by understanding these distortions. These children are assumed to be out of contact because their response patterns are dislocated temporally and orientationally so that their behavior is not seen as responsive by normal people. A response is relative to the framework of the observer. To have a world is to maintain and operate in a consistent relationship which reflects the order and operations of that world.

The hypothesized perceptual distortion in autism can actually be artificially approximatèd in a sound film of one of these children by delaying and repeating the sound track on a copy of that film to simulate the postulated multiple sound inputs. When this is done the child suddenly seems to be looking this way and that in precise response to these now delayed and repeated sounds. The child exhibits a systematic orienting response to random sounds which have been systematically delayed and repeated. In a sense, a distorted sound input system has been created artificially which systematically matches his actual response patterns. The systematic form of these relationships aids in clarifying his 'looking around' as orienting responses: an ordered relationship has been observed. The multiple entrainment has been found to occur across a wide spectrum of types of childhood dysfunction, from autism at the severe end to dyslexia at the mild end. The multiple orienting response seems to be characteristic of only the more severe autisticlike dysfunctions. These observations from the study of dysfunctional behavior were presented, again, to emphasize the 'order–continuum' between the brain and the surround. When the ordered continuity of this relationship breaks down the world becomes distorted and can even be lost.

Human history has been an illustration of the search for an identity — that of the self. There has been an on-going clash between systems of belief and believable systems (based on information gathering). Emergent information which gains assent has an impact on prevailing systems of belief, often forcing reformulations. Our age, perhaps more than any other, is characterized by people beginning to study themselves as objects of knowledge. This is related more to man as a person in societies of persons and not so much to his physical nature which has had a longer history of study. People themselves and all their behaviors are taken as objects of knowledge. They are assumed to be as fully determined as any other natural process, even though incredibly complicated. The study of verbal and nonverbal communication highlights this trend. These are only two illustrations among a vast number of such studies across many dimensions. We are information gatherers as other cultures were food gatherers of various types. Humans are only animals, although specialized by their degree of intelligence. They will be found to be more and more fully determined. All aspects of their existence are beginning to be scrutinized: their gaze patterns, their postures and movements, their intonational patterns, their verbalizations, their communicational leakages, their slips, their hesitations, their greetings, and their courtships and aggressions. And as their identity shrinks one wonders how they will come to view themselves and their purposes. These are questions which also need to be raised. Human communication does not exist in a vacuum and greater knowledge of human behavior will have consequences on how people view themselves.

A basic personal conviction that has emerged from the microanalysis of sound films, as I have probably overstressed, is that human behavior and communication are profoundly ordered and integrated across many dimensions. The following section will deal with some wider aspects of the organization of human communication but in a more speculative fashion. Synchrony and other forms of behavioral sharing express degrees of closeness or distance between interactants. The very important pioneering work of Scheflen on posture sharing and quasi courtship is well known (Scheflen 1973). Much further work needs to be done in this area, particularly exploring all the subtle forms that behavioral statements about human relationships can take. There is a constant waxing and waning of the nature of the relationship: there is approach and retreat, dominance and submission, closeness and distance, superiority and inferiority, and all the subtle explicit and implicit evaluations contained in them. I am convinced that interaction can have important and lasting effects on the 'inner life' of interactants, especially developmentally. Communication has an ethical dimension which needs to be made explicit. Three examples may clarify what I am referring to.

1. While shopping I observed the following episode. A black mother and her children were slowly moving down an aisle from table to table examining the clothing. A white mother and her children were doing the same from the opposite direction and on the other side of the aisle. As the two groups passed a girl from the black family smiled in a friendly way at a girl in the white family. The white girl grimaced and turned her head. The groups continued on. The black girl glanced back with a hurt look on her face. This episode lasted just a few seconds. A smile and a grimace and their timing are not just indifferent parts of the structure of behavior but can have an effect on the inner being of the interactants.

2. In a family there were lovely, teen-aged, twin daughters. One daughter was diagnosed as schizophrenic. A sound film was made of the mother and the twins talking with a psychiatric resident. In the film the mother either shared posture or moved in heightened synchrony with the 'well' twin over 95 per cent of the time. It was as if the so-called 'sick twin' was being excluded from the interaction. The mother would only briefly share posture or movement with her. There is a poignant aspect to some of the hidden features in this out-of-awareness interactional process. The mother might be sitting with her right hand on her chin. The sick twin would shift posture and bring her right hand up to her chin, thus sharing posture with her mother. The mother would almost immediately bring her hand down. This postural distancing happened many times in various ways, suggesting a consistent pattern of nonverbal rejection. There is no blame in this, the sick twin may not have been responsive to the mother as a child, etc.

3. One mother had several nonverbal and paralinguistic features which she characteristically displayed when talking about her four-year-old son. She would clear her throat in a rasping fashion just prior to referring to him or she might grimace markedly at that point or both. He was often present at these moments, which were many, and seemed painfully aware that they related to him. She constantly complained, in a narrow, squeezed voice, about how much of a feeding problem he had been. During one such episode, the young boy, who had been playing on the floor, got up and brought her a pillow as if in atonement. She coldly took the pillow and, as he turned away, glared malevolently at his retreating back.

Communication is not just a process of 'bits' of information traveling between people: it is as much an overarching domain of trust and distrust; the multitudinous and subtle ways by which people love and hate, praise and blame, accept and reject — themselves as well as others. As such they affect the inner being of others, there to aid or hinder, with greater or lesser consequences on that inner life. R. D. Laing (1969) speaks of the self's identity as partially dependent on how people think others view them. 'A person's "own" identity cannot be completely abstracted from his identity-for-others; his identity-for-himself; the identity others ascribe to him; the identities he attributes to them; the identity or identities he thinks they attribute to him; what he thinks they think he thinks they think . . .' In this Laing follows the views of Sartre and Kierkegaard. There are many levels and types of subtle 'indoctrination' both past and present, incessantly alerting interactants for clues of impending judgements. T. S. Eliot (1934) alludes to this:

> And I have known the eyes already, known them
> all —
> The eyes that fix you in a formulated phrase,
> And when I am formulated, sprawling on a pin,
> When I am pinned and wriggling on the wall,
> Then how should I begin
> To spit out all the butt-ends of my days and
> ways?
>   and how should I presume?

Thus we are born, participants, into a preexisting family in a preexisting culture with ordered, communicational processes across many subtle dimensions. Our lives, as we grow, pattern in response to the patterns that we meet: of love and hate, praise and blame, acceptance and rejection; and of all the other ordered ways of that society. And the inner life, the relation of the self to the self, thereby fatefully becomes defined. Erik Erikson (1964), one of the leading thinkers on the dynamics of the inner life, has the following to say.

Later in childhood comes the time when the child enjoys his autonomy, standing on his own feet, wobbly but his own. He becomes aware of a whole circle of approving eyes which makes the space he masters both safe and secure. He learns to suppress some of his willfulness for the reward of feeling at one with the will of those around him. But, alas, the moments of disapproval and shaming also come, when he is frowned upon and laughed at, and blushes in anger not knowing with whom he is most angry: his exposed self or the hostile watchers. This, then, is the second uprootedness, that awareness of an exposed self by which man becomes an outsider to himself. From here on he is never fully himself and never fully 'them'. He will try at times, to become totally himself by identifying with his rebellious impulses; or try to become totally the others by making their laws his compulsions; or he may do both, with the result that he doubts himself as well as the others.

These, then, are some of the inescapable inner divisions which come about as man, freed of his biological navel cord, finds his place in the social and moral universe. Much of what we ascribe to neurotic *anxiety* and much of what we ascribe to existential *dread* is really only man's distinctive form of fear: for as an animal, for the sake of survival, scans near and far with specialized senses fit for a special environment, man must scan both his inner and his outer environment for indications of permissible activity and for promises of identity.

What happens during interaction tends to reciprocally mold people into what they are. Communication is not an external or alien system which can be studied apart from its involvement in what it means and does to the communicants. It is a fundamental part of their existence and has profound consequences. Insofar as it has such consequences, it necessarily has ethical implications. 'The pursuit of knowledge apart from the pursuit of happiness is ultimately meaningless' (Woodbridge 1940). Nature does not need our knowledge or our equations in order for it to manifest its powers. Existence is for people to make of what they can aspire to, not just to fit into a preordained destiny or purpose. Much of human life is enslaved to past experiences and this is intertwined with a similar enslavement to culture; both are expressed in the behavior of our lives. We cannot totally escape them but we can be much more aware of them and their influence. Edward T. Hall, in his superb book *Beyond Culture* (1977), explores how we are driven by the way cultural forms dominate the times and spaces of our lives out-of-awareness, often leading to misconceptions when we interact with other cultures. Our culture seems to drive us in ways which prevent the fulfillment of human life. Alan Lomax (1977) appeals for cultural equity. There is a need to rise above our own narrow cultural form and recognize the right of other cultural forms. There is a great shallowness in most of the philosophies which are supposed to guide human destiny. The student of human behavior cannot remain aloof from the implications and promises of his studies. We can utilize our understanding of how all the subtle aspects of communication affect the inner life in order to create a society where the achievement of a meaningful existence is available to all.

NOTE

1. W. S. Condon is partially supported by the Medical Foundation (through the Dr. Charles H. Weed memorial award) which is the Research and Community Health Agency of United Way of Massachusetts Bay.

WILLETT KEMPTON

The Rhythmic Basis of Interactional Micro-Synchrony[1]

SELF-SYNCHRONY AND INTERACTIONAL SYNCHRONY

An analysis of microkinesic activity begins with recording human motion and speech on sound film or videotape. The film is viewed frame by frame, using a time/motion analyzer (or similar video device), which permits viewing of a single frame and short series of frames. If a linguistic microanalysis is to be done in conjunction with the motion analysis, a phonetic transcription is also made, using the sound track of the film. The speech is broken down in sufficient detail to associate a single phonetic symbol with each frame of film.

An early discovery of Condon's analysis was self-synchrony: during speech, various parts of the speaker's body move in time with each other and with the articulation of his speech. Although different body parts move at different speeds and in different directions, they tend to change direction at the same time. That is, most frames contain no change in body motion, while several points of change in direction of movement will occur on the same frame of film simultaneously with a juncture in speech articulation. The following example (Condon and Brosin 1969) of movement during the articulation of the word 'why' /uuᵊᵛᵊᵛeˀeˀiii/, which occupies nine frames in a 48-frames-per-second film, illustrates this synchronization:

As subject B articulates the /uu/, a voiceless, high back vocoid which is the syllabic consonant /w/ of 'why', his head moves right, forward and down slightly; while his eyelid begins to come down very slightly at the onset of the eye blink; while his brows go up slightly; while his mouth opens; while the trunk moves forward and right, while the right shoulder is locked, i.e. remains relatively still; while his right elbow extends; while his right wrist flexes slightly, while joints B and C of the index finger extend slightly and the finger adducts slightly; while joints A, B and C of fingers 2, 3 and 4 flex; while the thumb remains relatively still. Almost all of the above body parts sustain their direction of movement precisely across the emission of /uu/ then change to a new direction together at the onset of /əˠəˠ/. The right elbow, however, sustains its extension across both /u̯u̯/ and /əˠəˠ/ where it then pronates. Fingers 3 and 4 sustain their flexion across the first aspect of the word 'why' — /u̯u̯əˠəˠeˀeˀ/. When some body elements sustain direction of change longer than the rest of the body, they are accompanying a wider segment (817).

In the above description, 'while' refers to the same frame of 48 f.p.s. sound film; thus 'simultaneous' events occur at least within the same 20 millisecond interval.

Condon reports that the phrase is the largest unit across which body motion is sustained synchronously. At the gross level of phrase it is easy to see speech–body synchrony without the aid of instruments. It is a common observation that people 'gesture in time with their speech' at the phrase level.

These motion changes exhibit a hierarchical organization which corresponds to the hierarchical organization of speech. This hierarchy is illustrated in the above example by the change in movement of more body parts when there is a point of greater articulatory change; that is, some motions are sustained across higher linguistic segments. Hierarchical organization is also sometimes manifested in greater or lesser amounts of change within complex movements of a single body part.

A quite surprising discovery was made when films of people *listening* to speech were also subjected to microkinesic analysis:

The hearer's behavior is also organized self-synchronously, following the same principles as that of the speaker . . . The units of the hearer's behavior are usually formed by different body parts moving or the same body parts moving in directions different than those of a speaker, but *they sustain direction of movement as the speakers sustain direction of movement and change when the speakers change.* Interactional synchrony is defined by this *isomorphism of pattern of change* between the speaker [and] hearer. This isomorphism is difficult to detect at the normal speed of body motion (Condon and Ogston 1971: 159, emphasis added).

Interactional synchrony appears with frame-by-frame analysis as the precise 'dancelike' sharing of micro-body-motion patterns of change between speaker and listener (Condon and Sander 1974b: 459).

The transcription system illustrated in Figure 1 has been developed (Condon 1975a) to record this synchronization. Each horizontal line indicates movement of one part of the body, and arrow points signify a change in motion, with the actual direction of movement indicated by the letters above the line (e.g. R,D$_S$ is right and down slowly, F$_{VS}$ is flex very slowly, etc.). Note that although speaker and hearer simultaneously change movement eight times (i.e. there are changes between eight different pairs of adjacent frames), and they both sustain movement 16 times, only once does one interactant change movement while the other sustains (between frames 11,211 and 11,212 the speaker starts closing his mouth slowly).

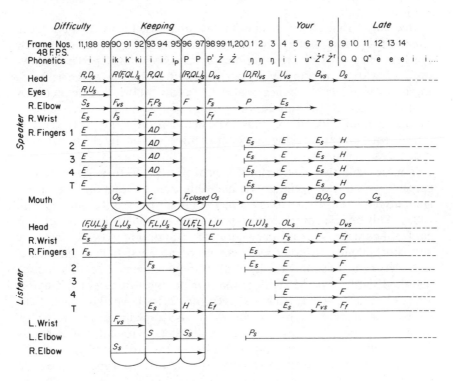

Figure 1. *Microkinesic transcription*

This 'interactional synchrony'[2] is most pronounced at the syllabic level, but occurs from the phone up through the word level, and in certain social settings characterized by 'heightened synchrony' it will occur at the phrase level as well. Interactional synchrony has been observed in *all* normal human interaction, including that of nonliterate peoples from diverse cultures (Condon 1968: 33–36), and in group interaction, where several listeners move in synchrony with one speaker (Condon and Sander 1974b: 459).

HOW CAN INTERACTIONAL SYNCHRONY BE EXPLAINED?

It may not be too surprising that a speaker coordinates the muscular activity of his speech production with his other muscular activity, but the finding that a listener also synchronizes with that speech (to within at least 20 milliseconds) is quite remarkable. It is illuminating to compare this phenomenon with other measurements of human response to auditory stimuli.

One might first try to explain interactional synchrony as the listener simply 'following' along with the speaker. The ability to follow speech has been measured by the experimental task known as 'speech shadowing', in which the subject repeats continuous speech as he is hearing it. Individuals are typically able to follow 500 to 800 milliseconds behind the speech they are hearing, with exceptional shadowers able to average within 250 milliseconds (Marslen-Wilson 1973: 523). This is clearly too slow to be the mechanism involved in interactional synchrony.

Is it possible that interactional synchrony is due to any *reaction to* speech? As a lowest boundary on plausible time of reaction to auditory stimulus, it is illustrative to examine the latency of the stapedial muscle reflex. This muscle contracts in response to loud sounds and protects the ear from damage, so from an evolutionary standpoint we would expect a very short latency. It should also react more rapidly than body parts such as fingers or arms simply on the basis of the relative number of synapses and the length of the nerve fibers that the impulse traverses (cf. Guyton 1971: 61, 72, 592–603). However, even this reflex latency is slower than the latency of interactional synchrony — the stapedial muscle reflex of different subjects ranges from 25 milliseconds to 130 milliseconds (Møller 1958). Thus, we must discard 'reaction to' or 'following of' articulatory changes as an explanation of interactional synchrony on the basis of these measurements of response to auditory stimulus.

A different sort of explanation for the remarkably close synchronization of speaker and hearer might utilize the fact that speech information is spread out: minor modifications in the speech stream indicate coming points of articulatory change. Perhaps the hearer has enough advance indication to be able to react by the time the change in articulation actually occurs. An explanation of this sort is severely weakened by several examples of interactional synchronization occurring with only visual contact. In one instance, two people who were facing each other went through a series of exactly synchronized movements in the absence of speech (Condon and Ogston 1971: 161). Several other examples (Condon 1963b: 7; Kendon 1970: 120; Davis 1973: 119) indicate that a visual channel alone is sufficient to maintain interactional synchrony.

In summary, interactional synchrony cannot be explained as a reaction or reflex to the sound or movement as it is being perceived. Unless we are prepared to propose some sort of extrasensory perception, we must hypothesize that synchronization occurs as a result of both interactants sharing *mutually known rhythmic patterns*. That is, interactants anticipate coming points of articulatory change or movement change by using prior change points in the utterance and their knowledge of the rhythmic patterns of human language (or the patterns of a particular language). We move together in all everyday interaction by using the same ability that allows us to dance with someone, or sing in time with another person's song (cf. List 1963).

If shared rhythmic patterns are the explanation for interactional synchrony, their structure is as yet unknown. The synchronized points of change are not at all equally spaced — interactants may sustain movement across three frames and change between the third and the fourth; then sustain across the next five, then across one, then across two, then two, then one, and so on[3] (cf. Condon 1973: Fig. 6). Thus, the rhythm of interactional synchrony is more than just the regularly timed beat discussed by Lenneberg (1967: 120); interactants must be following more complex rhythms which are not yet understood.

One could argue that the observation of interactional synchrony is an illusion — an artifact of the instruments or of the methodology used in analysis. The results of a number of methodological checks demonstrate that this is not the case. Different observers coding the change points in body motion show high reliability in their transcriptions.[4] In a test of the film equipment, a transcription was made of the synchronization of two people who were not interacting with each other, but rather with two other individuals off camera. If interactional synchrony was an artifact of the equipment it would have occurred in this situation, but in fact interactional synchrony was not observed (Condon and Ogston 1971: 158). Another test was performed by superimposing the sound track of one film onto another film of body motions made during different speech; this superimposed film displayed significantly lower self-synchronization than the normally recorded films (Condon and Sander 1974a: 101). An additional indirect verification of the technique is the observation that certain individuals who have been diagnosed as abnormal on other grounds also exhibit reduced or greatly changed interactional synchrony (Condon 1968, 1971, 1975b; Condon and Brosin 1969). In light of these explicit methodological checks and of the observation of dyssynchrony in certain pathological individuals, we must conclude that interactional synchrony is a real phenomenon; it is not an artifact of observational techniques.

The discovery of interactional synchrony provides a new perspective on human interaction, and suggests new methods of collecting data for the study of social phenomena. In addition to the obvious alternating transmission of discrete messages, there is a level of human interaction in which all participants actively and simultaneously share communicative behavior. A great deal of information may be carried by the rhythmic patterns of interactional synchrony themselves, rather than by overt words, expressions or gestures. These rhythmic patterns are observable and recordable (although their structure is not yet clear), and they should provide considerable information about interaction in diverse situations. A large part of the transcription process is mechanical (i.e. does not require subjective judgments), so we might reasonably inquire whether all or part of the time-consuming data collection procedures could be automated (cf. Kempton 1975).

NEONATE SYNCHRONIZATION AND THE QUESTION OF ACQUISITION

After observing interactional synchrony during adult interaction, our first inquiry might be: To what extent is this an innate ability, and to what extent is it acquired? Stark and Nathanson (1974: 340) independently discovered *self*-synchrony in four- to 19-day-old infants (they do not use this term, and seem to be unaware of Condon's work). After comparing sound spectrograms to frame-by-frame viewing of 16 f.p.s. film, they conclude that 'auditory features [of crying] do correlate quite highly with face, mouth and body gestures'.

Synchrony patterns exhibit cultural and subcultural differences (Condon 1968: 28, 36; 1973: 20, 23; personal communications 1973, 1975), so the socialization process must have an effect on interactional synchrony. However, it has been demonstrated (Condon and Sander 1974a) that the neonate has some ability to synchronize with speech of others immediately after birth:

This two-day-old infant displayed segments of movement synchronous with the adult's speech during the entire 89-word sequence . . . [this] precision of synchronization characterized the correspondence between adult speech and infant movement for all 16 infants [who ranged from 12 hours to 14 days old] . . . Chinese presented to American neonates was associated with as clear a correspondence as was American English (101).

The possibility of the adult synchronizing his speech with the infant's movement was ruled out by the use of tape-recorded adult speech. Thus, *some* ability for interactional synchrony is either acquired *in utero*, or is innate.

This synchronized neonate movement does not occur in reaction to all types of sound. The same group of neonates was presented with tapes of normal speech, vowels pronounced separately, and tapping sounds. The isolated vowels and the tapping sounds failed to show the degree of correspondence associated with natural, rhythmic speech (Condon and Sander 1974a: 101; 1974b: 461). It seems further that if a neonate is awake and alert, it will always move in time with natural human speech in its environment (Condon 1973: 19).

Since synchrony occurs from at least the first day of life, it is reasonable to expect that it provides an information channel for early socialization, as suggested by Condon and Sander (1974b):

If the infant, from the beginning, moves in precise, shared rhythm with the organization of the speech structure of his culture, then he participates developmentally through complex, sociobiological entrainment processes in millions of repetitions of linguistic forms long before he will later use them in speaking and communicating. By the time he begins to speak he may have already laid down within himself the form and structure of the language system of his culture (462).

The importance of rhythm in early socialization is also stressed by Tonkova-Yampol'skaya (1973), based on the careful analysis of infant vocalizations during parent–child interaction. He says that language learning begins with the intonational structure and that this constitutes the primary speech development during the first six months. New forms of intonation are acquired by contact with adults, indicating intonational interaction between the infant and parent (Tonkova-Yampol'skaya 1973: 137; cf. Weir 1966). The high frequency of special intonation in early socialization also suggests its importance — Blount and Padgug (1977) have found that between 52 and 78 percent of parental utterances to young children (9 to 22 months) are exaggerated in intonation. At this early stage, the acquisition of synchronization patterns surely combines aspects of 'learning the language' and 'learning how to interact'. Investigation of developmental changes in interactional synchrony should provide insight into this fundamental early socialization process.

Condon mentions cultural and subcultural differences in body synchrony and difficulties in cross-ethnic communication (1971: 20; personal communication 1975), but he does not report whether or not or to what degree adults can synchronize with the rhythmic patterns of a strange language. The presence of intergroup differences suggests a reduced ability to synchronize with the speech of a foreign language. If so, there is an interesting parallel between socialization into linguistic or cultural rhythms and the acquisition of the phonemic system. At one developmental stage every infant can produce the phones of all languages, but as sounds become categorized and combinations of them are associated with meanings, his ability to produce sounds is constrained by the phonemic system of the learned language (Jakobson 1941). If development of interactional synchrony is similarly channeled within the patterns prescribed for a particular group, the neonate would be expected to synchronize much better to a totally strange language than an adult could. In addition, if acquisition of a language improves the neonate's ability to synchronize with speech, adult language speakers would be expected to synchronize more closely to their own language than would neonates. These hypotheses can easily be experimentally verified, and should be tested.

CONCLUSIONS

The existence of precise synchronization between interacting individuals requires a view of human communicative activity as a shared rhythmic process, with listeners participating simultaneously with the speaker. If there is a delay in the synchronization of the listener, it is less than 20 milliseconds. Comparison of this maximum delay to other responses to auditory stimuli demonstrates that interactional synchrony cannot reasonably be explained as the listener following or reacting to the speaker. Motion synchrony can occur through visual contact in the absence of speech; presumably both sight and hearing provide rhythmic contact in most face-to-face interaction. It would be informative to examine body synchrony of congenitally blind and congenitally deaf individuals for comparison of the influence of these two perceptual channels. Synchronization with speech of different languages is observable on the first day of life, while synchronization does not occur with non-speech sounds. The facts of early ability and cultural diversity need to be resolved by comparison of neonate synchronization with adults listening to their own language and with adults listening to an unfamiliar language.

Other work, not reviewed here, suggests differences in synchrony patterns related to status, role, and interactional strategy (Condon 1963b, 1964, 1968, 1971, 1973; DeLong 1974; Kendon 1970, 1972). Condon (1973) claims that changes in interactional synchrony communicate 'closeness and distance, sympathy and understanding, acceptance and rejection, agreement and disagreement' (19). These very interesting subjective observations need to be supported with more explicit measurement procedures before they can be properly evaluated.

Interactional synchrony is the simultaneous sharing of changes in muscular activity between speaker and hearer. It constitutes an inter-individual coordination of much greater detail and complexity than we would expect from casual observation. By making this coordination visible, microkinesic analysis provides a time microscope for human interaction; it permits a close examination of the rhythmic forces which link individuals in social activity.

NOTES

1. Portions of this paper were first outlined in a seminar paper written for Mary Sanches at the University of Texas at Austin. This work has benefited from her suggestions and from comments by Ben Blount, Eliot Chapple, William Condon, Rebecca Field, Karl Fryxell, Frank Hall, Ann Millard, Cristina Monzón G. and Brian Stross, although not all of their criticisms have been answered here. Especial thanks to Andrea Meditch and Kathryn Dolan, without their early encouragement and numerous direct contributions this paper would not have been written.
2. This term is used by Chapple to denote a slower and substantially different interactional rhythm based on biological oscillators (1970, 1971).
3. It is interesting to note in passing that Birdwhistell's most 'micro' analysis missed the bulk of this synchronization phenomenon because of his methodological decision to examine only *every third frame* of 24 f.p.s. movie film (1970b: 241). He was still able to discern one example of synchrony across higher segments (1970b: 227), but he has not pursued this observation.
4. Independent coders ranged between 86 percent and 97 percent agreement (Condon and Sander 1974a: 100).

RUTH FRIDMAN

Proto-Rhythms: Nonverbal to Language and Musical Acquisition

Proto-rhythms is a line of investigation based on the sonorous–rhythmic expressions of the cry of the newborn. The present article is a continuation of previous studies (Fridman 1971, 1973, in preparation), and especially my recent book, *Los Comienzos de la Conducta Musical* (1974b). Three infants had been my first models of observation; later, four infants were observed: a boy who was born by Caesarean operation and triplets, a girl and two boys. The first group was studied from the moment of their birth up to their first birthday. With the second group I began by recording the beating of their hearts in fetal state (Fridman 1974a). They are three-and-a-half years old now. In addition to those infants, I have recorded many others to compare their rhythmic expressions. Lately I have analyzed the cries of six North American infants between 17 and 48 hours of age. [1] For the objectives of the present study I will present the data of Infant A and the triplets. As this work will develop the reader will be able to appreciate how proto-rhythms are the base for nonverbal communication as well as for future verbal communication and musical acquisition.

PROTO-RHYTHMS

When I was recording the observations and transcriptions of the first group of infants, I verified the existence of rhythms common to each of them. At that time, my objectives were based on the verification of the following hypotheses:
1. The first cry would structure intonated language.
2. Intonated language would be the basis for the development of articulated language.
3. Intonated language would be the basis for the development of musical activity.

After gathering the material from the second group (Infant A, and the triplets, B, C, and D) I began to analyze the rhythmic aspect of their sonorous expression. From the beginning, rhythm caught my attention. There is rhythm in the inspiration between cry and cry, there is rhythm in the values which structure cry or in the reiteration of some rhythmic values or in the appearance of new values, etc. Also of interest was the rhythm of the hiccough, cough, panting, sneezing, sucking, belching, etc. Afterwards, I verified that the former rhythmic values were expressed in a different way, as time went on. They were expressed not only through crying, but also apart from it. That led me to attach great importance to the rhythmic element (Fridman 1974c). The infant exercises in a thousand ways its own rhythmic schemes. Pre-linguistic phonology is formed by rhythmic values, which are included in the first cry. I started this study with the following hypotheses:

1. Phonology of the infant would be formed on a primary rhythmic net (proto-rhythms) of physiological origin, over which words similar to those of adult language would be constituted.

2. Rhythmic vocal expressions are of physiological origin that is genetically planned.

The analysis of the rhythmic expressions through musical notation revealed common rhythms in the infants. Unlike those who think that these utterances are only the expression of vital needs, I believe they must be considered as primary rhythms (proto-rhythms) for language development. Tempo, tone, and timbre, may vary, but any infant of any race has in its beginnings common rhythmic expressions.

The active principle of rhythm is its organizing function, whether in music or articulated language. (In music, timbre, tone sonority of a melody may vary, but this does not affect its recognition.) But if we modify its temporal internal relations it becomes uncognoscible. This also happens in language. Music is also constituted by proto-rhythms. Some minutes after Infant A was born he emitted the following rhythm ♪ ♫|♩. . This rythmic cell is used by Beethoven in his Fifth Symphony. It is also a common rhythmic structure of neonates' vocal expression.

THE FIRST CRY

The first cry is common to mankind from the biological point of view as it depends on breathing, a basic and vital need, and it is also the beginning of a functional possibility. Crying is not established immediately; it is generally preceded by explosive sounds or babbling promoted by the entrance of air. The first sonorous rhythmic vocal expressions of Diego (infant of the first group) were very impressive. They sounded like a melody which he repeated several times in certain intervals before he started to cry (Fridman 1974b, first example on the documentary record). At the beginning the cry is not organized, but as soon as the newborn gets it established it becomes firm and more effective. The infant seems to make less effort to maintain it. Rhythm gives form and structure and might be likened to what in music is called musical thought. The same happens with language. The expressions of Infant A's vocalizations are a product of his sensory-motor intelligence (Fridman and Battro 1977). They are the first expressions of Infant A, and the rhythm is undeniable. The different rhythmic values which appear in the analysis and the possible rhythmic combinations are most significant. Nobody teaches an infant how to cry. This fact, which is so simple, is most important. The word and the musical manifestation will arise from crying, having both a common origin: *intonated proto-rhythms*. Rhythm is physiological and it will vary according to physiological, metabolic and psychological states.

When the child becomes conscious of them, it becomes difficult for him, he has to learn them again. From this analysis we can gather the importance of re-feeding natural rhythms from the second month on, in order to make easier his future linguistic and musical acquisition. On this respect Key (in press) says 'the development of nonverbal behavior (paralanguage and kinesics) is crucial in the acquisition of language; there is evidence that disruptions of nonverbal behaviors may result in disruptions of acquisition of language.' All words and all spoken or musical thoughts have rhythm.

OBSERVATIONS BASED ON TRANSCRIPTION NO. 1

I have taken as the starting point for the demonstration of my hypothesis the first six minutes of Infant A's crying when he was born, as in Figure 1.
The following are illustrated:
1. The proto-rhythms expressed at the moment of Infant A's birth.
2. The rhythms he emits as his umbilical cord is sectioned.
3. The rhythmic schemes he begins to maintain and repeat.
4. Possible combinations of rhythmic schemes.

EXPLOSIVE SILENCE 3″ EXPLOSIVE SILENCE 2″ SILENCE SILENCE 4″ SILENCE 3″ SILENCE 4″ SILENCE 5″ VOICES INTERFERING UMBILICAL CORD IS SECTIONED SILENCE SILENCE 4″ THEY BATHE HIM SILENCE 6″ SILENCE 9″ SILENCE 4″ SILENCE 2″ SILENCE 5″ VOICES INTERFERING SILENCE 6″ SILENCE 3″ SILENCE 5″ SILENCE 4″ SILENCE 2″ SILENCE 2″

Figure 1. *Global structure of Infant A's proto-rhythms at birth: the first six minutes of his cry*

1. Explosive sounds.
2. He seems to cough.
3. Infant A became tense when the pediatrician received a radio message. Sounds were very high pitched.

Those who have some musical knowledge will be able to appreciate the importance of the rhythmic aspect. At first sight, we could say we have before us a little score, elaborated by a musician. These, however, are Infant A's first expressions. Even so, they must be considered as a first approach, as I only count with my audition and musical knowledge. I have only transcribed its rhythm, without taking account of its pitch; however, I will refer to it when I think it is important. The entrance of air at birth promoted in Infant A the emission of explosive sounds. After a silence of three seconds he emits sounds again. Then he expresses an isolated sound (♩); keeps silent for one second; and then emits sounds seventeen times in an explosive way (♫); and in a natural way (♫ ♪). He keeps silent for five seconds and expresses a new rhythmic scheme (♪ ♪). It is remarkable how he accentuates what could be considered musically as the first beat of a bar. The emissions of explosive character were expressed on an ascending 4th and a descending 5th interval. After the first silence of five seconds he starts to cry, with seemingly less effort when crying. When he establishes his cry, he does so on the 'notes' G, B, and D. Shortly after he varies the pitch passing to F and A (I am taking middle C of the piano as a base for this analysis).

A repeated general organic movement can be noticed when he cries. But, as he maintains the cry he seems to make less movement. In this respect Key says 'vocalizations and motor activity are intimately integrated, and in correlation with each other, though only recently they have been studied from the point of view that they are inseparable' (Key in press). I have also observed this fact and consider there is no vocalization without body movement (Fridman 1974b: 32). Condon and Sander (1974a) have demonstrated how neonate movement is synchronized with adult speech.

The most characteristic proto-rhythms are illustrated from Transcription No. 2 in Figure 2. These examples point out the combinations

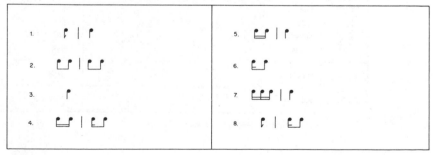

Figure 2.   *Rhythmic schemes of Infant A's cry*
TRANSCRIPTION NO. 2

Table 1.

Column (1) Child's rhythm	(2) Words of Mariano's language	(3) Real meaning in Spanish
♩♩♩	a-pam	avión
♩♩♩	um-úm	senala cosas
♩♩♩	co-có	pájaro
♩♩♩	fa-fá	paliza
♩♩♩	a-pié	fuego
♩♩♩	toi-tú	el pié
♩♩♩	pumpúm	tortuga
♩♩♩	papá	goalpear
♩♩♩	mamá	papá
		mamá
♫♫	coco-cola	coca-cola
♫♫	noni-noni	a dormir
♪♪♪♪	nenecayó	el nene se cayó
♩ ♩ ♩	a má-a	quiero
		dame
♩	ǵol	pelota
♩	chau	chau
♩	no	no
♩	tén	tren
♩	má	más
♩	pim	timbre
♩	si	si
♫♩	eto-qué ?	éesto que es ?
♫♩	epie-pié	el pié
♫	áme	dame
♫	agua	agua
♫	púmba	golpearse
♫	chiche	jugueta
♪♫	papáto	zapato
♪♩♪♩	acá-acá	ir a caballo

＊ These rhythms belong to the words of column 3

(4)   (5)   * (6)

In English	Adults real rhythm in Spanish	Social pressures : Affectivity-Objects Situations-Customs
plane shows things bird to spank fire my foot turtle to hit papá mamá	*(rhythm notation)*	Parents in Argentina say fafá to electric joints. Chás- chás to the action of hitting. Birds are usually called cocó.
coca-cola to sleep	*(rhythm notation)*	Parents use the word noni - noni when babies go to sleep.
The baby fell	*(rhythm notation)*	Babies at this age call themselves nene (baby).
I want give me	*(rhythm notation)*	
ball good-bye no train more bell yes	*(rhythm notation)*	
what is this ? the foot	*(rhythm notation)*	M. had both feet plastered, that's why he gave his feet so much importance.
give me water hits himself toy	*(rhythm notation)*	Adults say púmba to the act of hitting.
shoe	*(rhythm notation)*	
to ride horse back	*(rhythm notation)*	He hits his back imitating the action.

Ruth Fridman

Table 2.

Column (1) Child's rhythm	(2) Words of the triplets language	(3) Real meaning in Sp
♪♩♩	ETÓR	HECTOR
♪♩♩	COCÓ	CABALLO
♪♩♩	TETE	PULSERA
♪♩ ♫	COCOLA	COCA-COLA
♪♩♫	melélo	caramelo
♪♩♫	bobita	bombilla
♪♩♫	totúga	tortuga
♪♩♫	papáto	zapato
♪♩♫	bibita	Silvita
♪♩♫	petéta	Penitencia
♪♩♫	mamáno	hermano
♩	no	no
♩	pá	pan
♩	má	más
♩	tú	Ruth
♩	mis	gato
♫♩♫	aya aya	
♫♩♪	nene nf	nene
♫♪	agua	agua
♫♪	áto	auto
♫♪	Buki	perro (nombre)
♫♪	Yogui	perro (nombre)
♫♪	tilla	silla
♫♪	malo	malo
♫♩♩	bibibf	pajarito
♪♩♪♫♩♫	mamá, cocola	mamá coca-cola

* These rhythms belong to the words of column 3

4) In English	(5) Adults real rhythm in Spanish	*(6) Social pressure : Affectivity - Objects / Situations - Customs
HECTOR HORSE BRACELET	♪	Adrián and Silvina call Etór their brother. Héctor calls himself Etór. This is due to social pressure.
COCA - COLA	♪	Family imitates the expression
candy tube turtle shoe Silvita penitence brother	♪	Family imitates all these expressions. When the mother wants them to behave she says "I wont give you the melelo."
no bread more Ruth Kitten	♪	They call the Kitten "mis" by social pressure. Parents in Argentina use this expression to call this animal.
		Way of expressing the whistle of the train. They seem impressed by the sound. Although the station is far they point out the direction from where the sound comes.
baby	♪	They play with the word "nene", creating new forms of expression.
water car dog's name dog's name chair bad	♪	Rhythmic correspondence is exact. M. calls the car tutú. A very common expression in this country
bird	♪	Parents imitate the children's expression
	♪	The mother feels very happy with this small phrase. The triplets express the phrase well, without any difficulty

of the expressed proto-rhythms. Through exercising these schemes, the forming of holophrases or small phrases will take place. In this respect Masland (1972: 428) says, 'hour after hour the child practices the nonsense syllables of his own speech production. Inevitably there becomes established in his brain a pattern of certain associated events, namely, the sound of the phoneme, the motor activities associated with its production, and the closely related somesthetic, propioceptive, and kinesthetic input generated by his own movement.' Masland also asks the following question: 'Is it not probable that the child's own babbling provides him with the cues which draw his attention to the fundamental patterns of speech?'

The tables on pp. 82–85 point out the organization of proto-rhythms in infants between 22 and 24 months old. Table 1 represents Infant A and Table 2 the group of triplets. The four of them have been studied since the moment of their birth. The examples of the four infants will allow the reader to understand the importance of the rhythmic aspect in language. Most of the rhythms were present in the first cry of Infant A.

THE ORGANIZATION OF PROTO-RHYTHMS

I have said that proto-rhythms of vocal expression are motor structures which belong to the natural primary sonorous rhythmic net of the human being. What is the relationship between the proto-rhythms of a newborn and the rhythms expressed by the infants of Tables 1 and 2 in their language? We can take as a basis the proto-rhythms emitted by Infant A when he was born. In my opinion, they produce auditory sensations which continue up to the moment in which the infant organizes his locution. To do this, the infant will have to combine, as Fry says (1966: 190), articulation with vocalization; he will have to get respiratory control and establish the circuits to which the motor activity is firmly connected. Could the rhythm of the words be born through proto-rhythms? I think that the function of proto-rhythms is fundamental. It can be observed in babbling, crying, guttural expressions, vocal play, etc. But, what happens as the infant matures and produces expressions which are similar to the words used by the adults? He begins to organize them, but we will see that the infant does not emit or repeat just any word he hears. Imitation takes place when the group of syllables or phonemes he needs to express are present in the child. This means that the proto-rhythms' function has certain limits though they are determining. Tables 1 and 2 point out some aspects related to the hypothesis which I am going to develop. In the first place, it is interesting to see how rhythms are revealed through the vocal emissions of the words which the four infants emit, which reflect the exterior reality of the topics which continue through social cultural variables. We can see that Infant A, as other babies, talks about trains, mummy, daddy, bye, coke, feet, etc. In most of the examples the rhythms are adjusted to the real words, but there are some cases in which this does not happen. Proto-rhythms seem to be a guide, as they make the perception and reproduction of the adult's words easier.

In the aforementioned tables, we can appreciate how the phonological components of the vocal emissions can vary in their similarity to adult language. Rhythms usually correspond. There is rhythmic correspondence in *papato* and *zapato* 'shoe'; *ten* and *tren* 'train'; *e pié* and *el pié* 'the foot'; *papá*, *mamá*, etc. But they say *cocola* instead of *coca-cola* and *peteta* instead of *penitencia* 'penitence'. Even when the proto-rhythms seem to guide this process, they are not always employed by the infant, although he rhythmically possesses the capacity. What could be the reason for this? Infant A expresses the rhythm of the word *zapato* 'shoe'. The word *pelota* 'ball' could be expressed in that rhythm and Infant A should be able theoretically to say *pelota*; however he does not say it. Which factors could be influencing? I think that he, as any other infant, will have to acquire a certain grade of maturation to emit all the words he hears. Furthermore, the impact of the situation in which the word is presented, the rhythm of the whole expression and its action are very important. The affectivity which the object awakens is also important. Finally, generalization is common in infancy, for example, calling all men *papá*, and the balls *gol*. We must not forget that the child watches TV and listens to the radio from a very early age. During a football game the word *gol* 'goal' is used so often that he generalizes it to mean all balls.

I believe that the affective aspect is important. Infants tend to 'fall in love' with words they like, and repeat a thousand times those schemes which are agreeable to them. My youngest son called the horse *'caballo'* *vadereda* when he was two years old. The rhythm for *vadereda* is⌐♪ | ⌐♪, and the one for horse is ⌐♪ | ♪. My son played with this word he had invented, and it gave him a lot of pleasure. I approved his manifestation by repeating it, so he preferred it to the word for horse which had a different rhythm. I believe the infant practices the mechanism with which he will express himself. On this aspect McNeill (1966: 53) says 'even when the children's tendency to imitate their parents language seems to be very remarkable, they will not imitate the appropriate feats unless important parts of the syntaxis have been acquired.' If we take the examples of Infant A and the triplets we will be able to appreciate that the differences between them are not only determined by the proto-rhythms but also by the natural and personal disposition for the production of the language, and I fully agree with Papousek (1976) when he says that the 'complex preverbal cognitive processes have been shown to be affected by the quality and quantity of nutrition during this period.'

The infant always expresses itself rhythmically, through its locution (Engel 1972: 197). Adults tend to try to make the infant express itself in its own language, or to make it imitate, as much as it can, real language. In any case, they try to understand its lexicon, which is generally accompanied by gestures and different movements of the body. Bullowa (1976) says 'that mothers tend to "read" their infants' facial expressions from the first hours on.' This also happens with their cries or vocal play. Infant A began to organize words more slowly than the triplets, though the dissimilarities were leveled when they were two-and-a-half years old. However, in one case we have one son and a mother who is always ready to interpret, and in the other case we have three children and only one mother to take care of them. The fact is most important but not determining in what I am trying to explain. If we study carefully Tables 1 and 2, we will be able to appreciate how Infant A and the triplets emit words which are formed by the same rhythms. But, it is important to point out, that between the first and second year of life of the triplets, I observed that some words were expressed by only one of the triplets.

For this reason I have come to the conclusion that proto-rhythms acquire a certain grade of organization only if the infant is in condition to emit new forms of expression. Proto-rhythms cannot give form to something that does not exist. The infant modifies speech when he is able to hear the results of his own expression. Proto-rhythms are organizing elements not only in the auditory feedback, but also in the emission of new words. I believe that this is the real essence of proto-rhythms, for without them, the infant could not learn the acoustic effect of his expressions. Exercising them is the only way to obtain the acoustic pattern of what he hears. This fact becomes most interesting when the infant begins to give his 'first musical answers'. I have recorded examples of infants answering at six months of age. Examples of infants answering at nine months of age are given in Fridman (1974b: last example of the documentary record; 1975: 12–16).

PROTO-RHYTHMS IN EARLY MUSICAL ANSWERS

Early musical answers are also structured by proto-rhythms. The first six months are of crucial importance for learning music. I developed a methodology with which an infant can begin to sing a song he hears his parents sing. Infants can be sensitized to musical facts from birth on. This is the basis of support for the beginnings of their musical intelligence. Michel (1973) also says 'that the first six months represent the period in which a child learns to hear.' Early musical answers are important in that proto-rhythms begin their organization through very short musical answers. The infant does not learn proto-rhythms or the sonorous pitch of his expressions. They are inside him. What he learns is a system, a phonological and musical system formed by rhythms and sounds that belong to the social group in which he lives.

THE UNIVERSAL CHARACTERISTICS OF LANGUAGE

The theory of proto-rhythms reinforces those theories of contemporary linguistics where the fundamental problem is the universalities of language. Chomsky (in Smith and Miller 1966: 6) says:

Given a number of grammars for natural languages, we can ask to what extent they embody similarities attributable to the general form of language as such, wherever it occurs. These similarities, insofar as they can be shown to hold for human languages everywhere, are known as *language universals*. In a sense, language universals are not part of language but are prelinguistic and psychological. They are exactly the features of any language that need not be described as part of its grammar because they are the same for all grammars. And for that very reason it is plausible to assume that the language universals, whatever they should prove to be, are part of every human being's innate linguistic competence and do not need to be learned by a child who is acquiring competence in some particular language.

THE FORMAL CHARACTERISTICS OF PROTO-RHYTHMS

According to Chomsky, 'the study of the linguistic universals is the study of the properties of any generative grammar for a natural language. Definite suppositions about linguistic universals may belong to the syntactic, semantic or phonological component, as well as to the inter-relations between the three of them.' I refer to the phonological component in its essential structural aspect. I think that my hypothesis on proto-rhythms fits in with linguistic universals. If we start from the fact that proto-rhythms are sensory–motor structures which guide and prepare the child's locution, they could be considered as formal constitutive elements for the development of any language, for the following reasons:

1. They are not learned, and as they are expressed since the moment of birth, they would be genetically planned.
2. They belong to the sonorous expression of any infant.

CROSS-CULTURAL PROTO-RHYTHMS

Table 3 demonstrates some analogies between some proto-rhythms and the rhythm of the words which exist in different languages. Infant A's proto-rhythms can be associated with words in various languages.

Rhythms	Spanish	English	French
(1) ♪ | ♪	mamá papá	mamá bye‑bye	mamán papá
(2) ♫ | ♫	cola – cola mi mamita	dolly‑dolly mummy‑mummy	ma petite tigro‑tigro
(3) ♪	yo, si, no‑	I, yes, no‑	Moi, oui, non
(4) ♫ | ♫	Alleluya	Alleluya	Alleluya
(5) ♫ | ♪	a mamá	to mamá	a mamán
(6) ♫	Jorge	Georgie	Georges
(7) ♬ | ♪	ya voy a ir	I will be there	Je vais y alle
(8) ♪ ♫	zapato or papato	my dolly	mon arbre

Table 3. *Analogies*

CONCLUSION

As we can see, vocal rhythms and rhythms produced by human activity are important. No one teaches a baby how to cry. Vocal sonorous rhythmic expressions of an infant are not a product of the mind; they are part of his/her biologic inheritance. In the development of mankind, human beings learned, through historical and social evolution, to recreate what potentially exists inside them. In the first cry of a physically well-integrated newborn, rhythmic organization exists. From the first cry the word and the musical manifestation come forth, having both of them a common origin: intonated proto-rhythms.

Ostwald (1972) says that 'in studying infant vocalizations we are without doubt dealing with a very young science.' I believe he is right and I also think that studies from scholars of different fields that embrace human behavior can add significantly to the studies of infant vocalizations. Future research should be developed along these lines. Studies of proto-rhythms should be done in different countries in order to establish whether there are similar rhythmic patterns. Comparative studies will allow us, in the future, to judge whether those I am doing in Argentina may be generalized.

NOTE

1. The tapes were kindly made available by Dr. Evelyn Thomen and Dr. Victor Denneberg, from the Department of Biobehavioral Sciences, University of Connecticut.

CAROLYN LEONARD-DOLAN

A Method for Film Analysis of Ethnic Communication Style[1]

Human encounters would be markedly different if they were limited to an exchange of words. The printed word can be extremely sterile. The telephone conversation, lacking as it does the immediate presence of the other, remains only 'the next best thing to being there'. Words and language tell us much to be sure; however, they tell us even more when we are face-to-face with the individual saying them. Additionally, we have learned through experience that the same words spoken by different people may mean different things; that the same words spoken by the same person at different times may convey two entirely different messages; that different words may deliver the same message; etc. The person, the situation, the environment, the sound of words, what activity accompanies the words, and more, modify the meaning spoken and the meaning heard.

Human communication, then, requires more than a knowledge of language as those know who have tried to speak a second language or who have attempted conversation with a person who speaks our language but has learned it in a different culture. Somehow in these circumstances we are not quite comfortable or satisfied with the exchange. It is particularly relevant to this paper to note that our body movements while we speak and listen become an important dimension of the human encounter. This paper directs itself to that part of the communication process which involves speaking and listening behavior, events which involve both language: linguistics, and body movements:kinesics. Speakers possess a complex organization of linguistic–kinesic behaviors which they bring with them into any encounter with another individual. Some parts of an individual repertoire of these behaviors are consciously learned. Others apparently are not consciously learned, but are apparently learned and performed beneath the level of conscious awareness. It is the purpose of this paper to present methods for examining the complex organization of elements that results when, as two persons interact, their linguistic–kinesic repertoires meet and respond to each other.

Studies in the body motion aspect of human behavior continue to increase. Several must be mentioned because their use of film analysis relates directly to the content of this paper. Birdwhistell's studies (1970a, 1970b) have for over two decades provided methods for the systematic analysis of kinesic behavior. Paul Byers, at the annual meeting of the American Anthropological Association in 1971, presented a model for the use of sound film to analyze cross-culturally the behavior of men in groups, and his metaphor of 'simultaneous cultural performances', which as an image of the interaction process sheds light on the extreme mutuality and interpenetration of individual behavior styles in successful face-to-face communication.[2] Condon's studies (1968) of interpersonal synchrony, Kendon's studies (1970) of greeting behavior, Edward T. Hall's studies (1963) of proxemic behavior, and Erickson's study (1971) of interethnic communication patterns, have been especially helpful.

DATA INFORMATION

A series of dyadic interaction sequences of urban male students at a large midwestern university were filmed in 16mm sound. The series of films records the interaction of peers, strangers to each other — except insofar as they may have seen each other on campus. The students were selected from three ethnic groups: Mexican, Polish, Black; and combinations of 'same' and 'different' ethnicity were arranged. The individuals waited in separate rooms so that their first greeting occurred before the camera. The conversation topic 'What happens at registration' was suggested.

OUT-OF-AWARENESS BEHAVIOR

As has been stated, many behavior patterns are not consciously learned, but in fact have been acquired beneath the level of conscious awareness. The out-of-awareness linguistic–kinesic behaviors of the interactants can be analyzed from film record. Film analysis makes possible repeated viewing of the encounter at various speeds. Examined at 'slower-than-life' speeds and even frame by frame a film[3] reveals the organization of the intricate and complex system of out-of-awareness communication behavior paralleling those systems of behavior over which interactants have conscious control. As two individuals each possessing a distinctive repertoire of nonverbal behavior begin to interact with each other a new and complex system develops, a 'resultant' of the joining together of both the individuals' patterns.

NONVERBAL BEHAVIORS IN THE 'GREETING' PHASE OF INTER-
ACTION

The first behavioral event which occurs when two individuals meet and
greet each other may be initiated by one of them or by both
simultaneously. The beginning sound of a word, an eyebrow lift, an arm
movement, may be the behavior which opens the exchange. Or it may be
that a combination of linguistic–kinesic events taking place concurrently
in one or both persons sets the interaction going. Individual responses of
the two interactants will be various. Signals and responses increase,
overlap, merge, conflict as the interacting continues, as shown in Figure 1.

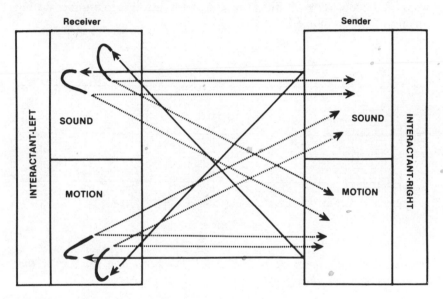

Figure 1.   *One-microsecond event*

METHODS OF ANALYSIS

Two general areas of analysis are possible: (1) Macroanalysis identifying
patterns in interaction process segments which vary in duration from a
few seconds to a few minutes; and (2) Microanalysis identifying degree of
mutual kinesic–linguistic involvement within the exchange across time
intervals of a microsecond.[4] A methodology has been developed for each
level of analysis for purposes of comparing sections within a film with

each other, or comparing sections in different films with each other. Both the 'macro' and 'micro' analytic strategies are closely interrelated since both are directed toward an examination of 'simultaneous performance' during the interaction process. At a 'peak' one or both of the individuals move several body parts concurrently or make a relatively gross shift in posture or 'proxemic' orientation.[5] Peaks in the out-of-awareness 'kinesic track' of interaction tend to recur in patterns. They are usually found to be accompanied in the within-awareness 'linguistic track' by a change of topic. The parts of a film where these kinesic-linguistic peaks or shifts occur serve as indicators for dividing the film into sections, called phases, for purposes of segment identification, closer examination, and/or comparison, as in Figure 2. For example, it was noted in one series of films that the phases increase in number during an interethnic exchange.

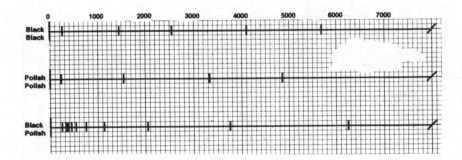

Figure 2. *Comparison of phases (each mark on line represents the beginning of a new phase)*

Microanalysis consists in viewing a *frame-numbered film*[6] a few frames at a time or frame-by-frame. (The use of a Bell and Howell projector with a crank attachment and an L. W. Athena projector [Kodak Pageant projector modified by L. W. Photo Products Company, Van Nuys, California] with a special gear mechanism facilitate this process.) At this 'slower-than-life' speed, it is possible to note exactly at which frame a body-part movement begins, changes direction, and ends, as in the handshake rhythm recorded in Figure 3. The frames are noted and graphed to give a visual representation and a summary of the body motion of both interacting individuals. The same procedure for the analysis of sound adds a further dimension.

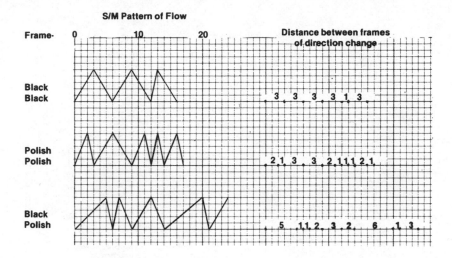

Figure 3.   *Handshake rhythm*

The resultant graph of a film segment (Figure 4) indicates when several body parts of one or both interactants move simultaneously. These concurrent movements are named 'sound/motion events', individual S/M and mutual S/M, which combine across time to produce an S/M pattern of flow. These patterns reveal the pace or rhythm of individual and mutual sound and movement at the level of a microsecond. When the S/M pattern is interpersonally symmetric the interaction is smooth and 'comfortable'; when the S/M pattern is interpersonally asymmetric the interaction is rough and 'uncomfortable' or even at times breaks apart.

To clarify this, consider what happens in a three-legged race. In order to move smoothly it is necessary to maintain an 'even gait'. When one or the other partner disrupts the even gait, the progress of the two is either temporarily halted by a 'stumble' from which they 'recover' or completely stopped by a 'fall'. Thus in the analysis of filmed dyadic interaction, as shown in Figure 5, an 'even gait' is a symmetric S/M which intrudes upon the interpersonally symmetric S/M pattern which has been established and then recovers interpersonal symmetry; a 'fall' is an interpersonally asymmetric S/M in which the pattern of flow established in

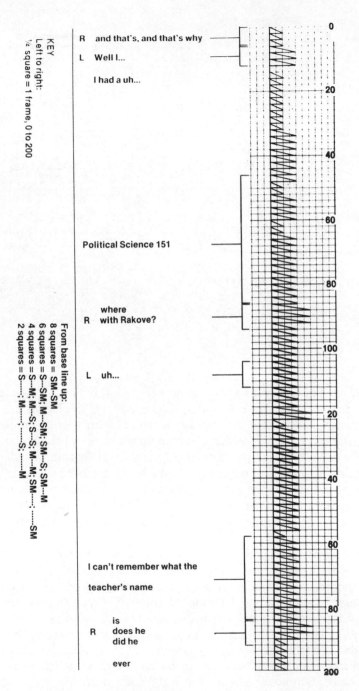

Figure 4.   *Graphic representation of mutual S/M*

the mutual behavior of the two individuals is not only brought to a halt, but persists in being halted — the mutual pattern of flow may not be reestablished for some seconds. These are the moments in a conversation that are especially uncomfortable, during which the interactants flounder.

3-legged race	*Summary designation*	*Symbol*
'even gait'	symmetric S/M	
'stumble'	asymmetric S/M which recovers	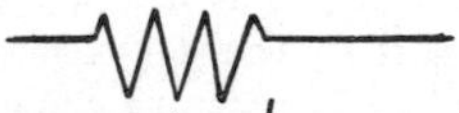
'fall'	asymmetric S/M which persists	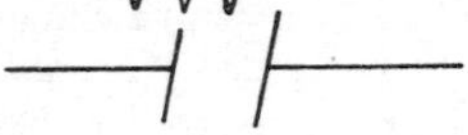

Figure 5.   *Analysis of filmed dyadic interaction*

Evidence produced through examination and comparison of symmetry and asymmetry in the flow patterns of individual and interpersonal 'sound/motion events' suggests that a person's kinesic and linguistic behavior, performed out of conscious awareness, influences the degree of successful communication in dyadic interaction. For example, microanalysis seems to indicate that the dyadic interaction of persons from the same ethnic background, even though they have never met before, may result most often in an 'even gait' and 'stumbles' from which the pair can mutually 'recover'. Relatively few 'falls' seem to occur in conversation between same ethnics. Same ethnics apparently manage to interrupt each other by either linguistic or kinesic behavior and yet maintain a fairly well-integrated pattern of flow. On the other hand, evidence seems to indicate that dyadic interaction between persons of different ethnicity may result in relatively frequent 'stumbles' ('clumsily recovered' from) and in 'falls'. An interpersonally symmetric S/M pattern of flow rarely seems to emerge and the interaction rarely gets 'off the ground'.

CONCLUSION — IMPLICATIONS

Since motion picture films segment behavior according to a constant time interval, (each frame of 16mm film = 1/24 of a second) both macroanalysis and microanalysis of frame-numbered films allow for comparison of films, of phases, of symmetric and asymmetric S/M patterns, etc. To some extent this comparison makes possible the distinction between 'idiosyncratic' and 'ethnic' behavior as well as the distinction between interethnic and intraethnic behavior.[7]

NOTES

1. NIMH project # MH 18230, MH 21460, under the direction of Dr. Frederick David Erickson.
2. Byers' 'cultural performance' metaphor, through which mutually appropriate behavior can be seen to create 'ensemble' in a conversation, provides a very different view of the communication process from the 'ping-pong' imagery implicit in the stimulus–response theory and learning theory.
3. Each frame of film is printed with a reference number during the production of a work print or answer print from the unnumbered original.
4. Each frame of 16mm sound film is exposed for 1/24 second. Hence, a 'microsecond' is 1/24 second or a multiple thereof.
5. Proxemic is the term coined by Edward T. Hall (1966) for the study of cultural patterns in interpersonal distancing behavior.
6. Each frame of film is printed with a reference number during the production of a work print or answer print from the unnumbered original.
7. Microanalysis also indicates that onset of body movement and sound occur at a regular pace, usually the number of frames between onset frames add up to numbers which are multiples of five or ten, a finding consistent with that reported by Byers (see note 2).

THOMAS J. BRUNEAU

Chronemics and the Verbal–Nonverbal Interface[1]

The major intent of this brief essay is somewhat ambitious, as it concerns offering some suggested answers to the question: What makes people tick? As a minimal understanding of the nature of time requires a frustrating wrestle with a long series of complicated and confusing problems, first it will be necessary to provide some definitional focus on the meaning of time. Since the gaining of conceptual clarity concerning the meaning of time could be reasonably compared to an electric eel attempting to discover its identity in a huge tank filled with such creatures, the definitional focus offered here will be necessarily limited. As it is the case that tempo concerns the entire spectrum of both verbal and nonverbal behavior, a second purpose of this essay will be to offer a description of the relational interface of verbal and nonverbal tempos — to describe the temporal interdependence of verbal and nonverbal communication. A third purpose of this essay will be to briefly define a new area of communication study to be called 'chronemics'. In this regard, a taxonomic schema will be offered which could be used in the study of human tempo as a primary dimension of human behavior.

DEFINITIONAL PROBLEMS

Two common viewpoints about the nature of time are in need of some discussion. A majority viewpoint is that time is objective; a minority viewpoint is that time is mainly subjective.

Most people who hold time to be objective, physical, external to themselves, or beyond their personal control: want time, need time, save time, waste time, give time, use time, pass time, have or do not have time, wish time would stop or hurry, fear time, and many such people hope for a long life. If one believes time to be objective, then the measure of time (clock time) is often accepted or assumed to be the only possible definition of time. Such a definition treats time as spatial points and intervals which are suspended in a constant and unidirectional, linear progression which never ends. Supporting such a viewpoint about the nature of time, one begins to search for regularities, constancies, and repetitive phenomena which support the point–interval assumption of an objective definition of time. If one unassumedly values a time-keeping device and unassumedly accepts the measure of time as the only kind of time (as millions do and have done), then perceptions, conceptualizations, and levels of consciousness can become biased toward observations which render the objective definition true and accurate. Also, once positive values are attached to these physical regularities, the referents for such regularities (clocks and time-keeping devices) can be accorded greater positive value. Such positive value may tend to discourage investigation into the assumptive basis of objective time. Under such a persuasion, persons who attempt to speak of the mythic nature of objective time can be viewed as odd, strange, or even blasphemous.

During industrial and technological growth, the positive value associated with clock time and objective forms of time (clocklike behaviors, tempo patterning, and conditioned pacing) can be heightened to a single-mindedness.[2] Consequently, people can come to value being 'on time' or 'ahead of time' and also may pride themselves on the accuracy of their watchfulness. Under such normative tendencies, certain irregularities, variabilities, and rhythms which are not easily unitized or do not easily lend themselves to accountability tend to take on negative value. Consequently, modes of perception which are different and levels of awareness which are on or beyond the temporal horizons of most people can be viewed with distrust, suspicion, and other forms of negation.

What often does not seem to be understood is that uniqueness in biological tempo appears to give rise to uniqueness in perceptual accommodation and assimilation. In other words, biological time variations give rise to variations in human perception which, in turn, give rise to variabilities in the 'time sense'.[3] In a milieu of objective temporality, variability in the time sense may be lost altogether — personal tempo becomes sacrificed to objective tempo. As John Cohen (1966: 257) has stressed: '. . . it is conceivable that our reliance on watches and other artificial aids has led to atrophy of our "sense of time".' What is not so apparent in an objective time milieu is that perceptions appear to tend toward stasis or repetition — being consistent is golden. In such a milieu, *déjà vu* can become common and the view of external reality can appear to recycle endlessly on a constant, dull, grey line of ennui. In such a milieu, perceptual novelty, perceptual *jamais vu* (always seeing fresh and new), and being aware of the rich hues of a dynamic nonverbal world can become retarded. In such situations, nonverbal illiteracy can occur.

It may appear to be speculative to propositionalize about the relationship between objective time environments and modes of consciousness. (Speculation, incidentally, is itself a mode of consciousness which has come to be distrusted and discouraged in many objective time environments.) However, it does appear reasonable to suggest that, just as objective time environments may discourage perceptual novelty, such environments may also discourage certain levels and kinds of consciousness.[4] Objective time environments appear to be most congruent with linear sequencing of information, the processing of information assumed to be discrete and capable of unitization, rational information, and other forms of information associated with the dominant hemisphere or committed cortex of the human brain.[5] It is conceivable that, in environments where objective tempo is paramount in the regulation of human behavior, certain modes of consciousness may become atrophied or become dysfunctional. Further, other forms of consciousness–unconsciousness may develop — such as daydreaming, mind-wandering, psychic fugues, nostalgic lapses, various forms of fantasy, etc. Perhaps such forms of mentation develop as compensations for the loss of other modes of consciousness.[6]

If we believe as did Du Noüy (1937: 133), that the nature of all reality concerns '. . . the manner in which time and space are conjugated', a popular objective view of temporality can have serious consequences concerning descriptions of both verbal and nonverbal behavior. Such consequences may have already obtained. For example, the growth of psychological behaviorism may be the most glaring indication of the growing faith in objective temporality. This growth will perhaps slow if, and when, the mythic bases of objective time are brought forth and widely understood. Such growth should also slow when it is deeply understood that temporal relativity may be the most basic mode of human individualism and personality. In this regard, Fraser (1966: xix) has commented: 'Tell me what you think of time and I will know what to think of you.' Unique tempo in personal behavior may be the difference which makes a significant difference. In this regard, the protest of the American poet, Walt Whitman, raised in his poem 'Song of Myself' seems appropriate here: 'I know I have the best of time and space, and was never measured and never will be measured.'

Relatively few people have advocated that time is subjective, individually unique, alterable, and that various kinds and levels of time-experiencing exist. While many people feel temporal relativity to be descriptive of their personal time-experiencing, few persons, save Bergson (1911, 1946) and Minkowski (1970) have given it such prominent focus. People with a belief in temporal relativity claim that time is created by them, that people are the true clocks of the world, and that personal clocks run both quickly and slowly in relationship to individual baselines of rhythmics. Such baselines of personal tempo may or may not resemble the objective tempo consensually accepted by others in the particular social and cultural orders in which one is expected to participate. If a personal tempo is noticeably different than the objective and standard tempo, one is not viewed as a 'regular person' or a normal group member. Temporal incongruence is not simply a problem of a traditional Yap or Ibo attempting to punch a time clock in a new business or industry; such incongruence also concerns people in technological societies who would enjoy slowing or stopping such clocks altogether. Yet, in an advanced technological society, the advocacy of slowing or stopping time clocks is viewed as anarchy by those who control such clocks. Conversely, those wishing to slow or stop the clocks would speak of a tyranny of time-keeping, time kept, or time stolen.

Persons who live a tempo and, consequently, a spatiality which is incongruent with the normative social and cultural tempos in which they attempt to participate often find regular living a little exasperating. Such people may tend either to abhor or wonder about two temporal signals or gestures which millions (perhaps billions) of others repeatedly, habitually, and regularly exibit: (1) the slight raising of one's arm, elbow bent, followed by an assuring flick of the wrist in order to render an object upon the wrist accessible to an eye gaze of approximately one second; (2) the casting of an upward glance of one's eyes to focus on an object suspended from a wall, vertical support, or housed in a tower — the focus lasting for approximately one second, the countenance of the observer taking on characteristics of irritation, worry, fear, awe, or, frequently, a look which might be mistaken for reverence. Persons who value personal time, as Wright (1968: 7) does, speak of an evolving and growing 'chronarchy', where the world is being controlled by master clocks which control slave clocks which, in turn, pace people toward greater and greater speeds and increased compliance with objective time standards — regardless of personal tempos and cultural customs of tempo.[7]

Persons who are extreme in their definition of time as subjective phenomenon may fail to see certain purposes of objective temporality. Advocates of a subjective definition of human tempo may overlook the social, political, and economical purposes of objective time: order, control, efficiency, and production. Such purposes can, of course, obtain in either positive or negative results in terms of the quality of life and living — depending on the rigidity of the definition of objective time and the degree of compliance expected. The danger of rigid objective temporal environments is that they can create invisible prisons filled with time-servers. These invisible prisons, while perhaps originally created from a necessary need for structure and a consequent structure hunger, can later perpetuate rigidly fixed, internal and external environments which discourage a lively dance of creative tempo through cell blocks and guarded spaces.

A definitional focus on the meaning of time as either objective or subjective is, of course, a simplistic dichotomy and a limited view of the nature of time. While such comparison can suggest some interesting points of departure for the further study of human tempo, such comparison only skims the surface of deeper problems concerning definitions of time.[8]

Time eludes definitive rigidity. The belief that time can be clearly defined is itself a temporal bias or, often, a temporal motive (see taxonomy). A person who clearly defines time or assumes its nature to be apparent or already formulated is like a person who builds theoretical monuments on dubious foundations. In this regard, the theoretical structures of some influential theorists of human behavior may warrant some careful examination of their foundations by building inspectors with keen eyes for temporal cracks, flaws, and fissures. A belief that time can be clearly defined often not only implies that time has *a priori* and discernible form or forms, but that the functioning of such assumed forms is consistent, regular, or subject to observational verification. However, definitive focus on the nature of time has usually involved only conceptual assertiveness or logical–symbolic gymnastics concerning notions of permanence and change — including the nature of their interdependence.

Definitional problems arise when assumptions concerning permanence and change are not examined in relationship to complex notions of duration and process. Further problems arise when duration and process are not viewed as relative human processes (involving attention, perception, conceptualization, and various modes of consciousness) of considerable temporal complexity. Complications in the definition of time also arise when durational and processual interdependencies (permanencies undergoing change) are not distinguished from their linguistic representations — concepts of space–time. Such complications appear to be chronic problems because it is most difficult to clearly separate temporal symbolism from temporal referents. This is especially so because the referents for temporal symbols are elusively complex.

Du Noüy (1937) aptly expressed this problem and the problem of using language to define time:

The majority of words employed to define an object, a force, or a tendency, necessarily imply the notion of time, for they evoke movements, relations, succession. The verb 'to be', which is indispensable, implies the idea of existence, and the idea of existence imposes the notion of time. All words are therefore inadequate, for one can only define a thing accurately by means of words which do not evoke ideas incorporating the very thing which has to be defined . . . The very existence of matter is inseparable from time by the mere fact that the word "existence" has been pronounced (125).

Gonseth (1972) appears to concur with this view:

One should not be surprised to see the problem of language . . . placed side by side with the problem of time and claim the attention of anyone who intends to treat the latter in particular . . . One may pretend to ignore its [time] presence; it nevertheless remains present behind all the words which one employs (15–16).

Even if a nondurational view of time were assumed and time symbolism were to be related to process, definitional difficulties would still arise. For example, if we accept Gale's view (1968: 5) that, '. . . time is a name which does not name', the supposed referents of temporal symbols become negated — the noun, time, would have no direct or indirect referents with physical attributes. The concept of time is a challenge to any student of symbolism. It appears to be even more of a challenge for those attempting to identify significant verbal–nonverbal correlations. The definitional problems surrounding the concept of time will be involved necessarily in the following discussion of temporal symbolism, temporal referencing, linguistic usage as temporality, and their relationships to nonverbal tempo.

TIME AND THE VERBAL–NONVERBAL INTERFACE

With a large number of languages in existence, including hundreds of technical, logical, and mathematical systems which might be classified as languages, it is most difficult to generalize about temporality in language. However, what can be reasonably said about most languages concerning their temporal characteristics may be deserving of mention here. Before any statements concerning the influence of temporal symbolism on nonverbal behavior can be made with any semblance of credibility, some discussion of certain significant relationships of time and language will first be necessary.

Languages are not merely 'time-binding', to use Korzybski's term (1966); languages appear to create and sustain particular temporal perspectives (past, present, future). Most, if not all languages, have forms and functions which at least implicitly indicate pastness, presentness, and futurity.[9] The very existence of linguistic codes and their expression implies time perspective. One uses representations for reference to previous events in the near or distant past and one expresses one's self linguistically when one anticipates the reception of a message in the immediate or distant future. The symbolic forms and functions of temporal perspective (linguistic tenses and tensings) in and of particular languages appear to vary in their degree of explicitness and orientational bias in time perspective.

Most languages appear to be weighted toward the *objectivization*[10] of processes related to memory functioning (past perspective). While the development of memory functioning is certainly related to the ability of humans to form representations, in both the individual and the species, such a complex relationship is too involved to discuss thoroughly here. Suffice it to say, as Whitehead (1929: 323) has outlined, that the representation of events and occasions concerns the alteration of process: An actual occasion is nothing but the unity to be ascribed to a particular instance of concrescence (objectification of process as a transitory mode). This concrescence is thus nothing else than the 'real internal constitution' of the actual occasion in question. The primary nature of representation, then, deals with the ability of humans to objectify process in relationship to short-term memory functionings. This primary ability appears to be mainly a matter of slowing process or altering process by the imposition of durations and intervals. Linguistically we appear to momentarily 'still' process. I have previously attempted to discuss this process of stilling processes as 'impositions of silence' (Bruneau 1973). An ability to impose discontinuities on process appears to create a condition whereby symbolic tags can be placed upon such durations (real or assumed) to accommodate the processing of later presentations of similar events. More importantly, such symbolic tags when placed upon objectifications can be used to represent such objectifications for purposes of communication. With such potential, abstraction becomes increasingly possible and people can increasingly represent past events while removed from the immediacy of such events. Fraisse (1963: 292) expressed this primary process simply: 'Change is transformed into an object. . . . This transformation is the symbol through which we affirm our domination of time'.

The primary process of representation is not only interdependent with the possibility of the retention of events in memory, it also helps to separate the observer from what is observed. Such a separation appears to be initially necessary for the development of personal identity. One can then establish one's self as either an object or subject among objects and the making of subject–object comparisons becomes possible. Once the primary process of representation is established, one '. . . is able to form representations of changes other than those he perceives in the present. . . . The representations of changes lead to representations of successions and durations . . . Man is then capable of relating all sequences of change and all temporal intervals independently of his immediate experience. We can thus gain [personal] control over change. . . .' (Fraisse 1963: 149). Russell (1915: 212) said the same thing more directly: '. . . past, present, and future arise from time-relations of subject and object. . . .' People, then, create time while creating themselves.

Because primary symbolic representation requires the imposition of durations on processes to create intervals, it should not be surprising to find that the majority of temporal symbols of languages tend toward spatialization of reality in their referencing of both internal and external tempos. The primary tendency of languages appears to be the establishment of a sense of permanency. Such permanence can then accommodate change. This view appears to be congruent with Cassirer's view (1953: 198–226) that true *Zeitwörter* (time-words) or verbs which actually refer to complex processes are late to develop in the genesis of languages and that only in highly developed languages does temporal symbolism begin to refer to human tempo in a complex fashion. While concepts of past, present, and future imply change, the basic foundations of most languages appear to be quests for permanency. This may be so because all change appears to be relative to a background of constancy or permanency. Without such a background, change would be meaningless (Benjamin 1966: 7).

It is important to note here the relationship between the primitivation of time and silence. When primitivation of time occurs, the real distance between subjects and objects degenerates or is lost altogether. When this happens, one becomes suspended in a concrete time-of-action which is essentially momentary or locked into the specious present (Werner 1940). Primitivation of time not only seems to dissolve temporal perspective in past and future modes, it eliminates the need to use symbolic representations of temporal perspective altogether. As one dissolves past and future perspectives, in other words, the need to say anything at all begins to become meaningless for, as Wittgenstein (1961: 151) has stated, that which is truly present can only be shown. The impatience hovering about words to be uttered (expectation) or the analysis of what has been said are removed in temporal primitivations. The tension of tense systems is removed in extreme present orientations — the language tends towards silence.[11] Anticipation and ego functioning (future orientations) are no longer necessary; analysis and retrospection become meaningless. The essential point being made here is that language is intricately related to temporal perspective as well as subject–object differentiations (which arise through temporal alterations). The silence which necessarily obtains through the primitivation of time seems to support the view presented here: The basic foundations of languages involve temporal alterations, perspectives, and functions which counteract the silence and null stances of rigid present orientations.[12] However, on the other hand, verbosity and verbal reasoning may be counterproductive to an awareness of the present moment and a here-and-now focus necessary for awareness of nonverbal behavior.

Languages can be said to vary in the degree to which time is referred to in spatial terminology. Languages also seem to vary in the degree to which temporal perspective is asserted. The assertion of temporal perspective appears to concern not only the degree to which the particular language is based in certain temporal assumptions, but also seems to concern the attitudes and values attached to various tempos in social and cultural orders. In other words, linguistic usage often asserts or reasserts the temporal biases and tempo of one's particular language and culture. Anyone who has heard a frustrated teacher of English as a second language attempting to teach English tense systems to a bewildered group of Micronesian or Oriental students would understand how bias in temporal perspective is asserted.

The manner in which words are used and especially how words are uttered can indicate the particular temporal biases, temporal perspective orientations, and the rigidity of temporal assumptions held by those expressing themselves. Linguistic usage in highly objective time situations, for example, may be replete with quickened motion toward states of certitude and states of being. In such situations, a result can be the common use of statements such as: 'I am!', 'You are!', 'We are!' 'It is!', 'It is not!', 'Is it!', etc. I do not believe a lexicon of temporal terminology exists in the English language. While the construction of such a lexicon would be arduous, the task product might be revealing, useful, and rewarding. Hundreds, or perhaps thousands, of clichés relating to the conception of time exist in the English language and, perhaps, many other languages. Examples of such clichés are: 'at this point in time', 'in a little while', 'it will be better in time', 'I wish I had time to . . .', etc. Even the phonetic and paralinguistic features of expressions can indicate the temporal beliefs, biases, and states of those expressing themselves. In this respect, anxiety, anger, frustration, and most human emotions have a particular tempo and rhythm in their expression. Such personal tempos often do not seem welcomed or suited to objective time restraints and constraints of constancy, order, and articulated fluency.[13]

Most people recognize that linguistic expression binds time. For example, certain expressions gain their artistic or creative impetus from the manipulation of the temporal features of expression. The timing of wit, the use of dramatic silence, pausings, and hesitations, the variations of rates with their alterations of vowel quality or extension are all involved in tempo alterations. Such timing appears to be based in the manner in which duration and process are blended linguistically. Such blending seems to be the basis of linguistic rhythm.

What is often not so apparent is that the tempo of expression may very well be highly correlated with the conception of time held by the expresser. The conception of time may relate not only to how a speaker or user of language has already conjugated space–time as an individual, but how such conception relates to his or her functioning and participation in social events requiring both verbal and nonverbal interaction.[14] The nature of interaction may relate more to the conception of the 'time of events' than it does to the signalic turn-taking cues used within the events. Event pacing seems to be essentially and primarily a matter of the conception of time held by those interacting in the event and the personal tempo of participants.

The degree to which time has been rigidly objectified by a person may relate to how one sees his or her self among others as a subject or object. The degree of temporal objectification may also relate to how a person has cut up his or her spatial realities as well as how a person articulates such realities while mobilized in such spaces among other people — whether private or public space. If one is convinced that time is spatial, one separates, divides, and otherwise cuts up his or her reality as if it were a geometrical pie or a very long piece of sausage to be sliced into distinctive and uniform pieces. The nature of environment is directly related to the temporality of the individual users of environment. In this regard, a static view of time may result in a view of reality quite different from a relative temporal view. A relative view of time, for example, may be related to perceptual awareness of environment. It is fairly well known that clock time appears to drag or remain constant when perceptions are not novel, when perception is habitual. It is also well known that clock time appears to fly like magic in situations of stimulus novelty. It seems to follow, then, that the degree of objectivity in personal tempo may affect one's sense of time and may interact with the manner in which environment is perceived and personally articulated. A spatial and objective personal orientation may be influential in producing motion through space in a habitual fashion. In this case, the environment is already clearly defined by spatial formulations and one's expectations for novelty can be reduced — certainty is well established. While time may seem to drag for persons in such situations, their movement through space may be either quick or regularized. Of course, this may not be the case in situations of stimulus sparsity or pathological boredom — both often being strangely interdependent. On the other hand, persons who hold time to be relative or less objective may move through similar space in an exploratory manner. In such a case, clock time would appear to move rapidly, perceptual novelty could increase, and movement through space would perhaps be slow.

In linguistic temporal environments, the same sort of situation seems to be common. For example, a lecture which is perceived as different, novel, or interesting appears to pass rapidly — the lecture seems to have ended without the use of much linguistic space or form. Conversely, a lecture which is perceived as boring, old hat, or not interesting appears to go on forever. In such situations the second hand on wrist watches may seem to have developed some form of paralysis. Some media events of high stimulus intensity seem to have an underlying purpose — to make clock time pass quickly or unnoticed.

Certain objections to these generalizations are certainly in order, as many variables are involved in the motion of biologically different persons through different kinds of space–time environments. The major idea being discussed here is that one's conceptions about time and one's temporal conditioning interact with one's personal spatiality and one's motion through informational space. It is certainly the case that there are widespread differences between individuals in their processing of different kinds of information and at different rates. These differences, however, also appear to be related to personal tempo and time orientations. It may be hypothesized that personal tempo interacts in many significant ways to yield particular space–time configurations in one's environments. It may also be hypothesized that habitual tempo in social and cultural situations interacts in significant ways with personal tempo. These propositions certainly deserve a great deal of focused investigation. Inquiry into the nonverbal meaning of time and human tempo has been curiously minimal. This may be due to the manner in which investigators have defined and conceptualized time. Newtonian time and its Siamese twin, Euclidian spatiality, are prone to the objectification of tempo. Highly objective views of temporality seem to produce highly objective, regularized, and spatialized modes of observation and methods of investigation. Such modes and methods unitize space and events for the purposes of control, the management of data, and observational verification. However, the assumptions concerning number (such as the meaning of 'one' and 'zero') and numerical progression (ordinal direction and motion) have been accepted without question by most students of human behavior. Such acceptance is perhaps unwarranted, as mathematical clarity concerning the meaning of number in ordinary mathematics is by no means established theoretically — without recourse to some rather tenuous assumptions about the nature of time. Statistics are based on such tenuous assumptions. Numbers and systems of numbers epitomize the language of objective temporality. Consequently, relative temporal environments appear to be neglected in the theoretical constructions and models concerning non-verbal behavior.

Human tempo as a relative factor may be a deeply hidden dimension. A rigid view of time can decrease awareness of relative human tempo and temporal environment. It may be that space is not the only 'hidden dimension' (Hall 1966) of human behavior. Relative tempo may be an equally significant dimension of human behavior. In fact, space appears to be *created* and articulated by both objective and subjective tempos. In turn, of course, spatial formulations can and do control and regulate subjective tempo. While the recognition that space and time should at least be hyphenated is a step forward, it should also be recognized that time is the primary dimension — time is the language of space. This may be so because relative spatiality is subject to the temporal inter-dependence of duration and process. In other words, that which endures or appears to endure becomes an object with relations to other objects. A static spatiality exists only as an abstraction. It is only in an objective stance that space is referred to as 'real' or unchanging — such space appears to exist only in symbolic, spatialized temporality. Spatial relativity, then, is only a special case of temporal relativity. 'Things' are never truly still — except in death — but even there, temporal relativity could enliven the situation.[15]

Linguistic objectification of time appears to complement the level of environmental objective tempo. This proposition is much more complex than it appears. The importance of this idea goes far beyond the notion that time affects the amount of information people exchange. McLuhan (1964: 143) suggested that clocks accelerate the pace of human association and, by coordinating and accelerating human meetings and goings-on, also increase the sheer quantity of human exchange. However, McLuhan's view implies that information between people in speeded environments is actually 'exchanged'. What is more likely is that increased compliance to clock-time acceleration tends to decrease the amount of information actually shared and understood. Compliance to demands of greater and greater speeds not only seems to reduce the amount of clock time allowed for communication, such compliance appears to have radical implications for the kinds of exchange and the forms of information which are possible or permissible.

In environments of speeded, objective tempo, the tendency toward task related statements appears to increase while feedback and interaction concerning such statements appear to decrease. In such temporal environments, the emphasis is placed on doing and finishing what needs to be done — regardless of the means involved. When motion toward finality and end products in such environments is highly valued, the acceleration of tempo is valued and objective tempo can be increased without protest. What is not so obvious in such situations is that communication relating to questioning, means alternatives, or contrary opinion appears to decrease. The acceleration of objective tempo, then, may be capable of consolidating or fostering organizational control and political power. To require everyone to hurry and scurry through their waking day not only produces fatigue, but also such demand reduces the possibility of inquiry, reduces the possibility of personal interaction necessary for the development of trustful relationships, and reduces the possibility of the formation of groups whose purposes may be contrary to organizational purposes. These conditions are, of course, relative to each particular organization and the pace or acceleration of objective tempo. Wittingly or unwittingly, the control of objective tempo can be a powerful persuasion tool. A proposition may be in order: Those who control or potentially control objective tempo also control space and motion through space. People who control clocks control people.

The use of objective time as a form of persuasion appears to gain its power because of certain factors. Objective tempo seems to be congruent with certain temporal values or motives (see taxonomy) held by people objectively paced: the value of speed, large numbers, consistency, order, timing devices, etc. Objective time as a persuasive force also can become powerful because temporal conditioning and habituation is pervasive in human behavior. Many persons never seem to question their characteristic rates of behaving or how they came to acquire such rates of behavior. In this regard, the pacing of people can be slowly accelerated, intentionally or unintentionally, without their understanding of its pervasive effects and its somewhat 'invisible' influence on their personal tempos. Another factor in the power of objective time as a persuasive force is that many people seem to measure their own self-worth and self-esteem in terms of their abilities to beat clocks, keep pace with a clock (John Henry myth), go faster than a pacing device, or regiment themselves with clock time. Self-discipline and personal identity are often related to association with clocks and time keeping or pacing devices. Such association can become so involved that some people's behaviors can become clocklike — a behavioral puppetry can be the result. Such behavior is reminiscent of the behavioral rigidity in the early Christian monasteries where time-keeping devices were first used to rigidly control social behavior (Wright 1968: 37–41). Perhaps one of the reasons that clocks are accepted so readily by so many is that clocks symbolize power, authority, and, frequently, deity.[16]

In summary, the temporal interface of nonverbal and verbal behavior is complex. The interface involves: the manner in which presentations are formulated; the manner in which presentations are represented; the nature of temporal symbolism and referencing; the interdependent tension of permanence and change; the interaction of personal and objective tempos; and the influence of imposed tempo on human proxemic and kinesic behavior. Time does not merely 'talk'. Time is intricately related to how people talk, the nature of communication environments, and the nature of communication events which mediate and sustain social order and organization. Time may be the basis of all nonverbal communication (Bruneau 1974: 665). The tempo of human behavior is deserving of the personal time of those interested in advancing the study of human behavior.

CHRONEMICS

I have recently attempted to outline a branch of communication study called 'chronemics'.[17] The main features of this outline may deserve repetition here along with the offering of other formulations which could be useful in the further study of human tempo.

Chronemics can be briefly and generally defined as the study of human tempo as it relates to human communication. More specifically, chronemics involves the study of both subjective and objective human tempos as they influence and are interdependent with human behavior. Further, chronemics involves the study of human communication as it relates to interdependent and integrated levels of time-experiencing. Previously, these interdependent and integrated levels have been outlined and discussed as: biological time; physiological time; perceptual time; objective time; conceptual time; psychological time; social time; and cultural time (Bruneau 1977). A number of classification systems exist in the literature of time.[18] However, such systems are not applied to human interaction directly. The above classification of levels of time-experiencing is, of course, arbitrary. Other levels such as 'linguistic time', 'psycholinguistic time', 'literary time', and 'creative time' could be added as bounded levels of time-experiencing or as subsets of other levels mentioned. The number of levels of time-experiencing involves the arbitrary placement of conceptual boundaries which serve only to contain a dynamic system of integrated and interactive tempos. Investigation into the nature of the interaction and integration of various levels of tempo, I believe, will result in the generation of new conceptions and theoretical constructs in the study of human behavior. More specifically, each particular level of time-experiencing, if bound with some degree of definitional relativity, may deserve and require years of further study. A classification system of levels of time-experiencing need not imply a hierarchy of temporalities. Each level of time-experiencing is so dynamically integrated with other levels as to make hierarchical distinctions appear to be nonsensical. Notions of hierarchy may hinder the development of temporal models — as hierarchy implies directional order and temporal sequencings which may not pertain to, for example, psychological tempo and some biological processes.

A taxonomic schema concerning interrelated levels of time-experiencing is offered below as a potential aid for the further study of temporal behavior. This initial attempt to construct a schema for observing chronemic behavior should be understood to concern systemic and highly integrated levels of analysis: [19]

Temporal drives: involving biorhythmic activity; hormonal and metabolic periodicities; ergic impulses (Cattell 1957, 1965); involving the reduction of physiological need tensions; etc.

Temporal cues: pertaining to the initial sensing and recognition of one's own temporal drives and those of others.

Temporal signals: involving the imposition of perceptual durations and intervals which give rise to individual sense of time; perceptual continuities and discontinuities which give rise to habitual and variable recognition of successions and durations; any durational or processual phenomena giving rise to the formation of perceptual information related to the pacing, control, regulation, or facilitation of human behavior; concerning the recognition of temporal characteristics of nonverbal behavior; etc.

Temporal estimates: concerning the sense of time and timing; the use of temporal signals for the purpose of establishing, maintaining, or changing the recognition of how quickly or slowly time is flowing in relationship to either some habitual personal baseline of tempo or some objective standard of tempo; estimates made concerning rates of personal tempo and/or the rates of behavioral events; etc.

Temporal symbols: pertaining to the symbolic representation of succession and duration, change and permanence, or of temporal perspective and orientation; concepts of subjective and objective tempos; relating to the representation of objective time, timing, and times; concerning linguistic representations and functionings related to levels of time-experiencing and all behaviors (including mental) subsumed under the taxonomic items presented here; etc.

Temporal beliefs: pertaining to assumptions held about the nature of time and space; concerning degree of rigidity in the perception and conceptualization of space–time behavior; concerning the validity of temporal cues and estimates; concerning the validity of temporal information arising from temporal drives, temporal signals, and temporal symbolism; pertaining to the validity and nature of temporal judgments (see below); etc.

Temporal motives: relating to psychological intention to influence temporal behavior; concerning the intention to alter personal and objective tempos; concerning the process of altering personal and objective tempos; relating to the influencing of drives, needs, and motivations; intention related to goals and goal behavior; etc.

Temporal judgments: pertaining to the validity of temporal beliefs, temporal motives, and temporal values (below) as exercised by individuals or groups of individuals in sociocultural contexts; etc.

Temporal values: concerning valuation and evaluation of tempo, times (events), and timing as they relate to personal, social, and cultural behavior.

NOTES

1. Some terminology in the text of this article may be unfamiliar or questionable. However, referral to the taxonomic schema in the last section of the article should help to clarify such terminology.
2. Concerning the increasing power of objective temporality see Mumford (1934, 1952) and Wright (1968).
3. On matters of perception and the sense of time see, for example, Fischer (1966, 1967, 1971a, 1971b, 1975) and Cohen (1967).
4. For views and reviews of consciousness which depart from objective and traditional conceptions see, e.g. Bruneau (1976 i.p.), Fischer (1974), Fischer and Rhead (1974), Fischer (1975) and Krippner (1970). Also see a relatively new journal, *Journal of Altered States of Consciousness*. A popular interpretation can be found in Ornstein (1972). A somewhat unusual view of the consciousness–unconsciousness continuum can be found in Lilly (1972a, 1972b).

5. On traditional notions of 'committed cortex', see Penfield (1958), Penfield and Roberts (1959) and Penfield (1966).

6. Cf., e.g. Singer (1966), Kleitmann (1963) and Bruneau (i.p.).

7. This view of the growth of objective tempo may appear to be sheer hyperbolism. However, spread of objective time throughout the world has been rapid and is growing. The significance of this movement might best be expressed in two hypotheses: (1) Objective tempo, when largely accepted, tends to destroy cultures which are based in subjective temporality; (2) The widespread adoption of standards of objective temporality tends to neutralize cultural diversity.

8. Another definitional viewpoint is that time does not exist. In response to such a view, Sherrington (1951: 212) said: 'Time may be an invention of the mind, but none the less the mind is integrated by it.'

9. Cf., e.g. Cassirer (1953: 198–226, language and concepts of space and time), Cassirer (1955: 104–140, time, myth, and religious consciousness), Cassirer (1957: 162–190, intuition of time) and Nilsson (1920, primitive time-reckoning).

10. In classical philosophical discourse, this word refers to the reality assumed to exist by those holding an objective view of the world. It is used here to stress the pervasive influence of 'looking backward'.

11. It should be noted here that extreme orientations in either past or future perspectives also can be movements toward silence. A person engrossed in his or her personal memories or in a speculative future can become isolated or alienated from interaction with others.

12. This is not to say, however, that all motion toward silence involves the primitivation of time. Silence has many forms and functions (Bruneau 1973).

13. While little has been said concerning the relation of time-èxperiencing and human emotion, some interesting possibilities for further study may be deserving of mention. Personal tempo in relationship to objective standards or a baseline of personal, habitual tempo appear to be radically altered during heightened states of emotion, during heightened states of attention, and during events related to self-preservation (physical or psychological threat). Personal tempo can be altered during certain human relations (e.g. dancing, communal activities, sexual intercourse, etc.), during certain forms of interpersonal closure (e.g. reduced physical distances between people, touching, positive and extended eye contact, psychological intimacy, etc.), and during emphatic projections with others who are immediately present or distantly so — as in mass media. Perhaps some interesting correlations of personal tempos and human relations may be in need of further investigation.

14. In terms of interaction, for example, a common occurrence of people functioning in quickly paced, objective time environments is the deferment of communication time, e.g. 'Let's try to get together . . .', 'Maybe we could talk again, later,' '. . . some other time', 'Maybe we could take a little while after a while to . . .', 'We have no time to talk about this now', etc.

15. Loren Eiseley's beautiful and moving account (1975) of temporal relativity in relationship to his own remembrances, aging, and on-coming death relates to the serious and hopeful side of this statement.

16. Cf. Alexander (1927), Brandon (1970).

17. Cf. Bruneau (1977). This source contains a representative bibliography of levels of time-experiencing and a 100-item glossary of chronemic terminology.

18. Cf., e.g. Doob (1971), Gioscia (1971) and Fraser (1975).

19. In relation to Pike's distinctions concerning etic and emic descriptions of behavioral systems (1954–1960 [1967]: 37–72), a field of study called 'chronetics' could complement the proposed field of 'chronemics'.

DONALD M. BAHR

The Role of Rhythm in 'Cementing' Meaning in Piman Songs[1]

Among the Piman (Pima-Papago) Indians of Southern Arizona, and apparently throughout the American Indian Southwest, there are three basic genres of oral literature: prose, chant, and song. Prose is the longest and freest in execution. Prose myths and legends typically run for hours. The freedom of prose is that a narrator may *paraphrase* episodes in his story from one telling to another.

Song is at the opposite extreme in length and freedom; chant is in the middle. A song text is normally less than a minute in length. In ceremonial use such as for curing, 'raindancing', etc., such a text is repeated several times with minor but systematic variation (e.g. to run a series of color or animal names through an appropriate 'slot' in the text). When song is used in conjunction with telling prose myth, which is its other major use in the Southwest, such repetition is usually lacking. In either case, however, the norm for execution is the same. Letter perfect accuracy is the rule in singing and resinging songs. There is no paraphrasing from one performance to the next and no room for the performer to tailor his song to the audience.

In effect meaning is cemented into songs. This genre provides Southwest Indians with their surest method of protecting a message from the ravages of time. Accordingly the singer is not viewed as the creator of a song, but as its custodian. Two different origins are attributed to songs, corresponding to their principal uses, in ceremonies and in telling myths. Ceremonial songs are traced to dreams or visions in the recent past and are understood as gifts from a supernatural. A singer may pass these songs on to other singers, but they are still explained as having come in the first place from spirits, animals, etc. In contrast, myth-telling songs are considered to be the preserved speech of ancient flesh-and-blood characters. They are interspersed 'as quotes' in a narrator's prose account of history. The prose narrative may vary considerably in fullness and emphasis from one telling to the next while the songs are much more stable. They are in effect the hard data around which the rest of the narrative crystalizes.

The above remarks apply to the Pimans in particular but they are felt to represent a strain through the Southwest in general. The remainder of this paper concerns the function of rhythm in fixing meaning into Piman songs, i.e. in assuring that each successive singing of a song will be the same as each previous singing since it was originated.

The key to Piman song is its steady beat. Because of this beat one finds when timing the repetitions of a given song (e.g. from a curing ceremony where it is repeated 16 times), that the repetitions vary by mere tenths of a second. I am told that Pimans hold a given tempo (e.g. 'allegro') more tenaciously than most Western orchestra conductors. This tempo, or underlying rate of pulsations, interacts with two things in the performance of Piman music: a percussive accompaniment by the singer himself with a rattle, rasp, or drum; and the sung text. As a rule the relation between percussion and the underlying beat is steadier and more monotonous than is the relation of text and the beat. The following examples of first lines from two ceremonial songs are typical and illustrative of my method of song transcription. Here the lower line of 'inch marks' represents the underlying beat pulses. The inverted 'v's' across certain inch marks represent percussive strokes, made in the present examples by striking an inverted cardboard box with a gourd rattle (to produce a sound not unlike that of the combination of base and snare drums as heard from a distant marching band). Sung syllables are written above; these will be discussed later.

(1) *sa   pi yoi   ni   ne si   si ya   li me*

∧ · · ∧   · · ∧ · ·   ∧ · · ·∧ · · ∧   · · ·

Free translation: 'It is not yet dawn'

(2) *si ya li we wiwewo po hi   m*

∧∧ ∧∧ ∧ ∧ ∧ ∧ · ·

Free translation: 'Towards the dawn they run'

We see a steady percussive accompaniment in both examples, and more diversity in the length of syllables in (1) than in (2). (1) is more difficult to learn to sing properly than (2).

Piman songs are highly textual, meaning that virtually every vocalization in them is cognized as part of a word which is part of a clause which is part of a multisentence discourse. Viewed as texts, the key fact about songs is that they are difficult for native speakers, even experienced singers, to understand on first hearing. There is a great difference between sung and spoken Piman. It is felt that songs are not meant to be obscure in the sense of a cabal against the uninitiated.

Rather, the difficulty that Pimans experience in understanding them may be viewed as a cost incurred from using songs as a genre specialized in letter-perfect textual reproduction — as 'native xerox machines'.

To know for certain what is in a song, one must learn it first and then reflect on it. Prior to learning it completely, one will certainly have an idea of what is in it, but that is not certain knowledge. It is my experience from trying to learn songs and from watching Pimans do the same, that the greatest difficulty is in apportioning the syllables of a word (or line) to a song's beats. The melody poses much less of a problem. It is a simple matter to sing the tune, once one can beat a song out, getting the words right.

The syllables of a sung word present a challenge because there is not a one-to-one correspondence between the shape or sound of a word in spoken Piman and that word's shape or sound in song. The word *gitwal*, 'swallow', for example, appears in the following forms (among others) in various 'Swallow Songs':

gi to wale
·   ·   ·

ñi to wali
·   ·   · ·

ñi ñi to wali
·   ·   ·   ·

ŋiŋi to wa li
·   ·   ·   ·

These different forms are due to the rhythmic patterns of the songs, not to anything intrinsic in the word itself except that sung 'swallow' must not be utterly unlike the spoken form. The problem then is: What sets the rhythmic pattern of a song? The following represents my current thinking.

The internal subdivisions of a song for analytical purposes are the strophe comprises a complete little story. Piman song is a narrative form. although, as was noted above, in ceremonial singing one finds substitutions at certain 'slots' when a strophe is repeated. In literary terms a strophe comprises a complete little story. Piman song is a narrative form. The nearest thing to it in my knowledge is the Japanese *haiku*. Like the latter, Piman songs tell stories covering an extremely short span of 'narrative time'. A film scenario based on a sung narrative would require only a couple of seconds to run. (The running time of the film would be much shorter than the already brief singing time of the song because the song's time is taken up with stating details that are on scene or in action simultaneously). As with *haiku*, what counts in Piman song is the selection and placement of details from the moment under narration.[2]

Internal to a strophe, tone, rhythm, and text cooperate to make it relatively easy to define *lines* and, internal to lines, to define *word* units which are analogous to musical measures. It should be noted that none of the above analytical terms are mirrored in the Piman technical musical vocabulary as it is now known. Pimans use a word 'song' (*ñe'i*) which corresponds in part to our 'strophe'; and they have words for the 'beginning' (*şon*), 'turning point' (*noḍ*), and 'end' (*ku:g*) of a song. In general their vocabulary appears to designate *points* within a song rather than *bounded segments*, hierarchically arranged, as is the case with Western musical vocabulary.

To return to the diverse forms of a word such as 'swallow', it is found that a given song will have a preponderance of words with a given number of beats, e.g. three-beat words or four-beat words. This is a fact of the structure of that song, and it explains the different beat lengths of 'swallow' as efforts to fit that word into a *dominant measure length*.

Within the dominant measure length, there are normally words of several different internal rhythmic and syllabic configurations, e.g. the two different four-beat configurations of 'swallow' in the above list. This is a second level of fitting, into a *dominant word shape*. It is easy to see that both of the above factors set up resonances in a song with the effect that it is easier for a learner or critic to determine whether a given song is being correctly sung. Also both factors involve the reshaping of words drawn from ordinary speech. For the sake of correct (or correctable) reproduction of text, there is a sacrifice in the ready comprehensibility of the text.

The dominant word shape is normally represented by one or more key words in the textual message of the song. Thus rhythm and discourse interlock. A further aspect of this interlocking is that the initial line of a song sets a pattern for the lines that follow. The dominant word shape is found in the first line and the line as a whole sets limits for the length and 'sound' of the succeeding lines. (This line incidentally serves to distinguish one song from all others. Thus, in indexing one singer's repertoire of over 200 'Swallow Songs', it was sufficient merely to enter the first lines on cards. Only two of the songs had absolutely identical first lines.)

The above processes indicate what I mean by 'the cementing of meaning', but they are confined essentially to one aspect of it, namely the modification of the form of words from spoken to sung Piman. Sounds and word order also change, to name two more aspects. The presumed purpose of the changes is to aid in memorizing or, perhaps more accurately, to aid in the flawless recall of a text from memory, a process which the Pimans call the 'taking out' (*wu:ṣad*) and 'standing up' (*ke:kiwa*) of a song. They speak of it as a nearly physical process.

To recapitulate, this process is aided by establishing a steady beat and by framing lines and measures in patterns determined by key words. We have treated the process as a technique more than an art, which is one-sided. It is necessary to point out that the dominant word shape is far from the only word shape in a song, and the pattern set by the initial line is not slavishly followed. Songs are not mechanical. At the present, early, stage of studying them I feel that the 'cognitive' approach advanced here holds greater promise than a purely esthetic one, i.e. granting that song metrics are not mechanical, it yields more to view their departures as attempts to *say something interesting in Piman* (such that it can be preserved), than to view them as attempts to *say something pretty in song* (such that it can be embellished).

NOTES

1. Funds for this research were provided by the Arizona State University Faculty Grant-In-Aid Program and the American Philosophical Society, Phillips Fund. Three Pimans who have been indispensable to it are Joseph Giff, Jose Manol, and Paul Manuel, a Pima, a Papago, and a Pima, respectively. The one analysis of a song set which has been completed to date is by Bahr and Haefer (1978).
2. The following are a *'haiku*-like' song and a famous *haiku* that is similar, both given it literal (but not metered) translation.
   Buzzard Song (Jose Manol):
   Black buzzard doctor,
   [Tree] stick end-on sits and coos (the sound made by the buzzard),
   East-towards greyly shines (ambiguous whether the subject is 'buzzard' or 'dawn')

   Haiku (Matsuo Bashō):
   Withered branch on
   Crow has settled —
   Autumn nightfall (published in Henderson [1958: 18])

PART III

Organization of Language and Nonverbal Behavior

STARKEY DUNCAN, JR.

Some Notes on Analyzing Data on Face-to-Face Interaction

It is both true and unfortunate that the relationship between nonverbal communication and sociolinguistics presents itself as a valid and important issue to investigators. Sociolinguistics has, for the most part, followed linguistics in its traditional definition of language, though not in the range of linguistic phenomena to be considered. It seems fair to say that sociolinguists have acknowledged the presence of 'nonverbal communication' but have not made extensive use of such phenomena in their analyses.

In a complementary fashion, investigators of nonverbal communication have concerned themselves primarily with what is typically left out in the work of linguists and sociolinguists: those actions, such as paralanguage, body motion, and proxemics, not included in the traditional definition of language.

One can argue that this separation of endeavor is strongly counterintuitive, that the phenomenon basic to all these disciplines is the conduct of face-to-face interaction. Considered as a whole, face-to-face interaction does not lend itself readily to the classical distinctions found in the literature. Rather, it may be best approached through a more integrated study of its various components. Such an argument implies that language use cannot be fully understood apart from both the sociolinguistic aspects of that use and the co-occurring 'nonverbal' phenomena. Similarly, study of nonverbal communication is inevitably incomplete when accompanying language use is ignored. This position contemplates, therefore, a synthesis of heretofore disparate research areas, aimed at the creation of a social science of face-to-face interaction. It would seem that the task at hand is to consider lines along which such synthesis may be possible. The concern of this volume is timely.

In achieving a more integrated study of face-to-face interaction, consideration must be given, of course, both to guiding conceptualization or metatheory, and to research method. Despite the fact that most of the current work on nonverbal communication is being done by social psychologists whose views of the relevant issues and phenomena appear to diverge sharply from those of linguists and sociolinguists, it is possible that metatheoretical issues do not present a serious obstacle to more integrated work on face-to-face interaction. An essentially linguistic (rule-based) approach to understanding face-to-face interaction as a whole was being articulated by investigators as early as 1955 in the work comprising *The Natural History of an Interview* (McQuown et al. 1971). The volume edited by Kendon, Harris, and Key (1975) contains the more recent work of a number of researchers concerned with the organization of interaction. Goffman (e.g. 1971, 1974) has considered the rule-governed and strategic aspects of interaction in considerable detail. Elements of a research-oriented metatheory for work on face-to-face interaction have been suggested by Duncan and Fiske (1977).

In any event, the concern of this paper will be methodological. Work on face-to-face interaction as a whole will undoubtedly require extensive consideration of method, for there are significant differences in this respect to be found between linguists and sociolinguists on the one hand, and investigators of nonverbal communication on the other. There are also significant differences between the methods used in many nonverbal-communication studies, and those proposed in the Duncan/Fiske monograph.

Among the many aspects of method meriting consideration, this discussion will focus on only one: the presentation of evidence with respect to descriptions of face-to-face interaction. I take it that descriptions of interaction are more precisely regarded as hypotheses concerning major sources of regularity in observed interactions. This being the case, the issue becomes one of adequately supporting (or documenting) such hypotheses. Sankoff (1974: 19) has stated the issue nicely: 'At the most general level, the basic problem is that of accountability of description of any behaviour to some data base . . .'

In considering this aspect of method, the discussion is offered in the spirit of on-going discussion of methodological issues. I do not propose to suggest to linguists and sociolinguists the methods they should be using. Rather, I shall discuss some methods and their rationale developed in a program of research concerned with the organization of face-to-face interaction (Duncan 1972, 1975; Duncan and Fiske 1977), though generally identified with 'nonverbal-communication' research. Both the general approach and specific methods to be described have been modified several times in the course of this research, and I assume that this development will continue. I would hope that continuing discussion of these issues would include the perspectives of linguists and sociolinguists using quite different approaches.

The discussion will begin with some broad distinctions and will proceed to consideration of specific techniques. Mention of these distinctions is not intended as an exhaustive account but rather as a means of emphasizing certain points. It may well be the case that some investigators will find themselves differing from the expressed views on both the broad and the specific levels.

SOME DISTINCTIONS APPLICABLE TO RESEARCH METHOD

Organization and strategy

I assume that research on face-to-face interaction is aimed at discovering, documenting, and describing regularities in the actions observable in actual interactions. The adequate description of face-to-face interaction as a whole will include consideration both of its organization (rules, etc.) and of the strategies that individuals and groups may be observed to take within that organization. The notion of 'organization' here is intended to be roughly equivalent to other, closely related terms such as structure, grammar, custom, convention, rule-governed behavior, and practice. Issues relating to the differences in these terms will not be considered in this discussion.

The notions of organization and strategy are joined in face-to-face interaction as two sides of a coin. Given an organization applying to some aspect of face-to-face interaction, participants operating within the framework of that organization cannot avoid becoming involved in a concomitant strategy. Strategy derives directly from the availability of options, and options are ever-present in organization. An obvious source of optionality in some rule sets is the provision for legitimate alternatives within the rules. But optionality is present in all rule sets — even those that do not permit legitimate options — because there is always the possibility of rule violation.

Although deeply interrelated, the notions of organization and strategy are conceptually distinct. It seems appropriate to maintain this distinction in descriptions of face-to-face interaction. Thus, a full description of some aspect of face-to-face interaction would include both a description of the hypothesized organization of that aspect, and a description of the strategies observed to be used within that organization, these two descriptions being clearly distinguished in the exposition. Of course, a single study might not attempt such a full description of interaction; it might, for example, focus exclusively on organization. But a study focusing on strategy would presuppose the availability of an adequate description of organization.

Finally, it seems useful to draw a clear distinction between the description of an interaction strategy (describable as patterns of option choice), and interpretations of the goals, motives, interactions and the like underlying that strategy. Describing a strategy is an empirical process, framed in terms of the organization of rules, etc., within which the strategy operates. The hypothesis of one or more goals of the observed strategy would seem a more complex endeavour, requiring information far beyond the observed interaction, such as assumptions regarding value structures in the society and intentions of the described participants.

Optional sequences and obligatory sequences

A second basic distinction will require the brief statement of two prior assumptions.

Source of data. I assume that research on face-to-face interaction is properly based on actual transcriptions of interactions, these transcriptions containing appropriate and sufficient detail relevant to the issues under investigation. Although this assumption seems unexceptional, it implies, among other things, that descriptive statements would not be justified by constructed examples, a practice that is fortunately quite rare in the sociolinguistic and 'nonverbal-communication' literatures.

Interaction sequences. I also assume that an essential aspect of face-to-face interaction is that it consists of sequences of action involving two or more participants. (For purposes of convenience, I shall frame the discussion in terms of two-person interactions.) Thus, investigators of face-to-face interaction will not focus their studies on the productions of individual speakers or interactants, but rather on the sequences of actions that occur between interactants. Of course, in many cases research on, say, the organization of interaction sequences will require information on the organization of individual interactants' productions within · those sequences. Similarly, hypotheses concerning the organization of interaction sequences will also involve hypotheses concerning the organization of individual productions. Nevertheless, the ultimate concern of research on face-to-face interaction is, by definition, sequences of action between participants.

The assumption regarding interaction sequences suggests that linguistics, in its traditional emphasis, provides useful information for interaction research but does not touch directly on its central concern. Similarly, because information on sequences is not included in the data of many 'nonverbal' studies relating such things as amount of gazing at the partner to sex differences or personality variables, such studies do not provide information on interaction sequences between participants, although the data of such nonverbal studies are gathered from observations of interactions.

We may now return to the distinction between optional and obligatory interaction sequences. Let us consider a two-part interaction sequence A-B, where A is an action by a participant, and B is a subsequent action by the partner.

The hypothesis of an obligatory sequence involves at least the claim that, given A, B definitely 'should' follow. An example might be response to the offer to shake hands. It would seem that the recipient of such an offer does not have a legitimate option to refuse, except under highly specialized circumstances (such as demonstrably dirty hands), for which apologies are given.

A stronger claim for an obligatory sequence is not only that B's must occur after A's, but also that B's must occur only after A's.

If the sequence A-B is said to be an optional one, then the interpretation is that B appropriately occurs only after A; but given A, B may or may not occur, depending on the choice made by the participant. In baseball the batter chooses to swing or not at a pitch. If the batter chooses not to swing, it is not considered to be a violation of any rule but rather the exercise of a legitimate option. In research on the exchange of speaking turns in some two-person conversation between adults (Duncan 1972; Duncan and Fiske 1977) the results were interpreted as indicating that there was optionality attaching to the auditor's response to the activation of the turn signal by the speaker. Given a turn-signal activation, the auditor may choose whether or not to take the turn. The turn signal was interpreted as indicating those points in the speaker's turn at which the auditor might appropriately act to take the turn, if so inclined.

The distinction between obligatory and optional sequences is commonplace in linguistics and sociolinguistics, needing no further elaboration here.

Probability of antecedent and probability of consequent

It is apparent that there are two general types of questions that can be asked of the *A-B* interaction sequence. The more familiar question is, given the occurrence of *A*, what is the probability that *B* will follow it? I shall call this the probability of a consequent. Such a probability would be calculated by dividing the number of times that *B* follows *A*, by the total number of *A*'s. Issues relating to such probabilities can be handled in a number of ways. For example, transition probability diagrams and Markov analyses are often encountered in the literature.

On the other hand, we can also ask the complementary question. Given the occurrence of *B*, what is the probability that *A* will precede it? I shall call this the probability of an antecedent. In this case, the number of times that *A* precedes *B* is divided by the total number of *B*'s in the corpus.

Given this formulation, several points seem clear. (a) Any set of observations of interaction sequences yields information on both the probability of consequents and the probability of antecedents. (b) There is an important conceptual difference between the two probability types. And (c) the respective values of the two types can be very different in a given data set. For example, let us say that there are 50 *A*'s in an interaction, and only 5 *B*'s; but each of these *B*'s occurs immediately after an *A*. The probability of the consequent *B*, given *A*, is only 0.10; but the probability of the antecedent *A*, given *B*, is 1.00.

The distinction between the two types of probability fades, of course, in various situations, such as when there is perfect association between *A* and *B*. In this case, both probabilities are 1.00.

Organization, strategy, and type of probability

To this point, three distinctions have been drawn: organization versus strategy, optional versus obligatory action sequences, and probability of antecedent versus probability of consequent. The interrelationships among these distinctions will be apparent. Consideration of these inter-relationships will return the discussion to its basic concern: the presentation of evidence in support of hypotheses in research on face-to-face interaction.

How does one gather evidence concerning optional rules in the organization of interaction? It seems that the appropriate approach is in terms of the probability of antecedents. Ideally, one would find for a hypothesized rule-governed, optional sequence *A-B* that the probability

of *A* preceding *B* is 1.00. (In the dust and confusion of actual interactions, however, such perfect performance may be somewhat rare.)

Conversely, given a hypothesized rule describing an optional sequence
in the organization of interaction, evidence on strategies taken with
regard to that rule is based on the probability of consequents. Thus, one
might find for the hypothesized optional sequence (even when it is
perfectly performed) that after Participant 1 produced *A*, Participant 2
responded with *B* 70% of the time; but that when Participant 2 produced
A, Participant 1 responded with *B* only 35% of the time. These findings
might be interpreted as different interaction strategies employed by the
two participants, both strategies being entirely legitimate within the
rules.

On the 'weak form' of an obligatory sequence (i.e. given *A*, *B* should
follow), the probability of the consequent ideally becomes 1.00: after
each *A*, there is a *B*. However, there may also be other *B*'s in the corpus
not preceded by *A*. In the 'strong form' of an obligatory sequence (*A* and
B perfectly related), both probability of antecedent and probability of
consequent ideally become 1.00: each *A* is followed by a *B*, and each *B* is
preceded by an *A*.

*Some statistical techniques for evaluating hypotheses of optional
sequences*

In studying optional sequences in the organization of interaction, one
hopes, of course, for perfect results (probability of antecedent = 1.00).
But of course perfection may not be frequently encountered in the
conduct of human affairs, in the formulation of hypotheses, or in the
gathering and analysis of observational data. How, then, does one
evaluate a set of imperfect results? This is obviously the province of
statistics. In papers proposing hypotheses regarding face-to-face interaction, it does not seem unreasonable to expect that these hypotheses
be evaluated in terms of appropriate statistical techniques, and that the
relevant data, together with statistical results, be provided for the independent evaluation of other investigators.

In this section are presented some statistical techniques that may be
used in a particular type of analysis. The brief comments in this section
are intended merely to provide some examples of the sort of techniques
that are available and not as an authoritative treatment of the area.

To this point, discussion has centered on the probability of an antecedent in evaluating hypotheses of optional rules in the organization of
interaction. But direct evidence regarding optional rules need not be

limited to such probabilities. Often, in testing a hypothesis on the organization of interaction there is some alternative action or event with which to contrast the hypothesized action. For example, in analyzing speaking-turn phenomena we could contrast the occurrence of smooth exchanges of the turn with the occurrence of simultaneous turns. The hypothesis was (a) that auditor attempts to take the speaking turn would tend to result in smooth exchanges of the turn when immediately preceded by an activation of the turn signal by the speaker; in contrast, (b) when such attempts were not preceded by the signal, they would tend to result in simultaneous claiming of the turn by the two participants. Similarly, in another study (Duncan and Niederehe 1974) a 'speaker-state signal' was hypothesized to be displayed in conjunction with beginnings of speaking turns, but not with vocalized auditor back channels.

For both the turn signal and the speaker-state signal, the data can be arrayed in the form of a 2 x 2 contingency table. Table 1 shows this array for one set of turn-signal results (Duncan 1972; Duncan and Fiske 1977). Although the data are reported in terms of frequencies, the table can be easily recast in terms of probabilities. Notice that in this table only information on the probabilities of antecedents is retained: the probability of a smooth exchange being preceded by a turn signal, and the probability of simultaneous turns being preceded by the absence of a turn signal.

Table 1. *Smooth exchanges of the turn and simultaneous turns resulting from auditor's turn-taking attempts when the speaker turn signal was present or absent*

	Turn signal present	Turn signal absent
Smooth exchange	(cell 1) 81	(cell 2) 0
Simultaneous turns	(cell 3) 7	(cell 4) 12

Given the hypothesis, a set of optimal results would yield a table in which cells 1 and 4 contain large numbers, and cells 2 and 3 contain zeros. That is, we would want no occasion of simultaneous turns to follow the turn signal, and no smooth exchanges to occur in the absence of the turn signal. As Bishop, Fienberg, and Holland point out (1975: 376), we need in this case a statistical measure that is symmetric;

that is, we are interested in the 'joint distribution of the two cross-classified variables'. Chi-square provides a test of the independence of the two variables.

In the data set shown in Table 1, a perfect probability of antecedents for smooth exchanges of the speaking turn was achieved: all smooth exchanges were preceded by a turn signal in the conversations observed. However, contrary to the hypothesis, some occasions of simultaneous turns were also preceded by the turn signal. Thus, the results did not perfectly conform to the hypothesis. A chi-square applied to Table 1 yields a value of 52.31; Table 1 has one degree of freedom.

Although chi-square is one of the more commonly encountered statistical techniques, users should be aware of certain difficulties attaching to it and to related measures of association, such as the coefficient of contingency. These difficulties are clearly described by Goodman and Kruskal (1954) and by Bishop, Fienberg, and Holland (1975), among others. In particular, it seems ill-advised to compare the strength of a chi-square or of a coefficient of contingency obtained in one data set with that obtained in another.

We may now consider a case in which an asymmetric measure is appropriate.

Although contrasting alternative actions as in Table 1 seems desirable, it is not always possible in practical research. Some of our work (Duncan 1975; Duncan and Fiske 1977) with auditor back channels (vocalizations such as 'm-hm', and 'yeah', and head nods and shakes) provides an example. We were seeking to test the hypothesis that a speaker 'within-turn signal' was associated with auditor back channels, these back channels being regarded as an optional response. Because responding in the back channel and acting to take the speaking turn appear to be two sharply contrasting actions an auditor may take, it would seem natural to use this contrast in the analysis. This could not be done, however, for the following reason. Although the speaker turn signal was hypothesized to have six cues and the speaker within-turn signal was hypothesized to have two cues, the two signals appeared to share one cue: completion of a grammatical clause. (For more extended discussion of signals and cues, see Duncan and Fiske [1977]). Thus, the hypothesis would hold that when that cue appeared, either a turn attempt or a back channel might appropriately occur.

Because no meaningful contrasts could be found between within-turn signals and other signals, it was necessary to draw up a 2 x 2 table contrasting (a) the occurrence or nonoccurrence of a back channel, against (b) the occurrence or nonoccurrence of the within-turn signal. Table 2 shows relevant figures for one set of data.

Table 2. *Auditor back channels and the presence or absence of the speaker within-turn signal*

	Within-turn signal present	Within-turn signal absent
Auditor back channel	(cell 1) 111	(cell 2) 14
No auditor back channel	(cell 3) 388	(cell 4) 272

To develop the notion of asymmetrical association, it may be well to consider Table 2 cell by cell. Optimally, we would want cells 1 and 4 to be large, and cell 2 to be zero. The first row contains information on the antecedent probability of interest: the probability of a within-turn signal preceding an auditor back channel. But what about cell 3? The hypothesis of an optional sequence does not concern itself with the extent to which a back channel actually tends to follow the signal (that is, the probability of a consequent). As mentioned above, that issue is a matter of strategy, not of the organization of interaction. Thus, cell 3 does not directly figure in the hypothesis. It is important only that cell 2 be small (ideally zero) while cells 1 and 4 are large.

This being the case, an asymmetric measure of association more closely reflects the hypothesis than a symmetric one. That is, we are more interested in the 'conditional distribution of one of the variables, given the other' (Bishop, Fienberg and Holland 1975: 376). There is an asymmetric measure of association readily available: the cross-product ratio. Following Bishop, Fienberg, and Holland, it will be denoted by *alpha*. The computation formula for *alpha* is simply cell 1 x cell 4, divided by cell 2 x cell 3.

The strength of association represented by *alpha* may be evaluated by *Q* (Yule 1900), computed by dividing (*alpha* − 1) by (*alpha* + 1).

Alpha is appropriate to the back-channel hypothesis because it reaches its maximum value (infinity), and *Q* reaches its maximum value (+ 1 or −1) when only one cell in the 2 x 2 table is zero. (This is, of course, not true for chi-square, as illustrated in Table 1.) Thus, *alpha* is said to be an asymmetrical measure of association. It may be seen that this provides a good test of the hypothesis applying to Table 2: the results are optimal when only cell 2 is zero. It is not necessary for cell 3 to be zero because it is hypothesized that the auditor back channel bears an optional relationship to the within-turn signal; the auditor may at times choose not to respond in the back channel upon activation of the signal by the speaker.

As noted above, Table 2, in contrast to Table 1, contains information on the probability of both antecedents and consequents. That is, one can derive from Table 2 the probability of the auditor's responding in the back channel, given a within-turn signal by the speaker. I have argued that this information on the probability of a consequent is not directly relevant to the support of hypotheses relating to optional sequences in the organization of interaction. It is conceivable, therefore, that a strong cross-product ratio resulting from the analysis of such a table may be due to the probability of a consequent, as opposed to the probability of an antecedent. This potential confusion may be avoided, however, merely by inspecting the respective cells of the table. As described above, an optimal result for a probability-of-antecedent hypothesis would be a zero in cell 2.. An optimally strong result due to the probability of a consequent would be obtained when there is a zero in cell 3.

Generalization of results

In proposing regularities in either organization or strategy, it is possible to distinguish claims made concerning the regularities in some set of observed interactions, from claims made concerning the extent of these regularities in the society as a whole. The work on speaking turn phenomena, mentioned above, may serve as an example. On the basis of detailed analyses of language, paralanguage, and body motion in two two-person conversations between adults, certain signals, rules, and other elements of an organization were hypothesized to relate to the orderly exchange of speaking turns. (This hypothesis was later supported in analyses of six other conversations.) That is, I hypothesized one social practice (presumably among many) used by the participants in the conversations observed. However, there is little in the available data that can help one in guessing how widespread the use of this practice is, despite the fact that six of the eight conversations analyzed were between previously unacquainted individuals. Obviously, to gather information on the extent to which the hypothesized practice is used within some group or subgroup, an appropriate sampling procedure must be used. Nevertheless, the strength of the results within the conversations studied may be evaluated in terms of chi-square and the coefficient of contingency, or in terms of *alpha* and *Q*. And in the case of *alpha* and *Q*, these results may be directly compared with those of other studies.

One may contrast the research strategy described above, with the strategy used by Sankoff (1974: 22). In that study a carefully stratified sampling of 'all Native French speakers resident in predominantly French areas of Montreal since early childhood' was carried out, permitting generalization of her results to that group.

SUMMARY

This discussion has touched on some issues related to the presentation of evidence in support of certain types of hypotheses in research on face-to-face interaction. Space limitations prevent a more extensive consideration of these and other relevant issues, as well as an examination of the various approaches to evidence presentation found in the literature of face-to-face interaction research. In addition, it is obvious that other types of statistical procedures may be useful in the analysis of data on face-to-face interaction. Nevertheless, several general points might be made on the basis of this discussion.

It seems reasonable to expect in a social science of face-to-face interaction that investigators present evidence in support of their hypotheses. Examples, even when taken from the recorded data (as opposed to constructed examples), are excellent communication devices, but they are entirely inadequate for evaluating the effectiveness of a proposed hypothesis for a given set of observations.

Statistical procedures, such as those described above, are available that are entirely appropriate for the type of data most commonly encountered in face-to-face interaction research: observations of discrete events. In many, if not most cases, these procedures will be simple to use and may be interpreted in a straightforward manner. However, a perusal of Bishop, Fienberg and Holland (1975) will reveal that procedures are available to handle more complex data structures.

Research results can be evaluated statistically. In the case of the cross-product ratio, different sets of results can be compared on the basis of measures of strength of association. Such comparison is valid, even in studies of one interaction or of a small number of interactions, when generalization to larger populations is inappropriate.

It is my firm impression that regularities resulting from the organization of face-to-face interaction (and potentially from interaction strategy) are quite strong. Hypotheses adequately reflecting these regularities should yield statistical results that compare most favorably with results obtained in other areas of social science.

VOLKER HEESCHEN, WULF SCHIEFENHÖVEL and
I. EIBL-EIBESFELDT[1]

Requesting, Giving, and Taking: The Relationship Between Verbal and Nonverbal Behavior in the Speech Community of the Eipo, Irian Jaya (West New Guinea)[2]

The aim of this article is to describe the relationship of verbal and nonverbal behavior during scenes of requesting, giving, and taking, in a nonacculturated society of Irian Jaya (West New Guinea, see Map). We will investigate units of verbal and nonverbal behavior in culturally relevant, nonmarginal scenes, i.e. in real-life situations of a non-Western society. As these units are meaningful in a society where communication is essentially face-to-face interaction, the data may contribute to future comparative studies. The bulk of the material has been collected in Western societies where, sometimes, the importance of face-to-face interaction is lowered to the degree of mere routines without impact on the overall picture of the culture as they are integrated into and constitute the lowest degree of more complicated systems of speaking and communication. Human ethologists have not yet tackled the task of studying the ways and meanings of speaking — the valuable hints they give concern the general function of bonding in feasts of exchange (Eibl-Eibesfeldt 1971 and 1972b: 80–81).

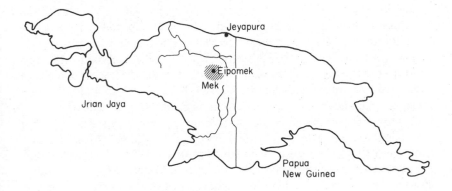

On the other hand, since Malinowski's statement (1923: 313, 315) that language either '. . . can only be understood from the direct function of speech in action', or that it serves '. . . the direct aim of binding hearer to speaker by a tie of some social sentiment', anthropological linguists have rarely specified this second function, called 'phatic communion' (but see Marshall [1961]).

An ethological interpretation of this function in relation to nonverbal means of communication was beyond the scope of their fieldwork. Finally, the functional approach to the evolution and deployment of species-specific activities like speaking, as is proper for the biologist and ethologist (for a recent survey see Hill [1974]), may well be combined with the functional view of language, as it has been developed since Malinowski in the London school of linguistics (Halliday 1973). For a survey of the functional approach to language see Robinson (1972: 42–56) or more recently, within the frame of the ethnography of communication, see Hymes (1972).

The guiding principle of this article is neither to describe single units of nonverbal behavior like paralinguistic features (Crystal 1974), proxemic behavior (Hall 1963, 1966, 1974; Watson 1974a, 1974b), eye-contact (Eibl-Eibesfeldt 1970a: 61–63; Argyle and Dean 1965), posture (Scheflen 1964), and the like. Nor does this study concentrate on single patterns of speech events, scenes or settings like speaking turns (Duncan 1974, 1975), sequencing in conversational openings (Schegloff 1968), directives, greeting and politeness formulas (Ervin-Tripp 1976; de Silva 1976; Ferguson 1976; Goffman 1972). In this article all these features so competently described by the authors mentioned center around a scene of everyday life and interaction: requesting, giving, and taking, essential in the bonding processes of a small community. Besides an attempted microanalysis of requesting, giving, and taking behavior between individuals, for the sake of comparison and contrast, we have included the description of organized giving and taking, of formalized exchange behavior among Mek groups (see also Mauss [1950]).

If we take for granted that the whole culture and social life of the Eipo build up the 'background expectations' (Gumperz 1972: 216), which we have tried to summarize in Sections 1.1 and 1.2, directing and managing the meaning and sequences of verbal and nonverbal behavior, these scenes are best described not as encounters, routines, or rituals (for a discussion see Hartmann [1973]) but as *'einfache Sozialsysteme'* (Luhmann 1972). In accordance with Max Weber (1956: I:1) we feel that the partners attach a meaning to their verbal and nonverbal actions and, more or less consciously, employ these actions in the pursuit of certain aims. The coming about of elementary interactions or simple social systems depends on (1) the mere presence of the to be partners, (2) the mutual perceptibility of the interactions, and (3) verbal communication (Luhmann 1972: 53–56). The first of these conditions eliminates all scenes of sharing and giving like feasts of exchange, which require varying degrees of planning. The second one is a prerequisite for nonverbal communication. The third, discourse, necessarily centers around a topic thereby structuring the interaction. Whether or not verbal and nonverbal communication are congruent is one of the questions we hope to be able to answer with our examples. One of the guiding hypotheses of this article, is that nonverbal acts are not only prerequisites, necessary accompaniments, or substitutes of language proper, but that they are means of action in their own right, the employment of which depends heavily on the different strategies in face-to-face interaction. Connected with this proposal is the second hypothesis that for human beings in general it is advantageous to have at their disposal two channels of communication: the verbal and nonverbal. Thus human beings are enabled to require, beg, approach, and make claims, which can be hostile acts or acts provoking repulsion and aggressivity, on the one channel, while maintaining the bonding process on the other.

Ultimately these hypotheses should be submitted to rigorous testing (Argyle 1972: 244). This, however, was not possible in the field situation. The methods employed therefore are those developed by Eibl-Eibesfeldt, that is the filming and subsequent interpretation of unstaged interaction scenes (Eibl-Eibesfeldt 1972a: 297–299) and those of anthropologists closely watching the behavior of people during participant observation. The materials on which this article is based are: 16mm films, partly with synchronized tape recordings of Eibl-Eibesfeldt, Heunemann, and Schiefenhövel, photographs taken by Heeschen and Schiefenhövel, tape recordings and field notes of Heeschen and Schiefenhövel. For the linguistic material these notes yield a large amount of evidence due to the fact that the approach was monolingual and that, as no work with the tape recorder was possible in the beginning, the situations in which the utterances were spoken, had to be noted carefully — a high percentage of the initial data were conversational openings relevant for the requesting-giving-taking system. The scattered, though ample data do not lend themselves to statistical treatment. Furthermore, one of the outcomes of working on the material at hand is evidence for the fact, that the different strategies and sequences of nonverbal and verbal behavior in the requesting-giving-taking system are highly subject to individual processing and monitoring by individuals, age groups, and constellation of the participants. The sequences we will describe are either sample scenes (Sections 2.1, 2.2, 2.3) or patterns generalized from a large number of scenes. To sum up, this study is explorative in character and tries to find ways of cooperation between human ethology and anthropological linguistics. The conclusions will have to await further confirmation and cross-cultural findings.

1. ANTHROPOLOGICAL AND HUMAN ETHOLOGICAL ASPECTS OF THE EIPO COMMUNITY

1.1 The people living in the valley of the Eipomek River in the highlands of Irian Jaya are neolithic horticulturists as are all groups in the mountain regions of New Guinea. Hunting, gathering, and pig-raising only supplement their staple diet, which consists mainly of sweet potatoes. The Eipo inhabit roughly the center of a larger area, where related dialects are spoken (see Section 1.2) and the same cultural pattern is found.

Eibl-Eibesfeldt (1976) summarizing the data which had been gathered by several members of the research team has characterized the Eipo as follows:

Neolithic planters; very martial; residing in villages, territorial through generations; village alliances; family-centered; cross-linking through clans; patrilinearity; [exogamous] marriages; babies caressed mainly by family members; high-ranking men as leaders, but no hereditary chieftainship; nonauthoritarian; cooperation in house building, warfare, and forest clearing; monogamous, [occasionally] polygynous, [rarely] polyandrous; boys very often play warfare, imitate adults [in other] games, girls play little, women never, men occasionally warfare with boys; taboos infringing sexual life, conspicuous timidity of men towards women; marked male conduct of men, clear separation of the two sexes in everyday life from childhood onwards, delousing in groups of same sex; children occasionally punished, encouraged towards aggression, often fights and violence within the group, between men as well as between spouses; no leisure time; ancestor worship; skull cult;[3] cannibalism (275).

This synopsis contains most of the important Eipo characteristics. It may be added that the Eipo are pygmies[4] and healthy, strong people with great physical stamina, cheerful, spontaneous, pragmatic, and tolerant in comparison with other Papuan groups.[5] Their warfare despite its spontaneity is ritualized and less determined than for instance that of the Dani west of them (Heider 1970). Verbal insults shouted towards the enemy, humiliating (anus presentation), and triumphing gestures (dancing with elements of genital presentation), play an important role in these fights.

Children's socialization is characterized by a long period of breast feeding (up to three years) during which girls and boys enjoy close body contact, caressing, and meals not infringed by taboos governing the eating of food for the boys after their initiation, which takes place when they are between about 14 and 15 years of age. Young people take an active part in working, feasting, and in discussions. At some occasions even a high-ranking man may be told off or openly corrected by a self-assured youngster, who does not have to fear any retaliation. The decisive roles in the community are played by the physically strong, the intellectually, socially, and supernaturally gifted, and the ones with particular ties to the mythological ancestors, which are part of a totemistic system. Festive ceremonies in connection with successful warfare, exchange of essential goods, which have to be imported, and religious cults act as bonding mechanisms even between groups which periodically have warfare against each other.

It is beyond the scope of this article to cover the elements of nonverbal communication which we have documented among the Eipo. We will therefore just list some of the typical behavioral patterns; the wide spectrum of the respective contexts in which the behavior occurs is merely hinted at in a cursory manner:[6]

. . . smiling, *sii lebna*, in friendly encounters, pleasant situations, during flirt, as part of the 'embarrassment syndrome'; laughing, *akwa*, in witty situations of humorous, obscene, malicious character, because of great joy, as part of the 'embarrassment syndrome' (Eibl-Eibesfeldt 1976: 191, 210); crying, *engene*, because of pain, in grief over someone or something lost, after being wronged by somebody; rage, *tulume, iibarya*, and other words as aggressive reaction to being wronged or not respected, with acts of auto-aggression (biting into own finger or hand) and aggression towards objects and persons (hitting, shaking, destroying, wounding, killing); scolding, *wane*, for wrong conduct; cursing, *mem sii lena*, in situations of great positive or negative surprise (*ngaluna*), using mainly obscene and sacred words; greeting (no general term) with establishing eye contact, eyebrow flashing, smiling, raising and waving index finger of erected hand, stroking of chin and scrotum (often in intention movements only, establishing skin contact, taking a grip on arm and shoulders; caressing, *iidiiana* (in public never among adults of opposite sex), with fondling, embracing, rocking (of babies), kissing (of babies, young dogs and piglets), mouth-to-mouth feeding (of dogs and piglets) with saliva and prechewed food; sexual intercourse, *fokna, kulubkulub*, and other terms with women also taking initiative (love songs); refusal of unwanted offers by turning the head away, lowering the eyelids, and pouting, *balume*; affirmation by eyebrow flashing and nodding, *ngang duukumana*; surprise reaction with fingernail clicking towards base of penis gourd, *sanyuum colobcolobana*, often accompanied by jumping movements in hip and knee joints in men and breast squeezing/milk squirting, *mum talena*, as well as touching of the pubic region with the same jumping movements in women; 'embarrassment syndrome', *alye*, with alternating smiling, establishing eye contact on the one side and cut-offs, face-hiding, self-embracing, finger-biting, and shaking-off movements on the other.

Many other elements of behavior through usage of objects as man's external organs, like songs of taboo, protest, grief, and magic performances e.g. will not be discussed here as well as physiological events with communication value such as sneezing, coughing, burping, yawning etc.

1.2   REMARKS ON THE LANGUAGE AND ON THE ETHNOGRAPHY OF SPEAKING

The Mek language family — formerly called the Goliath language (Schiefenhövel 1976: 265–266) — covers an area between approximately 139° 30′ and 140° 30′ eastern longitude. The southern boundary is the southern slope of the central range. In the north, Heeschen and Schiefenhövel found speakers of a Mek dialect in the hills south of the Idenburg River. The Eipo language is spoken in the center of these closely related languages, the percentage of shared cognates never falling below 50 percent. The Mek languages have been integrated into the Trans New Guinea Phylum (Voorhoeve 1975: 46; for critical remarks, see Heeschen [1977b]). Since the early word list of De Kock (1912), Bromley (1967: 299; 1973: 15–16) has contributed to the knowledge of these languages. Voorhoeve (1975: 116–117) relies heavily on Bromley's collections. Up to now no published work on the grammar of these languages is available.[7] (For some remarks see Heeschen [1977b: 650].)

From the background of continuous chatting only some few clearly distinct ways of speaking emerge: (1) the dancing songs, *mote*, requiring a special setting; (2) the songs, *diite*; (3) the incantations, *fuana*; (4) the *siidiikne*, the technique of enumerating terminologies and the special way the Eipo tell their stories; (5) the shouting of the warriors fighting and of the children playing war games is another distinct speech event. The daily stream of assertions, accounts, and larger bits of information can be interrupted by scenes of loud insults and noisy scolding.

Taboos govern the use of the 'real' names of certain persons, ancestors' spirits, and also of things, like sacred plants. The Eipo do not speak publicly of events which are of utmost importance to them, a fact which singularly contrasts with the normally unbound flow of verbal communication. The date when a dancing will take place (which at the same time is a feast of exchange, *niinye lii*, of giving and taking) is faintly hinted at. The men do not mention their departure to the hunting grounds openly, these regions are the abode of powerful spirits, those of ancestors and such of nature herself. The exchange of essential gifts is a matter of pure nonverbal communication. In the hunting grounds of the rain forests one has to speak in a low voice and in coded language in which the 'real' names for persons and things are replaced by others. Naming is a dangerous activity, inappropriately done it may arouse the anger of the hosts or the wrath of the spirits. The word, therefore, is something to be handled carefully.

1.3 SOME RULES FOR REQUESTING, GIVING, AND TAKING AMONG THE EIPO

To comment on someone's possession, e.g. rare food or precious things, is felt to contain a demand towards the possessor to share (compare Section 2.2). In some instances we, the strangers to the Eipo way of life, have misbehaved considerably in that respect, especially in situations when a group of people came back home from the forest laden with stringbags full of pandanus nuts or with game, usually small mammals and marsupials. We exclaimed: 'Look, our villagers with lots of pandanus fruits!', or 'Many animals they bring home from the forest!' Immediately we were told off: 'Don't talk! They will be angry with us!' So we all stood still and in silence watched the arrivals disappear in their family huts with their precious burden — no word was spoken, no gesture made. The tenseness of the scene was particularly felt as the Eipo, in every day life, are a loud chattering, cheerful lot.

The basis for this 'silence behavior', as we may call it, is the very mechanism just mentioned: to openly comment on something precious must be avoided. Otherwise it would induce the possessor to give of his wealth. Game, pandanus, as well as stone axe blades, etc., are rare. It is difficult, often dangerous, to get them. The possessor therefore must not be urged to share, he must be allowed to secure his load in his hut. He will often keep not a single piece for himself, for the game has been shot or snared for guests from another valley who are to perform a dance feast soon. But he will share according to his own decision. Sharing is so much an everyday pattern that in particular situations possessors have to be protected from the demands of others.

Do ut des, in an idiomatic Eipo phrase *arebminyura arebkinyura*, which happens to be an almost literal translation of the classic motto, is one of the essences of Melanesian life.

An impressive document of how even the younger children are encouraged to share has been brought home by Eibl-Eibesfeldt (1976:

190–191). A 16mm film sequence shows the following scene: a boy has a piece of taro. A younger girl, sitting beside him, tries to take it from him, but the boy turns away defending his possession. A woman's arm is stretched out; the boy hands over the taro piece, which is broken in half by the woman and given back to the boy, who now, looking at the two pieces in his hands, readily and out of his own decision presents one piece to the girl. This unstaged film captured a quiet, unpretentious educational act, showing how children are taught to share (see Plates 1–9).

Many a time when one of us strolled over the village ground or through the narrow paths between the huts a dark little face looked up inquiringly, and a child's voice said: *arebnangkin*, 'I will give you', and a tiny dirty fist stretched out with the bigger half of a sweet potato or another piece of food — everyday diet transformed into a delicacy by this altruistic gift.

To be *mako*, mean, not prepared to give readily, is considered wrong. *nuun mako niinye gum*, 'we are no mean people', the Eipo say when they give food or other presents. A generous person is classified *namin*, literally soft, friendly. To beg, to demand, is *morone*; there is no strict regulation on begging. On the other hand one often hears: *morone mem*, 'don't beg!' It is quite common to very frankly ask someone to share, to hand over, *arebnilyam*, 'give me!' Especially children are quite free to beg from anyone; close adult relatives mostly comply with their demands, whereas older children have often been observed to forbid the begging.

There are instances of giving and taking among the Eipo which we are too limited here to quote, we therefore just mention a few examples. People from distant villages arriving with goods gathered or produced in their area usually do not receive the counter-gift immediately but sometimes months or years later. Pigs, stone axe blades, string bags, cassowary feathers and many other items are exchanged over the ranges where one has to cross passes of 3,500 meters elevation. Big elaborate dance feasts often are elements of this exchange pattern. Prior to the biggest of such feasts we witnessed in Eipomek in March 1976 the hosts-to-be endlessly discussed, often in coded language, how much should be given. Giving more than others demonstrates superiority, and can thus be an aggressive act. Enormous amounts of food were given to the men who had come from several villages in November 1975 to help rebuild the sacred men's house, the religious center of the southern Eipomek valley Plate 10). The heaps of food we estimated to weigh several hundred kilograms. In April 1976 a procession of about 100 people walked to the village of Talim, each person carrying at least 10 kilograms of sweet potatoes and other food as relief gifts for the Talim people, who had suffered from a period of food shortage.

Particular relationship ties require particular generosity. The mother's brother, *mam*, for instance, is expected to give more often than other relatives to his sister's children. As we have tried to show, however, sharing and receiving in the Eipo society is not confined to special occasions. It is a pattern from early childhood.

2. ANALYSIS OF REQUESTING-GIVING-TAKING SCENES

2.1 *Interaction among girls while eating pandanus nuts (sequences from a 16mm film taken by Eibl-Eibesfeldt on September 29, 1975, field number 10, 25 frames per second)*

A description of macro- and microevents during this sequence is given first, an ethological interpretation at the end of this chapter.

In front of one of the family huts of the village of Malingdam some girls are sitting or standing close to each other, almost in a row. A short while before, the group had consisted of other members who are now gone. Bolma, a girl of about 12 years of age sits on top of one of the rocks. In her hands she has a sizable portion of a pandanus fruit consisting of several hundred nuts, locally named *win*. It grows in the rain forest above 2,200 meters.[8] With her teeth Bolma loosens the nuts and cracks them between her molars. She has already given some of these nuts to some of the girls who had been in the group a few minutes before. On Bolma's right side an unidentified girl, W, of approximately seven years of age leans towards Bolma, her hip resting against the rock (see Plates 11–37). Her skin is partially and at times in contact with that of Bolma. Bolma passes a nut to W. Both girls do not have skin contact at this moment, W remains in the leaning position besides Bolma. An unidentified little girl, X, of about three years of age is standing on the right side of W watching Bolma and W cracking nuts. The distance between the bodies of W and X is only about 10 centimeters, but there is no skin contact. W turns her head and shoulders to the right, very shortly (appr. 1/4 sec.) glancing at Karinto, about 13 years old, who stands at the right end of the row. Little X watching W crack the nut so close to her, raises both arms with the intention of reaching for the nut. The stretching out movement, however, is not completed. With hands and forearms having reached chest level, X draws them back to herself thus derouting the stretching out movement into one of self-embracing. X continues to watch W crack the nut. At the same time Bolma, who has just loosened another nut, turns her head and shoulders a little to the right and while cracking the nut between her teeth looks at Karinto. With her head slightly oblique and under continuing eye contact she offers the just-opened nut to Karinto. The gesture with which this is done has been observed by us several times: hand and forearm are in a vertical position, the angle in the elbow joint is appr. 90°. Karinto reacts to this offering gesture and stretches her left arm out to reach for the nut. Little X who is now the only one in the group without food turns her head and body towards Karinto looking at her with wide-open eyes. At this moment W who has just opened a nut and taken the contents out touches X in the axilla-region. X did not react to her offering the nut some seconds ago. Being touched, X turns back to W and takes the nut out of her hand. At this time all four girls are eating. In the next scene Karinto squats down at the right end of the row, on the left side Beayanto, a newcomer to the group, about 15 years old, squats down on the rock besides Bolma. She is eating a small sweet potato. For about two seconds W, X, and Karinto watch her eating; Beayanto does not share the small remaining piece with the other girls. Bolma continues to separate nuts. W leans towards her, her left arm and belly in skin contact with Bolma, her right hand at chest level, close to where Bolma is working with the nuts. X touches W's belly with her left hand. On the left side Beayanto sits in body contact with Bolma. Only Karinto has a little distance between her and X. Later Karinto leaves the group while the four others still sit or stand closely together. Bolma continues to eat nuts. For some while now she has not shared any of them with the other girls in the group. Beayanto, who does not stare at the nuts as W and X do, starts to talk to Bolma. At once both girls establish eye contact, Bolma tilts her head a little backwards, smiles towards Beayanto and performs a very pronounced eyebrow-flash (*Augengruß*). About three seconds later Bolma passes the nut pod to Beayanto who separates them with her teeth and passes the single nuts back to Bolma who cracks and eats one of them. W and X still watch her closely, their faces showing a begging expression. In the next scene Bolma receives more nuts from Beayanto who has finished separating them all. She does not keep one for herself. Bolma collects all the nuts on her lap and does not eat any of them now. W and X still have their eyes fixed on the nuts between Bolma's hands. Twice in the course of the next few seconds Bolma shows a tense and embarrassed expression in her face and she moves out of body contact with W and Beayanto by stretching her body backwards, returning to her former position. Beayanto, while separating the nuts, had body and head directed towards the open space in front of the girls, and her right knee touched Bolma. But, even during her passing over the nuts to Bolma, there had been no eye contact. Little X has turned her face away from the nuts in Bolma's lap and is now looking down to the ground. Except in the scene at the beginning W and X have not received any further nuts from Bolma nor has Beayanto. It should be noted that requesting, giving, and taking in this scene were not, except for the short conversation between Bolma and Beayanto, accompanied by speech acts.

The encounter between the five girls takes place outside of some family huts. The open group setting allows newcomers to join and group members to leave easily. Encounters taking place inside huts may require and/or favor a behavior more in line with the respective standards of conduct. Bolma, the possessor of the *win* nuts, occupies the top of the rock which is the spatial center of the group. She has complied with the rules to share by giving nuts to former members of the group, but she has done so not very generously. W, who maintains close proximity and almost constant skin contact with Bolma, receives a nut from her. During handing over the gift the two girls have no skin contact for a short while. We tend to interpret this to be a sign of a certain degree of tension between them despite the gift. This view is backed by the fact that Bolma does not give W any more nuts during the remaining sequence. Two close friends, according to what we have witnessed in other sharing scenes, would have remained in body contact, the receiver indicating his joy over the gift. W does not react in such an appreciation behavior. Little X performs the described derouted begging movement pulling her arms towards her before reaching the desired food. To watch this scene in slow motion provides an example of how subtle and expressive nonverbal behavior is and how useful is a documentation by movie film. It appears that X's behavior indicates her awareness of the rule that one should not snatch things away from someone else. As babies do not have inhibitions to take away things from others, this avoidance of taking away something is probably learned. That the derouted begging movement ends in self-embracing is ethologically interesting to us. Firstly, the transformation from a begging movement to that of self-embracement can be explained as '*Übersprungbewegung*' (displacement activity, Kortlandt [1940] and Tinbergen [1940], quoted by Eibl-Eibesfeldt [1969: 188–189]); secondly, to seek a hold on the body of another in stressful situations is a behavior pattern found in all cultures we have studied; it provides assurance, security, and comfort. Self-embracing seems to occur in moments when no other person is available or where the situation, for whatever reason, does not allow such reaching for someone's hand, arm, or body. It is remarkable that self-embracing, performed at different levels of intensity, is a pattern often found in depressive European (and other?) patients signalling their feeling of insecurity. Little X is constantly looking longingly, almost staring, at

Bolma, W, and (later on) Karinto, who eat. It is a strong nonverbal appeal which remains unanswered, except once by W. In the next scene Bolma offers a nut to Karinto, who is older than she and stands appr. one meter away. Establishing eye contact once again prepares the onset of the dyad. Then Bolma tilts her head into a slant position; this particular gesture has been described by Montagner et al. (1973: 8) as '*la posture de solicitation*'. During a series of experiments to assess common patterns of reaction towards a baby-and-mother unit we have also seen this head-tilt gesture. More data will have to be gathered for this behavior pattern, but the tentative interpretation may be put forward that a head-tilt gesture serves as an initial device for establishing contact and may basically be an act of turning the eyes and the normally horizontal line between them (the substrate of the menacing stare, '*Drohstarren*') into an oblique line, thus avoiding the menacing component. Yet more data are needed on 'offering gestures' in which the arm of the bidding person is not stretched out completely but held in a somewhat hesitating position, i.e. bent in the elbow joint, as if asking whether the gift is wanted or not. Even when Karinto reaches out for the offered nut, Bolma's forearm remains at the same angle as before. Little X directs her begging gaze at Karinto. With X's face away from her (and because of that?), W offers a nut kernel to X who is so much engaged in staring at Karinto that she does not realize W's hand is held out to her. Only after W has touched her repeatedly she reacts, turns, and takes the offer. With Beayanto joining the group — she is now the oldest of the girls — and taking a seat on the rock besides Bolma the group setting is newly defined. Karinto, who has not been in skin contact with a group member, leaves shortly after Beayanto has come. Bolma does not react to W's begging look, but bends her head backwards, smiles at Beayanto and performs a pronounced eyebrow flash (this particular face-to-face interaction pattern signalling readiness for contact, greeting, approval, etc., has been described by Eibl-Eibesfeldt [1972a: 185] among others; we will therefore not discuss it here). The only verbal encounter of some length during the filmed sequence takes place during this scene. Bolma and Beayanto have established a closer relationship than exists between Bolma and the others, though to our knowledge the two girls usually had no particular friendship tie connecting them in situations other than the described one. Beayanto has refrained from making any appeals for nuts from Bolma, this and the established friendly contact may have caused Bolma to pass the nut-pod to Beayanto for her to bite the nuts off. Still Beayanto does not make any moves to keep a little of the delicacy but hands all nuts back to Bolma and in doing so she avoids eye contact with her, thus controlling possible appeals of begging. Even though things have gone well for Bolma — the older girls did not make any demands for greater shares and the little girls restricted their begging to looking, touching and repeated proxemic shifts into body contact, thus leaving Bolma the choice to overlook and not react to these appeals — she apparently realizes the tense situation which arises, especially when she starts collecting the many nuts in her lap. The uneasiness apparently felt by her, as may be seen in her breaking body contact twice and her unusually tense facial expression, may stem from the conflict between the urge to keep the nuts for herself on the one hand and the (culturally reinforced) drive to share on the other. She has decided for egoism but her reaction betrays: the conflict is not fully solved.

2.2. *Indirect request during official visit*

The above described interaction between the five girls constitutes a typical everyday scene; we would now like to report an encounter in which requesting and consequent giving takes place in a more formalized way.

Babyal, one of the most influential men of the village of Munggona and at the same time one of the two war leaders, enters the village of Dingerkon, especially adorned for this occasion. He has come to perform a curing ceremony on Mangat, a man from the village of Malingdam, which belongs to the political unit headed by Munggona. Mangat had been seriously wounded during an ambush attack by warriors of the political unit Marikla/Dingerkon. The ambush had taken place near the village of Dingerkon. Mangat had finally been brought into the family hut of Ninke, the most influential man in the village of Dingerkon.

When Babyal squats down on the village ground (see Plate 10), about one meter away from Ninke, the two men start talking to each other. In the course of the conversation Ninke makes a remark about the bird of paradise feathers with which Babyal's string bag is decorated. The decisive words in his requesting are: *kwelib fotong teleb*, 'nice feathers of the bird of paradise'. Ninke and Babyal have eye contact during this scene. The conversation now covering other topics, Babyal bends down to his net and unties one of the feathers which he passes over to Ninke, who reacts to this gift with a long satisfied smile towards Babyal. There is no verbal equivalent to our 'thank you' in Eipo language. Ninke takes the feather and attaches it to the whitish leaves hanging down from the upper end of his bow. Eipo bows usually have this type of decoration (called *yin bata*); the bows are considered to be complete only when containing bird of paradise feathers. As these are not found in the Eipomek valley and have to be bartered for from outside it, these feathers are a very valued possession.

The requesting–giving encounter just described contains some elements which distinguishes it from similar scenes in everyday life. Babyal and Ninke are both leading men in their respective village communities, both have a share in the responsibility for the seriously wounded Mangat. Babyal had especially prepared himself for the curing ceremony and before climbing up the alpine track to Dingerkon had carefully adorned himself. Some days ago Ninke, after heated discussions as to where to bring the wounded warrior, had finally agreed to have him put into his house. His position as a leading man and his caring for one of the men of Babyal's political unit facilitate his request for the feather. Babyal does not hesitate to grant the indirectly expressed wish, thus thanking Ninke for his role in the care for the wounded, and at the same time, through presenting the gift, obliges Ninke to himself. The encounter between Babyal and Ninke is characterized by congruity between the two important levels of interaction: the interpersonal sphere, which is prepared by sitting and talking together, as well as establishing eye contact on the one hand and compliance with the culturally expected roles on the other.

2.3. *Giving and speaking as tension relievers*

The scene of nonverbal communicative interactions can be compared and contrasted with another scene which is characterized by the almost complete absence of any communicative acts at all. The people of Dingerkon (where one of the writers lived) had many relatives in the village of Wagidam situated in the neighboring Tanime Valley. Some of the Dingerkon people possessed gardens in Tanime and were living for two or three months in Eipomek and Tanime respectively. However, when a party arrived from Wagidam (the arrivals invariably appeared around noon, a time of the day when only some old men and some children and perhaps one or two men had not left for their gardens, and when there were almost no sweet potatoes or other food stuffs left over from breakfast) no greeting and politeness formulae like *yanmalam*, 'you are coming', or *Wagidam yanmalam*, 'you are coming from Wagidam', were uttered. The newcomers established contact by eyebrow flash, but during a time span of some minutes further eye contact was avoided and the two parties were keeping a distance of at least three meters. From the standpoint of ethology the silence and ongoing absence

3

of communication can be interpreted as hostility, arising when a stranger or another party penetrates another's territory. While the assumption that there is, during the first minutes of these encounters, a growing tension between the two groups rests on our intuition, the verbal and/or nonverbal responses to this precarious opening sequence support the view that the silence conceals the efforts to suppress or to control feelings of hostility. A humorous remark like *mane wik obmalam*, 'you have hunted many marsupials' (an allusion to the fact that the arriving party has passed through the hunting grounds on its way but has nevertheless not brought any game with it and will therefore depend on the hospitality of the hosts) may dissolve the tensions and initiate a conversation with all its consequences on the level of nonverbal communication, eye contact, proxemic shifts, etc. If one of the hosts happens to smoke a cigar or to eat sugar cane he will hand it over to one of the guests, thus removing whatever tension may have been left over and inspiring verbal communicative acts. In our view this exchange is the true equivalent of the Western type of greeting and politeness formulae. The third possible response to initial eye contact and subsequent silence — which indeed is the most frequent solution — is the guests making their way into the men's house, where, having stirred up the fire, they will be drying some tobacco leaves and where, the hosts dropping in one after the other, small gifts like cigars, sugar cane, or whatever is still available will be exchanged. The bonding system on the two levels, verbal as well as nonverbal has been started.

2.4. *Taking away as aggressive act, followed by punishment*

Now that we have analyzed a longer scene of everyday life (Section 2.1) and described the nonverbal vocabulary in detail, as well as the two visiting scenes (Sections 2.2, 2.3) which take place on a higher level of interaction, we will focus on shorter scenes which are created by spontaneous encounters in the village, less frequently, as we believe, in the family huts or the men's house than in the open.

Imagine that the interactional equilibrium (Laver 1976: 355–356) between the bonding and rejection mechanisms, as shown in Sections 2.1 and 2.3, has hardly yet been managed and that either the requesting party directly takes something without having asked for or without having established any contact or that this party makes a straightforward request. The first case is clearly an aggression. When Lekwoleb, aged 25, entered the men's house and took some bananas out of the net bag of his brother Ferengde, aged 30, the latter simply took a stone axe and inflicted a deep wound into the shoulder of Lekwoleb, who rushed into his hut and fetched his bow and arrows. While Ferengde stayed in the men's house, Lekwoleb raged for about two hours, shooting arrows against the men's house, crying, weeping, cursing, and whispering imprecations against his brother. Some older men and women prevented him from entering the men's house and from continuing the fight. In the following week the other men of the village watched carefully that the two brothers did not meet.

An aggressive act stops verbal interaction and the conflict can only be managed by the intervention of a third party, which in this case adduced verbally the norms and rules of appropriate behavior. This even holds true for minor aggressions like a simple refusal to share or menacing gestures.

2.5. *Direct request*

A fact which might be quite unsuspected is that in the taxonomy between the aggressive behavior and the bonding behavior a direct request ranges next to an aggressive act, when it has to be complied with by an adequate action by the addressee and where he has no choice and control over the interaction. Terban, a youth of about 15 years, used to apply this direct strategy. He straightforwardly came on to the potential giver, stretching out his right arm, looking into the face of the addressee, and gazing at the potential gift, saying: *bobnilyam*, 'give (it) to me', or *na ton*, 'me too', or *kwaning ton bobnilyam*, 'give me a sweet potato, too', or *saboka na ton*, 'tobacco for me, too', in a firm and loud voice. It was rare when the addressee complied with the request by handing over the object. Mostly the reactions to these requests have been observed to be the following: (1) The addressee turned away, having gazed at the addressor with an embarrassed smile, drew the object back and made an angle of at least 45° between the front of the two bodies, the angle between the two heads even bigger (compare Deutsch 1977). This movement could immediately be followed by the exclamation: *nonge*, 'mother', *na song*, 'I don't want (to give something to you)', *na like*, 'I object', or *basam kalye*, (a strong curse, referring to the abdominal fat of pigs used in religious and curing ceremonies). Some stronger refusals are *morone mem*, 'begging forbidden', or the interjection *bahai*, pronounced with varying degrees of pharyngealization, thus deriding the addressor. The verbal material displayed here shows perhaps the lowest degree of immediacy (Mehrabian 1972: 21–53). It is highly expressive of the negative or unwilling attitude of the speaker, it makes no reference to the partner, and the absence of any modal markers does not invite the addressor to a second turn. This vocabulary in the light of one of the primary functions of language, that of the 'phatic communion', is a simple nonbonding marker. (2) If the response of the addressee was only nonverbal the addressor could use the same verbal material to insult the person unwilling to share. (3) The scene comes to an end with a definite shift away from the other, with starting a conversation with a third person, or with continuing a conversation only interrupted by the direct request. Significantly, such conversation was started even if the third party was far away (up to 20 meters), which required shouting or a loud voice. A slight proxemic shift and singing a song was equivalent to the newly started dyads. (4) The questioner could start again mainly by a process of verbal arguing, saying e.g. *niirya areblum na teikyonok gum arebmanelam*, 'you have given (something) to all, but you don't give (something) to me'. The result of this renewed conversation depends on a multitude of variables not to be described here; again the function of language in this context is that of adducing norms of behavior and inter-action.

The description of this pattern is valid for spontaneous encounters between children, if the objects desired were sweet potato or tobacco, or between adults, if the object was tobacco.[9] The direct request was employed by the younger children among each other, one youth (Terban) and four adults in the village of Dingerkon. It proved to be the least successful.

That direct requests can be an offense has been documented also in other cultures (e.g. Eibl-Eibesfeldt (1972a: 114–115; 1976: 98–99 and 135)). To be polite means to allow the opponent to think over and even to refuse without destroying the bond. For this reason often special types of asking are employed. In Austria, for instance, the bridegroom-to-be asks his prospective parents-in-law whether they would agree to a marriage by asking whether he could receive a little tobacco from them. When the wish is granted, he knows he will be accepted. If not, he can still keep face. It was just tobacco and future relations are not severed. A lot more is known about such '*Verblümungssitten*', also from non-European countries. Demanding instead of asking is an instrusion which is responded to by cut-offs and refusing. Therefore the act of intrusion is often employed as a strategy of provocation.

2.6.   Childlike and submissive appeals

The questioner could improve his success by adding some paralinguistic features to the verbal requests. These features consist of lowering or heightening the voice and in prolonging the final vowel of the request, e.g. *na tone* [nʌ'tɔ nɛ: :]. The whole utterance could be slightly pharyngealized or nasalized or said in a whimpering tone. Alternative verbal sequences for the first turn are *na ka*, 'my in-law, my friend', or *na nii*, 'my father'. It is interesting to note that appeals to parental instincts are carried out by means of paralinguistic features as well as through the referential function of the word. These utterances occur with stretching out of the hand and stroking the chin or beard of the potential giver or with intentions to this gesture. The apparent advantages of these paralinguistic features are the following:

1. The questioner, by playing a childlike role or by stressing the fact that he is a child, submits himself to the person to whom he is begging and at the same time appeals to his parental instincts.

2. These utterances can be repeated in contrast to the direct request which we never heard to be brought forward a second time. Or they can be accompanied by smiles and continuous or repeated looking at the person in possession of the desired object. Generally this strategy is that of the children, but it is not uncommon to youths (e.g. Buk and Kwinirban), and even adults (Alalamde), though the adults mostly refrain from stroking the chin.

2.7.   Indirect requests

While in the foregoing scenes the requests were most explicit, the intentions of the requesting persons in the following scenes are stated with a diminishing degree of explicitness. Without verbal explicitness the intentions must be assumed and inferred from the schema of daily interactions with its system of expectations and interpretations (compare Section 1.3).

A slow proxemic shift towards the giver may indicate the intention. The preferred strategy of most of the children and some youths, among them Bingde and Melase, was to sit down at the side of the potential giver with close skin contact and a glance of about two seconds up to the person. An equivalent to this procedure was most frequently employed by youths and adults. After they had established eye contact and moved into the range of personal interaction, i.e. within a radius of one to three meters, they simply breathed in some air, thus producing a sound which may be described approximately as an intermolar, implosive and voiceless fricative, *leklekana*. In producing this sound, which may well be a ritualized sucking in, the airstream mixes with saliva. The Eipo often make this peculiar sound when eating hot spices like ginger and the leaves of a pepper species, or when smoking to indicate the savoring of the delicacy which had elicited so much saliva. Both procedures, proxemic shift and *leklekana*, however, are ambiguous. The first could stand for a kind of approach in general. The second one has the meaning of anticipating either the pleasure of consuming the delicacy or the delight the person would have if the object of joy were handed over to him. Neither procedure requires an immediate answer either verbally or nonverbally, the situation thus being in suspense. As the nonverbal openings are ambiguous in most cases the intention can be clarified by uttering the words as described in Section 2.5 or by the following statements: *naiye kwaning teleb*, 'my friend (lit.: father), a good sweet potato', *kwaning teleb dibmalam*, 'you are eating a good sweet potato', *teleb tong*, 'a good smell', *kwaning fatalonmanil*, 'I have been lacking sweet potatoes' (*kwaning* also stands for food in general), *fatan wik*, '(I have) a big hunger', or *teleb dibmalam na mune gum se*, 'you are eating well, I am hungry'. These remarks can be thrown in at any time during an encounter, though, normally, they follow the opening nonverbal sequences. The actual consumer now has the next speaking turn, but the decision to give up is not forced upon him by a direct request. Compare also Ninke requesting the feather from Babyal (Section 2.2).

2.8. *Indirect approach with requesting*

With regard to the verbal openings there are no clear-cut differences between the following scene and the preceding one. Between the openings which still refer to the gift and the wide range of conversational openings and assertions without such reference there are continuous transitions. The illocutionary force of the openings is more or less hidden. In a statement like *a bukmalam*, 'you are sitting there', reference to the food is still, though faintly, made if the person addressed is sitting and eating. Statements like *kedinge yuu*, 'the sun is blazing', refer to something edible only if the addressee has at his disposal some sugar cane, the juice of which quenches thirst.

The conversational openings may vary from simple assertions like *moke*, 'it is raining', *arukna*, 'it is cold', *sintam kelape yanganmak*, 'it is afternoon, the women will come home', and *asiik bulonmalam*, 'you have been staying at home', to more extensive accounts of what one has been doing or will do. The most successful strategy to ask for a gift is after the first speaking turn. A person most expert in this strategy was Dirban, aged 40, who invariably asked for something after a conversation had got on its way, with a short look into the eyes of his partner and a voice not contrasting with the natural stream of assertions. Invariably Dirban received the desired object. Once the conversational bonding process has been managed, the equilibrium can hardly be interrupted or disturbed by a request. If the focus is not upon sharing and giving, but on the maintenance of the conversational bonding, asking for something was most easily complied with. Again, as with the other scenes, at a closer look at the material, the distribution of this strategy over the age groups is not uniform.

Generally the big men of the village and the older men rarely ask for something. The three old men in Dingerkon never did, nor did Ninke, except in the indirect way (compare Section 2.2). The two other influential men, Wimde and Keblob, rather proceeded in the way described in Section 2.7. If they made a direct request, one always had the impression that they did not request for themselves, but enjoyed requesting insofar as it was their position in the society which entitled them to do so.

3. CONCLUDING REMARKS

The value of rules regulating requesting-giving-and-taking behavior in a hostile environment like the one the Eipo live in is evident, we believe. To be dependent upon one another provides security; having obliged others through gifts ties a net strong enough to protect an individual hit by bad luck or disaster. Besides constituting a safety device, sharing and receiving is an important factor in the bonding process, on the psychological level. It appeases, mediates, diminishes tension, or just simply helps to make friends (see Eibl-Eibesfeldt 1973: 241–244 and Marshall 1961).

We have found some evidence that the silence behavior with regard to requesting, giving, and taking on higher levels of the social organization correlates with the behavior in simple social systems. The best nonaggressive strategy on both levels is that of not mentioning, or not focussing upon, requesting, giving, and taking itself. The ways in which these two systems interrelate are unexplored. In addition, the following remarks are tentative as we have not presented all the material on the manner in which something is offered spontaneously and the way such a gift can be verbally or nonverbally refused. For the intervention of verbally aggressive acts during these scenes our material does not yield anything conclusive.

3.1. *Evaluation and discussion; verbal acts*

The findings concerning the verbal acts can be summarized in Table 1. The inclusion of nonverbal behavior in this table would be too redundant; thus, we will simply enumerate the elements of verbal communication according to their meaning and their function.

3.2. *Nonverbal acts*

1. Eyebrow flash and proxemic shift towards a potential giver are prerequisites for any contact. However, according to the background expectations of the Eipo the mere presence of a person not having food or not smoking may exercise an unmeasurable pressure on the possessor of food or tobacco to share.
2. Watching a person arriving is a prerequisite for making a choice on the side of the giver.
3. The arriving partner may avoid the eye contact with the possessor and addressee. Perhaps this means not to betray one's own intentions and not to embarrass the possessor by too close a contact.
4. The intention of the requesting partner can be made more explicit by a second slow proxemic shift towards the possessor (compare Section 2.7), leaning towards the possessor, skin contact, watching how somebody eats (Secton 2.1), *leklekana* (Section 2.7), prolonged and lasting eye contact, and a begging expression on one's face (for facial expression while begging, see Section 2.1).
5. The intention of the requesting partner is made explicit by stretching-out movements of the arm, touching the possessor, and pouting, in case nothing is given (Section 2.1).
6. Self-embracing (Section 2.1) may occur during the performance of the last two groups of nonverbal acts. It seems to be a displacement activity. Self-embracement probably has common roots with seeking a hold of the body of others in stressful situations.
7. Offering a gift is mostly accompanied by continued eye contact, stretching out the offering arm, and touching the addressee. If offering is done in an asking manner the head is in a tilted position and the arm is bent at the elbow joint (Section 2.1).
8. The refusal to give can be stated (or hinted at) by breaking skin contact with the requesting partner, making a proxemic shift away from him, drawing back the object, covering it with the hands, turning off movements of rump and head, continuing, renewing, or starting a dyad with a third partner. It may be accompanied by an embarrassed smile and/or avoidance of eye contact (Section 2.1).

Table 1. *Verbal acts in the requesting, giving, and taking scenes*

Verbal acts	Described in	Position in sequencing	Co-occuring with....	Alternative choices	Typical or possible responses	Preference by age group or in participant constellation	Meaning, function, or connotation
Direct request	2.5	first speaker turn	loud and firm voice, stretching out arm, gaze at potential gift and giver	(all other opening sequences)	refusal, turning away from addressor, drawing back object	all age groups, except old people	aggressivity
Direct request	2.8	after first speaker turns	short look into giver's face, normal voice, arm not fully stretched out	—	handing over the object	all age groups, except old people	bonding act, avoidance of interrupting discourse
Indirect request	2.2 2.7	opening sequence or later	*lekelekana*, shift toward addressee, skin contact, glance of approx. 2 sec. toward giver	direct request	handing over object, but not immediately	all age groups	politeness, request a speaking turn
Indirect request	2.6	opening sequence or later	prolonged eye contact, stretching out arm, stroking giver's chin, pharyngealization, nasalization, or whimpering tone of utterance	—	handing over object, but not immediately	children, but also youths and adults	can be repeated; submissive, childlike behavior appeal to parental instincts
Humorous remark	2.3	after preliminary contact and initial silence	renewed eye contact, shift towards each other	giving, and taking, change of scene	—	all age groups	initiator of assertion stream
Arguing	2.5	after refusal or aggressive act	—	teaching by example without verbal explanation	—	all age groups	appeal to norms and rules of social behavior
Exclamations	2.5	after direct request or refusal of direct request	movement away from addressor, drawing back object, embarrassed smile	starting a new dyad, continuing old one, sitting apart, singing a song	—	all age groups	non-bonding marker
Exclamation *bahai*	2.5	after refusal of direct request	pharyngealization turning away movement	—		all age groups	deriding the addressor

9. While simply taking an object is an aggressive act, giving has the general function and meaning of appeasement and tension relieving (Sections 2.3, 2.4).
10. Changing the scene (Section 2.3) is a strategy to avoid growing tension.

3.3. *Discussion of verbal acts*

A person requesting something from another person has a wide range of options how to contact the possessor and how to proceed. This supports the view that the verbal and nonverbal acts are means of action. Some of these acts are prerequisites for any contact at all, but most of them depend on the more or less conscious choice of the interacting partners, a fact, as we believe, which emerges from the system of alternative choices available to a requesting individual.

With regard to the second hypothesis the interesting question should be raised why direct verbal requests are made at all, if the continuum of giving and taking is best maintained, when the stream of talking does not focus upon requesting, giving, and taking itself. On the one hand the direct requests were typical for some individuals: the orphans Terban and Buk, low-ranking youths like Selwelengde and Dabuk, and low-ranking men like Alalamde and Dirban; on the other hand, the orphan Melase, a hard-working youth, who enjoyed the protection of one of the most influential men in the village of Dingerkon, Manang, and Bingde, the son of one of the big men, Keblob, never (or rarely) made direct requests. The requesting behavior, then, may directly depend on (1) the bare necessity of the requesting individuals to be supplied with food, tobacco etc., and (2) on the efforts of these individuals to maintain or to improve their position in the sharing–receiving system, which in our opinion, is an indicator of social rank.

The direct requests of the big men, however, are a display of high rank, a supposition which is confirmed by the observation that they rarely retained the objects handed over to them but most often and very soon passed them on to other individuals sitting near to them. If this correlation between rank and the making of direct requests proves to be correct, the evidence for the first hypothesis would be somewhat confined because rank in society would narrow the range of options and alternatives in the requesting-giving-taking system. The different strategies would no longer be a pure matter of personal choice but would also depend on rank and role.

Besides the different functions of verbal acts already mentioned (Section 2.5 and Table 1) the one crucial difference between a direct request and all other approaches deserves further explanation, which might have some bearing on the ongoing debate on performatives and illocutionary functions of utterances. A direct request in conversational openings requires immediate choice and answer, and the individual asked to share something has to make up his mind in a minimum of time. The approach of the requesting partner, which requires that the interactional equilibrium has to be managed, together with the direct request constitute perhaps too big an appeal, the consequence of which is that the addressee is irritated and turns off, not being able or willing to process the verbal and nonverbal stimuli immediately. In contrast with this strategy the other approaches offer the following advantages:

1. They all leave some time to the addressee of a request to choose among alternatives and to make up his mind.

2. In scenes where no verbal acts occur the possessor will act according to the background expectations and rules of his society (exemptions and violations do occur of course in every community!), but the precise moment of handing over the object is up to his decision. A number of times in the men's house we have observed a man, hesitatingly casting a last glance at the cigar or the sweet potato he was going to hand over to somebody else in the next moment.

3. Those direct requests, which co-occur obligatorily with paralinguistic features (Section 2.6), can be repeated; in our view it is this time-taking repeatability which assures the necessary processing time for the addressee.

4. Indirect requests and simple statements give the next speaking turn to the addressee. Thus, while the addressee takes the turn and takes part in structuring the bonding discourse around a topic he has, again, some time to make up his mind. This proposal can be linked to two other interesting findings. Clark and Lucy (1975) have shown that the reaction time of a hearer of an indirect request is longer than of a direct one. The hearer will first define the literal meaning of an utterance and secondly he will construe an interpretation according to the situation, making a guess at the intentions of the speaker. Whether this longer processing time is sufficient for the addressee and potential giver to come to a decision is not known to us. The ethological interpretation of psycholinguistic findings, however, clearly is a testable one. Ervin-Tripp (1976: 48) has proposed that one of the advantages of indirect requests and statements is '. . . that the discourse features of the surface expression can be taken up . . .' to maintain the 'continuity of topic'. This should be the case in questions and verbal expressions concerning mood, time, reference to participants, and setting (Sections 2.6, 2.7). However, in the conversational opening the linguistic form does not propose to

maintain a topic but it helps to structure the discourse around a theme. We hope to have given some evidence for the fact that the conversational bonding, and, consequently, the onset of conversation are the best means to guarantee nonantagonizing requesting-giving-taking encounters. Nonverbal behavior with its varieties in the sensory channels involved, and the subtle shades of its semantics, constitutes a well-structured system of communication in its own right.

The material presented in this article in our view also backs the assumption that one translates basic strategies of social interaction into speech. The relationship between nonverbal and verbal behavior has thus also a phylogenetic, vertical dimension.

NOTES

1. We would like to thank the initiators of the project, Dr. G. Koch and Dr. K. Helfrich, the German Research Society, the Lembaga Ilmu Pengetahuan Indonesia, the Universitas Cenderawasih, the Missionary Aviation Fellowship, the Unevangelized Fields Mission and all others who have assisted us.
2. Publication No. 17 Priority Program of the German Research Society 'Man, Culture, and Environment in the Central Highlands of West Irian'.
3. The ceremonies connected with the dead could perhaps be better described as 'tree-exposure of dead bodies and secondary burial of bones under rocks or in garden houses'.
4. Mean male length 146 cm according to E. Büchi.
5. We have drawn here from our experience with the Roro, the Pawaia, the people living in the deltas of the Kikori and the Era, the people on the shores of Lake Murray, the Biami, and other groups in Papua New Guinea.
6. A separate publication on the ethnography of communication is being prepared.
7. A manuscript on the Eipo grammar has been written by V. Heeschen; notes and manuscripts on other Mek dialects have been prepared by several missionaires.
8. The diet of the Eipo is very low in fat and protein, therefore the *win* nuts are a nutrient and, because of their good taste, a very much sought-after delicacy.
9. Dabuk, 25, also begged for sweet potatoes.

DESCRIPTION OF PLATES

I. Plates 1 to 9.

Teaching lesson on how to share

A ʋuy eats a piece of taro, his half sister tries to take the food away from him (1), the boy turns away (2), one of the mothers demands the taro piece, boy and girl look at her, note the self-embracing of the girl (compare 14, 15) (3), the mother takes the taro piece (4), breaks it into two halves (5), hands them back to the boy (6), who now has the two pieces in his hands (7) and without further interference from outside offers the girl the piece in the hand close to her (8), she takes it, both eat happily, the conflict is solved through a remarkable educational act inducing sharing (10). — From 16mm film by Eibl-Eibesfeldt.

II. Plate 10.

Three of the eight heaps of food which the men have just started to arrange. The food is a kind of payment for those helpers who participated in rebuilding the sacred men's house in Munggona. At the end the heaps reached three times the initial height and contained many hundred kgs of taro, sugar cane and saccharum edule. — Photo from slide by Schiefenhövel.

III. Plates 11 to 37.

Requesting, giving, and taking in group of girls

Bolma, W, X, and Karinto (from right to left) forming a group; Bolma possesses nuts of which she gives one to W (11); little X stares at W eating the nut and starts to raise her arms towards this nut (12, 13); before she has reached that far, however, X deroutes her movement into self-embracing — to snatch something from someone else is not allowed, X is aware of this and deroutes her arms in a displacement activity (compare 3) (14, 15); Bolma establishes eye contact with Karinto (16), offering her a nut with flexed arm and head tilt (17), Karinto takes the offer, Bolma still does not stretch her arm out (18), while Karinto gets the nut Bolma lowers her head again (19); little X turns to Karinto (20) and watches her eat the nut (21); W holds a nut in front of X (22), who is still looking at Karinto and is therefore touched on the shoulder by W (22), at this sign X turns (23) and takes the gift, all four girls are eating now (24); Beayanto has joined the group, Karinto now squats besides X who touches W while W leans toward the body of Bolma, who continues to eat nuts, X and W beggingly stare at her (25), especially W has a demanding look while pouting slightly (26), from Bolma's face she looks to the nuts in her hands (27) and then turns her head away in a cut-off and with more pouting, Bolma does not give her any more nuts, Beayanto does not look at Bolma's face or at the nuts in her hands (28); she starts talking to Bolma, both establish eye contact after Beayanto's head has turned towards Bolma (29), Bolma performs a pronounced eyebrowflash in another bonding behavior (30) and smiles broadly towards Beayanto while W and X still gaze at the nuts in Bolma's hands (31); shortly afterwards Bolma, again with her head in a tilt 'asking' position, hands the nuts over to Beayanto for her to bite them out of their pod (32), Beayanto complies with this wish, W and X still watch Bolma eating nuts (33), Bolma now has collected those nuts which Beayanto has loosened. She shows a tense facial expression as a sign of conflict (34), receives more nuts from Beayanto, who hands them over to her without eye contact, thus avoiding a possible begging appeal (35). The tense expression in Bolma's face has increased, she moves backwards and thus breaks out of the body contact with Beayanto and W (36). Beayanto, again without looking at Bolma, passes the last loosened nuts to her, W and X have stopped gazing at the nuts in Bolma's lap (37). — From 16mm film by Eibl-Eibesfeldt.

IV. Plate 38.

Babyal and Ninke, leading men of their respective villages during an official visit by Babyal (foreground), who has come to treat a seriously wounded warrior. Ninke has made a remark on the feathers bound to Babyal's string bag (just visible as oblique white stripes above the lower edge of the photo); after this indirect request Babyal gives one of the feathers as a valuable present to Ninke. — Photo from slide by Schiefenhövel.

Plate I

Plate 1.

Plate 2.

Plate II

Plate 3.

Plate 4.

Plate III

Plate 5.

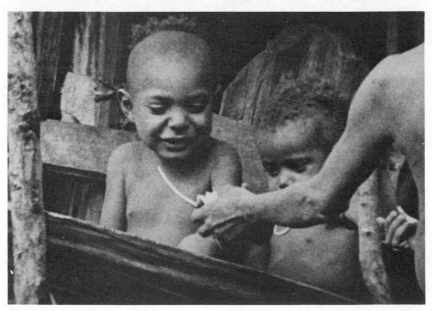

Plate 6.

Plate IV

Plate 7.

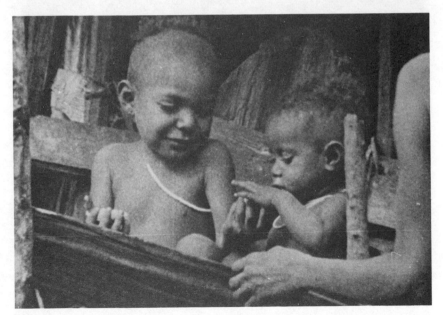

Plate 8.

Plate V

Plate 9.

Plate VI

Plate 10.

Plate VII

Plate 11.

Plate 12.

Plate VIII

Plate 13.

Plate 14.

Plate IX

Plate 15.

Plate 16.

Plate X

Plate 17.

Plate 18.

Plate XI

Plate 19.

Plate 20.

Plate XII

Plate 21.

Plate 22.

Plate XIII

Plate 23.

Plate 24.

Plate XIV

Plate 25.

Plate 26.

Plate XV

Plate 27.

Plate 28.

Plate XVI

Plate 29.

Plate 30.

Plate XVII

Plate 31.

Plate 32.

Plate XVIII

Plate 33.

Plate 34.

Plate XIX

Plate 35.

Plate 36.

Plate XX

Plate 37.

Plate XXI

Plate 38.

IVAN FÓNAGY[1]

Preverbal Communication and Linguistic Evolution

1. NOISE OR SIGN?

1.1. It is well known that the speech act, in everyday life as well as in poetry, shows a number of deviations from grammatical rules. We have to agree with Noam Chomsky that 'it would be absurd to try to incorporate these phenomena — i.e. distortions of an underlying grammatical pattern — directly into a formalized grammar (Chomsky 1962: 531). In fact, by means of the grammar, it is impossible to generate sentences at variance with the grammar. It has been suggested that such deviations are the products of a deficient output (Fodor and Garrett 1966), noise due to 'memory lapses and other formative difficulties' (Watt 1970: 140), or the result of limitations of our memory capacity (Chomsky 1965: 14ff.).

This type of solution is not satisfactory, for what may be noise from the point of view of grammar is frequently 'expressive' for the listener, and thus may be considered a message in a broader framework of reference. It is therefore understandable that attempts have been made to interpret purposeful poetic deviations from grammatic rules within the framework of generative grammar. This 'tour de force' was first attempted by Samuel R. Levin (1962).

Two types of solution are possible to account for poetic irregularities. One is the extension of the limits of grammar in such a way that irregular features could also be generated and interpreted within its framework, thereby ceasing to be irregular. In this case it is difficult to explain what determines when these 'new rules' are applied by the speaker (since they professedly cannot be applied in the same circumstances as other rules), and why we experience them as 'more expressive' than expressions generated by other rules.

The second solution consists of establishing that there are deviations, the extent of which can be determined. This is the approach adopted by Levin in later publications (e.g. 1965). It does not, however, explain how deviations come about nor how they become expressive.

1.2. In a previous paper I suggested a different solution (Fónagy 1971a). It was suggested that sentences created by the grammar in every case pass through a 'distorter' which contains as many levels as the grammar (phonetic, lexical, syntactical, and paraphrastic) but which operates according to fundamentally different rules. As opposed to arbitrary rules of grammar, the rules of the distorter are not arbitrary, they are motivated (symptomatic or symbolic), and may be assumed to be universal.

In the present paper, in keeping with the theme of this volume, the relationship of the two forms of coding will be examined from a dynamic and evolutionary viewpoint.

2. VOCAL STYLE

2.1.1. The radiocinematographic analysis of Hungarian and French emotive speech (Fónagy 1976; Fónagy, Han, and Simon, in preparation) clearly demonstrates that in both languages the variability of the articulation of the same consonants and vowels in identical contexts is extremely large. Thus, in a paradoxical way, in speech simulating hatred the /e/ is often closer than the /i/ pronounced in neutral speech. In speech simulating indifference, however, the /i/ may be more open than /e/ in neutral pronunciation.

Comparing the articulatory movements of French and Hungarian speech as reflected on the X-ray pictures, it appears that whilst the articulation of the 'same' vowel differs considerably in neutral speech, the same emotive attitude induces the same distortions in both unrelated languages. Thus, for instance, anger is expressed in French as well as in Hungarian by:
1. fast, spasmodic tongue movement (short transitions, the tongue is stiffened for brief periods in extreme positions);
2. highly increased muscular tension (increase of tongue and palate contact in plosives, strong contraction of the uvula etc.);
3. increased maxillary angle and labial distance (for /a/ increases on the average from 15.0 to 25.6 mm);
4. the tongue is withdrawn (as compared to its position in neutral speech) during the articulation of both vowels and consonants;
5. the mandible is withdrawn, the lower incisors retracted to a position considerably behind the upper incisors; the upper incisors bite on the lower lip in articulating the semi-vowel /w/.

Muscular tension further increases in hatred. (Thus for example the contact surface for /t/ increases from 3 to 10 mm.) The maxillary distance dramatically decreases, however, in contrast to angry speech. (Thus the maxillary distance for /t/,/v/ and /s/ is zero.)

The expression of tenderness differs significantly from that of anger and hatred:

1. articulation is smooth and continuous; transitions are slower and more gradual;
2. tongue and lip muscles are more relaxed, the uvula less contracted;
3. the tongue position is more advanced for the same vowels;
4. labialization of /i/ and /e/ frequently occurs;
5. alveolar plosives are more or less palatalized.

These data can be completed with the aid of myographic and tomographic analysis of phenomena observable at the laryngeal and thoracic level. During tender phonation, the laryngeal ventricle widens out. In angry phonation the laryngeal ventricle is constricted into a narrow passage, and completely vanishes on the tomographic image during the simulation of hatred as a result of extremely strong muscular contraction (Fónagy 1962). As a consequence, despite increased thoracic effort (the strong innervation of the expiratory muscles) the acoustic intensity is relatively low in the expression of hatred. We can confidently state that the ratio:

$$\frac{\text{acoustic energy}}{\text{physiological energy}}$$

is considerably smaller in the case of aggressive emotions than it is for tender (libidinal) affects.

2.1.2. This relationship is closely connected with data derived from acoustic analysis. It has been shown that in speech reflecting tender attitudes the duration of vowels increases, whilst in aggressive speech vowels are shortened and consonants lengthened (cf. Table 1). A· decrease of the quotient:

$$\frac{\text{duration of vocoids}}{\text{duration of contoids}}$$

points to the presence of aggressive feelings. Emotional contents with aggressive basis (e.g. disdain, irony, scientific discussion) show a decrease in the above quotient, whilst in the case of loving emotions (e.g. longing, coquetry) the quotient increases.

Table 1. *Mean duration of vowels and consonants measured in speech simulating tenderness and hatred (figures in parentheses are averages based on n<5 cases)*

		Vowels	Con-sonants	ptk	fsʃ	bdg	vzʒ	lj mn	wy	ptk fsʃ	bdg vzʒ	lmnj wy
Tenderness	S1	9.35	6.06	9.06	9.32	5.20	5.00	4.22	3.00	9.19	5.05	3.94
	S2	8.95	6.92	9.60	9.74	6.25	5.07	6.18	4.38	9.67	5.32	5.77
	S3	11.26	7.33	10.95	11.84	6.50	4.40	4.12	4.17	11.38	4.84	4.13
Hatred	S1	6.36	9.17	13.00	14.60	7.63	6.67	7.30	3.50	13.64	7.12	6.74
	S2	8.29	11.10	17.07	16.64	10.57	9.60	6.57	5.33	16.88	10.00	6.42
	S3	7.27	8.65	11.56	12.33	(14.67)	7.40	5.30	(2.00)	11.87	9.08	5.00

2.1.3. Numerical data and still pictures do not capture the most essential feature of expressive speech: movement. Thus for instance in the expression of disappointment during the articulation of /u:/ or /i:/ the initial raise of the tongue and the uvula is followed by a gradual slackening and slow deceleration of movement. In the expression of irony the articulation of /u:/ is commenced with the tongue moving backwards and approaching the uvula; it is then slightly lowered, then raised towards the border between soft and hard palate, and moves finally towards the pharynx. There is a strong correspondence between this tongue movement and pitch movement. The latter also starts at a low level, sharply increases and then falls to a very low level again.

Oral mimicry is particularly spectacular in the case of rolled /r/ pronounced in anger. The tongue is strongly erected and resists the pressure of outflowing air: it regains its erect position four or five times, whereas it vibrates only twice during neutral speech.

2.2.1. Emotive speech doubtlessly contains gestural elements. This is quite apparent in the case of tender labialization: tender lip rounding contains a preconscious allusion to kissing. The biting of the lower lips in anger, as well as the pushing forward of the upper maxillar containing the incisors, the unusually large mouth opening, the grinding of the teeth in repressed anger (hatred), are residues of an aggressive display. The violent contraction of all the muscles involved in articulation characterizing aggressive affects could be equally considered in the frame of reference of the Darwinian theory of emotions (1872; cf. also Crile [1915]) as a residue of general muscular tension in the preparation for fight. All these gestures are, however, grafted onto the arbitrary linguistic signs. The integration is so perfect that the duality of verbal and preverbal communication is never noticed. The secondary messages conveyed by means of distortion, an expressive manipulation of the sound patterns generated by the grammar, appear as 'manner of speaking', or 'vocal style'. Due to the high degree of economy which characterizes 'live speech' a single concrete speech sound fulfills two completely different functions. In spite of the distortion, with help from the context it identifies the phoneme, and by means of the distortion i.e. the gesture contained in the distortion, it expresses a content which differs fundamentally from the meaning of lexical or grammatical morphemes.

2.2.2. What we may call a 'meaningful manipulation of the sound patterns' covers a wide range of semiotic activities. The gradual slackening of the tongue accompanying disappointment may be considered its *symptom* signaling decreasing alertness. Tender lip rounding contains a preconscious *allusion* to kissing (as social gesture). Aggressive displays are equally allusive. Tender palatalization of alveolar stops implies an *identification* with the child, since children frequently palatalize alveolar stops and fricatives under a certain age. The displacement of the tongue position backwards (in anger and sadness), forwards (in joy and tenderness) suggests yet again a different mechanism. In such cases the tongue performs a *deictic* function: it represents the arm (or the whole body) which may point forwards and upwards — outward oriented gesture, approach towards the outside world — or backwards and downwards — inward oriented, negative, asocial, autistic attitude. Thus, the expressive manipulation of the vowels (shifted forwards or backwards) involves a *symbolic* relation between the tongue and the whole body, and transforms into a stage the oral cavity. The opposition between the expiratory muscles of the thorax expelling the air by means of violent contractions, and the muscles of the larynx impeding the outflow of the air, could be considered as a fight between antagonistic muscle groups.

2.2.3. The expressiveness of preconscious oral gesturing is enhanced by unconscious fantasies elicited by the activity of the speech organs. There is clinical evidence that the sphincter glottis may be cathected by anal-sadic libido, and that the unconscious identification of the two poles of the digestive canal may result in spastic disphony (cf. Weiss [1922], Ferenczi [1927–1939: III [1929], 448]). Anal cathexis of the glottal closure could account for the high frequency of glottal stops in angry speech, and more generally, for the predominance of retention, thus, the prolongation of occlusives and constrictives. Evidence from a number of sources indicates that the identification of the lips with the labia vulvae may contribute to the stylistic value of unusually open or unusually close rounded (labial) vowels (Fónagy 1970). Similarly, the strongly vibrating, stiffened, erect tongue in the articulation of rolled /r/ might be equated with phallic threat on an unconscious level. The inability to pronounce the rolled apical /r/ is especially frequent in boys with a neurotic background during the negative stage of the Oedipal phase (Fónagy 1970).

2.2.4. Thus, what we regard as the phonetic signal of emotional attitudes ('*Anzeichen*', according to Husserl's terminology [1922]) is in fact a complex process, involving numerous mechanisms. The secondary message integrated into verbal (linguistic) communication is pristine both from the point of view of its mode of expression and its content. This fact however implies that it incorporates various stages of the development that must have preceded linguistic communication.

3. DYNAMICS OF PHONETIC CHANGE

3.1. Phonetic change, in common with all forms of linguistic change, is a paradoxical phenomenon. In other types of semiotic systems the change of a sign has to be preceded by discussion and agreement. In the case of language, change occurs independently of the users of the code, against their will and without their knowledge. This paradox is only solvable if we assume that verbal communication is based on the integration of verbal and nonverbal communication. The double coding which gives live speech its liveliness is also a condition of linguistic change. The question is how alternation or variation becomes alteration or change.

3.2.1. To answer this question, it may be useful to have a look at expressive phonetic variations of the past, noted by grammarians and their contemporaries. The genital cathexis of labial articulation might have been responsible for the fact, reported by 17th- and 18th-century French and English grammarians, that the more open pronunciation (greater labial distance) of vowels was regarded as vulgar. Henri Estienne (1578 [1885]) pointed out that well-educated women preferred the close variant of E, /e/ to open /ɛ/, as the close variant did not force them 'to open their mouth indecently' (II: 253). William Lilly (1602–1681) also regarded as indecent the /ai/ diphthong, which replaced the close palatal /i/, because of the maximal opening of the mouth (Dobson 1957: 1, 7).

It might be of interest, from a sociolinguistic point of view, that according to three major phonetic studies of Modern French pronunciation (cf. Boumendil-Lucot 1977; Robert 1977; Houdebine 1977) the articulation of vowels is significantly more open in the speech of women than in that of male subjects. Male and female pronunciation is also compared by Key within the context of a general study of sex differences in language (Key 1975a).

The unconscious phallic cathexis of the rolled apical /r/ might have contributed to its development in a number of European languages, at first in the 16th-century court circles. The non-rolled, non-erect version of the /r/ was considered as a more 'delicate' and more 'refined' variant, thus the uvular /R/ gradually replaced the rolled /r/.

3.2.2. The stylistic value of a variant is at first determined by the articulatory gesture it involves. In the following stages of development of stylistic character, a determining factor is the distribution of variants in social space (social status, professional groups, sex and age, etc.). The unrolled *r* was probably adopted by court circles because of the restrictions it implied. Instinctual restrictions are part of 'good manners', signs of moral and social superiority, in sexual behavior, in eating habits, and perhaps also at the phonetic level. But once the unrolled *r* becomes associated with a particular social group, that link will determine its stylistic character.[2] Thus, a variant of *r*, the fricative /z/ acquired an 'affected', 'feminine', and at the same time 'vulgar' connotation in French in the 16th century, as a consequence of its adoption by courtiers on the one hand, and by Parisian petit bourgeois women on the other, according to Erasmus and some French humanist grammarians (cf. Thurot 1881–1883: II, 270ff.).[3]

3.3. Simplifying the complexity of the phenomena, we can outline the relationship between alternation and alteration in the following way:
1. In the first phase, with the help of context, the listener traces back the distorted speech sound to the corresponding phoneme. Thus, for example, the [z] in *père* is traced back to the /r/ phoneme. If the listener did not do this, he would interpret the word as *pèse* /pɛzə/ 'measuring weight'. The /r/ → [z] transformation is interpreted as an oral gesture containing a message:

/pɛzə/
    → /z/? No.   attenuation (*cs* level)
    → /r/? Yes. Hence: /r/ → [z] =
                                   emasculation (*ucs* level)

In fact, what we are dealing with is a phonetic metaphor:

| /r/ | /z/ | phonologic level |
| [r] | [z] | phonetic level |

The /z/ of *père* is not *z* and not *r* but rather a movement from *r* to *z*, a process of replacement.[4] The stylistic value of the transferred sound is determined by the direction of the transfer and the phonetic distance covered by it. As it is a contradictory, dynamic phenomenon, it contains within itself the possibility of change.
2. Change or alteration only comes about when the transfer 'sets' in a social group, and thus ceases to exist as a metaphor; in the case of the 'metaphoric' use of /z/, when a direct and stable relationship is created between the sound [z] and the phoneme /r/ or the phoneme /z/. We

know, for instance, that the word *chaire* (< Lat. *cathedra*) 'chair (seat)', 'rostrum', '(university) chair' oscillated for a long time between / ʃɛrə/ and / ʃ ɛzə/. When in certain 17th-century circles, such as the literary salons, the /z/ version came in general use, the phonetic metaphor 'froze', and while it lost its stylistic value due to the articulatory gesture it involved, it gained a new type of *evocative* stylistic value in the language community as a whole (cf. Bally 1921: I, 170–202). It became capable of evoking this social group and the speaker could magically identify with and become a fictitious member of the group by using this variant. Thus in this case we are dealing again with an archaic mental mechanism: incorporation underlying imitation (Freud 1940–1946: 118 ff.).
3. The new version might then generalize, due to various factors, including its original gestural character, and its social value (cf. Herczog 1913; Reichstein 1960; Labov 1972), as well as many other causes, most importantly the 'intern' factors which are a function of the linguistic system itself (cf. Jakobson 1971b; Haudricourt and Juilland 1949; Martinet 1955). The /ʃɛzə/ version of *chaire* generalized in the whole linguistic community with the meaning 'chair (seat)', whilst the /ʃɛrə/ version generalized with the meaning 'rostrum', (university) chair', 'professorship'. As pieces of furniture were more likely topics of conversation in the French literary salons than 'rostrum' or 'university chair' and since the archaic version occurred in sermons and lectures, the new version became associated with furniture, whilst the conservative pronunciation was retained for 'rostrum' and 'university chair'.

The process of phonetic change is considerably more diversified and complex than the above outline would suggest. For the present purpose, however, it is important to note that the phonemic structure of a language could not change if language were only *langue*, i.e. *'une forme, non une substance'* (Saussure 1915 [1976]: 157), if through the speech process it did not inseparably interweave with preverbal communication.

4.   SYNTACTIC GESTURING

4.1.1. Dual coding characterizes the concrete speech act at all levels. Expressive irregularities of word order are particularly striking and relatively easy to interpret. This 'disarrangement' of morpheme sequences conceals a double arrangement. The mechanisms of coding and decoding irregular sequences are similar to those involved with concrete speech sounds. The irregular order has to be 'identified' (Bally 1921: I, 105–139), i.e. traced back to the grammatical word sequence in order to identify the primary message of the sentence. From the reconstructed grammatical sentence we revert to discover the secondary message conveyed by the expressive modification of the grammatical word order.

The principles governing disarrangement of the sentence may again be of symptomatic and/or symbolic nature. The most important element of the message may 'run ahead' of the sentence in spite of the rules assigning to the word a less prominent place. Such a disarrangement reflects impatience, excitement:

Vite, donne ces alumettes.
(Quickly, give the matches.)

instead of '*Donne vite ces alumettes*'. The adverb is, in fact, ejected from the sentence and could be considered as a one-word-sentence, reminding one of children in the first period of language acquisition. The procedure could be considered as a momentary controlled regression to an early period of language development (Fónagy 1975a). Expressionistic and impressionistic poetic word order is a stylized version of symptomatic disarrangement (Reitz 1937; Fónagy 1964).

The impulsive, nervous dismembering of a sentence in live speech — the repeated separation of syntactically and semantically related words, may be a verbal analogue of the parapraxis consisting in tearing a sheet of paper into pieces in anger — an action of considerable symbolic significance (Freud 1940–1946: IV, 213–241). Such a disarrangement of the sentence is symptomatic as well as symbolic, in that the sentence is unconsciously identified with an inert or living object. On a poetic level, interruptions marked by commas are significantly more frequent in Verlaine's aggressive cycle of poems, the *Invectives* (15.8 per 100 words) than in the tender *Bonne chanson* (8.5 per 100 words).

4.1.2. Poetic word order may reflect the organization of objects of the world outside (Spitzer 1926:146 ff.; Fónagy 1964).

Qu'il va, stoïque, où tu l'envoies.
(That he goes, stoically, wherever you send him.)
Victor Hugo, *Trois ans après*

Moral isolation is depicted by means of the embedded sentence (hyperbaton) representing the lonely man. On the visual level the word *stoïque* is isolated by empty space, on the auditory level by silence. Thomas Mann in *Joseph*, Proust in *A la recherche du temps perdu* systematically use embedded sentences to represent on the verbal level the different layers of time. According to Leo Spitzer's interpretation, embedding in Proust's novel often opens a window through which the writer speaks confidentially to the reader (Spitzer 1926: 365–497). At other times, the hyperbaton is again symptomatically applied by Proust: it reflects the resistance towards particular themes, postponing the embarrassing statement by means of a long embedded sentence. Thus, the embedded clause describing his discovery that M. de Qu. is a homosexual extends to two pages (500 words).

4.2.   As with phonetic metaphor, the modified, expressive word order 'empties' as soon as the 'distorted' word is no longer compared with the grammatical order, since it has itself become regular, i.e. directly generated by the grammar. In Modern French the emphatic 'ejection' of the most informative element of the sentence ('dislocation') is becoming a rule in daily conversation, and, in a lesser degree, in written French (Bally 1921:I, 311–313; 1932 [1965]:210–212). As a result of this, and as is apparent from statistical analysis of French and Hungarian texts, 'dislocation' became a regular procedure of French sentence construction; it became much more frequent than in corresponding Hungarian texts, where this form of splitting is only present as expressive distortion (Fónagy 1975b).

5.   SEMANTIC GESTURING

5.1.1.   Less obvious displacements occur along the virtual paradigmatic axis, whereby a probable lexical item or grammatical category is replaced by an improbable, inappropriate one (tropes, figures). It is questionable whether the concept of preverbal communication should be extended to include lexical and grammatical transfers. I think, however, that a real understanding of the role that preverbal communication plays in linguistic evolution could hardly be reached without this extension of meaning. The structure (or mechanism) as well as the content of tropes show a deep analogy with those of 'phonetic transfers' and syntactic gesturing; and it is no mere chance that the term of 'transfer' or 'metaphor' proved to be helpful in treating expressive sound phenomena.

   Let us remember that the metaphoric process inevitably starts with a sudden but voluntary amnesia, followed by a momentary controlled regression to a preverbal stage. Thus the poet, a trope-maker, a *tropator* or *troubadour*, turns into an *in-fans* which literally means 'nonspeaker'. He rejects the word which is traditionally linked to the object he is setting out to rediscover, and substitutes for it an objectively incorrect but subjectively adequate term. As the term meta-phor (transfer) suggests, the metaphor is a mental movement, a semantic gesture, which is not identical with either the symbol, or the object symbolized, no more than with the elements they have in common (the *tertium comparationis*). Not unlike the expressive speech sound the metaphorically used sign is a *moving* morpheme. In Mallarmé's poem *Evantail* (or: *Evantail de Mademoiselle Mallarmé*) the *fen* appears as a bird, asking the Dreamer, the young girl (*'O Rêveuse . . .'*) to keep its wing in her hand (*'garder mon ail dans ta main'*). Throughout the poem we can follow up the mental movement associating the *fen* with the image of a captive bird: first wing beats (*'fraîcheur de crépuscule'*) in the first lines of the poem — vast horizon, unlimited possibilities (*'Vertige! voici que frisonne l'espace comme un grand baiser'*) — flight evasion — the flight is however fictitious, 'blank' (*'blanc vol'*, *'coup prisonnier'* /captive wing-beat/, *'subtil mensonge'*) — no real satisfaction (*'ne peut jaillir, ni s'apaiser'*), fixation to the verbal level, to imaginary flight — (because of?) fixation to a female relative (keeping the bird in her hand) — (in the last stanza) the wing transformed into a scepter leaned against the bracelet of the young girl (reminding one of winged phallic representation of Greek and Roman Antiquity, and of dreams identifying flight with intercourse, the bird with the male genital) — the wing transformed into a 'unanimous fold' (*'unanime pli'*) absorbing a laughter conceived as a liquid ('unanimously' evoking the female genital).

This tendency to condense preconscious and unconscious images applies equally in the case of scientific metaphor. An English phonetician, T. H. Pear (1931), not concerned with psychoanalysis, qualifies the different varieties of non-rolled *r* metaphorically as an 'emasculation' which undoubtedly contains an unconscious phallic, genital conceptualization of the rolled *r*. It is significant that during the early stages of development of a discipline, e.g. in Greek, Roman, Mongolian, early Japanese and early Western phonetics, metaphors are predominating (Fónagy 1963). In contrast to poetic metaphors, metaphoric terms used in prescientific phonetics, such as *hard, soft* or *moistened* (*'mouillées'*) consonants and *dark* and *light* vowels, did not replace existing terms — they were constructed to indicate an as yet invisible, still unknown object. The ancient grammarians were unaware of the articulatory features that motivated or underlay their metaphors. They did not know that (a) the tongue points upwards and outwards (toward the light) when articulating *light* vowels, and backwards (toward the dark regions) when pronouncing *dark* vowels; (b) the muscles of the tongue are more tense and the tongue is harder when unvoiced, *hard* consonants are articulated, and (c) there is increased contact between the moist tongue and the moist palate during articulation of the palatalized, *moistened* /t'/, /d'/, /n'/, /1'/ in comparison with the unmarked, *dry*, /t/, /d/, /n/, /1/.

This suggests that metaphors enable us to formulate preconscious and/or unconscious ideas (to say things we are unaware of), and that these preconscious and preconceptual messages can be correctly interpreted by listeners without conscious understanding. Thus the metaphoric process plays an essential role in the poetic and scientific discovery procedure.

5.1.2. The metaphoric mechanism goes back to an early stage of onto-genetic development— the period immediately preceding speech — and thus it is hardly surprising that operations underlying the metaphor are characteristic of cognitive development at the age of language acquisition. Thus there is (a) semantic inconsistency, whereby each metaphor casts a different light on the same object; (b) diffuse meaning; (c) sensuality, with the tactile and visual sense organs predominating; (d) projection, manifested in the animistic perception of objects; (e) subjective, impressionistic, narcissistic perception (*'Wahrnehmungsidentität'* as opposed to *'Denkidentität'*, in Freud's terminology (1940–1946: II/III, 571, 607); (f) false (infantile) perspective with inadequate size constancy (Fónagy 1965). The characteristics of metaphoric ideation are well illustrated by a statistical comparison of the semantic tendencies of metaphor as compared to the ontogenetically more highly developed simile (Fónagy 1975c).

5.1.3. What has been said about the metaphor in the narrow sense of the term (a transfer based on similarity) can be extended to all types of lexical transfer, to 'metaphor' in the Aristotelian sense. All forms of semantic transformations recognized by ancient and modern rhetoric (cf. e.g. Lausberg 1960; Dubois et al. 1970) correspond to aspects of infantile, archaic, paleological ideation. Thus, for example, (a) an object may be identified with parts of it; (b) an object may represent its principal quality; (c) a person may represent a quality; (d) an object may be identified with the person to whom it belongs; (e) the cause may denote its effect; (f) the dimensions of an object or event may be exaggerated; (g) an idea may be converted to its opposite, etc. For an infant of two or three years mommy's dressing gown may be a great deal more than a garment belonging to the mother: it may serve as a substitute for the mother. All types of early mental substitutions are analogous and comparable to later verbal substitutions.

5.1.4. The archaic character of the errors involved in grammatical metaphors is recognizable from the inadequately demotivated processing errors found in psychotic delusions. Uncertainty of identity and ego boundaries in schizophrenia correspond to the more innocent metaphoric use of personal pronouns. The verbal substitution of present tense for past tense appears in schizophrenics as a real confusion of past and present (Searles 1965; Sechehaye 1969; Roheim 1955). Hyperbole might be conceived as a demotivated form of the delusion of grandeur and fantasies of omnipotence in manic depressive psychotics (Hollos and Ferenczi 1922).

5.2. Semantic changes are extensions of the rules governing spontaneous lexical and grammatical transfers. Linguistic change starts where the transfer ends, i.e. when the speaker or listener, rather than pursuing the long and complex process of 'sensible distortion', creates a shortcut by forming a direct link between the new v forms of representation and its actual meaning. Thus, for instance, in the case of intransitive use of transitive verbs, instead of attempting to find the repressed object and the cause of repression which the incorrect use of the transitive verb suggests, they simply accept the grammatical polysemy, the fact that the same verb may be transitive as well as intransitive. Such a change is at the moment in progress in modern colloquial French. The correct form *je l'aime, je l'adore, je le connais* is more and more generally replaced by *oui, j'aime, j'adore, ah, je connais* which no longer need to be traced back to the original grammatical sentences. Thus they cease to be expressive, at most evoke a feeling of intimacy of style. An adequate model of grammar would have to include both the transitive and intransitive forms of these verbs (specifying the stylistic level which permits the use of the intransitive form).

This qualitative change from alternation to alteration is a direct consequence of the original expressivity of the transfer. The more expressive the transfer, due to its implications, the more popular it will be. That means: it will be used in an increasingly large number of contexts. The less context-dependent the use of the transfer will become, the less necessary it will be to restore the original undistorted form.

It was repeatedly (and rightly) stated that lexical units of everyday language are lively or frozen metaphors. We think less frequently of the metaphoric background of grammatical categories. In fact, everyday language and (even more) scientific language could hardly do without a considerable number of Mallarméan categorial transfers, objectifying by hypostasis negative attributes, such as *absence, lack, nothing, nothingness.*

6. PREVERBAL COMMUNICATION AND VERBAL EVOLUTION

6.1. This return of language to preverbal forms of ideation is inevitable. I should like to illustrate this using the semantic structure of possessive constructions as an example.

Linguists, philosophers and aestheticians have repeatedly pointed out the extraordinary polysemy of possessive constructions in English and other languages (Jespersen 1924 [1968]; Wagner and Pinchon 1962; Lees 1960; Empson 1930 [1953]; Quine 1952 [1962]; Gruber 1965; Fillmore 1968; Miller and Johnson-Laird 1976).

Comparative analysis of English, French, German, and Hungarian possessive constructions reveals that even the most economical classification must differentiate ten grammatical and nearly as many logical functions (Fónagy 1975b). The question arises here, just as in connection with lexical polysemy, as to what holds together these different meanings. (Cf. Bolinger 1965). What differentiates homonymy from polysemy? From a different viewpoint another question arises: how can one explain that whilst the linguistic sign is arbitrary, the semantic structures of linguistic signs in unrelated languages seem to have many elements in common? Thus, for example, the possessive construction in all the above languages, and in many others, can equally well signify ownership, family or love relations, part/whole relation, the relationship of creator and created, that of actor and action, the circumstances of the act, a causal relationship, the quality of an object, gradation, a relationship of similarity, or poetic equivalence.

Analysis of the semantic structure of grammatical and lexical signs suggests that what may appear to be diverse and unrelated meanings from the point of view of rational thinking, are in fact equivalent from the point of view of an archaic thought process. On a deeper level, for instance, love is a form of ownership; in an anthropomorphic perspective a quality of an object becomes its property (in the literal sense of this term) or a physical part of it; the product a property of its creator.

It is easier to understand the interrelationship of meanings and the unity of the meaning complex if we consider them within the context of their development. The phonetic metaphor leaves no traces — the new form replaces the previous one. A recurrent semantic transfer, however, enriches the semantic content of the sign, it does not necessarily absorb previous meanings. Each word, each grammatical item contains the subsequent meaning, just as each passing year is marked on the trunk of a tree. Since metaphor is never arbitrary, there must be some natural link between old and new meanings. As transfers are governed by unconscious as well as by preconscious associations, the analogy between the different meanings of a sign are not always apparent. The German word *schmutzig* has a dual meaning: (1) dirty, unclean; (2) sordid, stingy. We may create different links relating the two meanings ('he is saving even on toilet articles'); we come, however, to a deeper understanding of the real nature of the semantic unity of the German word, if we retrace dirtiness and stinginess to their common anal origin (Freud 1940–1946: VII, 203–209). The same holds for the Greek word *kakos* meaning (1) dirty; (2) ugly; (3) miserable; (4) wicked. A semantic distinctive feature analysis has to reckon with the existence of latent semantic features.

6.2.   Ancient rhetoric has a special term to denote necessary transfer (catachresis). In fact, semantic transfer is, in general, vital in verbal and mental evolution. There is no other semiotic procedure enabling the speaker or writer to create and to denote a new concept (concepts in progress). In a first phase, an erroneous judgment is made on the basis of a preconscious and partly unconscious mental processing. In the case of metaphors, this consists of a mistaken evaluation of an object or phenomenon. With grammatical metaphors the error is more general. Mistaken categories and mistaken types of judgment arise from out-of-awareness, e.g. causal relationships appear in the form of possession, as in *the tree's shadow* or *the echo of the shot*. Let us imagine that in the child's idiolect, or going even further back, in the language of a primitive society, causal connections have not yet developed. When, in a given situation, the speaker is confronted with a causal relationship, he pursues the same course of ideation as the ancient grammarian who could not differentiate between voiced and unvoiced consonants. He falls back on an information-processing mechanism older than language, but always present in its background, in which archaic mental functioning plays a very significant role. Freud termed it *primary process* in order to differentiate it from the rational and reality-principle based *secondary processes* (1940–1946: II/III, 593–614). A mechanism which is hardly adapted to reality provides the fundamentally erroneous possessive structure to describe the relation between shadow and tree. If the discrepancy between the suggested logical pattern and the real relationship is sufficiently large, consciousness recognizes the absurdity of the suggestion and we step into the next phase of verbal processing. Consciousness discards the possibility of possession and examines other existing uses of the possessive construction, such as the relationship of body and body part, of part and whole, etc. Since the causal relationship does not fit into any of the existing categories, it accepts a new form of usage, puts the data into a still empty (nondefined) category which progressively acquires a more definite semantic profile. Thus, an erroneous judgment becomes, through demotivation, the verbal expression of a newly discovered logical relationship.

6.3. Only in close relationship with preverbal communication can language solve the paradoxical task which Münchhausen brilliantly tackled by pulling himself out of the quicksand by his own hair. Natural language differs from other, artificial semiotic systems in that through the inclusion of preverbal communication it enables the users of this unique system to surpass themselves.

NOTES

1. I am indebted to Miss Vanessa Moore and to Dr. Peter Fónagy for their valuable comments on the manuscript.
2. The concept of 'social groups' comprises also virtual social groups, such as age groups, sex groups, professional groups. The frequency distribution of the variants in virtual groups equally affects the stylistic value of speechsounds. Thus, e.g. variants which are significantly more frequent in the speech of the age group 60–80 sound 'old fashioned', 'antiquated'.
3. The gestural aspect continues to affect the stylistic value of the variant. 'Parisian women are so affected that instead of *"père"* they say *"pèze"'*, writes Pillot in 1550.
4. It is surprising and reassuring to find this idea in an early writing of Roman Jakobson: *'La perception du mouvement est présente aussi dans l'aspect synchronique'* (1971a: 218).

ANA MARÍA MARTIRENA

Interruptions of Continuity and Other Features Characteristic of Spontaneous Talk

O. INTRODUCTION

The aim of this paper is to describe the linguistic behavior of speakers in a style largely neglected by linguists — spontaneous talk. It seems only natural that this style should be thoroughly described since it is in face-to-face conversations that most linguistic activity takes place. Although this study is based on conversations among speakers of Spanish, it is assumed that there are no significant differences across languages.

The syntax in conversations is not complex. Sentences are not long enough to include many embedded clauses or other syntactic devices which would make them complex. What is left after the syntax has been described is usually regarded as 'nonlinguistic', that is, unsystematic. This may not be so.

This is an attempt to present an analysis of some features characteristic of spontaneous talk. In face-to-face conversations, speech does not wholly consist of complete, well-built sentences (as described by most linguists) but rather of incomplete sentences, with a variety of repetitions, rephrasings, hesitations, etc.

The following extract from a conversation illustrates this point.[1]

A– *Graba bien y tiene una/*   *una fidelidad muy / muy buena.*
B–   *Una nitidez*
A– *Y lo que tiene de bueno es que es / eh no es pesado.*
B–   *Claro!*
A– *Y yo /*
B– *Es transistorizado.*
A– *Claro!*   *Y / . . . El otro día me anotaron en la boleta que*
B–   *Claro!*
A–*tenía una / un golpe. Casi me los como. Les digo ya tiene / ya tiene diez viajes acá al service y todavía / eh* (noise) *imagínese cómo no va a haber razón para que se me golpee.*

In the above passage there are eight utterances,[2] 75 words, five complete uninterrupted sentences (*'Claro!'*, *'Es transistorizado.'* *'Casi me los como.'*), several interrupted sentences, six interruptions by the same speaker (*'. . . una fidelidad muy / muy buena.'*, *'Y lo que tiene de bueno es que es / eh no es pesado.'*, *'Y / . . .'*, *'. . . tenía una / un golpe.'*, *'Les digo ya tiene / ya tiene . . .'*, *'. . . y todavía / eh . . .'*), two interruptions by the listener (*'Graba bien y tiene una / '*, *'Y yo /'*), two repetitions by the same speaker (*'una fidelidad muy / muy buena'*, *'Les digo ya tiene / ya tiene . . .'*), one repetition across speakers (A- *'Claro'*, B- *'Claro'*), two rephrasings (*'Y lo que tiene de bueno es que es / eh no es pesado'*, *'. . . que tenía una / un golpe.'*), some nonlinguistic noise (*'. . . y todavía / eh* [noise]*'*) and three hesitations (*'Y lo que tiene de bueno es que es / eh no es pesado.'*, *'Y / . . .'*, *'. . . y todavía / eh* [noise]*'*).

A free translation of this excerpt would read:

Graba bien y tiene una fidelidad muy buena. Y lo que tiene de bueno es que no es pesado. Es transistorizado. El otro día me anotaron en la boleta que tenía un golpe. Casi me los como. Les digo ya tiene diez viajes acá al service. Imagínese cómo no va a haber razón para que se me golpe.

The following is a description of some of the features characteristic of the original version.

1. FEATURES CHARACTERISTIC OF SPONTANEOUS TALK

A previous study was conducted on certain characteristics of informal conversation, which were called 'interaction markers' (Martirena 1976). These are words or combinations of words (or in cases, combinations of sounds not usually recognized as words) which are not within the messages of a conversation nor do they alter them, but rather they add something to the messages pointing to a dynamic relationship between the speaker and his audience. 'Well', 'see what I mean', 'you know', 'say', 'uh' are the English equivalents of some of these markers.

It was found that a speaker uses an interaction marker when:
1. He is searching for an adequate idea or expression.
'. . . y ese dinero va para un . . . COMO SE DICE . . . una ayuda para los estudiantes que no tienen dinero para estudiar.'
2. He has found the right idea or expression, has made a decision or has accepted a situation.
'Y . . . // BUENO, mirá, yo en general nunca tuve mucha opinión . . .'

3. He wants to keep the floor while thinking.

'*Y . . . // Bueno, mirá, yo en general nunca tuve mucha opinión . . .*'

4. He is anticipating the character of the information.

'*SABES, compró uno sencillo . . .*'

5. The following statement reflects a contradiction, an objection, or when he wants to change the topic of the conversation.

'*. . . y me decía PERO, ¿vos sabés los años que hace que estoy estudiando?*'

6. He wants to show his attention to the other person's speech, or his agreement (or disagreement) with it or with his own speech.

'*yo este semestre he entregado / NO, el primer semestre / he entregado . . .*'

7. He asks for agreement, repetition, attention.

'*Es solamente una cuestión de principios, ¿TE DAS CUENTA?*'

1.1 *Interruptions of continuity*

We intend to identify and describe separately the following characteristics of spontaneous talk and then point out how some of them combine in the corpus analyzed. These characteristics are:

1. Interruptions of continuity,
2. Rephrasings,
3. Incomplete words or sentences,
4. Hesitations,
5. Interaction markers,
6. Repetitions,
7. Nonlinguistic noises,
8. Overlappings.

An *interruption of continuity* is the point where a speaker breaks off, having uttered an incomplete sentence with a nonfinal intonation contour followed by pause.

Two kinds of interruptions have been found in the corpus:

1. The speaker himself interrupts his speech, leaving the sentence unfinished. After the interruption he may continue speaking.

'*Porque a mí para el / la lengua indígena me conviene la velocidad alta.*'

'*Ah, vos porque estás / te pensás que estás grabando.*'

2. The speaker is interrupted by the listener.

A– '*Comprás eh cualquier tipo de polvo anti /*'

B– '*Ah, ¿cualquiera de esos polvos?*'

1.2 *Rephrasings*

Very often a speaker utters a few words, pauses and *rephrases* part of his message. What has been first uttered is an incomplete statement and is always preceding an interruption of continuity (as above). The rephrasing may reflect either a grammatical or a lexical change.

1. A grammatical change. The speaker decides to order the elements of the sentence in a different way, to change to another verb tense, to use a different construction to convey the same information, etc.

> '*Realmente no / nunca lo entiendo.*'
> '*Dice que de cara está viejita / muy vieja, llena de arrugas.*'

2. A lexical change. The speaker in some way decides to make a change in the content of the information and does so by using a word or construction different from the one he has begun to utter.

> '*La señorita / la señora Inés.*'
> '*Sabés qué es malo, no solamente que los estudiantes / que un grupo de estudiantes . . .*'

1.3. *Incomplete words or sentences*

At times a speaker stops talking and leaves his *word or sentence incomplete*. As with the case aforementioned this feature always occurs along with an interruption of continuity.

1. Incomplete word. The speaker stops before he has uttered a complete word.

> '*Defi / No. No definida sino que eh fué algo que nunca me molesté en tener.*'

2. Incomplete sentence. The speaker leaves the sentence incomplete, making no attempt to rephrase what has been interrupted.

> '*Cuando dejé de pintármelas, claro ya ví que el /*'
> '*Era una cara que se prestaba para /*'

1.4. *Hesitations*

At some points, a speaker may *hesitate* and pause, either filling that pause or leaving it unfilled.

1. Filled pause. The hesitation point may be filled by either of the two forms speakers of Spanish use for this purpose: '*este*' and '*eh*', or by the lengthening of a final sound.

> '*Y* este *y* eh *pero dice de cara que está muy viejita.*'

'*Había mucho movimiento* eh/ *pro-Cuba, comunista.*'
'*Eh yo tengo* un·_ / *hongo debajo de una uña.*'
2. Unfilled pause. The speaker hesitates but does not choose either of
the above forms, remaining silent.
'*Y/ . . . El otro día me anotaron en la boleta que tenía . . .*'
'*Mirá. . . . El / una / no, dos terceras partes las tenía hace un año.*'

1.5. *Interaction markers*

In a conversation, speakers use certain devices to adjust the message to
the participation of the listener. These *interaction markers* have already
been described.

1.6. *Repetitions*

Speakers often make *repetitions* of phrases or parts of phrases which do
not add to the message at all. The following types of repetitions have
been identified:
A. By the same speaker:
I. Repetitions of words or groups of words, usually separated by pauses.
They seem to reflect some delay in sentence completion, as in (1), or
emphasis, as in (2), below.
1. '*Les digo ya tiene / ya tiene diez viajes acá al service.*'
2. '*Sí. Sí. Está muy diferente.*'
II. Repetitions of very short words, not separated by pause. These
repetitions appear to be accidental, implying neither (1) nor (2) above.
'*¿Dónde está el coso de de de Mau Mau?*'
'*Me trató de convencer de que no no harían ningún mal.*'
B. Repetitions across speakers. One speaker utters a word or phrase and
the other repeats what the former has said, usually adding or deleting
something.
1. A- '*Dos terceras partes tenía hace un año.*'
    B- '*Hace un año.*'
2. A- '*Así que viniste en agosto del 66.*'
    B- '*En / sí, en agosto setiembre del 66.*'

1.7. *Nonlinguistic noises*

While talking, speakers often interrupt the linguistic flow with *nonlinguistic noises* (other than hesitations and interaction markers), such as sighs, breathing, laughs, coughs, etc. The following are some of the nonlinguistic noises found in the conversations analyzed:

'*Una o dos palabras no las entendí y el tipo me dijo yo tampoco, así que* / laughs   *seguí de largo.* '
A- '*¿Fué compañera mía?* '
B- '*No, secundaria fué.* '
A- 'Tch, *¡Ah!* '

1.8. *Overlappings*

At some points, the listener does not wait until the speaker pauses or completes his utterance, and he takes the floor. In such cases, there is an *overlapping* of speech.
1. A- '*Entonces como ahora iba lento no me acordé que* / '
    B-   '*Lo acompañabas con el dedo también.* '
2. A- '*Nada más, porque no va a ir con el otro chiquito.* '
    B-   '*Claro, ya es bastante.* '

2.   POSITION OF ABOVE FEATURES

As already pointed out, some of the features described occur *only* accompanying an interruption of continuity. A careful examination of the corpus showed that all of the other features could also occur along with an interruption of continuity, though not only in that position. It seems of interest, then, to describe the occurrence of these features relative to the interruptions of continuity.

In order to make this description as complete as possible, some additional terms (which require no explanation) will be introduced. They are:
Interjections
Complete words
Completion of sentences
Pauses between speakers
Different messages

2.1 *Preceding an interruption of continuity*

The nonfinal intonation contour and the pause which mark an interruption of continuity may be *preceded* by:

1. A complete word. The utterance is interrupted after a complete word.

   '*El / una / no, dos terceras partes las tenía hace un año.*'

   '*La señorita / la señora Inés.*'

2. An incomplete word. The speaker stops before he has uttered a complete word.

   '*Defi / No. No definida sino que eh fué algo que nunca me molesté en tener.*'

   '*Un amigo mío que estaba en ingenie / Yo tenía quince años.*'

3. A hesitation. The most usual form of filled pause preceding an interruption of continuity is the lengthening of the final sound.

   a. Filled pause

   '*Si el problema es de · / digamos de velocidad . . .*'

   '*Esa era la que· / la de Los Muchachos Peronistas.*'

   b. Unfilled pause.

   '*Y para el miércoles no sé qué . . . / A mí me hartó.*'

4. An overlapping. Sometimes — but not very often — both speakers realize that there has been an overlapping of speech and they interrupt their utterances simultaneously.

   A- '*Yo estoy acostumbrada a que vaya a velocidad alta.*'

   '*Vaya más rápido.*'

2.2. *Following an interruption of continuity*

In the conversations analyzed it was found that the interruptions of continuity were *followed* by these features:

1. A rephrasing. This feature follows the interruptions of continuity within the speech of the same speaker.

   '*Tu trabajo lo juzgan en el mismo / al /como si vos estuvieras al mismo nivel.*'

   '*La señora de / que fué la directora.*'

2. A repetition. The same word or words are uttered before and after the interruption.

   '*Pero me falta / pero me falta mi disco de Mau Mau.*'

   '*Les digo que ya tiene / ya tiene diez viajes acá al service.*'

3. A different message (a new sentence). After the interruption, the speaker does not attempt to complete the unfinished sentence and starts a new one.

   '*Hablaron, discursos, todas esas cosas y en / Andaba este Fanta y Coca Cola.*'

   '*El que está siempre es / bah un profesor / vos no fuiste ahi*' (second bar).

4. The completion of the interrupted sentence. The speaker interrupts his speech, and after the interruption completes the unfinished sentence.

'Bueno, se puede tener interés eh político pero no / así, no dentro de la universidad.'

'¿Y después se re / retrogradó así?'

5. A combination of:

a filled pause		a rephrasing
(or)		(or)
an interjection	followed by	a repetition
(or)		(or)
an interaction marker		a different message
		(or)
		the completion of an interrupted sentence

'Ahora esto después lo voy a borrar porque / eh Yo tengo un hongo debajo de esta uña' (filled pause followed by a different message).

'A mí me fastidió mucho en la universidad la forma en que lo / bueno, en que se metieron' (interaction marker followed by rephrasing).

'El que está siempre es / ah un profesor . . . (interjection followed by the completion of the interrupted sentence).

6. The pause between speakers. The speaker voluntarily stosstops talking, leaving a sentence unfinished, and his interlocutor takes the floor.

a. A- *'¿Los compraste acá o en /?'*

   B- *'Sí, la verdad es que no tengo más tantos discos de Gradel como tenía antes.'*

b. A- *'Voy a ver si la próxima vez que lo llevo le hago cambiar chasis o /'*

   B- *'Sí, evidentemente, si el problema es de velocidad* . . .*'*

3. CONCLUSION

The study was undertaken with the aim of describing — from a linguistic point of view — the use of language in conversational style. Several features characteristic of this style were identified and described. It was found that one of these features — the interruption of continuity — could occur along with all of the others.

Two lines of research appear of interest next: (1) the study of these features in different styles: face-to-face, on the phone, lecturing, etc., and (2) the study of these features in larger corpuses for each style and the corresponding statistical analysis.

NOTES

1. Some conventions used in the transcription:
   / interrupted sentence
   . . . hesitation or incomplete sentence
   · lengthening of a sound
2. Following Fries (1952:23), an utterance is considered any stretch of speech by one person before which there is silence on his part and after which there is also silence on his part. In some cases, B's spontaneous reaction does not interrupt A's speech, nor does A pause deliberately to listen to B's reaction. In such cases, A's utterance is not considered as being interrupted, even though B's interruption is counted as an utterance. If, on the other hand, A pauses to get B's reaction, A's speech is considered as consisting of two separate utterances.

HOWARD M. ROSENFELD and MARGARET HANCKS

The Nonverbal Context of Verbal Listener Responses[1]

Prolonged conversations are common human activities that can serve a variety of personal and social functions. It often is difficult to determine the motives that are operating in any conversation or the mechanisms by which the substantive goals of participants are carried out. However, there is general agreement that a fundamental feature of conversations is complementarity of verbal participation by the actors involved.

Typically, at any given time in a given dyadic conversation, one person can be identified as the speaker and the other as the listener. It is generally assumed that the person in the speaker role is the dominant provider of information. However, listeners need not always be silent. In fact quite frequently they give brief verbal responses. Such verbalizations, while often technically qualifying as 'speech', are attributed to the listener role when they are presumed to serve primarily as feedback to the speaker rather than as attempts to take over the floor.

The contents of verbal listener responses can range from the simple 'mhm' to more complex utterances such as 'I think I see what you mean'. Just how complex a verbal response can be and still be classified as a listener response is a matter of controversy. The major arguments have been reviewed and evaluated elsewhere (Rosenfeld 1978).

Listeners are as active kinesically as they are verbally. They engage in a wide range of visible nonverbal behaviors, some but not all of which co-occur with their verbal listener responses. These include occasional shifts in posture, periodic changes in direction of orientation of the head and eyes, gesticulations of the hands and arms, and a variety of affective and emblematic reactions involving the face and head.

Presumably many of these nonverbal activities of listeners function to provide feedback about the adequacy of the presentations of speakers. However, little concrete evidence is available about the particular feedback functions that are served by variations in nonverbal responses of listeners, or about how these interact with the verbal components of listener responses. The following speculations are based upon evidence evaluated in the recent review by Rosenfeld (1978).

The most common form or component of listener responses, at least among American conversants, is the brief vocalization, particularly 'mhm'. It occurs frequently following phrase boundaries and phonetic junctures of speakers in face-to-face interactions, and it is a particularly characteristic listener response when communication is limited to the vocal-auditory channel, such as in telephone conversations. As noted above, more complex vocal and verbal forms also have been identified as listener role behaviors.

The most commonly identified kinesic form of listener responses is the head nod. Head nods may or may not accompany verbal listener responses. In fact they often occur in the absence of any verbal component, although the present analysis will be limited to consideration of listener responses that contain some vocal activity. An interesting difference between brief vocalizations and head nods is that the latter are much more likely to occur in listeners *prior* to the completion of a speaker's utterance. This difference in location may be attributed to the less interruptive consequences of nodding, versus talking, while another person is speaking. But a further possibility is that when the listener nods prior to completion of an utterance of the speaker, it indicates that the listener is processing information faster than the speaker is producing it. Such behavior could have important effects upon the subsequent type and amount of information provided by the speaker. There also has been some speculation that more complex forms of listener response, such as the combination of brief vocalizations and head nods, may communicate more complex feedback messages — for example, understanding or agreement rather than simple attention.

The empirical part of the present study inquires into some of the functions served by nonverbal behaviors which are temporally associated with verbal listener responses. Our questions include the following:
1. Do the nonverbal accompaniments of listener responses differ from the nonverbal accompaniments of speaker behavior? The initiation of complex speaker utterances should be more likely to be accompanied by cues indicating that mental encoding activity is occurring and that the speaker wants to remain in the dominant speaker role. Thus we would expect that listener responses would be less likely than would speaker responses to be associated with avoidance of visual orientation or with the initiation of incomplete gesticulations. Conversely, listener responses should be more likely than speaker responses to be accompanied by head nods. In other words, can nonverbal evidence be found to support the

distinction between speaker and listener made on verbal grounds?
2. What is the factorial structure — the major configurations — of nonverbal components of listener responses?
3. Do different nonverbal response configurations of listeners have different meanings? Specifically, are any configurations evoked by the prior nonverbal activities of the speaker? For example, does greater nonverbal activity by the speaker result in more complex listener responses? Also, are different messages communicated by different configurations of listener responses? In particular do they indicate different degrees of attention, understanding, and agreement? These three dimensions are emphasized in the present analysis because they seem to be generally applicable to conversations, although certainly not inclusive of all listener messages. A listener at any point in a conversation could be expected to respond along one or more of these dimensions, and any speaker probably would be concerned with his listener's positions on all of the dimensions.
4. Finally, what is the relationship between verbal and nonverbal components of listener responses? Do more complex verbal responses have more complex nonverbal concomitants? Do the verbal and non-verbal components contribute differentially to the messages conveyed by listeners?

METHOD

To answer the questions posed in this study, data were collected from a set of 20 independent seminaturalistic conversations.[2] Participants were adult males, native speakers of American English, living in a pre-dominantly middle-class university town, who had agreed to discuss a social issue (e.g. disarmament) in which they had strong personal in-volvement. Each dyad was composed of two unacquainted persons who had somewhat discrepant viewpoints on their topic. The conversations took place in a simply furnished $12\frac{1}{2}$ x $14\frac{1}{2}$ foot (3.8 x 4.4 m.) room. All participants consented to being videotaped. Separate cameras in corners of the room farthest from the participants enabled the split-image videotape recording of a frontal view of each participant from the head to the lap and knee areas, along with the audio track. Chairs were placed at the borderline of comfortable conversational distance — five feet face-to-face at a 135-degree angle — as determined by previous research in a similar setting (Rosenfeld 1965).

Two coders of the videotapes identified the listener responses of one member of each dyad, using an adaptation of Yngve's conception (1970) of 'backchannel' speech. That is, while the speaker retains his speaking turn, the listener offers brief verbal commentaries that enable the speaker to evaluate the effectiveness of his performance. Lengthy paraphrases, sentence completions, and commentaries were excluded. Approximately 85 percent of speaker utterances preceding the verbal listener responses scored in this study ended with a phrase boundary. To strengthen the inference that speakers indeed retained their 'turn' throughout the listener response episode, only those listener responses were selected that were preceded and followed by at least five seconds of undisputed floor-holding by the speaker.

A maximum of 20 listener responses was retained for any given dyad; if more occurred, the first 20 were used. Altogether 250 listener responses, representing all 20 dyads, were retained for further analysis, although the number per dyad ranged from one to 20. For purposes of analysis the 250 responses are treated as if they were independent events. Relationships of the responses to other variables are considered 'significant' if they have a probability of chance occurrence of 0.05 or less by two-tailed tests of inferential statistics. However, this criterion should be interpreted with caution inasmuch as there may be some violations of the assumption of independence in the data, and also because this statistical procedure does not separate intra-individual from inter-individual sources of variance.

A generally comprehensive and reliable set of 38 nonverbal categories was applied to the videotapes, based upon a broad and eclectic examination of the literature. Major categories and their associated coefficients of interobserver reliability were: forward postural change (67% agreement), gesticulatory activities — starts, holds, completions (82%), head nods (79%), head orientation — eight categories (70%), eye orientations (89%), eyeblink (63%), eyebrow raise and flash (83%), smile (100%), and non-speech-associated lip movements (70%).

Most categories were separately scored for performance by speaker and by listener during three different time intervals: prior to (Period 1), during (Period 2), and following (Period 3) the verbal component of the listener response.

Two additional sets of measures were constructed specifically for the present study. One was intended to assess the complexity of the verbal listener response, with minimal semantic inference. Three levels of complexity accounted for virtually all of the responses. Starting at the simplest level they were: (1) 140 instances of vocal identifiers or segmentals such as 'mhm' (Pittenger and Smith 1957); (2) 93 occurrences of simple lexical items such as 'Yeah', 'Right', and 'I see'; and (3) 16 cases of complex lexical items such as 'Yeah, okay', 'Right, right' and

'Fine, that's fine'. Among other possible complex categories there was only one occurrence of simple lexical items preceded by vocal identifiers, such as 'Um, okay' and 'Mhm, all right'; and there were no instances in the sample of complex lexical items preceded by vocal identifiers. While events in the last category did occur in the conversations, they were designated as more like turn-taking than listener responses (see note 2). Along with the above categorization of complexity, the listener responses also were scored subjectively for three levels of audibility: (1) minimally audible, (2) borderline clarity, and (3) clear.

The other set of additional measures was intended to assess the degree to which each listener response was indicative of three messages to the speaker. Four university students who were unfamiliar with the research were hired to judge each individual listener response from the videotape for the degree that it implied attention, agreement, and understanding. Each dimension was rated on a four-point scale, ranging from probable absence to presence of the message. Five of the six pairs of judges reliably agreed on judgments of attention ($p < 0.01$), four agreed on understanding ($p < 0.01$), and all agreed on agreement ($p < 0.001$). The average of the four judges was used as the best estimate of the actual scale value to each listener response on each dimension. A separate analysis was also performed using only the scale scores of the one judge who agreed most highly with all other judges. But inasmuch as virtually identical results were obtained from the two procedures, only the average judge scores will be considered further in this report.

RESULTS AND DISCUSSION

Nonverbal concomitants of listener responses

Our first question concerned the validity of classifying verbal behaviors as listener responses, rather than as dominant speaker behavior. We have assumed that the production of verbal feedback by listeners requires much simpler conceptualization than does the generation of utterances by speakers. Thus we would expect to find fewer nonverbal cues indicative of speech encoding being produced by the listener during his verbal response than are produced by the speaker during the resumption of his talking. The most common nonverbal speech-encoding cues are orientation of the eyes or head away from the other person and the initiation of gesticulations of the hand or arm. The relative frequencies of each of these speech-associated activities by the listener and speaker were assessed by comparing two locations in each of the 250 conversational segments analyzed in the present study — during the verbalization of the listener (Period 2), and during the first two words of speech of the speaker immediately following the listener response (Period 3).

Head movements away from the other conversant were performed by the listener during Period 2 in 2% of the segments, while the speaker moved his head away during Period 3 in 10% of the segments. Eye movements away from the other conversant showed a similar pattern — 9% (listener, Period 2) as opposed to 42% (speaker, Period 3) — as did initiation of gesticulation — 1% (listener, Period 2), compared to 6% (speaker, Period 3).

A further analysis was done within the listener responses — gazing away was compared between segmental and lexical listener responses. Only 6% of the segmentals were initiated with averted gaze, in comparison to 25% of the lexical listener responses. All in all, then, the coding of verbal behaviors as listener responses was validated by the relative absence of nonverbal indicators of complex speech encoding. In particular, the less 'linguistic' utterances of listeners were only rarely associated with overt nonverbal speech-encoding cues.

It is important to add that the above results are not attributable to a tendency for speakers simply to be more physically active than listeners, regardless of nonverbal category. The respective percentages of speaker and listener periods containing head nods were 11 and 75.

Our next concern was to identify the major varieties of nonverbal accompaniments of verbal listener responses. For purposes of statistical analysis we limited our attention to nonverbal response categories that occurred neither very rarely nor very often in the sample. Several response categories that were considered by the authors to be topographically or functionally similar to each other, or which occurred too infrequently to be considered separately, were combined for this analysis. [3]

Seven substantively distinct variables or configurations of speaker nonverbal behavior and ten of listener nonverbal behavior met our criteria. Each variable was marked for its temporal occurrence in the listener episode — prior to the verbal listener response (Period 1) and during the verbal listener response segment but prior to the continuation of the speaker's utterance (Period 2). Inasmuch as some variables occurred in both periods the total number of variables actually was nine for the speaker and 15 for the listener.

The nonverbal variables of *speakers* are listed below, along with the temporal period or periods in which they occurred, as well as the total frequencies of occurrence of any subcategories within them. These variables are listed vertically in Table 1a.

1. Termination cue, 1 (31 end of gesticulation, 208 juncture pause).
2. Orientation toward listener, 1 (9 posture forward; 18 head turn, 99 head point, 2 head cock — all in the direction of the listener; 19 small head nod).
3. Continuation cue, 1 (72 hold gesticulation, 12 frown).
4. Orientation away from listener, 1 and 2 (49 and 35 turn eyes away, 13 and 6 turn head away).
5. Questioning emblem, 1 (22 eyebrow raise, 17 eyebrow flash).
6. End of facial display, 1 and 2 (4 and 0 end frown, 6 and 5 end raised brow, 9 and 4 end smile).
7. Total effort, 1 (number of different kinds of nonverbal activities).

The nonverbal variables of *listeners* were the following, as listed vertically on Table 1b.
1. Head nod frequency, 1 and 2 (10 and 167 — excluding very small head nods).
2. Smile initiation, 1 and 2 (9 and 17).
3. Disengagement, 2 (5 end of small nods, 5 end of smile).
4. Posture forward, 1 (39).
5. Eyework 2 (144 blink, 3 raise and 7 flash eyebrows).
6. Self-directed energy, 1 and 2 (7 and 8 eye flicker, 9 and 16 non-speech-associated lip activities).
7. Head orientation toward speaker, 2 (8).
8. Withdrawal of attention, 1 and 2 (3 and 10 head away; 26 and 22 eyes away).
9. Begin small head nods, 1 and 2 (18 and 21).
10. Total activity (number of different kinds of nonverbal activities).

Nonverbal configurations

To reduce still further the number of nonverbal categories within the listener and speaker sets, each was submitted to a principal components factor analysis with varimax rotation of factors that had Eigenvalues greater than one.[4] This resulted in four speaker factors accounting for 64% of the variance in speaker nonverbal behavior, and seven listener factors accounting for 67% of listener nonverbal behavior. Major loadings of nonverbal variables with the factors are included in Tables 1a and 1b along with the percent of variance accounted for by each factor.

Among the speaker factors, Factor 1 was labeled 'active ending'. It was characterized by the following speaker behaviors prior to the listener verbalization: shifting of posture toward the listener, turning and pointing the head toward the listener, small head nods, initiation of

Table 1a   *Factorial structure of nonverbal speaker antecedents*

Variables	Period	Factors and Loadings			
		1 *Active ending*	2 *Floor maint.*	3 *Persist. display*	4 *Deactiv. ending*
1. Termination	1	0.<u>49</u>	0.17	−0.29	−0.20
2. Orientation toward	1	0.<u>71</u>	−0.07	0.12	0.00
3. Continuation	1	0.<u>51</u>	−0.42	−0.04	−0.05
4a. Orientation away	1	0.24	0.<u>76</u>	−0.04	0.05
4b. Orientation away	2	−0.01	0.<u>77</u>	−0.03	−0.05
5. Question emblem	1	0.21	−0.01	0.<u>71</u>	0.37
6a. End facial display	1	0.02	0.01	−0.02	0.<u>91</u>
6b. End facial display	2	−0.09	−0.03	0.<u>80</u>	−0.26
7. Total effort	1	0.88	0.14	0.09	0.32
% variance accounted for		23	16	13	12

Table 1b.   *Factorial structure of nonverbal listener responses**

Variables	Period	Factors and Loadings						
		1 *Norm*	2 *Pre- proc.*	3 *Min. rec.*	4 *Int.*	5 *Self dir.*	6 *Dis- eng.*	7 *Antic.*
1a. Head nod frequency	1	−0.03	0.<u>98</u>	0.04	0.00	0.03	0.01	0.04
1b. Head nod frequency	2	0.<u>90</u>	−0.03	−0.07	−0.05	−0.01	0.03	0.03
2a. Smile initiation	1	−0.11	0.12	−0.10	−0.06	−0.04	0.06	−0.<u>54</u>
2b. Smile initiation	2	0.06	−0.12	0.<u>83</u>	0.03	0.06	0.04	−0.16
3. Disengagement	2	−0.01	0.11	0.<u>91</u>	0.00	0.06	0.01	0.04
4. Posture forward	1	−0.07	0.05	−0.03	0.<u>56</u>	−0.14	−0.17	0.42
5. Eye work	2	0.38	0.05	0.05	0.<u>58</u>	−0.23	0.16	−0.07
6a. Self-directed energy	1	−0.02	0.09	0.07	−0.01	0.<u>80</u>	−0.18	−0.09
6b. Self-directed energy	2	0.05	−0.08	−0.04	0.00	0.<u>80</u>	0.18	0.13
7. Head toward	2	−0.01	−0.07	−0.03	0.17	0.08	0.<u>77</u>	−0.03
8a. Attention withdrawal	1	−0.06	0.06	−0.01	−0.<u>76</u>	−0.17	0.05	0.15
8b. Attention withdrawal	2	0.04	0.08	−0.01	−0.33	−0.11	0.<u>65</u>	0.02
9a. Small head nods	1	−0.28	0.20	0.<u>54</u>	0.00	−0.03	−0.03	0.28
9b. Small head nods	2	0.11	0.13	0.10	0.11	−0.13	−0.25	−0.<u>63</u>
10. Total activity	2	0.89	−0.07	0.14	0.32	0.03	0.10	0.09
% variance accounted for		17	12	10	8	8	7	6

*See text for fuller description of variables. Factors are based on varimax rotation. Loadings summed to construct factor scores are underlined.

frowns and the holding of gesticulations, and a clear pause. Also total number of different nonverbal behavior categories was highly loaded on this factor. This configuration of behaviors struck us as a highly coercive effort to elicit a reaction from the listener, but without relinquishing the floor.

Speaker Factor 2 was labeled 'floor maintenance'. It consisted of turning the head and eyes away from the listener both prior to and during the verbal listener response. We expected it to be much less likely to elicit a strong listener reaction than would Factor 1.

Speaker Factor 3, labeled 'persistent display', was comprised of eyebrow flashes and raised brows during the end of the speaker's utterance, and the lowering of brows and the termination of smiles during the subsequent verbal listener response phase. It appeared to imply a persisting, though rather perfunctory request for a listener reaction. Speaker Factor 4, 'deactivation ending', consisted of the termination of smiles, of frowns, and of eyebrow raises prior to the listener response. Inasmuch as Speaker Factors 3 and 4 did not significantly affect listener behavior, they will not be discussed further in this report.

Listener Factor 1, 'normal acknowledgement', was based upon number of normal head nods during the verbal listener response. It appeared to be a classic indicator of attention to, and acceptance of, the flow of the speaker's utterances.

Listener Factor 2 differed from the prior factor primarily in the location of head nodding. In this case, it occurred prior to the termination of the speaker's utterance. We labeled it 'preprocessing' on the assumption that it indicated that the listener was signaling understanding before the speaker had finished talking.

Listener Factor 3, 'minimal recognition', was composed of brief smiles and small head nods during the listener's verbalization. It appeared to be a less potent reaction than were the prior two types.

Listener Factor 4, labeled 'interest', was based on forward posture and visual attention prior to the verbal listener response, and the initiation of eyebrow raises or flashes or eye blinks during the verbal listener response.

Listener Factor 5, 'self-direction', consisted of eye flickering and non-speech-associated lip movements before and after the termination of the speaker's utterance.

Listener Factor 6, 'disengagement', included both gaze aversion and return of gaze during the listener response period.

Listener Factor 7, 'anticipation', contained a combination of prejunctural smiling and low amplitude post-junctural nodding. It was not involved in any significant findings and will not be discussed further.

Elicitation and perception

The next major question of this study concerned what influence, if any, speaker behavior exerted on listener behavior. Although such a question cannot be answered definitively from a descriptive study, heuristic approximations of an answer were sought from significant correlations between speaker behavior and listener behavior. Speaker behavior consisted in the first two speaker factors described above, with scores on each factor computed by summing the scores on the variables that were heavily loaded (see Table 1a). Total number of different activities by the speaker was analyzed separately, even though it was associated with the first factor.

Six listener factor scores were similarly computed (see Table 1b). Additional listener variables were number of different nonverbal behaviors, although this was associated with the first head nodding factor, and complexity and audibility of the listener response.

Major results are displayed in Table 2.

Table 2. *Significant correlates of listener behavior**

Speaker Nonverbal Factors	Listener Nonverbal Factors						Listener Speech	
	1 Norm	2 Pre proc	3 Min. rec.	4 Int.	5 Self Dir.	6 Dis-eng.	Com-plexity	Audi-bility
1. Active end.	0	+	+	+	0	–	0	+
2. Floor maint.	–	0	0	0	0	+	–	0
Judgments								
Attention	+	0	0	+	0	–	+	+
Understanding	+	0	0	+	0	–	+	+
Agreement	+	0	0	+	0	0	+	+
Listener Speech								
Complexity	+	0	0	+	0	0		+
Audibility	0	0	0	+	+	0		

*Direction of relationship denoted by plus (positive) and minus (negative) signs. All signed relationships significant at ≤ 0.05 level of confidence by two-tailed test. Speaker Factors 3 and 4 and Listener Factor 7 are omitted (see text).

Two of the nonverbal listener factors had significant positive relationships to judgments of attention, understanding and agreement by observers. These were Factors 1 ('normal acknowledgement') and 4 ('interest'). They were also the most easily interpretable and contained the most active configurations of nonverbal components. Factor 1 was based on number of regular head nods (excluding barely discriminable nods) during the listener response period, and Factor 4 contained discrete attentional acts before and during the listener period.

But the two factors were differentially evoked by nonverbal speaker factors. Listener Factor 1 (nodding) occurred following the absence of speaker gaze aversion (Speaker Factor 2). In contrast, Listener Factor 4 occurred after the presence of active nonverbal endings by the speaker (Speaker Factor 1), and was particularly related to the variety of nonverbal responses of the speaker.

It thus appears that common attentional behavior, i.e. head nodding, tends to be internally generated by listeners at junctures in speaker behavior, unless inhibited by speaker gaze aversion. We have interpreted gaze aversion as a floor-maintaining cue by speakers, but of course it also makes the speaker unavailable to receive nonverbal reactions from listeners. Discrete attentional cues by the listener appear to be evoked by similar types of attention-getting cues from the speaker.

Active nonverbal endings by the speaker (Speaker Factor 1) also significantly evoked two other listener factors — Factor 2 ('preprocessing' or early head nods) and Factor 3 ('minimal recognition' or smiles and small nods). Our original conception of preprocessing was that it should indicate that the listener understood the speaker before the speaker had completed an utterance. But our study found no relationship of Listener Factor 2 to judgments of listener understanding. A more supportable interpretation is that the early nodding is a reaction to coercive attention-getting cues emitted by the speaker prior to a speech juncture — regardless of the listener's actual comprehension, agreement or attention. Two of the cues in Speaker Factor 1 also were identified as predictors of prejunctural listener nods in an earlier informal study, described by Rosenfeld (1978). These cues were head movement and hand gesticulation.

It is not clear how much of individual differences in the probability of early nodding by listeners is attributable to the strength of the prejunctural coercive cues of speakers, rather than to individual differences among listeners in reactivity to such cues. Perhaps those listeners who are more offended by the coerciveness are the ones who are most likely to respond with the minimal recognition cues of Listener Factor 3. Other research has demonstrated that smaller head nods are interpreted by observers as less positive reactions (Rosenfeld and McRoberts 1977).

Listener Factor 5 ('self-direction' or lip movements and eye-flickering) was not related to either speaker antecedents or observer judgments. Perhaps, then, these responses function as 'adaptors' (Ekman and Friesen 1969) — nonverbal adjustments to discomfort generated by conditions other than the immediate content of conversation. Perhaps the containment of energy enforced by cognitive activity or by the listener role is uncomfortable, and discharge of energy through small, relatively unobtrusive behaviors alleviates the situation. Another possibility is that the listener intentionally emits some behaviors that are not controlled by the speaker or the conversational situation — a small but satisfying assertion of independence.

Listener Factor 6, consisting of eye movements both away from and toward the speaker during the listening period, had puzzled us. It turned out that this factor was negatively associated with judgments of attention and of understanding. Additionally, this factor was more likely to occur following either the absence of active endings by the speaker (Speaker Factor 1) or the presence of gaze aversion (Speaker Factor 2). A possible interpretation is that when the speaker averts gaze, the listener reciprocates the act but then returns to the normal visual attention that is characteristic of listeners. Although we have emphasized the well-documented function of gaze aversion by speakers as an indicator that effort is being expended in the encoding of speech, another documented function of gaze aversion should be noted — an indication of discomfort. Thus the reciprocation of gaze aversion may indicate an unwillingness of either participant to take on the speaker role, with resultant embarrassment over the prospect of extended mutual silence.

RELATIONSHIP BETWEEN VERBAL AND NONVERBAL COMPLEXITY

Our study provides some evidence about the relationship between verbal and nonverbal complexity of listener behavior. The two are not independent. First of all, more complex verbalizations also were more audible. Also verbal complexity was significantly associated with the occurrence of two strong nonverbal listener factors, Factor 1 (normal acknowledgment) and Factor 4 (interest). The aspect of nonverbal listener behavior that was most strongly related to complexity of listener speech was variety of nonverbal activities (Listener Variable 10, Table 1). Both verbal and nonverbal complexity predictably followed the absence of Speaker Factor 2 (gaze aversion). An estimate of the degree to which verbal complexity of the listener was predictable from antecedent nonverbal speaker cues was available from an additional statistical analysis of the present data. A hierarchical analysis of variance statistic (Gillo 1972), using the pre-factored speaker behaviors as independent variables, revealed that they cumulatively accounted for approximately 18% of the variance in verbal complexity of listeners.

Also the audibility of the listener response was significantly predicted by Speaker Factor 1 (active ending). And both verbal complexity and audibility were significantly associated with judgments of greater attention, understanding, and agreement.

To clarify further the effect of all listener behaviors — verbal and nonverbal — on judgments of attention, understanding, and agreement, the hierarchical analysis of variance statistic again was applied. The respective percentages of variance in the three judgments accounted for by the coded listener behaviors were 15, 20 and 25.

CONCLUSION

Clearly the present evidence indicates that verbal listener responses are intimately connected to a variety of nonverbal behaviors of both the listener and speaker — both co-occurring with the verbal listener response and during the preceding end of verbalization of the speaker. Judgments of responsiveness of listeners to speakers were predictable not only from the complexity and audibility of the vocal components of listener responses, but also from nonverbal activity — including concomitant head nods, eyeblinks, eyebrow raises and flashes, and forward shifts in posture. The concomitant head nods, which were the most common nonverbal components of listener responses, seemed to be initiated at the option of the listener, whereas a variety of other nonverbal components apparently were evoked or even coerced by a variety of active nonverbal cues of speakers at the end of utterances. These listener responses included early head nods, and very small head nods and smiles, in addition to the other listener reactions noted above. When speakers gazed away from listeners at the ends of their utterances, the listeners were likely to reciprocally avert gaze and to inhibit head nodding.

The amount of variance accounted for in predictability of listener behavior from immediately prior speaker behavior was significant although not large. Further research is needed to determine how much additional predictability could be obtained by predicting from a longer period of conversational antecedents of the listener response. And, of course, we have virtually ignored the predictive potential of the semantic implications of prior speaker behavior, Additionally, there remains the very real possibility that much of the explanation of the occurrence and complexity of listener responses lies in the personal information-related capacities of the listener rather than in the immediate conversational context.

The predictability of observer judgments about the listener's conveyance of messages of attention, understanding, and agreement also was significant, but modest in size. Again it would be of interest to know if assessment of a larger conversational context or a more comprehensive set of variables would improve the degree of predictability. Additional messages of listener feedback also should be explored.

Until quite recently, theory and research on conversation was based upon the assumption that the verbal channel carried virtually all of the significant information. The present study adds to a growing body of data that invalidates the older assumption. We now need to expand and refine our understanding of the separate and combinatorial contributions of verbal and nonverbal behavior to the regulation of conversational behavior.

NOTES

1. The research reported herein was conducted in the Social Behavior Laboratory at the Kansas Center for Mental Retardation and Human Development. Partial support was provided by Center Support Grant HD 02528 from NICHHD, and by University of Kansas General Research Grant 3909 and Biomedical Sciences Grant 4673.
2. The authors are indebted to Pamela Gunnell for her collection of the videotapes, the definitions of most code categories and the training of author Hancks in the reliable usage of the code. Gunnell's doctoral dissertation, which will emphasize the role of nonverbal behavior in speaker switching episodes in the tapes, is expected to provide complementary information to the present study of variations in listener backchannel responses.
3. Readers may wish to check the combinations of variables into categories, as well as the latter interpretation of more complex factors, against their personal intuitions.
4. The authors are grateful to Professor David Thissen for his helpful advice on factor analysis of the data.

ADAM KENDON

Gesticulation and Speech: Two Aspects of the Process of Utterance[1]

When a person speaks there is always some movement in the body besides the movements of the jaws and lips that are directly involved in speech production. This speech-associated movement may be slight and comprise not more than a minor bobbing of the head or occasional movements of the eyes and eyebrows. Quite often, however, movement may be observed in other parts of the body as well, most notably in the arms and hands. These movements may become complex and extensive and they are generally recognized as being intimately linked to the activity of speaking and are often regarded as part of the speaker's total expression. These hand and arm movements, here to be referred to as *gesticulation*, have been the object of attention by numerous workers. Early workers include Austin (1806), Bacon (1875), Ott (1892), and Mosher (1916) who were interested in gesticulation as a part of public speaking and their studies were mainly prescriptive. Systematic descriptive analysis is much more recent, although the most notable work still remains that of Efron (1941 [1972]).

Most workers have been explicit in noting that gesticulation, as we here refer to it, is to be distinguished from other kinds of bodily movement that can be observed in interaction, and several studies show clearly that it is an integral part of speaking. Thus Ekman and Friesen (1969) distinguished 'illustrators' and 'emblems' from movements in which the individual touched or manipulated his own body or his clothing, which were termed 'self-adaptors'. Freedman (1972) distinguished 'body focused' movements from 'object focused' movements and showed that 'object focused' movements occurred only during speech, whereas self-touching occurred at other times. Kimura (1976) in a recent paper has presented a number of observations which suggest very strongly that these movements are controlled by the same part of the brain that controls speech production. Thus she observed the movements right-handed subjects made during periods of speaking as compared to periods of silence and found not only that gestural or free movements only occurred during speaking, but that these movements were made predominantly by the right hand. This was in sharp contrast with self-touching movements which were observed to be made equally often by either hand. Right-handed subjects who, nevertheless, had gestured during speech mainly with the left hand, were tested for speech lateralization using the dichotic listening technique. She reports a significant relationship between hand preference in gesturing and lateralization of speech function as assessed by this technique. She also observed left-handers and found that they tended to use both hands during speaking. This is in accord with suggestions that speech is more bilaterally organized in left-handers than in right-handers. Kimura also reports a number of studies of patients with left hemisphere lesions with consequent aphasia, who also showed apraxia. In particular they had difficulty in copying sequences of gestures. The intimate relationship between speech and gesticulatory hand movements is further supported by recent observations that suggest that movements of the hands coordinative with movements of the speech organs may be present from birth (Trevarthen 1977), and Ingram (1975) has observed that children as young as three years engaged in gestural movements with the dominant hand when speaking in a conversation.

Movements that are closely associated with speech appear to be phenomenally distinct from other movements. Thus, Kendon (1976) showed 20 individuals a film of a New Guinea highlander addressing a large gathering. The observers who did not hear the sound track of the film, were asked to describe what movements they saw the man make. All of them recognized that he was speaking to a large gathering, all of them recognized the same segments of movement as being related to his speech and all of them distinguished these quite sharply from other movements that, they were all agreed, had nothing to do with his speech. Thus arm extensions, elaborate movements of the hands in the space in front of the body, were all recognized as belonging to his speech performance. Self-touching, postural movements, movements involved in the manipulation of an axe — these were all regarded as being quite separate.

In this paper we shall review findings from some detailed studies of the organization of these gesticulatory movements and how this is related to the organization of concurrent speech. As we shall see, this work shows that this bodily activity is so intimately connected with the activity of speaking that we cannot say that one is dependent upon the other. Speech and movement appear together, as manifestations of the same process of utterance. That is, in the translation of 'ideas' into observable behavior which may be read by others as being reportive of those ideas, the output that results is manifested in both speech and movement. While we shall here concentrate upon the phrasal structure of gesticulation and its relation to the phrasal structure of speech, we shall also take note of the way in which the 'ideas' being expressed in speech are also encoded in the movement patterns being produced. It will be clear that the manner of encoding is, in each case, quite different. In gesticulation we see patterns of movement that are enactive or depictive of the ideas being expressed, yet such expressions are concurrent with, indeed they often somewhat precede, verbal expression. This suggests that the formulation of ideas, in a form of action which is iconic or analogic to those ideas, is as fundamental a process as the formulation of ideas in verbal form.

THE RELATIONSHIP BETWEEN GESTICULATION AND THE STRUCTURE OF SPEECH

The movements of gesticulation and their relationship to speech may be analyzed by a close inspection of examples recorded on 16mm sound film. By use of a hand-crank operated time–motion analyzer, it is possible to examine and reexamine the film frame by frame or by short stretches of several frames at a time. A detailed map may be made of the movement patterns observable, which can be plotted on a chart to show their development in time to the nearest frame. Using standard sound-film rates, this means that we can analyze the behavior to the nearest twenty-fourth of a second. Such a map of the movement patterns may be matched with a phonetic transcript of the concurrent speech, which can also be plotted against the frames of the film it matches. In this way, the relationship between body-motion and speech may be examined to the nearest twenty-fourth of a second (or to smaller intervals of time, if the appropriate film speed is used). Details of these procedures were first described by Condon and Ogston (1966, 1967b) and an account may also be found in Kendon (1970, 1972, 1977).

The first work in which this approach was used was that of Condon and Ogston (1966, 1967b). In this work an extremely detailed study of the flow of movement in relation to the speech flow was undertaken. This showed that as the speaker speaks his bodily movement is rhythmically coordinated with his speech rhythm. One of Condon's principal concerns, in this work, has been to explore the degree to which this synchrony of speech and movement is precise. Its principal significance for our present concern is that it shows that the individual, in speaking, acts as a whole, that speech is not a disjunct action system but that it continuously mobilizes the muscular systems of the whole body.

Condon's work has been conducted at very fine levels of organization. He has examined the synchrony of bodily movement with speech at the verbal, syllabic and phonic levels of the organization of speech. Here we shall be concerned with much higher levels of organization. As Condon (1976) himself has pointed out, at the level of the phrase and above, we tend to observe parts of the body differentiating out in movement, so that the head, the arm or the hand, or at times the whole trunk performs phrases of movement that are sustained over syllabic groupings at the level of phrases and, as we shall see, at still higher levels of organization.

In the first study to be considered here, fully reported in Kendon (1972), an extended utterance was analyzed which was taken from a film made in a London pub in which eleven people, who had gathered over drinks with an American anthropologist, were discussing the differences between British and American national character. In the utterance analyzed the speaker maintained a continuous discourse for about two minutes. He directed his utterance to the anthropologist, but in such a way that it also served as an address to the whole group.

The speech stream was segmented into intonation tune units, following criteria given by Kingdon (1958). This yields units which are the equivalent of Tone Units, as these are defined by Crystal (Crystal and Davy 1969). The relationship between these Tone Units was then examined, and they were found to participate in four levels of organization. First, the Tone Units were found to combine into groupings termed *locutions*. These generally comprised complete sentences. Locutions were found to combine into Locution Groups and these in turn were organized into Locution Clusters. Locution Clusters may be thought of as the paragraphs of the discourse. They are set off from one another by a pause or by a marked change in voice quality, loudness or pitch range, and there is generally a clear shift in subject matter. The Locution Clusters are themselves combined into the highest level of organization of all, the Discourse, which is here the equivalent of one speaker turn.

It was found that each level of organization distinguished in the speech stream was matched by a distinctive pattern of bodily movement. Thus for the duration of the Discourse the speaker sustained a bodily posture that contrasted with the posture he sustained before and after it. For each of the Locution Clusters within the Discourse, he used his arms differently. Over the first of the three Clusters distinguished he used his right arm only, over the second Cluster he used his left arm only, while over the third he used both arms together. Within each Cluster, each Locution Group was contrasted in the way in which the head moved over each of the Locutions within it. Each Locution began with the speaker's head held erect or raised and tilted to one side. As the Locution unfolded the head was lowered to be brought to a low central position or to a lowered left tilt position. Locution Groups were distinguished according to whether the head movement pattern was a forward lowering or a forward lowering combined with a leftward tilt, over each Locution within the Group. Successive Locutions within a Group were distinguished from one another not only by the head movement cycle we have just described — each Locution starting with the head in a raised position — but also in the pattern of movement in the hand and arm employed. For example, in the second Group in the Discourse analyzed, over the first Locution the left arm was fully extended and retracted; over the second Locution gesticulatory movement was confined to forearm rotation and movement in the wrist and fingers; over the third Locution the forearm was raised by flexion at the elbow and a succession of lowering movements were then observed. Finally, at the level of the Tone Unit, distinctive movement patterns could again be observed. Thus over the first Tone Unit in the first Locution of the second Group, the left arm was fully extended, it was retracted over the second Tone Unit, and extended again over the third.

The paralleling of organization in the speech stream and gesticulatory stream revealed in this example, together with certain details having to do with the relative timing of the nuclei of the Tone Units and the nuclei of the gesticular phrases, led to the conclusion that it is 'as if the speech production process is manifested in two forms of activity simul-taneously: in the vocal organs and also in bodily movement' (Kendon 1972: 205). Analyses of other examples, taken from other sources, have served to reinforce this conclusion. Furthermore, some additional features of the speech–gesticulation relationship have become apparent that allow us to go further in our understanding of how far back in the speech production process the organization of concurrent bodily movement has its origin.

We shall now consider some findings from some other analyses of gesticulation structure in relation to utterance structure. Space does not permit a full presentation which will be reserved for another publication. In this new work a number of examples of extended utterances have been analyzed, all of them taken from a film made in Philadelphia at the Eastern Pennsylvania Psychiatric Institute. The film, known as ISP 001 63, is of five psychiatrists and a social worker meeting to discuss a patient that the social worker and one of the psychiatrists had been interviewing. The film contains many examples of extended utter-ances, with a good deal of gesticulatory activity.

In this work the speech in selected extended utterances has been analyzed into Tone Units and their various groupings according to procedures already described in Kendon (1972) and outlined briefly above. In analyzing the structure of the gesticulation, however, we made use of the concept of the Gesticular Phrase.

In forelimb gesticulation the limb is typically lifted away from the body as it performs one or more complex movement patterns, and then it is returned to what may be called its *rest position*. Gesticular Units, thus, may be demarcated as extending from the moment p begins the excursion of the limb to the moment when the limb is finally at rest again. Within such an excursion the limb may perform one or more *phrases* of gesticulation. A phrase of gesticulation, or G-Phrase is distinguished for every phase in the excursionary movement in which the limb, or part of it, shows a distinct peaking of *effort* — 'effort' here used in the technical sense of Rudolf Laban (Dell 1970). Such an effort peak, or less technically, such a moment of accented movement, is termed the *stroke* of the G-Phrase. It is usually preceded by a *preparation* — that is, by a phase in which the limb moves away from its rest position to a position at which the stroke begins. The stroke is then succeeded by a *recovery* or *return* phase in which the limb is either moved back to its rest position or in which it is readied for another stroke.

Gesticular Phrases, like Tone Units, may be grouped in various ways, so that a Gesticular Unit, or G-Unit, may contain more than one G-Phrase, and sometimes more than one grouping of G-Phrases. Description is further complicated by the fact that both limbs may be used simultaneously, at times performing in unison, but at other times showing considerable differentiation in the way they are employed.

Several of these features will now be illustrated with a specific example. In Figure 1 a G-Unit and its internal structure is diagrammed in relation to the speech it co-occurred with. In Figure 2 three sketches of S are presented to show his general posture and two main features of his gesticulation. The example is taken from the film ISP 001 63 already mentioned. In this example, the psychiatrist who is presenting the case, S, is commenting on the difficulty he has had in getting the patient in question to give a coherent account of herself. The passage we are concerned with is as follows, transcribed to show its organization into Tone Units:

this patient has been a *prob*lem/ so far as a *his*tory is concerned/uh y'know a very *form*al one/ uh or *any* kind of a history/ cos she talks very very *rap*idly/and *moves* very quickly/from one area to *another*/

We are concerned here with the gesticulation that occurs in association with the final five Tone Units in this passage.

It will be seen from Figure 1 how a single G-Unit extends during the passage of speech in question. It is recorded as beginning at frame 11084, the earliest point in which gesticulatory movement can be observed, in this case in the left hand, to frame 11250, when both limbs have returned to a stable, non-gesticulatory position.

This G-Unit, however, will be seen to contain three manual G-Phrases, regarded as being organized into two groupings or Parts, the first Part containing two G-Phrases, both enacted by the left hand; the second Part contains one G-Phrase only, enacted by the right arm. These G-Phrases are regarded as belonging together in a single G-Unit because, in the first place, between G-Phrase 1 and G-Phrase 2 the hand does not return completely to its rest position. Secondly, as will be clear from the diagram, G-Phrase 3 begins before the recovery phase of the preceding G-Phrase is completed. G-Phrase 1 and G-Phrase 2 are grouped into Part I because they are very similar in form and in the space they make use of. G-Phrase 3 is regarded as belonging to a separate Part, in this case because it is enacted by a different limb. In other examples, where the gesticulation is confined to one limb only, distinct Parts are recognized if the limb moves to an entirely new spatial area for enactment, or if it engages in a sharply distinctive movement pattern.

G-Phrase 1 and G-Phrase 2 are very similar. For both, the fingers of the left hand are extended and spread to assume an 'umbrella' hand form (i.e. with palm facing down, all digits are extended and abducted, but all are partly flexed at the A-joints). At the same time this development of the 'umbrella' form occurs, the wrist extends slightly, lifting the hand away from the chair arm on which it has been resting (see Figure 2). In each of the two G-Phrases, this development of the hand posture and the concurrent wrist extension is regarded as constituting the *preparatory* phase of the G-Phrase (p_1 and p_2 in Fig. 1). In the *stroke* (S_1 and S_2) in each G-Phrase, the wrist is flexed rapidly, moving the 'umbrella' hand sharply downwards. In both, the stroke is followed by a *hold* (h_1 and h_2) in which the hand, still in its 'umbrella' form, is held still in the position it reached at the end of the stroke. Thereafter, in G-Phrase 1, the fingers slowly flex and draw together into a 'loose bunch' form. This is regarded as a *partial recovery* (Pr_1) because the hand does not return all the way to the position it was in before the onset of the G-Phrase. After the hold (h_2) following the stroke in G-Phrase 2, however, the fingers are drawn fully together, but, at the same time, the arm is moved off the chair arm, into S's lap. The forearm is then supinated and the hand spread, to form a support for the folder S is holding (see Figure 2). Note that in this case

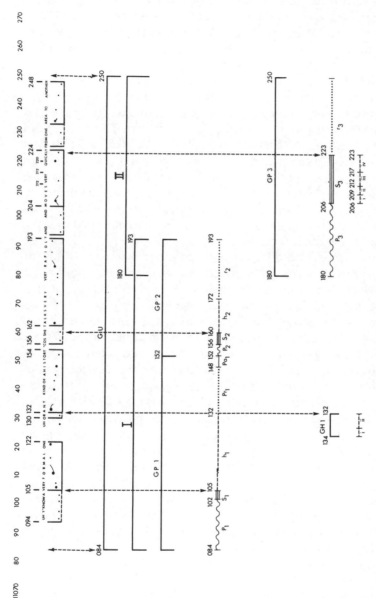

Figure 1.   *Diagram to show the organization of a Gesture Unit and its relationship to the vocal aspect of the utterance. The utterance is taken from the film ISP 001 63, frame nos. 11070–11270. The boundaries of tone units are shown by solid vertical lines immediately below the text. The head section of each tone unit is marked by a continuous horizontal line, the pre-head section by a dotted line. Intonation patterns for each tone unit are written below the text. GU = Gesture Unit; GP = Phrase; P = preparation; S = stroke; h = hold; Pr = partial recovery; Pa = pause; r = recovery; GH = Gesture Phrase in Head. Vertical broken arrows indicate relationship of components of the gesture phrases with components in the vocal aspect. For further explanation see text*

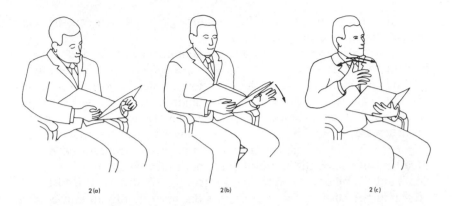

2(a)   2(b)   2(c)

Figure 2. *Tracings from ISP 001 63 to illustrate the hand positions in the Gesticular Unit diagrammed in Figure 1. (a) Position of hands prior to the Gesticular Unit; (b) 'Umbrella' form of left hand in G-Phrase 1 and G-Phrase 2; the arrow shows the direction of movement in the stroke phase of the Phrase (c) position of right hand in G-Phrase 3; arrows indicate pattern of movement in the stroke of this Phrase*

the limb is moved, not to a rest position, but to a position in which it is employed in a non-gesticulatory activity.

G-Phrase 3 is likewise analyzed into a preparatory phase (P_3), in which the arm is lifted upwards through flexion of the upper arm (at the shoulder joint); a stroke (S_3) in which the upper arm is rotated inwards and outwards twice, serving to sweep the hand in to the center of S's gesture space and out again; and a recovery phase r_3 in which the arm is lowered again, and then moved to reassume the position it had before, supporting the folder. The stroke, in this case, is a *complex stroke*, analyzable into four components.

Finally, note should be taken of the segment marked GH1, which occurs during h_1 in G-Phrase 1. This is a gesture of the head, in this case a *head-shake*. As may be noted from the diagram, it is integrated with the gesticulatory activity in the limbs and, as we shall observe later, it bears the same relationship to the speech structure as the other gestural units do. However, for the present it is convenient to treat head gestures separately and we have not considered this as part of the gesture phrase organization described for the forelimbs.

A detailed analysis of the relationship between the phrase structure of the gesticular flow and the organization of the speech flow has been carried out on five extended utterances from the film ISP 001 63 from three different participants. There are three general statements that may be made from these analyses.

First, just as we found in the analysis summarized earlier and reported in Kendon (1972), so here, in the two examples in which there were divisions in the discourse at the Locution Cluster level, these Clusters contrasted in their concurrent gesticulation in terms of the way the limbs are involved in gesticulation. Thus in F42, an extended utterance by the social worker, which divides into four Clusters, over the first she uses only her left arm in gesticulation, over the second she uses both arms equally, while over the third she uses both arms, but the right arm is dominant. Similarly, in S134 (an utterance of the psychiatrist who presented the case to the group), the discourse is divisible into three Clusters. Over the first, which is very short, S uses his left arm; over the second, he uses his right arm; and over the third he again uses his left arm.

Second, in all of the examples we have analyzed so far, each Locution has its own G-Unit. That is, boundaries of Locutions are associated with the gesticulatory limb either at the rest position, or with it being in the phase of return to that position. Furthermore, within each G-Unit, the pattern of movement observed is different. This also confirms what was found in the previous analysis: each Locution is associated with a distinctive unit of gesticulatory activity.

Third, whereas in the previous example, as we saw, each Tone Unit was differentiated with a distinct pattern of gesticular organization — each Tone Unit was found to be matched with a distinct G-Phrase — in the other examples we have analyzed this relationship between Tone Units and G-Phrases has been found to be somewhat more complex. In F42, for example, in which there were 26 Tone Units, twenty of these had a corresponding G-Phrase. Of the other six Tone Units, three, occurring in succession, shared a single G-Phrase (which extended over the entire sequence of the three), while the other three Tone Units each had associated with them not one but two G-Phrases. Likewise, in D43, and in S134, we find groupings of Tone Units covered by a single G-Phrase.

An examination of just which Tone Units are grouped by a single G-Phrase and which co-occur with one or with more than one G-Phrase suggests that the G-Phrases are manifestations of the 'idea units' the utterance is giving expression to and are linked to the output of Tone Units only as closely as this itself is linked to the expression of 'idea units'. For example, in F42, Locution 4 is as follows:

(10)   (11)   (12)
/but all *through*/ you you *sensed*/ that she and *fa*ther/
           (13)   (14)
      are being very se*duc*tive/ with each o*t*her/

(nuclear syllables of each Tone Unit are in italics). A single, though complex G-Phrase occurs over Tone Units 11 to 14, in which the forearm is moved back and forth in front of the body, with the hand held with the palm oriented inward. This movement would seem to embody two items in an interplaying relationship with one another. Thus, though it takes a succession of Tone Units to specify 'patient' and 'father' and their 'relationship', a depiction of their relationship is here given in a single G-Phrase. On the other hand, also in F42, we have the Tone Unit 'and supposedly re*buffs* her' and in association with this two G-Phrases are performed. In association with 're*buff*' the hand is held with the palm facing the body, the upper arm rotated inward at the shoulder so that the forearm crosses the body. As the nuclear syllable of 'rebuff' is uttered, the thumb is moved rapidly outwards in a pushing-away movement. This, however, was preceded by a movement of the whole arm, in which the arm was raised and then lowered slightly and also moved towards the body. However, as it is so moved it also is moved in a series of rapid, in-out motions of small amplitude. This rapid back and forth movement is not uncommonly seen in association with expressions such as 'partly', 'more or less', 'somewhat'. Here it appears, thus, that in the single Tone Unit in which the idea of 'rebuff' and of its *supposed* character is given expression, these two aspects are given separate expression in two G-Phrases.

In D29 and D43 we find examples of a single G-Phrase, here taking the form of a sustained hand position, being held over two or three Tone Units which are all linked by a common theme. In D43 and also in S134 we find groups of Tone Units in which only one conveys new information, the others serving to link this piece of new information with the previous or succeeding argument of the Discourse. Here a G-Phrase associated with the new information is performed, but it co-occurs with the Tone Unit grouping (Locution) as a whole, and does not mark out the separate Tone Units.

A further instance is provided in the example given in Figure 1. There, it may be noted, there are five Tone Units but only four G-Phrases. S says that the patient moves very rapidly from one area to another, taking two Tone Units to express this, but there is only one G-Phrase, G-3. This is a complex phrase in which the hand is moved back and forth quickly from one place to another. A rapid back and forth movement of the hand, thus, embodies in one unit of movement the idea that is also expressed in two units of speech.

The degree to which the different levels of organization in discourse are marked by separate G-Phrases appears to be a matter of some variation, at least below the level of the Locution, and further analyses will be needed before we will be in a position to specify anything about what factors might be related to this. However, it would appear that whereas the structure of the movement pattern in gesticulation is closely integrated into the rhythmical structure of the co-occurring speech stream (Condon and Ogston's work has shown how very close this is), in terms of the phrasal organization of the gesticulation a distinct phrase of gesticulation is produced for each unit of meaning or 'idea unit' the utterer deals with. This means that the phrases of gesticulation that co-occur with speech are not to be thought of either as mere embellishments of expression or as by-products of the speech process. They are, rather, an alternate manifestation of the process by which 'ideas' are encoded into patterns of behavior which can be apprehended by others as *reportive* of those ideas. It is as if the process of utterance has two channels of output into behavior: one by way of speech, the other by way of bodily movement.

FURTHER ANALYSES OF THE RELATIONSHIP BETWEEN SPEECH UNITS AND GESTICULATION UNITS AND PHRASES

An examination of the relationship in time between the nucleus of a Tone Unit and the stroke of its associated G-Phrase shows that the stroke of the G-Phrase is completed either before the Tone Unit nucleus, or just at its onset. This phenomenon was reported in Kendon (1972) and it is confirmed in our later analyses. Thus in F42, in which there were 22 Tone Units with a matching G-Phrase, in 15 instances the stroke was completed either before or simultaneously with the onset of the tonic syllable; there were six instances in which the stroke was completed by the end of the tonic syllable; and only one instance in which the stroke continued after the tonic syllable. In all instances the gesture phrase *began* well before the tonic, and in most instances it began before the onset of the head of the Tone Unit. In none of the material we have analyzed is there an instance of a G-Phrase *following* its associated Tone Unit. It either co-occurs with it or precedes it. Where we are dealing with the first Tone Units of a Discourse, furthermore, if gesticulation occurs during the first such Unit it always begins before speech begins. Usually only the preparatory phase of a G-Phrase is enacted before speech, but occasionally complete phrases are enacted. An example of this was described in Kendon (1972).

Once again, this point is illustrated in Figure 1. There, it will be seen that the stroke of G-Phrase 1, GH 1 and G-Phrase 2 is in each case completed before the onset of the head section of the Tone Unit with which it is associated. G-Phrase 3 is enacted concurrently with the head of Tone Unit 4 but, as we noted above, in its form it expresses the idea the verbal expression of which is not completed until the completion of Tone Unit 5, in this sequence.

The appearance of G-Phrases somewhat in advance of the appearance of speech phrases with which they are associated means, of course, that the G-Phrase must have been organized at least at the same time, if not a little in advance of its associated speech phrase. Thus the G-Phrase must be seen as originating simultaneously with the origination of speech and not as a product of the speech production process.

Further indication that the gesticulation associated with speech is an alternate manifestation of the same encoding process is provided by an examination of the relationship between G-Phrases and speech phrases in which there are pauses or hesitations. For example, in many cases where a Tone Unit has already begun, and a pause occurs between the prehead and the head onset, if a G-Phrase is also underway it may continue to completion despite the interruption in the flow of speech. Indeed from several examples we have analyzed it seems that the speech is only resumed once the stroke of the G-Phrase has been completed. In these cases it would seem that, despite the pause, p had already organized the *semantic* structure of the next part of the utterance, for the G-Phrase that is performed in the pause is well formed, clearly embodying the content of what is also produced in speech. Such within Tone Unit pauses where kinesis continues reflect, thus, an interruption in the *speech* production process but not an interruption in the process of utterance.

An example may be given to illustrate this phenomenon (full details must await another publication). The example is F2, taken from the beginning of the film ISP 001 63, where the participants are settling in their seats and discussing in an informal fashion what is going to happen in the main part of the session. F makes a joke based on a scene in Wilder's *Some Like it Hot*. She says: /they wheel a big *tab*le in/ with a big with a big (pause) *cake* on it/ and the *girl*/ jumps *up*/ (here someone else fills in for her with the phrase 'with a machine gun').

This speech, which here comprises but one Locution, may be divided into four Tone Units. For the first three of these there are three corresponding G-Phrases, and the form of movement in the stroke in each of them has a clear relation to the content of what F is saying. Thus in G-Phrase 1 F sweeps her left arm inward in a horizontal motion — this is associated with 'they wheel a big table in'. In G-Phrase 2, co-occurrent with Tone Unit 2, F makes a series of circular motions with the forearm pointing downwards and with her index finger extended, here describing in movement the shape of a cake. In G-Phrase 3 she raises her arm rapidly until it is fully extended vertically above her. This is clearly a 'jumping up' movement, the action taken by the girl she refers to, though this action, it will be seen, is not referred to verbally until the last Tone Unit, during which F is only recovering from the previous G-Phrase, not producing a new one.

Looking at the relationship in time between the components of these G-Phrases and the flow of speech, it appears first that the stroke of G-Phrase 1, the horizontal inward movement of the left arm, commenced precisely at the same moment that F's speech began, but its preparation, the lifting of the arm to the position from which it commences the inward sweep, began 19 twenty-fourths of a second before this. This exemplifies the anticipatory character of gesticulation mentioned above. Second, it will be noted that the second Tone Unit is broken up. The prehead is spoken twice and then there is a pause of 26 twenty-fourths of a second before the rest of the phrase is uttered. It is during this pause that the rotary movements of the second G-Phrase are produced. The head section of the Tone Unit, '*cake* on it', is uttered as the limb recovers from the stroke. Here, then, though speech was arrested, this portion of the utterance was continued to completion kinesically.

In the next G-Phrase, as we have seen, F raised her arm rapidly to a vertical position. This movement matched precisely the tonic of the Tone Unit — this is the word 'girl' — but, as we have also already noted, the form of the movement referred, not to the girl but to her action of jumping up which is nevertheless given verbal expression in the next and final Tone Unit. Thus though in terms of phrasal organization F's speech and gesticulation become once again aligned, in terms of the semantic content the gesture was well in advance of the verbal reference.

As we have seen, phrases of gesticulation tend to appear a little in advance of their associated speech phrases, and their preparation begins sometimes well in advance. This suggests, as we have said, that the processes of speech-utterance and gesture-utterance begin at one and the same time. The temporal priority of gesture may partly be due to the fact that for a given idea to be expressed in words it must be strung out in time, whereas the same idea may be expressed in gesture within a single movement or pose of the hand. However, the observation that speech production may be interrupted while gestural production is not, may also suggest that the process of gestural encoding is more readily accomplished than that of verbal encoding and so may be faster for this reason.

MODES OF IDEATIONAL REPRESENTATION IN GESTICULATION

We have argued that gesticulation is a second output of the process of utterance. Insofar as utterance makes use of the vocal channel, use is made of a complex code, language. In the kinesic channel, however, the movement patterns that are employed in gesticulation do not appear to have properties that are like the lexical and syntactic character of spoken language though they do appear to share, in the dynamics of their organization, some of the prosodic features of speech, at least in the speakers of English to which this sort of analysis has been confined. Thus we have seen how gesticular phrases may be distinguished in terms of nuclei of kinesic emphasis, much as Tone Units may be distinguished in terms of nuclei of vocal prominence. There is also some reason for thinking that intonation tunes may have their parallel in kinesic organization. Thus Birdwhistell (1970a) has reported that a lowering of a gesticulating body part co-occurs with a falling terminal juncture in speech and that where a gesticulating body part is sustained or held at the end of an utterance, the pitch of the voice is also either sustained or raised. Several examples of our own, which will be reported in detail elsewhere, show that in questions in which the pitch of the voice is raised or held, concurrently the head or hand is also raised or sustained.

However, gesticular movements, although shaped in part in parallel to the prosodic structure of the concurrent speech also are patterned in ways that are clearly related to the content of what is being expressed. Furthermore, in the various poses the hands may assume, we can also see manifestations of aspects of the content. The relationship between the content of gesticulation and the content of speech is a highly complex one and we cannot undertake a detailed review of this here. To date the most thorough treatment of this still remains that of Efron (1941). Here we will cite a few representative examples from our own material to show that the mode by which ideas are encoded in gesticulation is quite different from the way in which they are encoded in language.

First, p may depict in gesture some object or action he is referring to in speech. Thus in the 'cake' example F2, given above, F performed movements that were analogous to movements that would be made of wheeling in a table or jumping up; she also made a movement that outlined the shape of the cake she was talking about. Movements characteristic of aspects of action are indeed very common. In F42, which we already have alluded to, F continues her description of the patient's relation to her father by saying 'and she doing things to annoy him, to attract his attention, to outrage him'. Over each of these three Tone Units she moves her hand outward in a rapid 'slapping' movement, which has the dynamic character of actions that, addressed to another, would provoke or tease him. In D43, in asking why both the psychiatrist and the social worker F had had difficulty in getting the patient to tell her history, he says '. . . maybe it's because *Pete* doesn't want to *nail* down this attractive bit of *fluff* or something'. As he says 'nail down' he raises his right arm, hand posed as if it is holding something, and he performs a series of forward thrusts, an action sequence which has the character of knocking nails into something, as one might if one were nailing a notice to a door.

In these examples p appears to be creating a gestural form *de novo* to suit the immediate utterance. Sometimes, however, he makes use of a gestural form that is more or less conventionalized. Thus, in the example just mentioned, when D says 'bit of fluff' he raises both hands, palms facing inwards, and performs sinous in–out movements, thus performing a well-known gesture which means 'shapely woman'. Such conventionalized patterns may take on the status of gestures which can be given a meaning when presented in isolation. These have been termed 'emblems' by Ekman and Friesen (1969).

Gesticulation does not only depict objects, actions, or behavior styles of others that are being described. It may also be used to encode more abstract features of the utterer's discourse. For example, it may refer to the overall theme of the utterer's discourse, rather than to particular parts within it. For example, in the first part of D43, D says: /How about this *his*tory business/ you *Pete*'s having trouble getting a history/. As he says this, his hands are held forward, palms facing each other in a 'framing' arrangement. This double hand frame was sustained throughout the series of Tone Units in this part of the utterance, which are linked together by the theme of 'getting a history'. In other instances a sustained hand position may be observed which appears to mark the *kind* of utterance that is being produced. Thus we have collected many examples in which a sustained position of an open palm extended forward marks a question or an utterance in which p is putting forward an example for discussion.

Gesticulation may, in various ways, make visible the organization of the discourse. We have already referred to the way in which body use is differentiated in association with different segments of the discourse. However, at times one may observe gesticulatory patterns that appear to have this function particularly. Thus in a discourse recorded in the film TRD 009 (not described in Kendon 1972) the utterer, x, describes certain features of the British Northerner. As he does so, each Tone Unit is associated with a distinct rotary movement of the right arm, while he holds his left arm forward and slightly bent at the elbow. This is sustained for this segment of the discourse, apparently framing or tying together the separate statements he is making.

The foregoing is intended to suggest that there are many different ways in which gesticulation may be related to the content of an utterance. Gesticulation and speech work together in an intimate relation of great flexibility and subtlety. However, as we have already suggested and as these examples must make clear, the mode of encoding of content is quite different in gesture from the mode of encoding in speech. Whereas in language highly conventionalized forms from an already established vocabulary are used, which are organized sequentially according to grammatical rules, in gesticulation encoding is presentational. Though conventionalized forms may be used, the utterer has considerable freedom to create new enactments which do not then pass into any established vocabulary. As far as can be seen at the moment, gesticulation is not composed of elements which are formed into constructions according to a syntax. They occur, rather, as a succession of enactments whose sequencing is governed by the order of presentation of ideas in the discourse.

The enactments of gesticulation described above are broadly of three sorts. There are movements of the sort performed in the 'cake' example in which the form of an object may be suggested. There are movements which consist in actions, which are the actions being directly described. There are also movements which suggest the arrangement of objects in space, the organization of space into sections or compartments, or the moving about of objects in space. Here the gesticulation seems to consist in the operations of spatial organization and reorganization of elements of the discourse themselves. It is as if, in the movements of the hands we can observe overt manifestations of the objects, actions and their organization into arrangements and sequences by which the goal of an utterance may be achieved.

Several recent lines of investigation have suggested that the process of thought often involves operations on mental images which are directly parallel to physical operations on actual objects (Metzler and Shepard 1974; Huttenlocher 1975). McNeill (1977) has described how, when subjects are asked to give an account of how they carried out a mental paper-folding task of the sort described in Metzler and Shepard (1974), as they spoke they performed enactments in gesticulation of the operations they were describing in words. In utterance, thus, one makes manifest in overt behavior the operations one is performing on one's mental representations of objects or actions. This is done both directly, in gesticulation, and also by means of speech.

It is of great interest to note, in this connection, that Blass, Freedman and Steingart (1974), in a study of hand movements during speech in congenitally blind individuals, found that these consisted in complex movements in which the fingers of the hands were continually touching themselves. The mental representations of blind persons are largely haptic. If gesticulation is indeed the manifestation in movement of the operations one is performing on one's mental representations of objects or actions, whereas these are spatial in seeing persons, one would expect them to be tactile in blind individuals, as the observations of Blass et al. would suggest.

We earlier noted that Gesticular Phrases tended to emerge in advance of the segment of speech in which the same idea is encoded. This observation, also recently reported by Butterworth and Beattie (1976), suggests that Gesticular Phrases originate at a very early stage in the process of utterance. The way in which the content of the utterance appears to be manifested in the Gesticular Phrase suggests that the process of utterance has its origin in the organization and manipulation of mental representations of images and actions directly and not, initially, in the organization of forms that can be derived only from verbal language.

Recent developments in linguistic theory have led many to the view that it is the semantic organization of an utterance that is the starting point for the processes by which its surface structure is eventually generated (Maclay 1971; Leech 1974). Most particularly, in this connection, we may mention the views of Chafe (1970) who has argued explicitly for the position that the process of utterance generation proceeds through a series of stages, starting with the organization of semantic structures. The work on gesticulation we have reviewed here would suggest that this earliest stage in the process of utterance formation has, or can have, a direct expression in gesticular action.

DISCUSSION

The foregoing analyses are all based on occasions when a speaker is also engaged in obvious gesticulation. However, such gesticulation is not always present, and it would be very helpful for our further understanding of its significance if we knew more about the circumstances in which it is likely to appear.

Several writers have suggested that since the mode of representation of ideas in gesture is more primitive it is likely to be resorted to where the speaker is finding it difficult to express what he has to say in words (De Laguna 1927; Mead 1934; Werner and Kaplan 1963). In this view, it is supposed that the prior enactment of ideas in movement facilitates their transformation into sentential form. Kendon (1972) described an example of an apparent working out in gesture of a complete utterance during a period of highly dysfluent speech. The observation reported above when F described the shape of a cake in movement during the pause in her speech that preceded the production of this word could also be interpreted in these terms. Butterworth and Beattie (1976) similarly suggest that gestural enactment may play a part in the facilitation of word search. Elzinga's observation (1978) that Japanese in conversation with other Japanese gestured much less than when they were conversing in English with Australians could also be interpreted in terms of this idea. Dobrogaev (1931: 127) reported an experiment in which subjects 'had to talk, trying to completely inhibit the gesticulatory movements of their extremities, their head, and mimic movements of the face — in general, the whole body. It turned out that no one could carry out such an inhibition completely . . . /furthermore/ the speech . . . lost its intonation, stress and expressiveness; even the very selection of words needed for the expression of content became labored; there was a jerkiness to the speech, and a reduction in the number of words used'.[2]

On the other hand, Ekman and Friesen (1972) have suggested that gesticulation is more likely to appear, the more excited and enthusiastic the speaker is, and the more dominant his role in the interaction. Consonant with this, Baxter, Winter and Hammer (1968) have reported a study in which they found that speakers produced more gesticulations when they were talking fluently on a topic with which they were familiar, than when they were talking about something they knew less well.

These observations and suggestions are not incompatible. If, as we suppose, the tendency to enact in movement the ideas that are to be encoded in speech is always present, the above observations and suggestions indicate some of the conditions in which such a tendency is enhanced. On the one hand, an increase in the energy level that someone engaging in an utterance employs will lead to the overt manifestation of gesticulation. On the other hand, where the speech component is inhibited or blocked, this same tendency again is enhanced. It is notable that children who are born deaf spontaneously resort to gesture as a mode of linguistic expression at the earliest opportunity (Goldin-Meadow in press; Goldin-Meadow and Feldman 1977). Where gesture is then sustained as the only mode of linguistic expression available, it becomes much elaborated and organized into a fully linguistic system (Kuschel 1973; Stokoe 1960, 1972; Friedman 1976, 1977).

Does gesticulation function communicatively? It is remarkable how few investigations there are that have tackled this question. Cohen and

Harrison (1973) compared the number of gestures used by a speaker in giving directions to another over a sound intercom system and the number employed when the directions were given face-to-face, and found there was an increase in the latter condition. This suggests that a speaker may add in gestures if the circumstances are such that they could be appreciated by his recipient. However, only Graham and Argyle (1975) appear to have tested directly the question of whether gesticulation improves the effectiveness of communication. In their study, subjects were faced with the task of describing geometric figures to recipients who had to draw the shapes described. A comparison of the degree of similarity of the shapes described and the shapes drawn in response to the descriptions served as a measure of communicative effectiveness. Twenty-four English and 24 Italian subjects took part. All subjects described one set of shapes with any gestures they liked, and another set without using gestures. It was found that for both English and Italian groups there was some improvement in communication when the gestures were used, but this improvement was much more marked for the Italians than for the English. This indicates that gestures may be used for information by recipients, at least those that serve to describe shapes. It also suggests that there may be cultural differences in the extent to which such gestures are attended to and made use of. Efron (1941) described the pictorial nature of Italian gesticulation, and there are several other authors who have discussed the propensity for the use of gesture by Italians (de Jorio 1832; Efron 1941; Lyall 1956). It is interesting that the findings of Graham and Argyle's study are in line with this.

Despite these findings, the fact that people can very readily carry on conversations over the telephone, or in situations of poor lighting where gesturing is hard to see, suggests that where speech is available gesticulation is not usually of central importance for linguistic communication. This makes its intimate and deep connection with speaking all the more striking.

In a previous paper (Kendon 1975), to which the present one is heavily indebted, it was suggested that this connection between speech and gesture is not incompatible with the idea recently revived by Hewes (1973a, 1973b) that the first form in which language emerged was gestural and that the development of vocal activity for language functions occurred at a later stage.

The fact that gesticulation tends to anticipate speech, that speech may be readily disrupted when concurrent gesticulation appears to go forward smoothly, and the fact that on occasion a gestural response may be given first before any speech whatever is begun, does perhaps provide a hint that the gestural channel is easier and more readily called upon, that the process by which an idea is transformed into linguistically functioning public behavior is more swiftly accomplished gesturally, that there are fewer steps to the process than there are when a formulation of the 'idea' into speech language is to occur. The least we can say about this is that we would not, perhaps, expect a more elaborate and time consuming method of utterance to be the one that was first developed in language evolution. In these respects, thus, the findings reviewed in this paper are fully consistent with Hewes' argument in favor of a gestural origin for language.

NOTES

1. This paper includes material originally published in Kendon (1975). I am indebted to W. S. Stokoe, the editor of *Sign Language Studies* for allowing me to do this.
2. Translation by Margaret Kendon.

CHARLES E. OSGOOD

Things and Words

The title of this paper is a deliberate, and appropriate, reversal of the title of Roger Brown's well-known early book (1958) on psycholinguistics. I say 'appropriate' because the most gross working principle underlying the general theory of cognizing and sentencing I am presently writing on (*Toward an Abstract Performance Grammar*) is this: *both in the evolution of the species and in the development of individual humans, the cognitive structures which interpret sentences received and initiate sentences produced are established in prelinguistic experience, via the acquisition of adaptive behaviors to entities perceived in diverse action and stative relations.* One might also call this an 'article of faith', I suppose. However, it follows directly from what would seem to be two rather obvious assumptions: (1) that, before they had language, humanoids must have had capacities (a) for cognizing the significances of states and events occurring around them and (b) for learning to behave appropriately in terms of such significances — if the species were to survive; (2) that, before they acquire language, children of contemporary humans display exactly the same capacities for acquiring the significances of perceived states and events and reacting to them with appropriate intentional behaviors. A recent paper of mine, 'What Is a Language?' (Osgood i.p.), elaborates on this theme.

This axiom leads in turn to what I call the Naturalness Principle. Naturalness *in cognizing* involves notions deriving both from Representational Neobehaviorism (to be sketched below) and from psychological intuitions about *what is natural* in the prelinguistic cognitive processing of young children — in contrast to linguistic intutions about *what is grammatical* in adult sentencing. Naturalness *in sentencing* involves another notion that is more axiomatic than specifically predictive — namely, that *the more sentences produced or received correspond in their surface structures to the cognitive structures developed in prelinguistic experience, the earlier they will be acquired by children and the more easily they will be processed in both comprehending and expressing by adults.* In what follows I will also be making the following assumptions: (1) that this 'deep' cognitive system is essentially semantic in nature, with syntax involved solely in trans-formations between the structured semantic system and the surface forms of sentences produced and received; (2) that this 'deep' cognitive system is shared by both nonlinguistic (perceptual) and linguistic in-formation-processing channels; and (3) that sentencing (comprehending and producing) in ordinary communication is always context-dependent, influenced probabilistically by contemporary linguistic (conversational, discoursive) and nonlinguistic (situational, social) factors.

A CAPSULE LIFE-HISTORY OF BEHAVIORISM

Since many readers of this volume will have mainly affective stereotypes about behaviorism — as well as being entirely unfamiliar with its more recent and complex variants — I feel that this brief orientation is necessary. At the outset it must be emphasized that BT ≠ LT (i.e. behavior theory, or behaviorism, is not the same thing as learning theory); rather, BT *includes* LT, but along with innate structural and functional determinants of behavior as well. One might even, and quite appropriately, say that learning theory is to behavior theory in psychology what syntax is to grammar in linguistics. Behaviorism had its origins in British Associationism, but in its primitive stages it was peripheral stimuli and responses that were associated rather than the central meanings or ideas. What I will call the 'Classic Behaviorism' of the 1930s and 1940s was one of the stepchildren of logical positivism and a hypothetico-deductive theoretical system, modeled quite explicitly on physics: antecedent (input) and subsequent (output) *observable events* in some natural or experimental situation were to be identified with the *abstract constructs* (overt S's and R's but also inferable convert s's and r's) with which the underlying postulates (principles) of the theory were expressed; these postulates, particularly in their dynamic interactions, were to lead to certain *deductions* (explanations or predictions) which could be unambiguously *confirmed* or *disconfirmed* — disconfirmation (in principle if often not in practice) leading to revision of the postulates. It was this type of theory building that gave impetus to the evolution of behaviorism.

Primitive Single-stage ('empty organism') Behaviorism

As an aid in exposition, I will make use of the notion — not of a Little Black Box, but of a Little Black Egg, this being more appropriate for biological entities. The evolution of behaviorism can be viewed as increments in the number and complexity of the theoretical mechanisms that are put *into* the Little Black Egg. In revulsion against what could fairly be called the 'junkshop theorizing' that characterized much of late 19th-century psychology, around the turn of the century a group of American behaviorists (Watson, Weiss and Kantor), and later Skinner, went to the other extreme: *there is nothing whatsoever inside the Little Black Egg that is the proper business of an objective behaviorist*! This was not strictly true, of course; even the most adamant Skinnerian would admit that it is not external stimuli (S's) and overt movements (R's) that are associated in learning — which would obviously be nonsense — but rather the patterns of neural events at the more central termini of the sensory (s's) and motor (r's) projection systems. So what Single-stage Behaviorism really should be called is $\dot{s} \rightarrow \dot{r}$, not S→R, psychology. Only the outer layer of the Little Black Egg (see Figure 1 (I)) was filled, however.

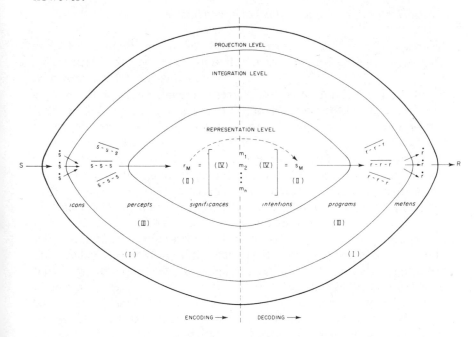

Figure 1.   *Evolution of the Little Black Egg of behaviorism*

Although Primitive Behaviorism proved to be a healthy antidote for the loose mentalism that it largely replaced during the 1920s, it was severely limited in the problems it could handle. Rats replaced humans as subjects — or humans were reduced to rat-level performances. But even at the 'rat level' of human behavior replicable phenomena began appearing that were impossible for a single-stage theory to handle. One such was *semantic generalization* — where, having learned to make some novel response like finger-flexion to some word like JOY on a prior list, the same response would occur on a subsequent list to semantically related words like GLEE but not to phonetically related words like BOY — therefore generalization in terms of similar meaning; another was *semantic satiation* — where rapid seeing/saying repetition of a word, like CANOE-CANOE-CANOE . . ., produces a loss of meaningfulness (as measured, e.g. with the semantic differential, cf. Osgood, Suci and Tannenbaum [1957]), but repetition of a nonsense overt response having the same shape, NÚKA-NÚKA-NÚKA . . ., does not. Both of these phenomena were very embarrassing for a theory that dismisses 'meaning' as a mentalistic ghost.

Classic Two-stage ('mediational') Behaviorism

Insufficiencies of this sort were the 'why' of the evolution into Classic Two-stage Behaviorism, best exemplified in the theorizing of Hull (1930, 1943) and Tolman (1938, 1948). What was the 'what'? As shown in Figure 1 (II), Hull put into the Egg a replica (some might prefer to say a 'graven image'!) of the peripheral S-R (s-r) relation, but for reasons that will become apparent, here reversed as $r_M - - \rightarrow s_M$(where the use of lower-case letters (r and s) indicates unobservable (hypothetical) responselike and stimuluslike events, the subscripts indicate merely 'mediational', and the dashed arrow indicates an automatic, unlearned dependency relation). The mediating process itself *is* a single, albeit complex, event (presumably in the cortex), but as a *dependent event* (in comprehending) it is functionally a 'response' and as an *independent* (antecedent) *event* (in expressing) it is functionally a 'stimulus'. For Tolman, the equally hypothetical mediation process was called (anticipating a theory of meaning) a 'sign-significate expectancy'. What both Hull and Tolman had done, in effect, was to break the S-to-R relation into two, *separately manipulatable*, associations, $S/s \rightarrow r_M$ and $s_M \rightarrow \dot{r}/R$, the former involved in comprehending and the latter in expressing. This greatly amplified the explanatory/predictive power of behavior theory.

But what was the 'how' of the anchoring to observables? Hull was much more explicit on this than Tolman. Here is a paradigmatic demonstration and, following, a Hullian explication:

A rat is in a glass-fronted box that has an electrifiable grid for a floor and a turnable ratchet-device on a side wall; a buzzer is sounded intermittently, always followed in five seconds by shock. On early trials our subject 'pays no attention to' the buzzer, but is galvanized by the shock into waltzing about on its hind feet, clawing at the walls, squeeking and no doubt undergoing autonomic glandular, heart-rate, etc., changes — in the course of which the ratchet is turned, shutting off the shock; a bit later the rat *begins* waltzing to the buzzer and moving in the general direction of the ratchet, promptly turning it when the shock comes on; and, finally, our subject waits near the ratchet, standing up and turning the ratchet *before* the shock comes on, thus avoiding it. (And our rat still later may become a bit cocky, delay too long, and get shocked again!)

As shown in Figure 2, the shock-*significate* (using Tolman's terminology), S, is associated single-stage (innately and/or via past learning) with the waltzing, clawing, etc., which I symbolize as R_T (total behavior to the thing signified); the buzzer-*sign*, S, gradually acquires *some* of the behavior (notice, *not all*, e.g. not the frantic clawing) produced by the significate, clearly indicating the anchoring of mediating (r_M) to observable (R_T) behavior; but since these *overt* mediators drop out, while the mediated behavior, R_X (turning the ratchet), remains, we assume that this adaptive behavior is now being mediated by unobservable *covert* 'replicas' of the overt mediators, the r_M - - → s_M process. This is the basic mechanism for development of two-stage (mediational) behavior out of single-stage behavior, and note that in Tolman's terms this mediating process is the *significance* of the sign — the buzzer comes to 'refer to' the shock — hence the symbol r_M for Tolman, as later for Osgood, would stand for a 'meaning' response, not simply a 'mediating' response.

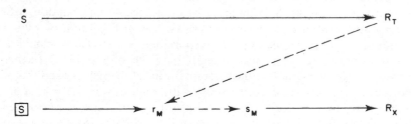

Figure 2. *Development of two-stage (mediational) behavior from single-stage behavior*

Three-stage ('integrational, mediational') Neobehaviorism

There were two very general, and significant, insufficiencies of the solely 'mediational' theories of Classic Behaviorism, and they both came down to the fact that the principles of such theories dealt only with S → R (s → r) associations. The first gross insufficiency was incapability of handling the phenomena of *perceptual organization*, so amply documented in the literature of Gestalt Psychology (e.g. the phenomenon of perceptual *closure*). That such phenomena are functions of experience, as well as having their innate determinants (which was the main thrust of the Gestaltists), is clearly indicated by the extensive evidence for an inverse relation between the frequency-of-usage of words and their tachistoscopic thresholds — the more frequent in experience, the lower the threshold. But since it is S-S learning that is involved here, no strictly S-R-type theory could handle it. See Osgood and Hoosain (1974) particularly the Discussion section, for an up-dated review of the controversy over S-S versus S-R interpretations of the tachistoscopic word-threshold data. The second gross insufficiency was inability to handle the phenomena of *behavioral organization*, the formation of central motor programs for complex behaviors like piano-playing and talking — as argued so forcefully by Karl Lashley in his Nixon Symposium address (1951). But since such behavioral organization involves R-R learning, again no strictly S-R theory could handle it.

By the mid-1950s I had become convinced that something else had to be put into the Little Black Egg if a behavior theory — of language performance, certainly — was to make any claim to adequacy. But, again hewing to the parsimony principle, this 'something' had to be the minimum necessary. As shown in Figure 1 (III), I proposed an Integration Level of processing between the Projection and the Representational Levels, on both sensory (encoding) and motor (decoding) sides of the equation. Since projection systems are essentially isomorphic and unmodifiable by experience ('wired in'), surface stimulations (S's) can be viewed as being in one-to-one relation with more central patterns of sensory signals ($\dot{s}, \dot{s}, \dot{s}$ in Figure 1), or what I would now call *icons*, and surface respondings are similarly related to patterns of more central motor signals ($\dot{r}, \dot{r}, \dot{r}$), or *motons*. I further assumed that these signals at the central termini of the sensory and motor projection systems have connections with neurons in the still more central sensory and motor integration systems (the newly postulated Integration Level) — probably in what are called the sensory and motor 'association areas' of the brain. The former ($\overline{s\text{-}s\text{-}s}$) I would now call *percepts* and the latter ($\overline{r\text{-}r\text{-}r}$) *programs* (after Lashley). Note that the relations *between* projection-level signals and integration-level events are *not* assumed to be isomorphic, but the relations *among* integration-level events *are* assumed to be modifiable by experience — *hence S-S (s̄-s̄) and R-R (r̄-r̄) learning.*

Without implying any particular neurology of the matter (however, cf. Hebb [1949] and elsewhere, for one possibility — formation of 'cell-ensemblies'), the following functional principle was proposed for learning at the Integration Level: *the greater the frequency with which icons* (ṡ, ṡ, ṡ) *or motons* (ṙ, ṙ, ṙ) *have co-occurred in input or output experience, the greater will be the tendency for their post-projectional* (s̄-s̄-s̄) *or pre-projectional* (r̄-r̄-r̄) *correlates to activate each other centrally as percepts or programs respectively.* This principle can be viewed as a behavioristic attempt to account for the phenomena of perceptual organization (long the stronghold of Gestalt Psychology) and of motor organization (highlighted by Lashley). What it says, in effect, is that redundancies in either sensory input or motor output will come to be reflected in *evocative integrations* ('closures' resulting from higher co-occurrence frequencies) or *predictive integrations* ('tunings up' resulting from lower co-occurrence frequencies) in the nervous system.

This hypothesized three-level functioning of the nervous system would provide higher organisms with what might be called 'Three Mirrors of Reality' on both encoding (sensory) and decoding (motor) sides of the information-processing coin: on the comprehension side (1) a mirror of *what is*, by virtue of unmodifiability via experience (ṡ, ṡ, ṡ), (2) a mirror of *what ought to be*, by virtue of predictive closures on the basis of past redundancies of often scanty information (s̄-s̄-s̄), and (3) a mirror of *what is signified*, by virtue of the representing relation of r_M (elicited by a sign) to R_T (elicited by its significate); on the production side, and always via feedback loops, (4) a mirror of *what is intended* as a communicative act (s_M), (5) a mirror of *what is programmed* (r̄-r̄-r̄) for skilled execution, and (6) a mirror of *what is actually done* (ṙ, ṙ, ṙ). An intriguing example of the interaction between Mirrors (1) and (2) in my own experience is what happens when, due to power failure, the old banjo clock on my living room wall stops (and, because it can't be re-set, we have to wait until time catches up); every so often I will glance at the clock 'to see what time it is', *see the second-hand moving* (the mirror of *what ought to be*), say to myself 'that can't be', look again 'to inspect it', and *see that it is NOT moving* (the mirror of *what is*)!

THE UNIQUENESS OF REPRESENTATIONAL NEOBEHAVIORISM

There are two quite distinct types of mediation theories — one viable as a paradigm for *language behavior* and the other clearly not. The nonviable version is *nonrepresentational mediation theory*: this two-stage model is essentially an extension of Skinnerian single-stage theory; it is characterized by the fact that the source of the mediator (a subvocalization) is the overt *linguistic* response (symbolized by R_X in Figure 2 above) made to some sign. The viable version is *representational mediation theory*: as a two-stage model, this is directly traceable to Hullian behaviorism (see particularly Hull's use of the anticipatory goal response, r_G, in his paper (1930) titled 'Knowledge and Purpose as Habit Mechanisms'); it is characterized by (a) the source of the mediator being the overt *nonlinguistic* responses (symbolized by R_T, total response, in Figure 2 above) made to the significate (that which is signified by the sign), and by (b) the mediating process itself being componential in nature.

The source of representational mediation processes

Both mediation models provide for the *nonobservability* of the mediating process — a nontrivial characteristic demanded by the facts of symbolic behavior. But here similarity ends. Whereas formation of the representational mediating process is *historical* (occurring during the original learning of signs), formation of the nonrepresentational mediator is contemporary with its (subvocal) utilization *as* a mediator in each performance situation. Whereas representational mediators could be entirely *central* — cortical events, having no formal resemblance to their overt behavioral sources (which I think is almost certainly the case) — nonrepresentational mediators are explicitly assumed to have formal resemblance to their overt sources, being equally *peripheral* occurrences albeit with greatly reduced amplitude. Fodor's critique (1965) has effectively demonstrated the insufficiency *in principle* of nonrepresentational mediation theories as far as any account of meaning or reference is concerned, thereby doing Neobehaviorism a service — by pruning out one of its less powerful alternatives.

The componential nature of representational mediation processes

Referring back to Figure 1, it will be noted that there is a fourth 'level' in my Little Black Egg — which is not really a level but rather an elaboration on the nature of representational mediation processes. On both the encoding and the decoding sides of the mediational coin, the $r_M - - \to s_M$ process is assumed to be *componential* in nature. Just as the total behaviors made to things signified are typically a *set* of overt responses which together constitute an 'act', so also are the mediation processes derived from these overt behaviors, and now elicited by the signs of things, a *set* of mediator components. *Thus* r_M (in comprehending) *and* s_M (in producing) *are summary symbols representing meanings-as-wholes, and they are analyzable into sets of mediator components* [m_1, m_2, . . .m_i . . . m_n].[1] Such mediator components are strictly analogous to *semantic features*; this, I think, is the entrée of Neobehaviorism to a theory of meaning and reference — and, with structuring of the semantic system, ultimately to a theory of sentencing (which is what my forthcoming *Toward an Abstract Performance Grammar* will be all about).

Just as the phonemes and sememes of linguistic theory are componential in nature, being exhaustively analyzable into sets of *distinctive features* (see, e.g. Jakobson, Fant and Halle 1951 [1963]), so it is postulated in Representational Mediation Theory that global mediation processes (r_M's) are exhaustively analyzable into sets of *distinctive mediator components* (r_m's). Note also that both phonemes and mediator components are *abstract entities*, unobservable in themselves but necessary as theoretical constructs for interpretation of what *is* observed: one never hears or produces the phoneme /k/, but rather always some contextually determined *allophone* of /k/ (e.g. with flattened lips in *key* and rounded lips in *coo*); analogously, one never hears or produces the meaningful distinction carried by a mediator component (r_m) but rather it is always a semantic distinguisher within some contextual set (r_M) which conveys the whole meaning of a form (e.g. some common affective feature is distinguishing *rage* from *annoyance, joy* from *pleasure*, and *yearning* from *expectation*, but we can only call it vaguely + Potency).

Figure 3 is a componential elaboration of the global mediation process ($r_M - - \to s_M$) represented in Figure 2 above. It also illustrates three other crucial aspects of this neobehavioristic theory: (1) a shift in a single mediator component can change the entire meaning, and hence the function of the mediation process in behaving — thus the change from component m_i to m_j, as shown in this symbolic representation, occasions the shift in *significance* (r_{M_1} to r_{M_2}) and hence in *intention* (s_{M_1} to s_{M_2}) of the entire process, all other components remaining constant; (2) signs associated with the same global mediation process (here, $\boxed{S}_1, \boxed{S}_2$, and $\boxed{S}_3$ with r_{M_1}) will have the same *significance*, and hence be functionally equivalent, and, similarly, behaviors associated with the same global mediation process (here, $\boxed{R}_1$, $\boxed{R}_2$, and $\boxed{R}_3$ with s_{M_i}) will express the same *intention*, and hence be functionally equivalent; (3) signs and behaviors associated with different and incompatible global mediation processes (here $\boxed{S}_2$ and $\boxed{S}_3$ as well as $\boxed{R}_2$ and $\boxed{R}_3$) will necessarily be *ambiguous* as their significance (in comprehending) and as to their intention (in expressing). For language as well as other behavior, differentiation of the effects of signs upon dependent

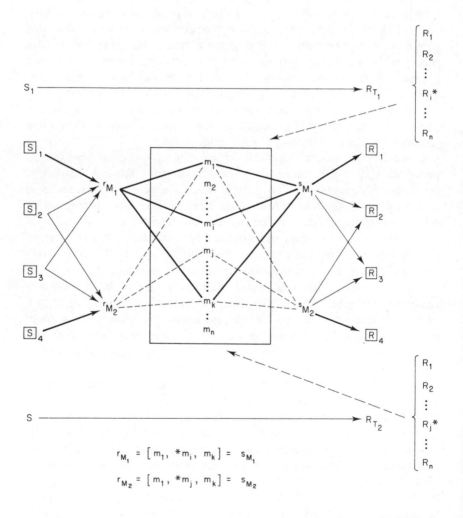

Figure 3. *The componential nature of representational mediation processes*

behaviors ((1) above), functional equivalences among signs as well as behaviors ((2) above), and ambiguities of both signs and behaviors ((3) above) are precisely the phenomena that require postulation of central mediating processes having the functional properties of $r_M = [m_1, m_2, \ldots m_i \ldots m_n] = s_M$. The two mediation processes displayed in componential terms at the bottom of Figure 3 are *distinct as wholes* because their derivational histories are from *different* significate-behavior relations, $S_1 \rightarrow R_{T_1}$, vs. $S_2 \rightarrow R_{T_2}$, as shown by the dashed R_T - - - $\rightarrow r_m$ arrows.

Another paradigmatic type of experiment — conducted by Lawrence (1949, 1950) with the humble rat as subject, and entitled 'Acquired Distinctiveness of Cues', but in principle applying equally to the child acquiring its phonemic and semantic systems — would seem to be in order at this point:

In a simple T-maze, with the upper 'arms' at the choice-point having both BLACK versus WHITE walls and CHAINS versus NO-CHAINS (soft curtain) distinguishing right from left sides (but with random right–left locations across trials), members of one group (of the four actually used) are rewarded with food-pellets at the end of the 'arm' if they choose the BLACK side and punished by sudden loss of support (being dropped into a net) at the end of the 'arm' if they choose the WHITE side. [Referring to Figure 3, BLACK would be $\boxed{S}_1$ (acquiring a 'hope' significance, distinguished by our m_i) and making $\boxed{R}_1$ (acquiring an 'approach' intention) while WHITE would be $\boxed{S}_4$ (acquiring a 'fear' significance, distinguished by our m_j) and making $\boxed{R}_4$ (acquiring an 'avoidance' intention).] For this group the CHAINS versus NO-CHAINS locations are random with respect to this differential reinforcement, and hence must become signs having ambiguous significances ($\boxed{S}_2$ and $\boxed{S}_3$) generating ambivalent, cancelling intentions toward behaving ($\boxed{R}_2$ and $\boxed{R}_3$). Being reasonably bright little fellows, these rats rapidly learn to get food and avoid falls. The crucial thing in this experiment is this: after this training experience, *they will learn to approach WHITE and avoid BLACK* (reversing the significance of the cues) *much more rapidly than to approach CHAINS and avoid NO-CHAINS* (shifting from originally irrelevant to now relevant cues).

In other words, in this paradigmatic situation (and many experiments bear this out), the humble rats have learned to 'pay attention' to those differences that make a difference in meaning — here anticipated reinforcement ('hope') versus anticipated punishment ('fear') — and to 'disregard' differences which do not make a difference in meaning. In this connection, it is interesting that, although many linguists and most psycholinguists assume that phonemic and semantic feature distinctions must be acquired via experience (given the obvious fact that languages differ in just *what* features will come to 'make a difference'), I have searched in vain for any theoretical explication of the crucial 'how' of such learning.

The present theory offers two interrelated functional principles here. The first is the basic sign-learning paradigm for global meanings (which is probably prior to the acquisition of distinctive features in both species and individual development): *when a percept which elicits no predictable pattern of behavior is repeatedly paired with another which does* (e.g. SIGHT OF COOKIE followed by EATING COOKIE), *the former will become a sign of the latter as its significant, by virtue of becoming associated with a mediation process* (r_M/s_M) *that distinctively represents the behavior produced by the significant* (R_T) *and therefore serves to mediate overt behavior appropriate to* ('taking account of') *the significate* (R_X, e.g. salivating and reaching for perceived COOKIE OBJECT). This principle suggests how, bit by bit, LAD acquires what he 'knows' about his world. The statement assumes that we are dealing with primary (usually perceptual) signs, but these in turn become *surrogate significates* — having 'prefabricated' mediation processes as predictable response patterns — in later linguistic sign learning (e.g. heard 'cookie' now paired with COOKIE percept). And, bit by bit, LAD acquires what he 'knows' (semantically) about his language.

The second is the *feature-learning paradigm,* which — once a componential conception of the mediation process replaces an undifferentiated global conception — is a logical extension of the sign-learning paradigm: *to the extent that differences in signs as stimuli* (perceptual or linguistic) *are associated with reciprocally antagonistic differences in behavior, the central representations of these differences* ($^+r_{mi}$ versus $^-r_{mi}$) *will become those semantic features which distinguish among the significances of signs* (first perceptual and later linguistic). The Lawrence research on 'Acquired Distinctiveness of Cues' above illustrates both global sign- and distinctive feature-learning paradigms — but are they feasible for human children? Moeser and colleagues (Moeser and Bregman 1972; Moeser and Olson 1974) report that children acquire an artifical language easiest when the 'words' (nonsense syllables) refer *consistently* to nonlinguistic entities in a perceptual–object reference field and the syntax of the 'sentences' is lawfully related to the semantic classes which differentiate the perceptual reference field.

THE INTIMATE PARALLELISM OF NONLINGUISTIC AND LINGUISTIC
COGNIZING

William James characterized the mental state of the new-born infant as
'a bloomin', buzzin' confusion'. He was thinking of the infant's
awareness of the external environment, but we could similarly characterize the infant's awareness via feedback of its own behavior as 'a
bumblin', fumblin' chaos'. How, in behavior theoretic terms, is order
brought out of perceptual confusion and behavioral chaos? On the
perceiving side, we may first note that the infant is born with certain
Gestaltlike dispositions — innate tendencies to perceptually group
stimulus elements having similar sensory *quality*, spatial *contiguity,
continuity* of contour, and *common fate* as organism and environment
move in relation to each other (thus the flesh-colored, spatially contiguous and contoured stimuli emanating from the infant's own chubby
hand as it moves as a whole in front of its eyes, and similarly the more
patterned stimulation of the mother's face). As Campbell (1966) astutely
observes, first perception and then language tend to follow Aristotle's
advice and 'cut nature at her joints'. And this advice is also followed on
the *behaving* side: the infant comes equipped with many reflexive
behavior units (like sucking to appropriate stimulations of the lips,
fixating and tracking figural visual stimuli with the eyes, and grasping
when the palms are suitably stimulated); these, along with an array of
vocalization patterns, are to become components in the complex
behavioral skills of childhood and adulthood.

Order out of chaos: integrations and representations

Given such innate 'building blocks', the mechanisms postulated in
Three-stage Neobehaviorism also operate to bring order out of chaos in
prelinguistic, and later linguistic, perceiving and behaving. Redundancies
in *icons* (stimulus patterns) and *motons* (response patterns) give rise,
through operation of the Integration Principle, to *percepts* ($\overline{s\text{-}s\text{-}s}$) and
programs ($\overline{r\text{-}r\text{-}r}$) — which can fairly be called perceptual and motor
skills, respectively; but these skills, in themselves, are *meaning-less* (or,
referring back to Figure 1, significance-less and intention-less). Still
further reduction of confusion is brought about via the association of
percepts with *significances* (r_M's) and of *intentions* (s_M's) with programs
for behaving, following the basic sign- and feature-learning principles
described above and represented symbolically in Figures 2 and 3; in this
way percepts and programs become *meaning-full* (or, referring to Figure

1 again, acquire significance and reflect intentionality, respectively). Prelinguistically, this development is evidenced by *appropriateness* in behaving toward the signs of things — the 'representing' or 'taking account of' criterion (thus reaching and salivating at the *sight* of the baby bottle, ducking the head when the *visual image* of an object increases rapidly in retinal size); linguistically, for example, this development is prerequisite for the shift from phones to phonemes (differences that make a difference in *meaning*).

The 'emic' principle in Neobehaviorism

Icons and percepts variable; significances constant. By virtue of the fact that both things and organisms are mobile with respect to each other, along with the fact that environmental contexts are changeable, *it follows that the distal signs of things* (and the icons and percepts they produce) *will be variable through many stimulus dimensions*. Thus MOTHER'S FACE will vary in retinal-image size as a function of distance from the child and in both brightness and hue as a function of time of day, from mid-day through twilight. However, since the $S \rightarrow R_T$ relation will hold regardless of these variations (eventually mother cuddles child), *there will be extension of the common mediator,* $r_M\text{-}\text{-}\text{-}\rightarrow s_M,$ *across such classes of distal signs* (via replicated sign-learning facilitated by stimulus generalization). Therefore, these will be percept differences which do *not* make a difference in meaning. *This common significance* (r_M) *is the constancy phenomenon* — familiar to psychologists — the 'thingness' and 'thatness', and in this example the 'who-ness', in perception. In Figure 4, the heavy convergent arrows relating a variable set of perceptual signs to a common significance (r_M) represent this constancy paradigm. In behavior-theoretic terms, this constitutes a *convergent hierarchy* and indicates the functional equivalence of the set of signs with respect to the common mediator — they all signify the same entity.

Intentions constant; programs and motons variable. The heavy divergent arrows relating the common *intention* (s_M) to a variable set of responses constitute a *divergent hierarchy* and indicate the functional equivalence of the set of different responses with respect to the common intention (these responses are *not* necessarily equivalent with respect to other stimulus antecedents, as will be seen momentarily). This is the behavior-theoretic representation of the fact that the same intention may be expressed in a diversity of ways (e.g. one may express an interpersonal 'recognition' intention by vocalizing 'Hi, there!', by an upward bobbing of the head plus smile, by a salutelike forward wave of the hand, and so on). It should be pointed out that this combination of convergent and divergent hierarchies of functionally equivalent classes of signs and behaviors with respect to common mediators is *not* a special case, but rather *the general case in cognizing.*

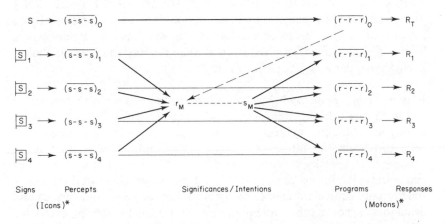

Signs   Percepts   Significances / Intentions   Programs   Responses
(Icons)*   (Motons)*

Figure 4.   *The 'emic' princple in behavior theory. *Not diagramed to reduce complexity*

Control and decision in Neobehaviorism. We are now in a position to show how these two types of hierarchies interact in adaptive behavior. Let $\boxed{S}_1$ be the perceptual sign of a desired APPLE on a table some distance away (small retinal image), $\boxed{S}_2$ its percept at a bit more than arm's length, $\boxed{S}_3$ at crooked arm's (normal inspection) distance, and $\boxed{S}_4$ at a few inches from the face (very large retinal image); correspondingly, let R_1 be a locomotor response of approaching, R_2 a response of reaching for, R_3 a response of grasping, and R_4 a response of mouth-opening and biting. Now note that each of the *percepts* ($\overline{s\text{-}s\text{-}s}_1$ through $\overline{s\text{-}s\text{-}s}_4$) is associated *both* with the common 'apple' significance (the 'thatness') *and* with the distinctive response appropriate to the distance of an object having the real size of an APPLE-object (the 'thereness'). Both of these associations are crucial for effective behavior (no one in his right mind 'reaches for' the source of a percept signifying A RED-HOT COAL or 'bites at' the percept of an APPLE on a table six feet away).

The *convergence* of the distinctive percepts (s-s-s's) plus the common 'apple-getting' intention (s_M) upon alternative responses (R's) determines the smooth sequencing of the observed behavioral act[3] —

locomoting toward the distant APPLE (R₁), reaching for it when almost near enough (R₂), grasping it and bringing it to crooked arm's distance (R₃) (perhaps inspecting it briefly for possible bugginess!), and only then initiating a biting response (R₄). This is what I mean by *control* in Neobehaviorism. On the other hand, *divergence* among alternative responses — either different meanings (r_M's), e.g. HOT COAL versus APPLE, RIPE versus ROTTEN APPLE, HARD APPLE versus SOFT TOMATO, or different instrumental responses (R's), as here — always requires *decision*. In Neobehaviorism, as in Classical Behaviorism, 'decision' is a probabilistic function of the numbers and weights (habit-strengths) of convergent associations.

Why an 'emic' principle? Just as the emic principle was the conceptual 'breakthrough' that made a science of linguistics possible, so I think an analogous principle makes Neobehaviorism feasible as a science of behavior, including language behavior. Not only does it provide an answer to Chomsky's critique (1959) of Skinner on the matter of inadequate definitions of 'stimulus' and 'response' (here defined as the functionally equivalent classes of signs having the same significance and behaviors expressing the same intention), but it further demonstrates the intimate parallelism between nonlinguistic and linguistic cognizing. Just as classes of physically different phones (as received) 'converge' upon common phonemes (differences in sound that make a difference in meaning) and these 'diverge' into classes of contextually determined phones (as produced) — and similarly for morphs to morphemes and most relevantly semes to sememes — so do classes of signs 'converge' upon common meanings (in comprehending) and these 'diverge' into classes of contextually determined behaviors (in expressing).

But more than this, one can claim that there is a *syntax of behaving* just as there is a syntax of talking — and the former is earlier in development. For a child to make biting, then grasping, then reaching responses in that order (all in thin air) as he approaches the desired apple would be just as 'ungrammatical' as it would have been for Caesar to announce '*Vici, vidi, veni*'! And note the strangeness of **he ate the apple, grabbed the apple, and opened the cupboard* as compared with the naturalness of *he opened the cupboard, grabbed the apple, and ate the apple*. There is increasing evidence that conjoined clauses ordered in terms of naturalness (i.e. in orders corresponding to prelinguistic ex-periencing of related events) are easier to process than when ordered otherwise. There is also a *semantics of perceiving* just as there is a semantics of word-combining in sentencing — and again, the former is earlier in development. The child reaches for a BALL OF BLACK

THREAD on the floor and suddenly it spreads and starts moving — a sudden shift to SPIDER-object meaning occurs, along with a radical shift in programs for behaving!

The 'ambiguity' principle in behavior theory

Icons and percepts constant; significances variable. The signs discussed above and diagrammed in Figure 4 are *unambiguous*; one significance–intention mediation process has very high probability for all members of the constancy set of signs and all other alternatives have negligible probability. Figure 5 represents in behavior-theoretic symbols the converse situation: a single sign ($\boxed{S}_Y$),[4] and its resultant icon and percept (ṡ, ṡ, ṡ$_Y$ and $\overline{s\text{-}s\text{-}s}_Y$, sketched in here for reasons that will become apparent) is associated with a divergent set of significances — and hence is *ambiguous* in meaning. This is the condition for *perceptual homonymy*. Just as most words in a language are to some degree polysemous (including homonymy) — *he went to the BANK, it was a LIGHT one, the SHOOTING of the hunters was terrible* — so too are most nonlinguistic signs polysemous, not only the familiar ambiguous figures like the Necker Cube, but also the meanings of facial expressions of men in a picket-line.

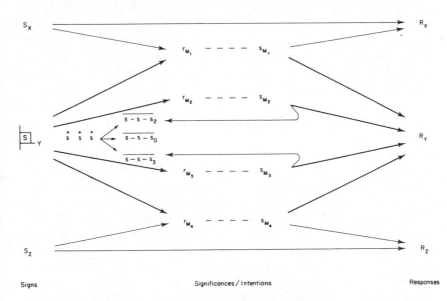

Signs   Significances / Intentions   Responses

Figure 5.   *The 'ambiguity' principle in behavior theory*

Intentions variable; programs and motons constant. On the other side of this behavioral coin (the right side of Figure 5) we have represented the fact that observed communicative behaviors may be ambiguous as to the intention behind them — to the listener/recipient, of course, not the speaker/initiator. Thus, linguistically, 'he was a *Colt* until this year, but now he's a *Bear*' as spoken is quite ambiguous (to a non-'sportsaholic', at least!) and the intention behind '*can* you open the window?' is ambiguous as to being a request or an inquiry about the listener's physical competence; nonlinguistically, the combination of a tight-lipped smile with the shaking of a fisted hand is ambiguous as to whether the intent is to threaten or to express successful completion of some effortful task.

The disambiguation of perceptual and linguistic ambiguities. Given the ubiquity of ambiguity for signs in both linguistic and nonlinguistic channels, why aren't we hopelessly ambiguated most of the time? As indicated by the S_X and S_Z in Figure 5, potentially ambiguous signs (and responses by others) are nearly always *disambiguated by other contextual signs* — which may be either perceptual or linguistic in their relations to the signs and responses in question: *linguistic/linguistic — he ROWED to the bank, it was a light PLAY,* and *the shooting of the hunters BY THE NATIVES was terrible* are essentially unambiguous; *perceptual/linguistic* — when my friend exclaims 'duck!' in a barnyard, I'm likely to respond by looking around for that bird, but passing by a busy sandlot baseball field I'm likely to 'duck' my head; *linguistic/perceptual* — as is notoriously the case on television, interpretations of facial expressions (e.g. of the men in the picket-line) can be easily modulated from 'rage' to 'determination' by the parallel commentary of an announcer; *perceptual/perceptual* — the tight-lipped smile plus shaking of a fisted hand *by a boxer* will be interpreted as 'threat' just before the fight but as 'prideful satisfaction' just after his winning it.

Perceptual patterns vary in their degrees of ambiguity, as of course do linguistic forms, from the near-infinite potential meanings of nonsense signs to completely unambiguous single-meaning signs (see Osgood 1953, Chapter 5). For most of my students, the two forms in Figure 6-A approach infinite ambiguity (LOOK BEFORE READING FURTHER!): interestingly, when I say of A(1) 'this is a fat janitress washing the floor, as seen from behind' and then of A (2) 'this is a soldier and his dog passing by a hole in a picket fence', they find it almost impossible to interpret them any *other* way — as if one $\rightarrow r_M$ had suddenly shot out to a probability of 1.00! Figure 6-B is a sketch of the kinephantoscope used by Miles (1931) to generate a large number of alternative perceptual meanings of roughly equal strength: as the 'fan', brightly illuminated from behind, revolves, its sharply etched shadow may be reported as 'pirouetting' (clockwise or counter-clockwise), then suddenly as 'arms stretching out and pulling in', then as 'arms flapping in front' (or in back), as 'turning sideways and then coming back', and so forth. Significantly, when the experimenter gives the above quotes as *linguistic suggestions*, the observer finds it almost impossible to inhibit shifting to what he is told to perceive.

Figure 6-C(1) is one of the best-known, reversible figure–ground displays, with 'vase' and 'identical twins looking at each other' as the highest probability alternatives (although there are others — e.g. 'two bosomy ladies holding a conversation beneath a balcony'!): as shown in C(2) and C(3), the probability and persistence of the 'vase' versus 'twins' meanings can easily be influenced by adding contextual cues (the S_X vs. S_Z in Figure 5). Figure 6-D shows (1) the famous Necker Cube, which in two-dimensional outline form keeps flipping back and forth between (2) the 'from the side' and (3) the 'from above' solid percept integrations: there are studies demonstrating that *satiation* on one of the solid forms inhibits that meaning of the subsequently shown ambiguous two-dimensional form, the other alternative typically appearing first and persisting for longer periods than is the case for control subjects: As far as I know, the most interesting experiment here remains to be done — to see if one can satiate ambiguous *percepts* similarly with *words* (e.g. repeating 'block' versus 'tower' here, or 'vase' versus 'twins' above); positive results would strongly support the case for an 'intimate parallel' between nonlinguistic and linguistic processing.

The effect of meaning upon salience in perception and language. The final sequence in Figure 6-E illustrates what Gestalt psychologists have discussed as the competition between 'restraining' (peripheral) and 'cohesive' (central) forces in determining what one perceives; in my terms this would be competition of *icons* (mirrors of *what is*) and *meanings* (mirrors of *what is signified*) in the determination of *percepts* (mirrors of *what ought to be*). In the ordinary phi-phenomenon, if two spatially separated lights go on and off alternately at an appropriate rate, they are perceived as a single light moving back and forth. Brown and Voth (1937) developed an apparatus in which two *pairs* of lights are alternately flashed, each pair being at the ends of two bars whose angular relation can be varied (see Osgood 1953: 206–208): when the bars are at right angles to each other, E(1), and hence the distances among them being equal, the observer is equally likely to see *either* a single bar 'tilting' vertically (like a baton held upright in the hand) or 'teetering'

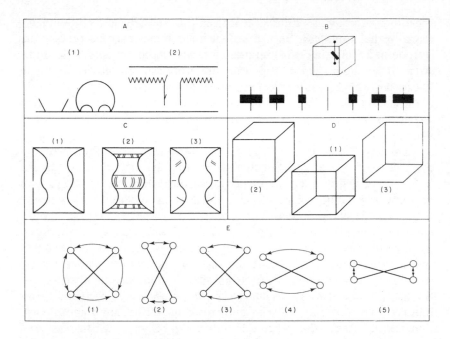

Figure 6. *Some perceptual ambiguities and their disambiguation*

horizontally (like a seesaw); when an observer is first shown the display with the lights vertically aligned, E(2), he *always* sees a rapid 'tilting'; as the angle between the bars is gradually increased, the observer *persists* in seeing 'tilting' *through* the equi-distance 90° angle, E(3), and well past it, E(4) — holding on to his existing perceptual interpretation — until at some point, E(5), he suddenly shifts to seeing a rapid horizontal 'teetering' (and the same happens if we go in the opposite direction, of course).

My neobehavioristic interpretation of this phenomenon would be that the pattern of icons (ṡ, ṡ, ṡ)'s set up by the stimulations of E(2) yield a shifting pattern of percepts ($\overline{\text{s-s-s}}$)'s which has the unambiguous significance (r_{M_2}) of A BAR TILTING BACK AND FORTH; as the angle passes through and well beyond 90°, the persisting *feedback from this meaning* (s_{M_2}) — see the feedback arrows in Figure 5 — maintains the salience of this percept (s-s-s)$_2$ despite its increasing deviance from the iconic input, until the discrepancy becomes too great (mirror of *what is* versus mirror of *what ought to be*!) — and there is the sudden shift *in meaning* as well as in percept to A BAR RAPIDLY TEETERING BACK AND FORTH.

What about meaning and salience in language behavior? Salience of visual–verbal units can be indexed by their tachistoscopic thresholds. Osgood and Hoosain (1974) reported a series of experiments designed to demonstrate the salience of words and wordlike larger units (having distinctive meanings as wholes) as compared with other units:

1. Monosyllabic words (*salt, mend*, etc.) had significantly lower thresholds than monosyllabic morphemes having much higher frequencies of visual usage (*-sult, -ment*), and the same held for multisyllabic words (*dashing, harmony*, etc.) and nonwords (*famness, henette*);

2. Wordlike nominal compounds (*stock market, stumbling block, real estate*, etc.) had significantly lower thresholds than ordinary noun phrases (*street market, copper block, city estate*) but the latter had only slightly lower threshold than nonsense compounds (*shade market, sympathy block, post estate*);

3. Most significantly for present concerns, although prior presentation of both ordinary noun phrases and nonsense compounds lowered the subsequently tested thresholds for their single constituent words markedly, prior presentation of *nominal compounds* did not lower thresholds for *their* constituent words at all — the word-forms *stumbling* and *block* were presented N times *physically* but they did not have the same meaning in the compound *stumbling block*, hence the feedback ($s_M \to s$-s-s) was not that associated in prior experience with tuning up either *stumbling* or *block* percepts.

THE 'DEEP' COGNITIVE SYSTEM SHARED BY THINGS AND WORDS

In introducing the Discussion section of my 'Where Do Sentences Come From?' in the volume on semantics edited by Steinberg and Jakobovits (Osgood 1971), I stressed the complete insufficiency (as an answer to this question for a performance theory) of the symbol S that tops every 'tree' in a generative grammar. S represents the set of all grammatical sentences in language L that can be generated by successive application of the re-write rules of that language; however, this fails to meet the pragmatic criterion that sentences produced be appropriate to contextual conditions — humans don't produce sentences *ad libitum*. The reason is that such a grammar does not, *and need not* (being a *post hoc* description), provide any account of selection among alternative re-write rules possible at each node in a 'tree' — including, crucially, final selections from the lexicon. Which is not, of course, to say that there are no problems for linguistic theory *per se:* for example, whenever one sentence (clause) is embedded in another, superordinate S_1 obviously constrains subordinate S_2 to some subset of all grammatical sentences in language L (e.g. *it is a fact that* . . . permits . . . *the water is hot*, but rules out . . . *water the lawn!* or . . . *is the water hot?*). It is also obvious *psycho*linguistically that for most illocutionary sentences the speaker must have cognized S_2 (e.g. . . . *Mary is pregnant*) before he can select among (e.g. *I know (think, doubt, pretend) that)* for S_1!

The semantic nature of the shared cognitive system

Function Notion IV in my developing performance theory of cognizing and sentencing (*Toward an Abstract Performance Grammar*, in preparation) states that there are two basic types of relations among perceived entities in prelinguistic experience: Stative Relations [M$_1$ (Figure) - - ($^+$Stable) - - > M$_2$ (Ground)] and Action Relations (M$_1$ (Source) - - ($^-$Stable) - - > M$_2$ (Recipient)], with both entities and relations being defined semantically. Donning one's 'booties' of early childhood, it seems intuitively obvious that the Figures-of-States will usually be more salient psychologically than the Grounds-of-States (e.g. perceiving CAT IS ON PILLOW BY WINDOW but not WINDOW IS BY PILLOW UNDER CAT, and ditto for later sentencings) and that the Sources-of-Actions will be more salient than the Recipients-of-Actions (e.g. RABBIT RAN INTO BUSHES but not BUSHES 'RECEIVED' RABBIT, and similarly for more natural Active versus Passive sentencings).

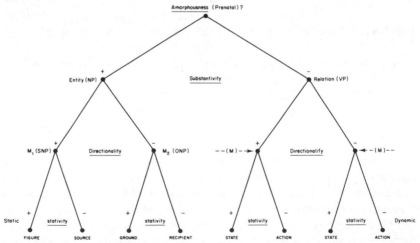

Figure 7. *A semantic characterization of the constituent structures of simple cognitions*

I have proposed a *semantic characterization* of the most basic syntactic distinctions made for simple (single-clause) sentences, a characterization which holds equivalently for nonlinguistic cognizings. As diagrammed in Figure 7 — without any claims as to whether these basic semantic distinctions are innate or acquired (probably both bases are involved) — we begin with complete semantic *Amorphousness* (prenatal state?). The three most primitive semantic (syntactic) features are postulated to be $\pm$*Substantivity* (distinguishing 'thinglike' Entities ($+$) from non-'thing-like' Relations ($-$)), $\pm$*Directionality* (distinguishing $+M_1$'s (SNPs) from $^-M_2$'s (ONPs) as Entities, on the one hand, and 'naturally' directed $^+- - (M) - ->$'s from 'unnaturally' directed $^-<- - (M) - -$'s Relations (VPs), on the other), and $\pm$*Stativity* (distinguishing the components of $^+$Stative Relations, FIGURE - STATE - GROUND, from those of $^-$Stative (Action) Relations, SOURCE - ACTION - RECIPIENT).

These very primitive features are only the beginnings of complex human semantic systems, of course, but they do imply a presumably universal Naturalness Principle for human cognizing and sentencing (e.g. that only a $^+$ $^+$ $^+$ M_1 related by a $^-$ $^+$ $^+$ $--$ (M) $-->$ to a $^+$ $^-$ $^+$ M_2 will be a 'natural' Stative Cognition and that a $^+$ $^-$ $^-$ M_2 related by a $^-$$^-$$^-$$<--$ (M) $--$ to a $^+$ $^+$ $^-$ M_1 will be an 'unnatural' Passive Action Cognition). It should be noted that this is a set-theoretic semantic system, hence akin to systems proposed by, e.g. Smith, Shoben and Rips (1974) and more recently by Tversky (1977). This Naturalness Principle also makes a very strong claim about human languages — namely, *that the prelinguistically based ordering of components in cognizing will be universally SVO* — a basis for sentencing we are presently testing cross-linguistically.

Evidence for the Naturalness Principle — priority of the perceptual channel

From thinging to wording. Even at the lexical level there is ample evidence that prelinguistic cognizing and categorizing of entities predetermines what Rosch et al. (1976) call 'basic objects' — naming categories whose members (1) have many perceptual features in common (e.g. *chairs* as compared with superordinate *furniture*), (2) are used by means of similar 'motor programs', (3) possess significantly similar shapes, and (4) can be identified from averaged shapes of exemplars. Experimentally, Rosch et al. have demonstrated that priming with such basic object names (e.g. *hammer*) facilitates detecting flashed pictures but priming with superordinates (e.g. *tool*) does not and that verification of a picture as being an instance of a just-previously named object was fastest (for both 'true' and 'false' reactions) for basic-level terms and slowest for subordinate (exemplar) terms, with superordinates falling in between. It would be expected that such 'basic object' names should be acquired earlier than either their superordinates or subordinates, and age-of-acquisition studies by Carroll and White (1973) have shown this to be generally the case. Along related lines, Potter and Faulconer (1975) have shown that deciding whether an object is in a given category such as 'furniture' or not takes significantly *less* time when a picture of it (e.g. CHAIR) than when its name (*chair*) is flashed tachistoscopically.

Naturalness in sentencing. Evidence for Naturalness in Simply Describing *simplex* cognitions, both Stative and Action perceptual relations, was overwhelming in the Osgood (1971) study: despite the grammatical availability of Ground - State - Figure sentencings (like *a plate is* holding *a ball, a spoon and a poker-chip*), these rarely occurred (equivalents of *a ball, a spoon and a poker-chip are on a plate* were given by 20 of the 26 adult subjects); despite the grammatical availability of ordinary passives (like *the tube was hit by the orange ball*), they rarely occurred (*the orange ball hit the tube* being given here by 21 of 26 subjects). Again donning the 'booties' of early childhood, it seems obvious that, when a preverbal child perceives a prototypical transfer event, the so-called Direct Object is cognitively a part of relation and the so-called Indirect Object is the 'real' Object or Recipient — as when little Suzie sees [BIG BROTHER/GIVES-THE-BALL-TO /BIG-SISTER]; in a paper titled 'Will the Real Direct Object in Bitransitive Sentences Please Stand Up', Osgood and Tanz (1977) tested this 'naturalness' prediction, both cross-linguistically and with American-English adults in several psycholinguistic experiments, with satisfyingly positive results. A recent paper by Yau (1977) makes the interesting point that, although sign languages may display either SOV or SVO *temporal* ordering of signings, the *spatial* ordering of the former is also likely to be SVO — with S and O signed with spatial separation *and then V* (the Relation) *signed in the space between them.*

The Naturalness Principle also makes certain predictions about the ordering of complex cognitions, i.e. of clauses in conjoined sentences — namely, that where there is a natural order in prelinguistic experience with complex events, this ordering in sentencing will be either required or preferred. Thus, for the causal mode, *it was raining and John got wet* but certainly not *John got wet and it was raining*, and note the 'mind-bogglingness' of *Mary went to bed and got undressed!* Although the use of adverbial substitutes for basic *ands* and *buts* (which must be centered) makes possible clause permutation, our principle must predict that centered adverbials that maintain natural clause order will be easiest to process (*Mary put on her prettiest dress BEFORE she went to the party*) and that preposed adverbials requiring unnatural order will be the most difficult (*BEFORE John went to the party he took a shower*). Opačić (1973) confirmed this (and finer predictions), but also found, for five different modes of conjoining, that where two orders are possible, one Natural (N) and the other Unnatural (U), NN (Natural-given and Natural-retained) had the shortest processing times, UN were next easiest (i.e. where the subject *restores* the Natural order), UU came next (literal recall of Unnatural order as given) and NU (shifting from Natural *to* Unnatural ordering) was the rarest and most time-consuming.

Evidence for interaction between perceptual and linguistic channels

Casual (but convincing) observations. Imagine how flabbergasted one would be if, while riding up in an elevator, the only other occupant were to suddenly say 'Pick it up!'. Commands of this sort imply some appropriate nonlinguistic context (a dropped banana peel, say!). Similarly, pointings, lookings, head-bobbings and the like normally accompany conversings — often substituting for phrases ('I could SLITTING MOTION ACROSS THROAT the bastard!') or even whole clauses ('They've got our car back in the shop again, so PRAYERFUL HAND POSTURE PLUS EYES LOOKING HEAVENWARD). It is also significant that nonlinguistic gestures typically parallel linguistic stress ('I will not/HAND BROUGHT DOWN SHARPLY wear that ridiculous tie!') and appear utterly ludicrous if displaced from stress points ('I will not wear that ridiculous tie/SAME GESTURE!'). In a paper titled 'The Relationship of Verbal and Nonverbal Communication', Key (1974b) provides many illustrations of such interactions, and I'm sure other papers in this volume will elaborate on this theme.

Redundancy deletion provides further evidence for this intimate interaction. Although anaphoric pronouns (*the three little bearded old men* becoming simply *they* in later sentencings), reflexives and quasi-reflexives (*John cut himself; one black ball hit another*) and other such linguistic devices serve to reduce redundancy, nonlinguistic devices often serve the same purpose — upon asking my wife where our poodle Pierre is during a Christmas shopping spree, she simply smiles and points to him on Santa's lap! Morgan (1975) provides many illustrations of how, in ordinary conversations, one uses the other's utterances as bases for redundancy deletion — example (p. 294), PERSON A 'What does Trick eat for breakfast?'; PERSON B 'Bananas.' — and Morgan's paper (titled 'Some Interactions of Syntax and Pragmatics') nicely illustrates the recent shift of interest on the part of many linguists away from studying sentences-in-isolation toward studying sentences-in-context. The dependence of listeners on nonlinguistic context for selecting among literal or nonliteral intentions of speakers provides a nice illustration here: as written, out-of-context, *can you take Pierre out for a walk*? is ambiguous as to the intent of the 'speaker' — is it a literal inquiry as to competence or an indirect request?; when I ask this of my wife when she's down with a bad cold, *can you* is probabilistically interpreted as *are you able to*, but when she's feeling fine and knows I'm very busy preparing a lecture, *can you* is interpreted as *please*.

Some experimental evidence. Early studies by the late Theodore Karwoski and his associates, including myself as an undergraduate at Dartmouth (e.g. Karwoski, Odbert and Osgood 1942), made it clear that auditory–visual–verbal *synesthesia* is not a freak phenomenon in people whose 'sensory wires are crossed', but rather a fundamental characteristic of human thinking, involving lawful translations from one modality to another along dimensions made parallel in cognizing — auditory LOUD going with visual NEAR rather than FAR (and similarly for the words *near* and *far*), auditory TREBLE being visually UP and BASS being DOWN (as well as verbally *high* and *low*). In a paper titled 'The Cross-cultural Generality of Visual–Verbal Synesthetic Tendencies' (Osgood, 1960), I reported data indicating that — when Anglo, Navajo, Mexican-Spanish, and Japanese subjects 'rated' words like *happy, lazy, excitement, weak, grey*, etc., by simply pointing to binary visual alternatives on cards (e.g. a COLORFUL versus a COLORLESS design, a BLUNT versus a SHARP form, a LIGHT versus a DARK circle, a VERTICAL versus a HORIZONTAL line, a LARGE versus a SMALL circle, and so forth) — there is high cross-cultural agreement on visual–verbal 'metaphors'; *happy* is 'universally' COLORFUL, LIGHT (rather than DARK), and LARGE, but *weak* is THIN, LIGHT (rather than DARK), HAZY (rather than CLEAR) and CROOKED (rather than STRAIGHT).

Using a somewhat modified version of this binary pictorial task, Sheinkopf (1970) was able to demonstrate that anomic aphasics perform very much like normals — pointing appropriately to the visual alternatives when given the test words — despite their manifest difficulties in naming and word-finding (here, they were unable to even describe the visual forms). There are other subject populations, of course, for whom a valid Graphic Differential — valid in the sense of yielding semantic profiles correlating with those obtained with the usual verbal Semantic

Differential — would be a most useful instrument, for example, nonliterates, normal members of illiterate cultures and children younger than six years. After much testing and pruning of visual polarities used in earlier studies, French (1977) has come up with a 15-scale (5 for each affective factor, Evaluation, Potency and Activity) Graphic Differential which seems to satisfy this requirement: 60 concepts (both abstract and concrete) were rated on both GD and SD scales by 30 subjects, the GD/SD correlations being 0.98 on E, 0.77 on P, and 0.67 on A. A theoretically (if not methodologically) related study is reported by Potter, Valian and Faulconer (1977): 96 spoken sentences were each immediately followed by either a word or a drawing probe, with the subjects to decide whether or not the probe was related to the meaning of the sentence; response times did not differ for the types of probes, and the authors conclude that '. . . the meaning of a sentence or a probe is not represented in a modality-specific format but in an abstract conceptual format . . . [this representation being] directly accessible from either verbal or pictorial stimuli (1)'.

Evidence for parallel processing across channels

Ordinary communicative competences. The ordinariest of human communicative abilities — and those most often used in one form or other in research with young children — are Simply Describing and Simply Acting Out, and both involve parallel processing of semantic information in the shared cognitive system. In Simply Describing, the meanings of nonlinguistic perceived states and events must be encoded 'up' into this 'deep' semantic system (comprehension) and then these cognitions be decoded 'down' into semantically equivalent verbal expressions (production); in Simply Acting Out, the meanings of linguistic words and sentences must be encoded into the same semantic system (comprehension) and then these cognitions be decoded out into nonlinguistic behavioral operations upon appropriate entities in the environment (production). A speaker's everyday reportings ('Hey! There's a great big, wolf-like dog on the lawn!') and directings ('The book you want is the thick red one on the third shelf.') are instances of Simply Describing — as are the rapid-fire descriptions of a sports announcer. A listener's behaving appropriately to everyday commands ('Get me the big pliers on the tool shelf in the cellar!') and requests ('Please pass me the gravy bowl.') are instances of Simply Acting Out. But my favorite example is this: two co-eds, walking along a campus path, see a third girl approaching with a *mini*-mini-skirt on; after she has passed, one says to the other, 'She also dyes her hair!'. The use of anaphoric *she* implies a prior cognition (which could only be perception-based) and the *also* identifies it as something like [THAT GAL / IS WEARING / A REALLY SHORT SKIRT].

Undoubtedly the most basic competence, as well as earliest in individual human development, is *communication of affect* (feeling), and here we have extensive evidence for sharing of the same primitive semantic system. It was M. Brewster Smith who first, in 1960, pointed out to me the essential identity of the factors (Evaluation, Potency and Activity) we were finding for American-English speakers using the Semantic Differential to Wundt's three dimensions of feeling (Pleasantness, Tension and Excitement); Schlosberg in 1954 had named them Pleasantness/Unpleasantness, Attention/Rejection, and Activation/Sleep, and in a paper of my own (based on labeling of posed live expressions in a demonstration/experiment at Yale in the early 1940s) I was to name the same three factors Pleasant/Unpleasant (E), Controlled/Uncontrolled (P), and Activated/Unactivated (A) — see Osgood (1966) for details. Over the past near-20 years our Center for Comparative Psycholinguistics has collected data from (now) 30 language–culture communities around the world, using comparable SD instruments, and the evidence for universality of the E-P-A affective meaning system is impressive (see Osgood, May and Miron 1975). Reciprocal facial gesturing by speakers and listeners is the most common parallelism of nonlinguistic and linguistic channels — smiling with the happy utterances, looking astonished with the surprising utterances, looking sorrowful with the sad utterances — and it is quite unsettling in ordinary conversation if either speaker or listener 'dead-pans' it (interestingly, one of the clearest clinical signs of abnormal dissociation is inappropriateness of facial/verbal expression pairings).

Extraordinary parallel processing in psycholinguistic experiments. Early research reported in Osgood, Suci and Tannenbaum (1957:275–284) had demonstrated that the E-P-A values of phrasal adjective-noun combinations (e.g. *shy secretary, treacherous nurse, breezy husband*) were predictable to a fairly high degree from the measured affective meanings of their single-word components via the congruity formula of Osgood and Tannenbaum. Hastorf, Osgood and Ono (1966) found that the affective meanings of different posed facial expressions of an actor (CEO sans mustache!), when fused in a stereoscope, could also be predicted from the meanings of the separate expressions; Ono, Hastorf and Osgood (1966), using the same posed facial expressions, were able to show that the more incongruent the expressions paired in the stereoscope, the greater the likelihood of the viewer experiencing binocular rivalry (e.g. COMPLACENCY/RAGE yielding more rivalry than DISMAY/REPUGNANCE). In his doctoral thesis Cuçeloĝlu (1967) used 60 'outline faces' (all combinations of four eyebrow types, three eye types, and five mouth types), these 'faces' being rated for degrees of likeness to 40 emotion-names by high school subjects in American, Japanese and Turkish cultures; factor analyses in all three groups yielded Pleasantness, Activation and Control as the three dominant factors, with MOUTH CURVED UP versus MOUTH CURVED DOWN, with WIDE-OPEN versus CLOSED EYES and with DOWNWARD-BENT (.\/.) versus UPWARD-BENT (/. .\) EYEBROWS as the most distinctive facial features for E, A and P respectively. Most recently (as part of his doctoral thesis), Hoosain (1977) has demonstrated both that conjoining congruent 'outline faces' (with 'and') takes less time than conjoining incongruent ones (with 'but') and that conjoining 'faces' with sentences (e.g. a SMILING, DOWN-TURNED EYEBROWS, WIDE-OPEN-EYED face with either 'I passed the exam' or 'I failed the exam') is much faster for congruent than for incongruent pairs — all consistent with earlier Hoosain studies with conjoined sentences.

There have been many psycholinguistic experiments in recent years where comparative parallel processing of cognitions in linguistic and perceptual channels has been required — one well-known example being the paper by Chase and H. Clark titled 'Mental Operations in the Comparison of Sentences and Pictures' (1972), where a sentence like 'the star is below the circle' must be verified against a picture as either 'true' or 'false'. Potter (1975) has shown that when viewers briefly glimpse pictures presented at rates up to eight per second, they recognize a target picture in the flashed sequence as accurately, and almost as rapidly, when they are only given the 'basic object' name (e.g. *a boat*) as when they have seen the picture itself in advance. Finally, I must note a recent study on 'modeling semantic memory' by Rosenberg and Simon (1977): when subjects were presented with items in different modalities (including a pictures-and-sentences condition) and subsequently given items (either identical or semantically similar) and asked if the latter were identical with the former, they frequently accepted items semantically consistent; and the authors conclude — most gratifyingly! — as follows: 'The results can be explained by the hypothesis that subjects integrate information across modalities into a single underlying semantic representation. A computer model, embodying this hypothesis, made predictions in close agreement with the data.'

Inescapable conclusions

The evidence summarized in this concluding section — for dependence of linguistic cognizing on prior cognizing in the perceptual channel at all levels, and for intimate interactions between these channels in both ordinary communication and diverse experimental situations as well for parallel processing in both channels in both ordinary communicative competences and extraordinary psycholinguistic experiments — leads back to the assumptions I made near the beginning of this paper, but now as inescapable conclusions: (1) that the 'deep' cognitive system is semantic in nature, (2) that it is shared by both nonlinguistic (perceptual) and linguistic information-processing channels, and (3) that sentencing in ordinary communication is always context-dependent. I would view the shift in recent years of linguists toward Functionalism and Pragmatics as steps toward developing *linguistic theories of performance*. However, there is little in this recent philosophical, linguistic and psycholinguistic (for that matter) literature that offers any *theory* of how nonlinguistic signs and contextual cognitions can have meanings and interact with language-based cognitions. Such a theory is central to the *Toward an Abstract Performance Grammar* I am working on (to be titled *Lectures on Language Performance*).

NOTES

1. See Figure 2 and the accompanying text for a paradigmatic case of such analysis. Since the process symbolized by r_M - - -> s_M is a single (albeit complex) central event — only *functionally* r and s respectively — I represent mediator components here simply as m's.
2. I use CAPS in text when I am referring to nonlinguistic, perceptual signs and events, and the usual *italics* when referring to linguistic signs and sentences (or quotes if vocal behavior is being specified).
3. Although I haven't added it to an already complicated diagram, sensory feedbacks from prior movements are also convergently operative here.
4. Here, and in Figure 5, I deliberately use an ambiguous symbol, $\boxed{S}_Y$, combining symbols for perceptual ($\boxed{S}$) signs and linguistic signs ($\boxed{S}$), to emphasize the 'intimate parallelism' of information processing in these two channels.

PART IV

Acquisition of Communicative Behavior

EDWARD C. TRONICK, HEIDELISE ALS, and
T. BERRY BRAZELTON[1]

The Infant's Communicative Competencies and the Achievement of Intersubjectivity

Human communication is a process in which message displays are interchanged by the communicants. These messages have two aspects. A content aspect and a regulatory aspect. The content of the message may refer to any event or object. The regulatory aspect of a signal contains information about a communicant's acceptance, rejection, or modification of the current state of the reaction. The content portion is similar to what Watzlawick et al. (1967) call the report aspect of a message and the regulatory portion is similar to what they call the command aspect. The regulatory aspect of behavioral signals is a meta-communication: a communication about a communication.

It is now recognized that the ability to communicate about the state of a communicative exchange is the necessary condition for successful (referential) communication to occur (Habermas 1969; Ryan 1974; Bruner 1975). This is the pragmatic basis of all communication as contrasted to the more limited syntactic or semantic bases of linguistic communication. Pragmatics refers to how two communicants behave in a fashion that allows for the exchange of messages. Its focus is not on grammar but rather on interaction as a form of communicative skill (Kaye in press; Ryan 1974).

In our work we have chosen to study the development of infant communicative competencies and the structure of infant–adult face-to-face communications (Brazelton et al. 1975; Tronick et al. 1977b; Tronick et al. 1978). This communicative system is unique as contrasted to adult–adult interactions. Since neither language nor objects are incorporated into it, it does not yet contain a referential or content function. Rather, it appears that the messages exchanged in the interaction are purely regulatory in that they refer primarily to the ongoing state of the interaction. In that sense the communication is its own content; the messages refer only to the communication process.

This raises the question as to what communicative competencies the infant has for regulating mutuality. Three initial capacities seem to be required for achieving a state of intersubjectivity (Bruner 1971; Lashley 1951). First, there must be organized units of behavior that convey the messages of the infant. In the prespeech child these messages are not carried by words, but by the expressive modalities of face, voice, eye, body, head, and hand. Second, there must be the arousal of an intention or goal in the presence of an appropriate object which will govern the selection of messages and the ongoing directionality of the interchange. Third, a syntax or set of rules is required that orders the sequence of constituent expressive behaviors. These capacities are required for any skilled performance although the constituent units would be different but communication requires additional capacities. Such a jointly regulated activity requires coordination between the two participants. Both communicants have to *share* the meaning of the constituent expressive behaviors, *share* a syntax that governs their exchange of messages, and then *share* an intention to engage in the interchange. This is the problem of intersubjectivity (Tronick et al. 1978; Tronick and Brazelton in press; Trevarthen 1977).

An understanding of these pragmatic communicative competencies of the child requires detailed description of what goes on in face-to-face infant–adult interactions. Ryan (1974) has argued that what is needed to understand infant communicative capacities is an 'analysis of the development of different forms of intentional behavior in the child, combined with detailed descriptions of the preverbal dialogues and other reciprocal interchanges that adults and children participate in.' The descriptive system presented here is an attempt to do that. It segments the interaction in expressive units called Monadic phases. From this segmentation we hope to be able to characterize the structure of such interactions and to thus gain a better understanding of infant abilities.

The Monadic phases are assumed to be the basic structural units of the interaction. They attempt to describe the full range of infant and adult behavior and to allow for the analysis of the dynamic relations between the infant's and the adult's behavior.

Briefly, the system of describing the interaction involves three steps. The first is to videotape a period of face-to-face interaction between an infant and an adult. The second step is to categorize each expressive behavior of the participants on a second-by-second basis from the videotape. The third step is to transform the combinations of expressive behaviors into Monadic phases. The Monadic phases are considered to be the structural units of the interaction and analysis of the interaction is then carried out on them.

METHODOLOGY

Subjects: The subjects were five infant–mother pairs. The infants ranged in age from 80 to 92 days of age. Three of the infants were boys, two were girls. The pairs were part of a larger study of social development that began during the newborn period.

Procedure: Each pair came to the laboratory for a recording of three minutes of face-to-face interaction. The mother was simply instructed to play with her baby. Videotaping is carried out in a laboratory setting (see Figure 1). The infant is placed in an infant seat that is set on a 30-inch table. The infant seat is surrounded on three sides by curtains to form an enclosed alcove which shields the infant from visual events. The adult comes from the side of the alcove and seats herself on a stool in front of the infant. Two video cameras are used. One camera is focused on the infant, the other on the mother. The outputs from the two cameras are fed through a special-effects generator, then through an electronic digital timer and then onto a single video tape recorder. The resulting output is a split-screen image with a frontal view of adult and infant each on one side of the image and the digital time displayed along the base of the image (see Figure 2). Scoring is done from the video recording. This allows for numerous reviews of the interaction at normal speed, in slow motion (1/7th normal speed) and by stop frame (up to 60 frames per second) with full resolution even when the tape is stopped. These options are available because of the use of a four-head video deck (Sanyo-1200) as opposed to the more typical video decks which only have two heads.

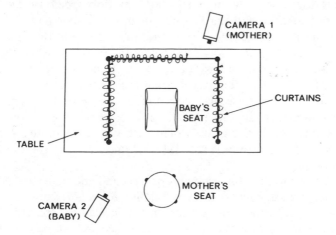

Figure 1. *Schematic view of the laboratory*

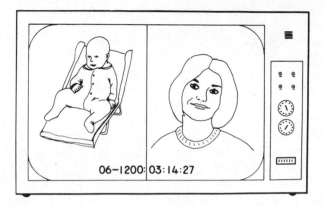

Figure 2.   *Split-screen video image*

Table 1 lists the categories of each of the expressive modalities scored. The infant modalities scored are facial expression, vocalization, eye direction, head position, and body position. The same modalities are scored for the adult with the additional category of specific handling of the infant. The categorizing of the behaviors is done by two observers as the tape runs at slow motion speed. Reliability is maintained at 90 percent absolute agreement for each category when rating is done by the two observers together and when it is done by different observers recoding the tape.

Scoring the tape as it runs in its slow motion speed allows for the 'expansion' of time and the viewing of an event that had a real-time duration of one second for seven seconds. The actual duration is known because the digital timer was simultaneously recorded when the event was initially recorded. The two observers score one expressive modality such as infant eye direction or maternal facial expression on each slow motion run. When each second of the tape is categorized for a particular expressive modality, another modality is chosen and a new slow motion run is begun. Vocalizations are scored with the tape running at normal speed, then categorization is recoded on computer data sheets for later processing.

The tape is started at the beginning of a second and then stopped at the end of that second. The expressive modality is categorized as it occurred throughout the second, and not just in single frames separated by one second in time. This technique was chosen because we believe that expressive behaviors.are plastic transformations of the stimulus arrays and not static configurations (Gibson 1966). The transformations of face and

Infant	Adult	Infant	Adult
1. *Vocalization:*	1. *Vocalization:*	4. *Facial Expression:*	4. *Facial Expression:*
1. none	1. abrupt shout	1. cry face	1. angry
2. isolated sound	2. stern, adult narrative	2. grimace	2. frown
3. grunt	3. rapid tense voice	3. pout	3. serious, sad, sober
4. coo	4. whispering	4. wary/sober	4. lidded
5. cry	5. little or no vocalizing	5. lidding	5. neutral flat
6. fuss	6. rhythmic sounds with little modulation	6. yawn	6. brightening
7. laugh	7. burst-pause talking	7. neutral	7. animated
	8. single bursts in rapid succession with wide pitch range	8. sneeze	8. simple smile
	9. burst of sound that peaks with much change of modulation and pitch	9. softening	9. imitative play face
		10. brightening	10. kisses
		11. simple smile	11. exaggerated
		12. coo face	12. broad full smile
		13. broad smile	13. 'coo' face
2. *Direction of Gaze:*	2. *Direction of Gaze:*	5. *Body Position:*	5. *Body Position:*
1. towards mother's face	1. towards infant's face	1. doubled over or complete away	1. turns body full away
2. away from mother's face	2. towards infant's body	2. arching	2. sits back and still
3. follows mother	3. away from infant but related to interaction	3. slumped	3. slumping
4. looking at toy or hand mother is using as part of interaction		4. off to one side	4. neutral-slight forward
		5. neutral or being adjusted	5. sideways shifts
		6. up into vertical	6. slight rocking
		7. up and off backrest	7. large sideways shifts into line of vision
		8. body vertical and extended	8. medium close forward
		9. leaning forward with back straight	9. going close and staying close
			10. large shifts forward and back
3. *Head Orientation:*	3. *Head Orientation:*		6. *Specific Handling of the Infant:*
1. head towards, nose level	1. towards and down		1. abrupt shift of baby's position
2. head towards, nose down	2. towards and up		2. abrupt but no shift
3. head towards, nose up	3. towards and level		3. jerky movement of limbs
4. head part side, nose level	4. part side and down		4. no contact
5. head part side, nose down	5. part side and up		5. gentle containing
6. head part side, nose up	6. part side level		6. small rhythmic backing
7. head complete side, nose level	7. away and level		7. rhythmic movements of limbs
8. head complete side, nose down	8. away and up		8. intensive movement, fast rhythm
9. head complete side, nose up	9. away and down		
	10. thrusting		
	11. nodding		
	12. nuzzling		
	13. cocked head		

body and voice carry the information that specifies the meaning of an expression. Transformations require time to occur and to statisize them would degrade the information available.

Each second-by-second combination is then transformed into one of seven Monadic phases according to predefined categories. Figure 3 schematically presents this process of transforming combinations of expressive modalities into Monadic phases. A complete manual of the transformation process is available (Tronick et al. 1977a). The Monadic phases are the same for adult except for adult Avoid and infant Protest, and adult Elicit. For Avoid and Protest the definition is the same: a negative facial or vocal expression along with attempts to orient away from the partner, but because adults never used behaviors such as crying, the label 'Protest' seemed inappropriate.

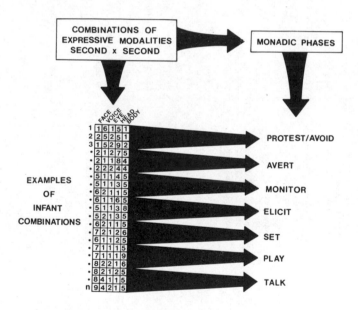

Figure 3. *Schematic presentation of the process of transforming combinations of expressive modalities into Monadic phases*

In Avert an interactant has a negative facial expression with orientation partially away from the partner. In Monitor the facial expression is negative to neutral while orientation is toward the partner. Elicit involves a wide range of facial expressions with orientation toward the partner and vocalizations and movements that are attention getting. This is only an adult phase. In Set, body and head are toward the partner and faces are neutral to positive. In Play, facial expressions are positive and body and head are oriented toward the partner, while in Talk vocalization occurs in addition to Play behaviors. Examples of the Monadic phases can be obtained by keying the numbers of Figure 3 to the numbers in Table 1 under the specific expressive modality. For example, combination of expressive modalities # 1 which is transformed into Protest has the infant with a cry face (Face # 1), with fussing vocalizations (Voice # 6), with eyes toward (Eye # 1), with head part side down (Head # 5), and with body completely away (Body # 1). The other combinations are similarly keyed to illustrate how sets of combinations are transformed into one Monadic phase.

RESULTS

The Monadic phase analysis was applied to the expressive modality data for each of the interactions. The data reported here will focus on the underlying organization and order of the interactions studied rather than on individual differences. However, it should be emphasized, and it can be seen even in the data reported here that the behavior of each interactant and the resulting interaction were uniquely structured despite the underlying orderliness and organization.

The rhythm and flow of Monadic phases for each interaction is presented in Figure 4. Each second of the interaction is plotted on the abscissa and the Monadic phases are plotted on the ordinate. When the data line for a communicant is horizontal it indicates the duration of time the communicant was in a particular phase. When the data line is vertical it indicates that the communicant was changing from one monadic phase to another. For each communicant one can see a cyclic, or rhythmic quality of moving through the monadic phases. The cyclic change rate is unique to each of the communicants as can be seen in Table 2. The infants' average change rates among Monadic phases vary from once every 1.9 sec. to once every 5.3 sec., and for the mothers from once every 2.2 sec. to once every 5 sec. Underlying this rhythmicity is the finding that the infant typically changes between phases that are one step apart (see Table 2). [2] For example, the infants move from Play into Talk, or Play into Set but seldom from Play into Avert or Set into Protest. Thus no matter what the infant's predominant Monadic phase, he moves amongst the phases in a highly predictable fashion. A similar transitional orderliness holds for the mothers except that their modal value is either 1 or 2 with a median value closer to 2 (see Table 2).

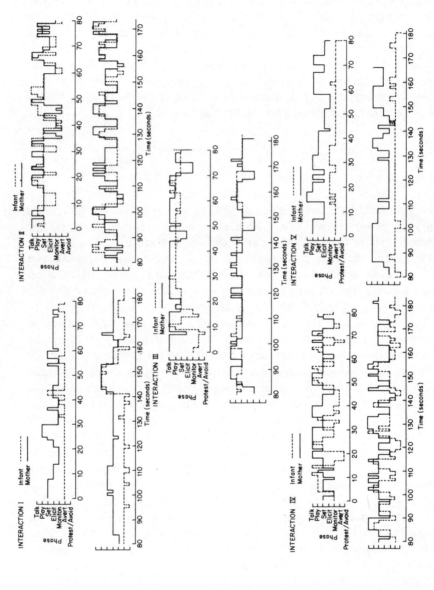

Figure 4.   Infant and mother transition among the Monadic phases over the course of their interaction

Table 2. *Proportion of each step size transition between Monadic phases and the rate of change**

INFANT		Step Size				Mean rate of change
		1	2	3	4	
Infant	# 1	84% (31)	11% (4)	3% (1)	3% (1)	5 sec.
	# 2	47% (41)	39% (34)	13% (11)	1% (1)	2
	# 3	51% (25)	31% (15)	10% (5)	8% (4)	3.7
	# 4	52% (51)	27% (27)	12% (12)	9% (9)	1.9
	# 5	100% (35)	—	—	—	5.3

MOTHER		Step Size				Mean rate of change
		1	2	3	4	
Mother	# 1	65% (26)	33% (13)	3% (1)	—	4.6 sec.
	# 2	34% (27)	51% (40)	11% (9)	5% (3)	2.2
	# 3	50% (19)	42% (16)	8% (3)	—	4.8
	# 4	27% (22)	62% (51)	10% (8)	1% (1)	2.2
	# 5	17% (6)	72% (26)	11% (4)	—	5

*Numbers in parentheses are actual frequency.

From this level of individual orderliness we went on to examine the relationship of relatedness between the infant's and mother's performance. We defined three joint states of relatedness that the interaction could be in at any point in time. The first state, Match, was defined as the times when mother and infant were in the same state with Play and Talk considered to be a match. The second state, Conjoint, was defined as infant and mother being one phase apart, i.e. Set and Play/Talk, Set and Monitor, Elicit and Set or Monitor, Monitor and Avert, maternal Avert and infant Protest or maternal Avoid and infant Avert. The third state, Disjoint, was defined as infant and mother being more than two states apart, e.g. Protest and Monitor/Elicit/Set/Play/Talk, and Set/Play/Talk, Play/Talk/Set and Avert/Avoid, etc. In addition, we defined three kinds of transitions among the states on a second by second basis. An Adjust transition was defined as a change from the Disjoint state to either the Conjoint state or the Match state. A Diverge transition was a change going from Match or Conjoint to Disjoint. The Stay transition occurs within any state when the pair stays in the same state from one second to the next.

Figure 5 presents the data on the joint states achieved in each of the five interactions. The size of each box represents the proportion of time spent in each joint state and the numbers above the lines the proportion of each kind of transition. Clearly there are large individual differences among the interactions in both the proportion of time each joint state

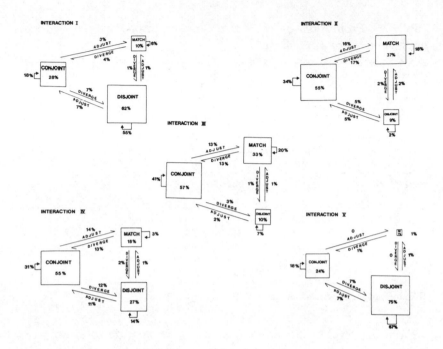

Figure 5.   *The proportion of time spent in the joint states of Match, Conjoint and Disjoint and the transitions amongst the states*

was achieved and in the proportion of each kind of transition. However, there are two striking features of these figures. First, is the proportion of time that the infant and mother are able to achieve a joint state of Match, with the exception of interaction V. Second, is the orderliness in the transitions amongst these joint states. In all the interaction there is an extremely small proportion of transitions between the joint states of Match and Disjoint. Rather the most common pathway for becoming either Match or Disjoint is through Conjoint. This characteristic provides a high degree of organization to the interaction.

In order to understand the nature of the coordination between the partners we carried out the following analysis on the Adjust transitions. We asked if the Adjust transitions were coordinations in which one partner followed the lead of the other or if the Adjust transitions were made up of both partners changing together at the same time. Table 3 shows that most Adjust transitions were accomplished when both partners changed together at the same second rather than when one partner changed and the second partner did not change until the next second. Thus there is a striking proportion of simultaneous coordinations occurring between mother and infant.

Table 3. *Proportion of adjust transitions which were follows* and those which were simultaneous***

	Follows	Simultaneous
Interaction: 1	12	88
2	17	83
3	13	87
4	19	81
5	7	93

*Follow: an Adjust transition that occurs when the partner who had not changed at one point in time changes Monadic phase in the next second.
**Simultaneous: an Adjust transition in which both partners change at the same time.

DISCUSSION

The Monadic phase analysis of mother–infant face-to-face interaction provides a detailed picture of several levels of organization and orderliness in such interactions. First, it demonstrates that the different expressive modalities of the infant, as well as those of the mother, can be 'packaged' into organized interactive units. Second, the orderliness of the rate and size of changes of expressive behavior for infant and mother is illustrated. Third, at the level of the interaction the analysis demonstrates the degree of relatedness that can be achieved in an interaction. And fourth, it shows the ability of the partners to simultaneously coordinate their behaviors. These characteristics begin to provide a basis for an understanding of the development of the communicative competencies and the achievement of intersubjectivity.

As hypothesized by Bruner (1971) the achievement of the intersubjective state and the communicative competencies required can be viewed as a skill. Skillfull performance requires units of behavior that are ordered by a syntax toward a goal. The Monadic phases seem to be able to segment the interaction into such units. They follow the Darwinian principle (1872) of antithesis: opposite emotions are expressed by opposite behaviors. The infant in Play sits up straight, raises his head and 'uplifts' his face into a smile. In Protest, the infant looks away, turns his body away and 'drops' his face into a frown. Thus by three months of age the infant is in possession of a well-organized expressive system.

One way to view this expressive capacity is simply as the Anlage of certain linguistic capacities. However, this would downplay the importance of this system by making it only the precursor of a later system and more importantly would mask the fact that this system continues to operate even after language is achieved. The expressive system available to the infant can better be viewed as the constituent units of communicative skill that are used for regulating the state of the interaction. They can be seen as a pragmatic lexicon which conveys the messages of 'stop' (Protest/Avoid, and Avert), 'change' (Monitor, Set, and Elicit) and 'continue' (Play and Talk). Thus the Monadic phases may be both the constituent units that have to be skillfully organized and the units of a shared lexicon of regulatory meanings required for joint regulation of the interaction (Tronick, Als, and Brazelton in press).

This interpretation is supported by other work on infant abilities. Brazelton et al. (1974) have observed that infants behave differently toward objects than they do toward people by three weeks of age (see also Bower et al. 1970). When presented with an object, the infant's limb movements are jerky, come in bursts and are embedded in a prolonged focused period of looking at the object. In contrast, when interacting with his mother the infant's movements are smooth and accelerate and decelerate in a modulated fashion. His facial expressions show a wider range than with an object and he looks toward and looks away from his mother in an on–off cycle of 4–5 times per minute. Furthermore the infant behaves differently with different people. Yogman (Yogman et al. 1976) and Dixon (Dixon et al. 1976) have described how infants behave differently with their fathers than with their mothers and differently from both their parents when compared to a stranger. Thus the infant clearly has different constituent behaviors in different contexts.

The organized quality of the infant's (and mother's) transitions among the phases provides data that supports the skill requirement that a syntax governs the sequencing of the phases. Neither communicant moves randomly amongst the phases but rather changes in a highly predictable fashion. Such sequencing is also clearly illustrated in experimental studies of face-to-face interaction in which the interaction has been perturbed. Tronick, Als and Adamson (in press) had the mother remain still-faced while sitting facing her infant. The infant greets the mother but quickly sobers when she fails to respond. Then he greets her again but this greeting is foreshortened and he turns away with a sober face and his chin tucked. He glances toward and away from her occasionally with brief smiles, but with her continued failure to respond he slumps in his seat with a sober expression and turns to self-comforting behaviors. Similar disturbed reactions have been noted by Stechler and Latz (1966), Carpenter (1974), and Trevarthen (1977).

This finding furthermore supports the requirement that there is a goal or intent governing the performance as well as the additional requirement of jointly regulated activities that the goal be shared by both communicants. When that goal is experimentally perturbed, as in the above example, the infant attempts to reestablish that shared goal. In the interactions analyzed here the joint organization is illustrated by the achievement of the joint state of Match, by the pattern of transitions through the Conjoint state, and most importantly by the simultaneity of the Adjust transitions.

The interaction between mother and infant appears to be a mutually regulated syntactically governed sequence of behavioral units that have a shared meaning. The communicative capacities are a major achievement of the infant in the first quarter year of life. They provide the basis for the incorporation of objects into the interaction and later still for the exchange of referential meanings in the form of language. Thus prior to language and prior to any form of reference the infant has achieved with nonverbal communicative means the necessary ability for successful communication.

NOTES

1. This research was supported by a grant from the Grant Foundation. The authors would like to express their gratitude to Susan Palmer, Cathy Larned and Joyce Peppi for their unique contributions.

   Some of the ideas in this paper are included in a forthcoming article.

2. The Monadic phases of Figure 4 and for the analyses are arranged in terms of their similarity. Similarity refers to the number of behaviors that are shared between any two states. Play and Talk share many behaviors but neither one shares many behaviors with Avert or Protest, although these share many behaviors. This arrangement produces the 'one-step transition' finding. If the states were not arranged in terms of similarity but were at least always in the same order we might have found a 3-step transition, or a 4-step transition etc. The important point is the regularity and order found regardless of the step size.

MORTON WIENER, ROBERT SHILKRET, and SHANNON DEVOE[1]

'Acquisition' of Communication Competence: Is Language Enough?

In a variety of literature reviews over the last decade, we have been surprised to learn how few studies have appeared which deal with the relationships between verbal and nonverbal communication, or with changes, over age, in the use of nonverbal communication behaviors (Wiener and Devoe 1977a, 1977b). While it is, perhaps, understandable that investigation has been focussed on verbal communication rather than nonverbal communication, it does not necessarily follow that since verbal communication behavior is of central importance for most, if not all, communication groups, nonverbal communication is, therefore, unimportant. Nevertheless, it appears that in stressing the importance of verbal communication, investigators seem also to have assumed the unimportance of nonverbal communication, and to have bolstered this assumption with at least three kinds of arguments. The first argument seems to be that since the 'significance' of any nonverbal communication behavior can be translated into verbal form, then nonverbal communication behaviors are nothing but more primitive, less adequate, or less explicit forms for expressing what can be expressed verbally. The second argument seems to be that, since verbal communication forms can occur in the absence of nonverbal communication forms (as in writing), nonverbal communication behaviors, when they occur, are unnecessary, or at best redundant with verbal forms. The third argument seems to be based on observations that very young children emit some nonverbal communication behaviors prior to verbal communication behaviors, but that these early nonverbal communication behaviors decrease in frequency of occurrence with increasing age and increasing verbal fluency. On the basis of such observations, it has been concluded that nonverbal communication behaviors occur only when appropriate verbal forms are unavailable, or that nonverbal communication behaviors, when they do occur, are considered to be nothing but early precursors of later verbal forms. Given these arguments, that nonverbal communications are merely primitive, inadequate, redundant, or unnecessary, and a view of communication as primarily verbal, it is not surprising that investigations of nonverbal communication, or of changes, past the age of five, in the use of nonverbal communication behaviors and in the relations between verbal communication and nonverbal communication have not been pursued.

If, on the other hand, one adopts the view, as we have, that communication for both children and adults includes the simultaneous indexing of a number of events in multiple modalities or channels, investigations of nonverbal communication, of relationships between verbal and nonverbal communication behaviors, and of changes in both these domains become more important, indeed absolutely necessary.

The term 'channel' as we use it is defined nontechnically (Wiener and Mehrabian 1968), as any behavior or set of behaviors (more traditionally, behaviors at a particular bodily locus) which an investigator considers to be used in encoding and decoding information. It is assumed: (1) that, in principle at least, any channel can be used in encoding an entire communication message, with no inherent limitations on the kind of information which can be indexed within a given channel; (2) that communication typically involves a matrix of channels, with channels differing in degree of articulation and of specialization for any communication group or subgroup; (3) that the principle for describing relationships among channels could best be described as combinatorial, rather than additive, much as words in sentences are seen as combinatory rather than additive; and (4) that groups and subgroups differ not only in terms of which channels are relatively elaborated or articulated, but also in terms of which channels are typically used in encoding and decoding particular kinds of information, and in terms of the combinations of components and/or channels typically used in encoding. Given these assumptions, we would predict that the 'significance' of a component in one or another channel might differ from the 'significance' of that component in combination with another component, and that for different groups or subgroups the 'significance' of combinations of components might differ even where the 'significance' of individual components appeared to be the same. Some data have been generated which indicate that children do respond to co-occurring nonverbal channels and that subgroups appear to differ in the 'importance' of information in the different channels. Brooks, Brandt and Wiener (1969) had equal numbers of children from middle socioeconomic backgrounds and working-class backgrounds 'play a game' — after Gewirtz and Baer (1958) — in which the child was to be an 'astronaut' and 'drive a spaceship' by putting marbles in one of two holes. There were six groups. When a child in any one group made an appropriate response by putting a marble in a particular hole, the child heard, via earphones, one of the following: (1) 'Good' or 'Right' said atonally, (2) 'Good' said with an 'approving' tone — that is, long vowel and slight upward inflection of the middle vowel, (3) 'Good' or 'Right' said in a 'disapproving tone — that is, with a short vowel and a guttural tone for the end, (4) 'Bad' or 'Wrong' said atonally, (5) 'Bad' or 'Wrong' said in an 'approving' tone, or (6) 'Bad' or 'Wrong' said in a 'disapproving' tone. The findings were that children responded quite differently to the various combinations of word and tone, and that the socioeconomic subgroups differed in terms of the particular kinds of combinations of channels, that is, to the particular word and tone pairing. Specifically, for working-class children, tonal variations seemed to be focal. These children did not respond to positive or negative words said with a neutral inflection, but did respond to the word whenever a tonal variation was present. In contrast, for middle-class children, tonal variations seemed to be responded to as indexing semantic information — that is, positive or negative information. To be more specific, noncongruent combinations of word and tone were not responded to; it was as if the 'information' in each of the channels, when contradictory, cancelled each other out, although congruent word–tone pairings were effective reinforcers, as were words alone. Interestingly, when a parallel study was done with adults (Brooks, Brandt, and Wiener 1969), similar patterns of differences both for conditions and for communication groups were also found.

Blumberg (1971), in a subsequent study, systematically varied a set of facial variations — judged to be positive, negative or neutral, presented both singly and in combination with the words 'Good' and 'Right' or 'Bad' and 'Wrong', all said atonally. The task and procedure were the same as in the Brooks, Brandt and Wiener study reported above. Again, the data showed: (1) that children responded differently to the different face, and face and word combinations, that is, that different facial components, and different combinations of face and word resulted in different rates of learning, and (2) that there were significant differences in responses to these combinations of contents in the two channels by children from the different socioeconomic (and presumably different verbal language) groups. For middle-class children, any appearance of a face acted as a reinforcer, as did words alone, and any *congruent* combination of face and word; for lower-class children, only positive and negative faces, alone and in congruent or incongruent combinations with words, acted as reinforcers.

The results from these studies seem to be consistent with our assertions that (1) nonverbal components are responded to by children as having communication significance, (2) nonverbal components, when these co-occur with verbal components, are not simply redundant with the verbal components, (3) the significance of a particular verbal or nonverbal component varies, depending on other co-occurring communication components, and (4) the significance of a given component or combination of components is neither universal across cultures, nor even constant across subgroups within what is ostensibly the 'same' language group.

Our approach posits that the indexing of any event may occur in different channels (e.g. a deictic gesture, frown, or a tonal inflection or raising of an eyebrow) both ontogenetically and/or for different communication groups. Thus, although one could impose verbal 'equivalence' for any instance of a communication behavior in nonverbal channels, the 'equivalence' is to be considered more like a translation from one language to another, rather than a synonymous verbal form.

Since one of the major foci in our approach is included in the view of translation equivalence rather than verbal equivalence, it is important for us to try to explicate and expand this point. When an investigator explores nonverbal channels, the medium used most often to 'describe' and 'explain' the nonverbal communication behavior is in a form in which the verbal component is focal. Once we begin to translate 'meaning' from one channel to another, it is all too easy to come to believe that the nonverbal form is 'just' a less explicit variant of the verbal communication, and then to come to the conclusion that this nonverbal form is only a precursor to the verbal form. This belief seems to be enhanced when one notes that children use some forms of tonal variations and other nonverbal patterns prior to the occurrence of verbal forms, and certainly prior to occurrence of systematic language forms, and that many of these early forms do seem to 'disappear'. However, any thought about this issue will show the untenability of a view of nonverbal behaviors as nothing but less than ideal substitutes or precursors for later verbal forms. If we take ASL as an example of nonverbal communication (e.g. as a completely articulated communication system which utilizes the hand and arm movement channel instead of the verbal–vocal channel) we find that 'translations' from vocal language to ASL involve the same kind of changes as when one goes from one channel to the other. Incidentally, while the predominant locus of ASL appears to be hand and arm movements, as Baker (1976) has so nicely reported, eye and other facial variations contribute systematically to the 'meaning' of ASL forms. Despite the possibility of translating from verbal language forms to ASL, few would hold that verbal forms are nothing but 'primitive precursors' to ASL; we suggest that it is equally illogical to argue that nonverbal forms are 'primitive precursors' to verbal language forms merely on the basis that it is possible to translate from nonverbal forms to verbal forms. In fact, we would argue that verbal forms are as much a substitute for nonverbal forms as the converse, and that translations from nonverbal forms (e.g. a palm-up movement) into verbal form (e.g. an index of 'not in disagreement necessarily' with a listener) lose as much in translation from one channel to another, as metaphor or idiom lose in the translation from one language into another.

More importantly, it seems that we all too often 'forget' that the graphic verbal forms — often taken to be the epitome of communication — are relative newcomers to the communication scene. We would argue that to learn to write or read requires one to learn to translate many of the other co-occurring communication channel behaviors into this one channel. As educators report, it is a most difficult task for children to comprehend a passage even if they learn the 'decoding' of words, if they do not 'phrase' or 'chunk' the verbal material. From our perspective, this difficulty can be accounted for by noting that in addition to 'decoding' a whole new set of visual cues to be 'equivalent' to some earlier auditory form, one must also, at the very least, 'impose' the tonal variations on the graphic forms, if such forms are to be 'comprehended'. It also becomes important to learn to write so that this stressing and chunking, in addition to other contents usually carried nonverbally (e.g. tentativeness) become readily 'apparent' to a reader. Making such cues available by phrasing, punctuation, context, or 'meaning' is no easy task.[2]

If one looks at language behaviors ontogenetically for a language group or for an individual, what seems to occur first is language embedded in a matrix of other channels, i.e. a communication with multiple channels. Subsequently, when one learns to 'read' or 'write', one is required to learn to *substitute* verbal forms for the omnipresent tonal, facial, hand and arm movement variations which are part and parcel of the earlier communication patterns. As noted above, to index tentativeness or uncertainty, often carried tonally (e.g. upward or open inflection), or gesturally (e.g. palms up, or circling), or bodily (e.g. shrug), or facially (e.g. eyebrow rise), a writer has to include a verbal equivalent such as 'I think', 'I believe', 'It seems'. In cases of use of 'single' channel in reading or writing, often a longer message is required. It is further evident that once a speaker masters the verbal channel and can use this channel well in reading or writing, the spoken forms of the communication do not then show any apparent decrease in the use of the other channels despite the 'mastering' of the verbal channel. We do not resort to the use of the verbal channel only, once we have mastered that channel. In fact, were we to do so, communication would be extremely inefficient. In sum, to argue that nonverbal behaviors do not seem essential for communication in written forms and that therefore they contribute little or nothing when they do co-occur with spoken verbal forms would seem to invoke an underlying logic which is strange indeed.

It may be worthwhile to report some data we have generated in another context which seems to bear on the issue of multiple channel usage — even in reading. Cromer (1970), and Wiener and Cromer (1967), using this framework, examined the reading behaviors of groups of individuals identified as good and poor readers. Two groups of poor readers (college students) were identified. One group seemed to 'identify' words in a text in a word-by-word manner (i.e. they read aloud almost as if they were reading a list), but showed good verbal fluency on a vocabulary test. The second group of poor readers had low verbal fluency, that is, they scored poorly on a vocabulary test, but read the text with phrasing. It was hypothesized that controlled presentation of visual materials in linguistic phrases, rather than in the more usual sentence and paragraph form, would improve the reading comprehension of the first group of 'nonorganizing' poor readers, but not the reading comprehension of the second group of poor readers. When this kind of linguistic organization was imposed explicitly on a new text by visual display, the reading comprehension of the first group of word-by-word poor readers *improved* to a level not significantly different from that of a group of matched 'normal' readers, while for the second group of poor readers, the visual 'chunking' did not significantly change reading comprehension.

In some subsequent work, Shilkret and Wiener (1972) reasoned that some 'poor readers' might be more appropriately thought of as 'poor organizers' of language instances, that is, when the organization is not given in a *text or in a spoken passage*, they do not impose it systematically. It was hypothesized that such 'poor readers' would have more difficulty than good readers in comprehending a *spoken* text in which the usual cues for linguistic organization (i.e. patterns of stress, pitch, and pause) were absent. When a text was presented in spoken form, but without many of the usual tonal components, to groups of fourth grade 'poor' and 'good' readers, the poor readers had more difficulty comprehending the atonally spoken text than good readers, and this difference between good and poor readers seemed to increase as the complexity or length of the sentence increased. The results of this study are quite consistent with a view that in going from spoken communication to written communication, one must impose on the written form some of the 'multichannel' regularities usually associated with the spoken forms but not indexed explicitly in the graphic forms.

It could be argued that the inflection, pauses, and stresses 'missing' in written forms are merely paralinguistic features of language, which do not constitute a communication channel in and of themselves, that our conclusion about reading as a multichannel activity is unwarranted, and that, in any case, explicit indexing of paralinguistic features could easily be supplied in graphic form (e.g. by placing a question mark in front of a sentence, as in Spanish, rather than at the end of the sentence, as in English). While we would agree that some of the comprehension difficulties might be ameliorated by systematic graphic indexing of some features of organization, we hold that the tonal variations which typically co-occur with spoken verbal forms often provide semantic information as well as organizational cues, that this semantic information must also be brought to a written text by the reader, and that this kind of information is considerably more difficult to index in graphic form than are the cues for linguistic phrasing. For example, the significance of 'I love you' can vary considerably depending on whether the 'who', the 'what' or the 'whom' is stressed, as in '*I* love you' versus 'I *love* you' versus 'I love *you*'.

If we are to investigate nonverbal behaviors as components within a communication matrix, and as systematically emitted by and responded to as having communication significance by most, if not all, members of a given group or subgroup, it becomes important to discriminate nonverbal communication behaviors from nonverbal noncommunication behaviors (e.g. socially patterned behaviors learned as part of the social matrix such as patterns of walking typical of males or females in a given group, and nonsocial nonverbal behaviors such as swatting at a mosquito). Unfortunately, from our perspective, few investigators of nonverbal behaviors have been concerned with discriminating between nonverbal communication behaviors — that is, nonverbal behaviors which, like verbal behaviors, are part of a code used by members of a group in communication behaviors — and nonverbal behaviors which an observer can use as a 'sign', that is, as behaviors from which an observer can make inferences about the behaving individual. Wiener et al. (1972) note that a review of the extensive literature of nonverbal behaviors indicates that most investigators seem to be concerned with the significance which some observer can attribute to a particular behavior; that is, the emphasis seems to be primarily on decoding. Given this decoding approach, there has been little consensus about any set of nonverbal behaviors which can be considered communication behaviors and the literature consists, for the most part, of a fragmented and unsystematic array of reports, with almost any conceivable behavior considered by one or another investigator to be a nonverbal 'communication'. Thus, such diverse movements as body or head positions, lint picking, foot kicking, scratching, gross postural shifts, and hand and arm movements such as palm-up during a verbalization, have all been considered equally cogent and relevant for an investigation of communication.

In addition, to the extent that many investigators of nonverbal behaviors have been concerned with using nonverbal behaviors as a basis for inference about the sorts of 'information' with which psychotherapists have been concerned (e.g. inference about 'personality' or other long-term 'traits', and inferences about transitory 'moods' and 'affective states') and to the extent that such concerns almost always include the domain of 'emotionality', it has been all too easy for investigators to come to view nonverbal behaviors as 'primitive' or 'undifferentiated' 'expressions' of what would later (perhaps after successful psychotherapy) be 'expressed' in 'more differentiated' verbal forms. That is, given a concern with 'affect', and the joint assumptions that affect will be 'expressed' nonverbally if it is not 'expressed' verbally and that verbal 'expression of affect' is preferable to nonverbal 'expression of affect', it has been easy to make the further assumptions that all nonverbal behaviors are nothing but primitive expressions of 'unconscious' contents which, when conscious, will be expressed in verbal form, and that nonverbal behaviors are nothing but primitive precursors of verbal forms. (It is interesting to note that investigators of nonverbal behaviors of adults and of nonverbal behaviors of children have both come to the same conclusions about the importance — that is, the unimportance — of nonverbal behaviors in communication, albeit from different starting points and via different sorts of 'logic'.) On the other hand, if, as we hold, nonverbal communication behaviors occur in a variety of channels, for different groups or subgroups, and may well change over age, it is important to leave open the issue of the kinds of events which may be indexed in a given channel, for a given group, rather than assuming, as many investigators seem to have done, that the information indexed nonverbally is restricted in significance to the domain of affect or personality (see Wiener et al. [1972] for more extensive discussion of these two issues and others relating to investigation of nonverbal communication), or is restricted to earlier ages.

To the extent that we are to explore 'acquisition' of nonverbal communication over the life span of individuals in a group, it becomes necessary to make explicit some of our assumptions about 'acquisition'.

For if we look at the literature reporting the 'acquisition' of verbal language by children, we find terms and concepts which seem to invoke metaphors about acquisition and communication which present us with problems.

For example, the very phrase 'language acquisition' in the acquisition literature seems to suggest that language is some fixed 'thing' which is acquired. This kind of metaphor of acquisition seems to require an investigator to describe his/her concerns in terms of 'something' — that is, some 'things' or 'elements' accumulated during the course of ontogenesis, and seems to entail a characterization of changes in language use during ontogenesis in terms of some linear accretion of components with increasing age.

There are, for us, several problems associated with this metaphor. The first problem is with the notion of accretion, which can be understood to mean that a form, or element, once 'acquired', remains forever unchanged. However, as others have also noted (e.g. Piaget 1955) there are changes in the ways items or forms are used which seem at least as important in describing changes in language usage during ontogenesis as any cataloguing of the first appearance of particular items. For example, 'so' as in 'so big' is used by very young children, 'so' as in 'so I went to the store, so I went back home, so I had some ice-cream' occurs as a temporal connective for somewhat older children, while 'so' as a causal or teleological connective, as in 'I wanted someone to go to the movies, so I called Sue' appears still later (Bennett 1974). In addition, it has been noted (e.g. Brown 1976) that early language usage may be characterized in terms of the 'indexing' of specific objects and events in the immediate environment (e.g. 'ball', 'rain'). Later usages seem, however, to include not only an increased explicitness in such labelling (e.g. 'basketball', or 'sleet') but may also include an explicit indexing of the relationships between events. That is, in later usage a term may be used not only to index some particular object or event, but a set of objects or events which may note a relationship, e.g. a contrast with some other set of objects or events. We believe (1) that these same kinds of changes in usages also include very different nonverbal communication components and (2) that similar changes can occur for any one particular verbal or nonverbal form (e.g. a pointing behavior).

Incidentally, these examples illustrate yet another point which we feel it is important to make; namely, that once a child comes to use 'basketball' or 'sleet', or 'so' (as a teleological connective) this does not mean that 'ball', 'rain', or 'so' (as an adjective) are no longer used. Rather, the less 'complex' usages seem to be appropriate for a more restricted range of instances than the later, more complex forms. That is, 'ball' can be used to index a 'basketball' when only a basketball is present in the context in which speaker and addressee are communicating, while 'basketball' can be used in this context as well as in contexts where there are a number of balls present, or in a situation where the basketball is not-here-not-now for the speaker and/or the addressee. However, the availability of 'basketball' does not preclude the use of 'ball' for particular situations.

We can cite a simple example of the kind of change in the verbal domain which explicates our perspective by noting the changing patterns of usage for one word, 'no', for a young child. That is, these 'different' usages seem to be different communication patterns rather than just another instance of a usage of the word. Incidentally, since the *same* word is used, and the example does not involve any change in the number of verbal elements in the communication, we can also use these same instances to explicate our notion of 'new combinations'. Consider these three usages as used by a child: 'No cup' (don't want it); 'No cup' (cup is not here or is gone); and 'No cup' (not the cup, but the glass).[3] If one observes the tone, the hand movements, and/or facial patterns when these three 'communications' are said, one will note marked variation of tonal and gestural forms even with the verbal components ostensibly held constant. We hold, then, that even when an utterance may include some identical elements (e.g. 'No cup'), the same number of components (e.g. 'No' with a head shake versus 'No' with a shrug), the combinations index something quite different from any component alone; in fact, it is the *combination* that 'indexes', not some addition of the components. From our perspective, it is important to spell out the ways in which the combining of components is changing rather than simply noting the number of components which change, or the kinds of components that change. Given our biases, any view of 'acquisition' of communication patterns as including only the accretion of new, additional, or 'better' verbal (or for that matter, nonverbal) forms, would seem to omit from consideration much of the kind of change in communication behavior which seems to occur during ontogenesis.

The acquisition metaphor presents still a further problem for us. The term 'acquisition' seems to suggest some common end-point beyond which only minor change may occur and beyond which all 'competent' members of a language group are ostensibly interchangeable. However, a group of adults, all of whom have presumably acquired 'language', are not all equally likely to produce and comprehend poetry, metaphor, or proverbs; nor can it be taken for granted that all will 'comprehend' the 'same' nonmetaphorical, nonproverbial or nonpoetical statement in the same way; nor even that the same person will comprehend the 'same' statements in the same way at different times, e.g. on repeated readings of some particular book or article. Given these kinds of considerations, it would seem to be essential to include, in concerns about 'acquisition', some statements about explicit criteria of mastery which specify what kinds of forms or combinations, for what kinds of contents, in what communication matrix, in what kinds of communication contexts, for what kinds of audiences, for what kind of speakers.

A similar problem arises when investigators recognize the difficulty of characterizing language solely in terms of elements and turn to characterizations of language in terms of 'grammars' or 'rules of combination'. Unfortunately, the view of language acquisition as an acquisition of the 'rules' seems to share many of the problems associated with the view of language acquisition as an acquisition of elements or forms. That is, using a concept of rules does not seem to mitigate the problem of either linearity of accretion or a presumed end-point. Phrases such as 'the child acquires the rules' or 'the child's verbal productions are rule-following' seem to invoke a notion of 'rules' as elements to be acquired in addition to forms to be acquired, with the 'rule' when acquired seen as being somehow 'in' or 'possessed by' the child.[4] We suggest that this sort of spatial metaphor is confusing and hold that if a spatial metaphor is to be used at all, it would be preferable to say — as we believe many linguists would say — that the rule is 'in' the principles invoked by the investigator, rather than 'in' either the communicator or the behavior.[5] For us, then, 'rule-following' is a phrase which describes the regularity and predictability of individuals' behaviors in contexts, and not a 'thing' which is acquired in addition to the behaviors them-selves. That is, regularity and predictability of communication behavior are not statements of what the child 'knows' but statements of whether or not the child behaves consistently as assessed by some social norm. In sum, then, 'rule-following' is for us only a categorization of behaviors and/or of individuals, but gives no data about antecedents or concurrent behaviors. It is, in our view, a descriptive category, not an explanatory principle, and can as readily be applied to concerns about nonverbal communication as to verbal communication behaviors. The important issue for us is that, as far as we can determine, the data are not yet generated which will make it possible to specify what shall be taken as regular and predictable *nonverbal* behavior at different ages, for par-ticular contexts, for the different communication groups.

This last point leads us to a further confusion. We, and others, sometimes talk about nonverbal behaviors as if these were universal, that is, as if they were similar or even identical over communication groups or even subgroups. However, if nonverbal communication behaviors are 'learned' rather than taught explicitly, then we would expect considerably more variation over subgroups for nonverbal communication behaviors than for verbal language behaviors, which appear to be relatively more systematically 'taught' to children.

As we have begun to show (Wiener and Devoe 1977a), groups of individuals who ostensibly speak the same verbal language do not always use the same nonverbal forms in their communications, nor do the groups necessarily index the same sorts of information via the same channels (see, e.g. Brooks, Brandt and Wiener 1969; Blumberg 1971). Similarly, in an ongoing study, we seem to be finding a pattern of downward tonal inflection combined with a palms-up gesture for lower-class males, and of upward or open inflection combined with palms-up gesture for middle-class males. As far as we can determine, for the lower-class males, the palms-up gesture in the combination indexes some attribution of power or status relationships of the communicators, while for middle-class males, the palms-up gesture combination appears to index some semantic information of uncertainty or tentativeness about the content.

To the extent that subgroups differ in terms of what is indexed, in what channels, or in what combinations of channels, it becomes important to investigate, for children within each of the subgroups, the sequence of occurrence of the forms or combinations, and to begin to specify the consequences of such differences for cross-subgroup communication exchanges. If one focuses on the differences in verbal channels for different subgroups (e.g. Bernstein 1971; Schatzman and Strauss 1955), one may overlook quite interesting differences in what is being emitted and/or responded to in other channels.

In sum, then, many of the assumptions typically associated with the metaphor of acquisition, whether of 'rules' or of 'forms', would seem to us to be less than heuristic when one is attempting to investigate the 'development of communication capacities'. Even if the view of language acquisition as the *sine qua non* of communication competence is accepted, it would seem that investigations must focus at least as much on the changes in language usage occurring somewhat later during ontogenesis as on the early language usage of the child in naming or indexing objects or events, as well as focusing on the changes in the channel co-occurrences that accompany the verbal changes. That is, it cannot be taken for granted that whatever is involved in the 'naming' activity of the young child is the prototype for later changes in language usage. Similarly, it cannot be assumed that whatever is involved in the nonverbal communication indexing by young children is the prototype for later nonverbal communication. Further, to the extent that we posit that much of what is communicated after the early periods of acquisition involves not just indexing of objects and events, but a specification of relationships between objects and events, with corresponding changes in the forms used in such communication, the most important focus of investigating early communication usages, for us, would be that of investigating what kinds of objects, events, qualities, the child is indexing. It is, then, less momentous that a child uses specific forms (e.g. 'yesterday') or uses predictable forms (e.g. formation of past tense) than that the child has begun to index time, and indexes time in a variety of ways which may change during the course of ontogenesis.

Having come to this view, we are beginning to look at children's communication behavior in a different way than we had previously. Now we are less concerned about when some form appears, but rather are more concerned with such questions as (1) are different forms used at different ages, or (2) does the same form combine with other communication components in different ways at different points in the ontogenetic sequences.

We may make this distinction clearer by describing briefly the perspective and findings in two studies which looked at verbal behaviors of children in these terms. Our investigations of changes in verbal language usage (Wiener and Shilkret 1977) over the course of ontogenesis have focused on specifying the kinds of changes in the indexing of different kinds of relationships between objects and events, using the concept of 'complexity' as a way to characterize similarities and differences among language forms in examining language changes. Complexity as used by Wiener and Shilkret is the number of *simultaneous* discriminations which can be inferred as being indexed by a particular usage. As an example, consider two events, 'He waxed his car' and 'It rained'. The occurrence of these two events may be coordinated in several different ways. The statement, 'He waxed his car and then it rained' could be regarded as a 'simple' indexing of the two events, with only a temporal relationship indexed explicitly. We could also index this temporal relationship in the form, 'As he waxed his car, it rained'. The use of 'as' conjoins the two predications in a temporal form as well as indicating a spatial relation between the actor and the activity when it rained. In that the latter usage entails a greater number of simultaneous discriminations, it would be regarded as more complex than the simple indexing of the events and would be expected to occur later in ontogenesis.

Using a concept such as 'complexity' has made it possible for us to try to scale instances of verbal communication behavior. Bennett (1974), for example, investigated the increase in the frequency and variety in the use of connectives by children from kindergarten through the sixth grade. Children were asked to tell a story about a series of pictures. The verbal productions of the child were analyzed in terms of connectives used to relate this cartoon series. Bennett found a change over age from juxtaposition, to simple coordinations, to sequence, to simultaneity, to antithesis, to subordination or dependent relationships. More importantly, while Bennett found increases in the number of connective words used by older children, she also found that the *same* connective was used in different ways over age and seemed to index different relationships. For example, children seem to use the form 'when' as a temporal connective at an early age, with the use of 'when' as a conditional term occurring somewhat later. We have already noted change, over age, in the uses of 'so' as described by Bennett.

Rubano (1974), using 'complexity' in a similar sense, looked both at connectives and at other verbal forms which specified relationships about two predications (e.g. had to, wanted to, I think). She then studied the occurrence of such relational terms used by fourth, sixth and eighth grade children from a middle socioeconomic group in their verbal descriptions of different pictorial stimuli. She found, first, that the scale, as described, showed acceptable reliability when applied by independent scorers to the protocols produced by children, and, second, that the level of complexity increased with age, as might be expected — although the effect was more marked from fourth to sixth grade than from sixth to eighth grade. When the same task was used with children from working-class backgrounds in another study, differences in these two language groups were also clearly evident. As in Bennett's study, these latter investigations also showed an increase in the number of terms which index relationships among objects and events more explicitly, as well as providing evidence that the relationship indexed by a single word does change during ontogenesis.

This same kind of approach can also be extended to the investigation of nonverbal forms. We have just begun to investigate changes in the use of forms in nonverbal channels using the concept of complexity, predicting an increase in complexity with increasing communication 'competence' for *any* channel of the communication matrix. While such a statement may seem straightforward, even trivial, it seems to be in contrast with other views of the occurrence over ontogenesis of such nonverbal communication behaviors as gestures.

In a study reported by Jancovic, Devoe and Wiener (1975), an analysis of the complexity of communicative hand and arm movements was used successfully in predicting the occurrence of specific forms used by children ranging in age from four to 18 years. It was predicted that young children would emit less complex communicative hand and arm movements than older children; that is, we predicted changes, over age, in the forms used, if not in the frequency of use of the channel. Children watched a cartoon and then described the film while being video-taped. The communicative hand and arm movements of the children were then categorized as deictics, pantomimics, or semantic-modifying, or relational gestures. Jancovic, Devoe and Wiener found that the use of both deictics (i.e. pointing movements denoting or specifying the spatial location of a usually here-and-now concrete object or event) and pantomimics (i.e. movements which copy or mimic some visual or kinesthetic attribute of a concrete object or event) *decreased* from four to 18 years of age (expressed both in absolute terms and as a percentage of total gestural usage), but that the use of semantic-modifying and relational gestures (e.g. arhythmic chops which are 'decoded' as an emphasis on the speaker's verbal point; a palms-up movement, taken to indicate that the addressor is open to, and recognizes the possibly divergent views of the addressee — see Wiener, Devoe, Rubinow and Geller (1972) — *increased* over this period. Furthermore, in contrast with the suggestions of other perspectives, it was found that there were not only changes in kind of gestures over age but also an overall *increase* in number of gestures used. We are currently utilizing this same approach in investigating changes, over age, in children's use of communication components in the tonal and facial channels, and in children's use of or response to regulator or turn-taking behaviors in communication. That is, we analyze the number of simultaneous discriminations required for appropriate use of a particular behavior in a particular context, using this analysis as the basis for predicting order of occurrence over age. So far, we are finding that, in nonverbal channels, just as in the verbal channel, both the number of forms and the complexity of usage of a specific form increases (e.g. when young children point they are indexing here and now events; when older children point they sometimes index, but they may also reduce via a point ambiguity of a verbal referent such as 'he' when several males are present; adults may in addition also point when indexing not-here-not-now past or future events. Similarly, children's pantomimes often seem to be equivalent to a verbal naming, while adults' pantomimes more often seem to index some particular attribute or facet of the verbal utterance).

We have thus far been discussing changes over age in nonverbal channels in much the same way that earlier we had warned against — as if something is being 'acquired', albeit in a different channel rather than in the verbal channel alone. Unfortunately, the bulk of research dealing with nonverbal communication seems to stop with this 'one channel at a time' kind of analysis — and we are equally 'guilty' of this kind of oversimplification. However, in that we assume that communication can be characterized in terms of a combinatory system of channels, this assumption includes the view that what may appear to be the 'same' component may, in fact, index quite different information when it occurs with different components within the same channel or with other components in another channel. Further, we assume that combinations of channels are not merely either redundant, or additive in any simple way. In fact, we hold that the ways in which channels are combined vary in complexity; thus, we would expect changes, over age, in the use of combinations of channels. The simplest form of channel combination appears to be that of redundancy, where information indexed in one channel is further 'stressed' via use of another channel. For example, the verbal statement, 'As he washed his car, it rained' said with tonal emphasis on 'As' seems to stress the simultaneity of the two events. The next most complex form in our model of combination would be that of complimentarity or clarification, where ambiguity in the information indexed in one channel is lessened or eliminated by the information indexed in another channel. For example, 'As he washed his car, it rained', accompanied by a point to index which of several possible males is being referred to in the verbal utterance. The next most complex form of combination appears to be that of additional information, where different information is indexed in each of two or more channels (e.g. 'As he washed his car, it rained', said with a smile on 'rained' and 'read' as the speaker's enjoyment of the washer's predicament). The most complex form of combination appears to be that of contrast[6] in which information indexed in one channel is contradicted by information in another channel (e.g. 'As he washed his car, it rained', said with both a lengthened vowel and raised pitch on 'rained', in this instance 'read' as the washer's dismay, with the smile indexing the speaker's enjoyment). Sarcasm, of course, involves such a juxtaposition of contradictory information in two or more channels (e.g. 'You're a real winner' said with a 'glare' and a 'sneer'). It is not surprising, from our perspective, that children do not appear to use or respond appropriately to such 'complex' combinations. We would expect then that in examining any communication channels or in examining any combination of channels, one will find an increase in the occurrence of and response to complexity of forms with age, or experience, even if these new combinations include some of the 'same' verbal and nonverbal forms that may appear earlier during ontogenesis.

Working with this kind of analysis, it was predicted that the introduction of 'redundancy' in a nonverbal channel would lead to more 'comprehension' by children of a 'complex' verbal form than would occur for that verbal form without the redundancy. Shilkret, Viets and

Wiener (1977) found that a stress or emphasis pattern on the words 'before' and 'after' facilitated young children's (four- and five-year-olds) comprehension of sentences which were temporally 'inverted' *vis-à-vis* the 'real time' order of events (e.g. 'Do B after A'). That is, children behaved more correctly when the term was marked tonally, than with a corresponding sentence in which the temporal word was not marked with a stress pattern. For children, such 'stress' seems to be responded to as a marker of the verbal form, while for older speakers stress patterns may well indicate a concern with the relationship, or other information not given in the verbal message, rather than marking some aspect of the verbal components. For example, in the sentence, 'You don't *listen* to me', the stress is responded to as indicating that the addressee consistently fails to understand and that the speaker is 'annoyed'; the stress here would be categorized by us as including supplemental information.

Similarly, exploring the tonal variations of adults in speaking to children, some interesting patterns can be noted. In one recent study (Shilkret, Andrews and Wiener 1976) it was found that mothers, as well as adults (college students) who had had considerable experience with young children (preschoolers), use more stress in speaking to young children than do adults who have had relatively less experience with children, but also use greater complexity of verbal forms than do adults who are inexperienced with children.

We hope to explore other changes in the numbers and combinations of channels used by mothers in their exchanges with a child and we would predict a systematic increase in the number of channels used and in the complexity of combinations of channels used. Again, looking at everyday communications, we have noted that when mothers or other adults address questions to infants (who, in any case are not expected to respond), they do not typically include the kinds of pitch levels, intonations, stresses and eye contact behavior which typically accompany questions when these are addressed to older children or adults. If one explores the intonational patterns of adults when speaking to children versus to other adults, one will, we predict, recognize significant differences in stress, pause, and inflection, with considerable change in communication 'significance', without, necessarily, any change in the 'referents' indexed in the verbal portion of the communication.

One additional point requires our explicit exposition. To the extent that we hold that variations in channel usages will occur differently for different communication groups, we should expect to find differences not only in verbal language and nonverbal channel occurrences, but also differences in the kinds and patterns of multichannel communication. As we have noted above, we have, in our beginning investigations, found that the communication patterns of children and adults from different socioeconomic groups are different in terms of the use of forms within a given channel (i.e. the kinds of connectives used by fourth, sixth and eighth grade children from middle and lower socioeconomic groups) and in their responses to particular combinations of channels (i.e. positive, negative, and neutral tonal inflections with positive and negative words; positive, negative, and neutral facial expressions with positive and negative words). In addition, these groups appear to differ in their use of nonverbal turn-taking forms which regulate the interaction of speakers during a communication exchange (Robbins, Devoe and Wiener 1976). That is, turn-taking behavior of working-class subjects — at least in the groups studied — showed behavior which allowed the listener more options about participation or interruption than did middle-class speakers who invoked more 'floor-holding' behaviors (i.e. filled pause, eye gaze away) and allowed the listener fewer options for participation or interruption.

The differences we have looked for come from a perspective which attempts to relate the noted differences in communication patterns to the varying ways in which different groups live in the world, a view not consonant with a concept of defect or deficiency for one or another group. As other investigations have also noted, and as we hope to emphasize here, it will be frustrating or fruitless to consider acquisition primarily in terms of the learning about forms, if one is concerned about 'competence' as a communicator. It would seem essential to include something about other information the child (or the adult) 'knows' or 'uses', including information about what is 'appropriate' for what social contexts. In this sense, not only do we suggest that we consider non-verbal components and their combinations important, we hold that communication 'competence' involves 'knowledge' not usually included under the rubric of language or even communication. In this framework, Cormier (1975) showed that the comprehension of an 'identical' text (i.e. same words, same linguistic organization, same nonverbal components) presented auditorily via a tape recording was easier (that is, the sixth grade children comprehended more of the passage) when the text was entitled as a description of something 'familiar' (i.e. a passage about a washing machine) than when the text was entitled as a description of something less 'familiar' (i.e. a passage about a paper-making machine). Given findings that 'knowledge about' the communication forms alone does not account for the comprehension of a communication, if we are to pursue the problems of 'acquisition' or 'competence', we can no longer focus solely on the forms used, or on the acquisition of particular forms, or even on the combination of forms used, in single or multiple channels.

Perhaps we can exemplify the importance of 'living in the world' even if we cannot specify 'what' about this world or 'how' the learning occurs. A spokesman for the deaf community (albeit one who became deaf after learning how to talk) noted that one major problem of people born deaf is *not* that they do not hear language, but rather that they do not have an opportunity to learn 'background information' about the kinds of things that are 'talked about' and how one 'talks' about them in the sense of what one notes, not what words to use. As another example, it is clear that children are required to 'learn' that one does not talk about some bodily activities, e.g. excretory activity, at least not in any explicit way, but that one may 'talk about' headaches or pains in quite direct terms. Children seem to recognize that one does not talk about some domains (e.g. sex) because such discussion is taboo; but that one does not talk about some other domains (e.g. politics) because no one else is interested. More at issue for us in this forum is that nonverbal communication patterns of children (or, for that matter, other subgroups within a communication group) appear to co-vary with changes in communication participants and communication contexts. For example, children may be more successful having their requests granted when the tonal components are appropriate for the individual or context (an 'assertive' tone with a sibling versus a 'subservient' tone with an adult).

Despite our attempts to expand our concerns about communication to nonverbal channels, we are still left with the broader question of 'What is acquired?' For us it seems that an answer cannot be given solely in terms of a linear accretion of forms, no matter how many channels or interrelationships among channels are considered. A question such as 'What kinds of "experiences" are essential for what age children to come to use certain communication patterns?' seems to us to be an appropriate question, but one for which we have no simple answer. We have nothing more to offer at present than what we take to be an heuristic approach concerning how one may investigate 'communication acquisition', even if such a phrase is taken only in the narrow sense of communication forms or combinations. For us it seems essential, at the very least, to include multiple forms and multiple channels for different groups and social contexts. However, we hope that by raising these kinds of questions as well as our still unspecified concerns about the relationship of living in the world to communication, other approaches to 'acquisition' and 'competence' will be more clearly articulated also, and that from a range of perspectives, we can investigate more systematically differences and similarities in communication patterns, within and between groups, for nonverbal as well as verbal components.

Morton Wiener, Robert Shilkret, and Shannon Devoe

NOTES

1. Much of the work reported here has been supported in part by grant NIMH 25775 from the National Institute of Mental Health and by grant NIE-74-G-0017 from the National Institute of Education. We are indebted to a large number of colleagues who have in many ways contributed to the ideas offered here. We are particularly indebted to Judith Cormier who contributed in many ways, and assisted greatly in adding to whatever clarity there is in the paper.

2. As an example of how 'overlearned' these 'chunking' behaviors are for visual users of a communication pattern, we encourage the reader first to 'say' the following sentence first as a sentence, 'The boy went to the store to buy some candy'. Secondly, the reader is asked to say each of the words in the sentence as if it were on a list. Thirdly, the reader is asked to read the words in the sentence backwards as if they were also on a list. It should quickly become apparent that there are remarkable differences in the tonal variations — that is, phrasing, stress, pitch variations — in the three patterns. In fact, most 'good' readers have a quite difficult time reading a sentence as if it were a list. It is important that we recognize that what appears to be a 'single' channel of verbal forms in writing and reading — that is, we can write or 'see' each word as if it were independent of the other words — is anything but single channel activity.

3. We are indebted to Sarah Bennett who brought this example to our attention.

4. Such usages of rule and rule-following are currently often associated with a view of the child as a linguist who 'samples the data' available, 'forms hypotheses' about the 'best fit' of the data and 'develops strategies' for 'testing hypotheses', all of which seems rather formidable activity for a two-year-old, or even an adult, and, further, involves an unnecessary assumption of awareness. A common alternative to the view of the child-as-linguist seems to be that of the child-as-computer, with linguistic data as 'input', neurological structure as 'processing mechanism', and language production as 'output'. While this view avoids the issue of 'awareness' as a problem, we fail to see how an analogy to a computer in describing children's 'acquisition of rules' contributes, in any substantive way, to our understanding of communication behaviors.

5. A similar point can be made in terms of 'acquisition' of elements. For example, the point at which an observer decides a child is beginning to talk is the point at which the observer takes a particular sound pattern to be a word. A child may produce close approximations of 'apple', for some time before the observer recognizes the approximation. Thus, while an observer will say that the child has acquired a vocabulary of n words, it might be more appropriate to state that the observer now categorizes n sound patterns as words.

6. There may well be other equally complex relationships between channels which have not been exemplified here; the sequence as described is viewed by us as illustrative, but not as exhaustive.

D. JEAN UMIKER-SEBEOK

Silence is Golden? The Changing Role of Non-Talk in Preschool Conversations

1. INTRODUCTION

Silence is anathema to the adult, middle-class American con-
versationalist, who tries to obey the rule that, in spontaneous conversation, 'someone's turn must always and exclusively be in progress'
(Goffman 1963:136). Adherence to this maxim must be accomplished
within a form of interaction where neither turn order nor turn size is
determined in advance, but through the unrestricted operation of a set of
rules for turn allocation[1] which in no way prevent — and in some respects
even foster — gaps in talk at many key points throughout the interchange. Gaps are to a certain extent encouraged by the sequencing
rules of spontaneous conversation, which allocate turns one at a time and
where each such allocation involves a set of options open to participants.
The current speaker, first of all, has to decide whether or not to select the
next speaker himself, and at what point in his turn. If he does not select
next speaker, the listener must decide whether or not to self-select, and,
if he decides to take a turn, must project ahead to a likely termination of
current speaker's turn and select an appropriate turn-entry device.
Finally, the current speaker must decide if he will continue speaking if no
listener has self-selected. At each of these decision-making points,
participants may choose not to take a turn. In this sense, gapping, like
overlapping, is a result of the conversation being a system of self-
management, where turns are assigned through the direct interaction of
participants.

On the other hand, gapping is inhibited by the fact that current
speaker may select next speaker or may continue his turn should no one
self-select, by the fact that self-selectors are encouraged to begin early in
the current speaker's turn to plan for the start of their own turn, and by
the fact that the current speaker, knowing that self-selectors will begin
their self-selection at the earliest possible moment, is encouraged to select
next speaker at an early point in his turn (Sacks, Schegloff and Jefferson
1974: 705).

Silences in adult conversation are, then, as systematically imbued with significance as signs where the signifier has an overt verbal or nonverbal form, and adequate conversational performances require that interlocutors be able to interpret and employ such 'zero-signifiers'[2] correctly. This paper addresses the question of the extent to which preschool children 'read' and behave toward conversational silences in ways similar to those of their adult counterparts. The data discussed here were collected over a period of five and one-half months, during which daily naturalistic observations and shorthand recordings were made of the spontaneous conversations between children and between children and adult teachers in three classroom groups.[3] The first consisted of fifteen three-year-olds (average age 40 months) in a private preschool in Highland Village, Indiana, the second of eighteen four-year-olds (average age 52 months) in the same preschool, and the third of twenty-nine five-year-olds (average age 66 months) in a Bloomington, Indiana, public-school kindergarten. All of the children were white and from middle- or upper-middle-class homes. The fathers of the youngest children had an average of 3.6 years of college education, those of the four-year-olds 4.0 years, and those of the oldest 6.7 years. Fathers of the children in the first two groups were employed in professional or semi-professional positions, those of the five-year-olds almost entirely in professional ones. Thirty of the children were male, 32 female. The eight adults were white females.

Clues to the preschool child's judgments about silences — namely, techniques used to avoid or acknowledge them — would seem to indicate that he is far from having acquired the adult semiotic system for the interpretation of conversational non-talk, yet the five-year-old is in several respects closer to the adult model than the three-year-old. Given the turn-taking rules for spontaneous conversation, the first obvious method for avoiding a gap at the end of a construction unit is for the current speaker to select the next speaker himself, the earlier in his turn the better. Probably the most common way to accomplish this is through the use of adjacency pairs, or units of discourse where the first pair-part 'sets constraints on what should be done in the next turn (e.g. a 'question' making 'answers' especially relevant for next turn)' (Sacks, Schegloff and Jefferson 1974: 717). Question and imperative sentence forms, as well as 'double' adjacency pairs, where the second pair-part is also a first pair-part of a second adjacency pair, were a pervasive part of preschool conversations, but, since they are being treated separately (Umiker-Sebeok in preparation), they will not be included here (see also Ervin-Tripp 1970; Ervin-Tripp and Miller 1977; Garvey 1977a, 1977b; Garvey and Ben Debba 1974; Garvey and Hogan 1973).

The second major resource for avoiding gaps in conversation at turn-transition relevance points is the creation of a buffer zone immediately prior to and/or after one's turn. On a single-turn level, signs used in this way are called either turn-entry or turn-exit devices, also known as *prestarts* and *post-completions* (Sacks, Schegloff and Jefferson 1974: 716–718). On the level of multi-turn conversational sequences, these are commonly referred to as openings and closings (e.g. Jefferson 1972, 1973; Schegloff 1968; Schegloff and Sacks 1973), which themselves may contain several turns. The one type of post-completion examined in the present study — tag-questions — is discussed elsewhere (Umiker-Sebeok in preparation), as are multi-turn sequence buffers associated with, for example, greetings, conversational openings, closings, side-sequences, and narratives (Umiker-Sebeok 1976; in press).

2. TURN PRESTARTS

This paper focuses upon the operation, in preschool conversations, of turn-entry (or turn-continuation) devices, or prestarts. The children's prestarts discussed below[4] are extremely frequent in adult conversation. They may be employed by someone who has been selected by current speaker as next speaker, by a self-selecting participant, or by a current speaker taking advantage of his right to continue talking when no self-selection has occurred. Consider, for example, the following conversation between a five-year-old and an adult:

(1)

Child:	I'm gonna shoot you!
Adult:	Oh no! Don't! Or I'll shoot you with this [Pointing pencil at child]. It's a weapon too! It shoots beams that go right through you.
Child:	*Yeh. But* . . . [Breaks off].
Adult:	*And* then your blood will turn to ice, N you'll be a big popsicle!
Child:	*Yeh. But this will go right through you!*
Adult:	Are you a monster or something? Batwoman?
Child:	I'm a good girl!
Adult:	*Oh!* You're a good guy, huh?
Child:	Yes.
(No response)	
Child:	What are you writing?
Adult:	That they're pretending that the blocks are a batmobile. That's what it's supposed to be, isn't it?
(No response)	

Adult: *And* now I'll write that bad Meera came over and tried to shoot me!
(Child pretends to shoot adult)
Adult: It really shoots! How did you make that?
Child: I put this on this, see, it fits on here? N then I push this.
Adult: Here. Shoot my hand.
(Child does so)
Adult: *Yes*. It really works.
(Child leaves)

Prestarts are, first of all, essentially 'deletable' conversational objects in the sense that, should they not be heard, for example, due to overlapping talk, the interpretive flow of talk need not be interrupted. The speaker may continue talking, and his turn may be heard from its beginning. It is the beginning of a turn, as noted above, which, by indicating the type of construction unit the turn will possess, often provides the information upon which listeners may begin to plan how and when they will attempt to enter into a turn of their own.

Should the speaker whose prestart has been overlapped yield the floor to another participant, as in the first conversational example above (lines 5–8), he may nevertheless be seen by his interlocutor(s) as having first priority for self-selection at the next turn-transition relevance point, thus contributing to the smooth transition of speakership at the next self-selection. It also makes it more difficult for the person who has taken the floor to change the topic of talk or in some other way move the conversation beyond a point where the unsuccessful self-selector can finally make his contribution. Even were this to happen, however, the fact that the prestart does not give any details about the subject or type of conversational work to be accomplished in the intended turn means that, when the person finally gets the floor, he is not committed to a certain line of thought, but can adapt his turn to the current state of conversational development.

Prestarts may also be used to respond to a potential gaplike silence, in which case they make it possible for someone to move to take the floor without as yet having a definite plan in mind for taking a turn. An intra-turn silence, or one which occurs other than at a turn-transition relevance point in talk, for example, may be filled by the current speaker's use of a device such as a hesitation marker, possibly followed by a continuation of his turn. An example of this is provided in line 8 of the following conversational sequence between a group of five-year-olds and their teacher:

(2)

Child₁:	Mrs. Keenan!
Teacher:	Yes?
Child₁:	Someone put some gum in with the tadpole!
Teacher:	They did? If someone has to spit, they can [?].[5]
Child₂:	It could have made the tadpole sick!
Child₃:	What's a tadpole?
Teacher:	Well, [?].
Child₂:	It's . . . *uh* . . . something that turns into a frog.
Child₁:	It hasn't turned into a frog yet.
Child₂:	I know.
Child₄:	You'll be lucky if it lives.

(Teacher calls them to attention and exchange ends)

A person who has been assigned the floor by the current speaker may, if he has not planned a turn, use a prestart in order to have time to formulate one, as in the following conversations between three-year-olds (3) and five-year-olds (4):

(3)

Child₁:	Hi Matt, what ya doing?
Child₂:	*Well . . . I'm [?] my cows.*
Child₁:	[?]
Child₂:	This is a black cow. This is a brown cow. This is a white cow . . . brown cow.

(No response)

(4)

Child₁:	You've got to kill those monsters!
Child₂:	*Well . . . (pause) . . . they're made out of [?] and its no use.* (Going over to inspect the 'monsters' and then returning). *Well . . . there's something that will kill them!*
Child₁:	What?
Child₂:	Only I don't know what it is yet! (Running away).

Silence after the completion of a construction unit may be filled by the current speaker's use of a prestart, in which case he makes it possible for a self-selector to make a bid for the floor or, if no one should do so, allows him to continue speaking with a minimum of silence between his earlier talk and its continuation. Consider, for example, the following exchange between three five-year-olds:

(5)

Child₁: In first grade the only place you can go is the bath-
                 room . . . (pause) . . . N . . . (pause) . . .
Child₂: To the library.
Child₃: *Yeh. N to the cafeteria!*
(No response)

A self-selector may also make use of a prestart in order to allow another
interlocutor an opportunity to take the floor and, if not, to take a turn
himself, as in the exchange below between three five-year-olds, where
Child₂'s lack of response (which itself constitutes a kind of turn) prompts
Child₁ to cue an answer to her question with *well*, although to no avail:

(6)

Child₁: Hey Eric [Child₂], what do you have on your lip?
(No response)
Child₃: On your lip. (Pointing to Eric's lip)
(No response)
Child₁: *Well . . . (pause) . . . what is it?*
(No response)

In some cases, current speaker may use a preturn before a continuation of his talk in such a way that it leaves the impression that,
instead of being in response to silence, his further talk follows some work
accomplished by his interlocutor(s), as in the following four-year-old
conversation, where the italicized utterance implies that Angie responded
with an utterance such as 'What is it?':

(7)

Child₁: Are you Angie?
(Child₂ nods)
Child₁: Cause I've got a nice present for ya.
(No response)
Child₁   *But I'm not gonna tell you what it is!*
(No response)

Prestarts are also useful conversational tools because they may be
repeated, unlike most conversational units, so that the speaker is certain
he has the listener's attention before actually beginning his turn, as in the
following exchange between a five-year-old and his teacher:

(8)

Teacher:	Now I did this [i.e. rearranged the children's chairs] so that you children will be on your best behavior this morning.
Child:	Well why did you change all the kids away from their friends!?
Teacher:	I did that so that they won't talk so much.
Child:	*But . . . but they'll talk so much about moving!*
(No response)	

Similarly, prestarts may be combined with one or more other prestarts to form sometimes quite lengthy strings, and this combinatorial possibility allows participants to improvise according to the demands of the changing conversational context. Adults are notorious for long stretches of hedging (G. Lakoff 1972) such as *Well you see I mean . . .* or *Well . . . uh . . . I think . . .* and the like.[6] In my preschool materials, combinations were restricted to affirmatives or acknowledgments plus a connective, as, for example, in conversations (1) and (5) above.

2.1. *Preturn connectives*

The connectives *and, but, well,* and *so,* are 'extremely common, and do satisfy the constraints of beginning. But they do that without revealing much about the constructional features of the sentence thus begun, i.e. without requiring that the speaker have a plan in hand as a condition for starting. Furthermore, their overlap will not impair the constructional development or analyzability of the sentence they begin' (Sacks, Schegloff and Jefferson 1974: 719). In the present study, the prestart connectives *and, but, or,* and *because* were found in 3.4% of preschool turns, increasing from 1% at three to 3% at four and five.

The variety of connectives as prestarts also increased with age. At three, only *and* was found in preschool turns, at four *and, but,* and *because,* at five *and, but,* and *or.* The frequency of occurrence of *and* remained stable from three to five years, with the rate of *but* showing the largest increase with age of the four connectives.

In the majority of cases, a connective-initial turn was one in which the immediately preceding turn by an interlocutor was the turn which was built upon in the sense of adding information (e.g. with an *and*-initial turn) or contradicting an assertion (e.g. with *but* as the prestart), as in the following examples:

(9)

(Three years)

Adult:	Does anyone know what day it is today?
Child₁:	Halloween!
Child₂:	*N it's my Mom's birthday!*
Adult:	It is?
Child₂:	It's really my Mom's birthday.

(No response)

(10)

(Four years)

Child₁:	Once we went on a train!
Child₂:	*N we did too!*
Child₁:	A train crashed into a car [?].
Child₃:	Once upon a time my Daddy and Mommy . . . (pause) . . . my Mommy took me down to a circus. N I saw my old teacher. N there was Kevin n Doug n Tim.
Child₄:	We didn't go!
Child₃:	*Well . . . most of the time it was Kevin n Doug.*

(No response)

The connective-initial turn may have referred, however, to a preceding turn by Ego, usually one which immediately preceded Alter's intervening turn. While almost any conversational turn by addressee can serve as the reference turn for a connective-initial turn by a self-selecting participant, a preceding turn by Alter was used in a more restricted set of circumstances, such as:

1. If Alter has self-selected as next speaker before Ego has had an opportunity to complete his turn; this was commonly found in the case of narratives, where the addressee would self-select in order to furnish the narrator with feedback in the form of an acknowledgment of the narrative;

2. If Alter has misreplied, in Ego's estimation, either through misunderstanding or contradiction, to Ego's preceding turn, or if he has emphasized the wrong aspect or presupposition of Ego's turn;

3. If Ego's first turn is a preliminary step to his second one, such as in example (7) above;

4. If Alter appears to be losing interest in what Ego is saying or his attention is drawn away from Ego during Ego's first turn in which case Ego may pause, continuing with his second, connective-initial turn only when he sees that he has his interlocutor's attention once again. Consider some of these uses in the following examples:

(11)

(Three years)

Child₁:	This is Heather.

Child₁: This is Heather.
Child₂: I know that's Heather.
Child₁: *N I'm Sherri.*
Adult: How are you today?
Child₁: Fine. I'm three. (Holding up three fingers)
Child₂: N I'm four. (Holding up four fingers)
(Children leave before adult can respond)

(12)

(Five years)

(Child₁ raises her hand to be acknowledged by the teacher)
Teacher: Tracy?
Child₁: I got this a long time ago. (Holding up cologne bottle)
Child₂: What is it?
(Child₁'s answer is unclear)
Child₂: I couldn't see it.
Child₁: *N I used it up but there was still some smell in it.*
              [?] water.
Teacher: OK. Kathy? Do you have something?
(Kathy shakes her head)
Child₁ remains standing in front of the group)
Teacher: Oh! Tracy isn't through yet. I'm sorry.
Child₁: *N now I got this.* (Holding up a silver spoon)
Teacher: What is it? A spoon. What does it say on it?
(Teacher reads name on spoon and then calls on another child)

2.2. *Preturn* well

Preturn *well* was recorded in 1.4% of all preschool turns in the present study.[7] At age three, they preceded 0.7% of the children's turns, at four 0.5%, and at five 2%. *Well* was one of the common ways in which the preschool children in the present study could modulate an assertion, or 'hedge', indicating 'the speaker's degree of certainty about his statement' (Gelman and Shatz 1977: 39, following G. Lakoff 1972).[8] R. Lakoff (1973) has noted that *well* was used in adult conversation to preface questions and rejoinders to questions. In the present study, it prefaced responses to commands (4% of the examples) and simple declaratives (73%) as well as questions (22%). The interjection is employed, she writes 'in case of an insufficiency in response, either by the respondent himself or by someone else' (464). That is to say, *well* may refer to an insufficiency in the forthcoming turn by the speaker (for example, an answer to a question) or in a preceding turn by Alter. Consider, for example, the following conversational fragment which took place in the three-year-old group:

(13)

Child₁: Teacher, tell him [Child₂] to get down.
Child₂: *Well . . . (pause) . . . I'm not gonna get down right now.*

In this example, the insufficiency is in Ego's response to the indirect command of Child₁. On the one hand, Child₂ is refusing to comply with the other child's instructions; on the other, he implies, by adding 'right now', that he intends to comply at some future time.

Consider also the following exchange between three four-year-olds and their teacher:

(14)

Teacher: What color's a Siamese cat?
Child₁: Beige.
Child₂: *Well . . . our cats are Siamese.*
Teacher: [?].
Child₂: *Well Shirley's not afraid of dogs!*
Teacher: The funny thing at our house is that our dogs are afraid of our
               cat.
Child₃: You have dogs *and* a cat!
Teacher: Yes. We have two dogs and one cat.
Child₃: Where are they?
Teacher: At my house.
Child₃: *Well . . . where do they live?*
Teacher: Where do we live? Do you know where the big College Mall
               shopping center is?
(Child₃ hesitates)
Teacher: We live far away. Some day you'll have to come over to our
               house.
Child₃: I'd sure like to come to your house . . . Cause then I could play
               with some [?].
(No response).

In this example, the insufficiency is an Ego's manner of framing his question. The child meant to ask, by 'Where are they?', not where the adult's pets were at the moment, but where they (and, presumably, the adult) habitually live. The response of the adult, 'At my house' does not therefore provide the child with the information he was seeking, and hence the *well* followed by a rephrasing of his original question.

In the following (five-year-old) fragment, the *well* introduces what can be seen as an insufficient rejoinder to Child$_1$'s question–accusation. According to one interpretation, Child$_2$ signals to Child$_1$ that, although he knows that it is not a part of the rules of free play to incarcerate a classmate in a closet, he nevertheless feels partially justified in doing so as an act of revenge for a past infraction of that rule when he was the victim and Child$_1$ the aggressor. According to a second possible interpretation, Child$_2$'s ambiguous feeling about his response comes from the fact that the earlier event which he describes never took place, so that his justification of his present behavior is, in fact, pure fabrication (as the other child's retort implies).

(15)

Child$_1$:   Are you gonna put me in the closet?
Child$_2$:   *Well . . . you caught me once N put me in there.*
Child$_1$:   Now you know I wouldn't do that.
(No response)

In all of the examples, *well* implies that the speaker is 'compromising' in some way. If the addressee has made an error, he corrects without direct complaint or accusation, and, if the speaker himself is in error, his treatment of himself is equally gentle. Notice that *well* is thus a valuable tool for indicating misunderstandings (partial or otherwise) or misrepresentations without disrupting the flow of turn-taking in spontaneous conversation.

From the individual's point of view, *well* shares with *oh, uh,* and *um* the ability to hold a turn for a self-selecting or appointed next speaker because, like the hesitation markers, it signals that the speaker is 'working on' the production of an appropriate turn. I have already noted above (see examples (3), (4), and (6)) the function of *well* as a means by which an appointed next speaker may delay the beginning of his turn, or by which a listener may give others an opportunity to self-select and thus avoid a gap in talk, or, finally, a self-selecting speaker may make the first claim to the floor without actually having to begin his turn immediately. The effectiveness of *well* in holding or securing a turn for its user may be seen by the fact that, in 45 of the 46 examples recorded in the present study, the speaker did in fact take his intended turn without interruption.

Gelman and Shatz (1977: 38) have noted the use of *well* by four-year-olds in order to close down a conversational topic (cf. R. Lakoff's discussion). *Well* also served such a function in the preschool conversations in the present study, beginning at four years of age. The following example indicates that *well* as a prestart may signal the speaker's intention that his turn be considered the 'last word' on the topic under discussion, one reason why a large number of the *well* prestarts were found to occur in children's arguments.

(16)

(Five years)

Child₁: Boys are stronger!
Child₂: Girls are [?].
Child₃: Just because we're girls doesn't mean we're pretty.
Child₂: *Well just because they're boys doesn't mean they're better.*
(Exchange continues with another topic)

2.3   *Affirmatives and acknowledgments*

The affirmatives and acknowledgments used as prestarts by the children in the present study include *uh-huh, hm-hmm, yeh/yes,*[9] *oh* (a short *oh*, with moderate pitch and a downward intonation contour), *right*, and *I know*. Like the forms discussed in Sections 2.1 and 2.2, these expressions reveal little about the substance of the turn which is to follow. Unlike them, however, these forms are ambiguous in that they may also serve as phatic communication, or a back-channel signal, when the user does not actually intend to take a more 'substantive' turn immediately (in which case the affirmative/acknowledgment appears to function more as a prestart to a continuation of talk by current speaker).

Prestart affirmatives and acknowledgments were found in 3.5% of all conversational turns. They were not used by the three-year-olds, by four-year-olds in 0.6% of their turns, and by the oldest children in 4% of theirs. Children preferred the following four types of affirmatives: *yeh/yes* (46% of all examples by children), *oh* (17%), *I know* (13%), and *uh-huh* (10%). The variety of affirmatives used by children increased with age, from none at age three, to four at age four, and five at age five.

Affirmatives and acknowledgements were followed by one of three possible events: (1) Neither speaker nor listener took a turn, as in the following exchange between four-year-olds:

(17)

Child₁: Ya know whose birthday it is now?
Child₂: No.
Child₁: Kathy's! [i.e. Child₂'s]
Child₂: *Oh.*
(No response)

(2) The person to whom the prestart was directed continued to speak, as in the following interchange between four-year-olds:

(18)

Child₁: Hey Angie!
(No response)
                 Angie, I want to tell you something.
(Child₂ — Angie — looks over at Child₁)
Child₁: I have a black-haired sister who used to be five. N yesterday she had a birthday N now she's six.
Child₂: *Hmm.*
Child₁: N I'll be five soon too.
(No response)

(3) The person using the prestart (either a self-selecting listener or a current speaker about to continue) takes a turn, as in the following five-year-old conversations:

(19)

Child₁: Once we had [?] goldfish N we had to flush them down the toilet cause a lot of them died.
Child₂: *I know. N we [?].*
Child₁: You had to bury all your fish?
(Teacher interrupts this exchange)

(20)

Child₁: When am I going to first grade?
Teacher: Next fall.
Child₁: Next fall?

Child₂: You see . . . summer's a big giant holiday. (to Child₁)
Child₃: *Yeh, summer's a long time! So's spring.*
Child₂: *Uh-huh. But you can come to school in the summer to play on the playground.*
Child₁: You know there's 40,000 years in the summer, N 40,000 years in the winter N . . . [Breaks off]
(Class is moved to another room and conversation ends)

The use of affirmatives and acknowledgments for prestarts by children increased with the age of the child. None of the examples served such a function at age four, but they did in 65% of those found at age five. Overall, 60% of the children's examples were prestarts.

When a participant utters an affirmative or acknowledgment which is not in response to a question or imperative and which is situated at a turn-transition relevance point, he merely indicates that he may take a subsequent turn. If he does not, the implication is that the current speaker should continue to develop the line of thought of his preceding turn. The likelihood that a preschool child would in fact continue to speak in such a situation increased with age. At three, children took another turn in 40% of the cases where the adult did not follow her affirmative or acknowledgment with a turn. At four years, children continued speaking in 50% of such cases, and, at age five, in 76%.

2.4. *Hesitation markers*

A small number of preturn hesitation markers were found in the transcripts of the present study (none at age three, only one — produced by an adult — at age four, and six at age five, four by children). The only examples used by the preschool children were in exchanges with an adult. Three forms of hesitation markers were found — *oh, uh,* and *um* — with children using all three.

The *oh* discussed here was longer, lower-pitched, and with a more level tone pattern than the *oh* mentioned under Section 2.3 above. This second hesitation *oh* is the type one could imagine in the following hypothetical answer to the query 'How many people witnessed the accident?':

There were . . . oh . . .ten or eleven people in the street when it happened.

James (1973: 10) describes this *oh* as signaling that 'the speaker is choosing one out of several alternatives, and that he feels that there is no one correct or accurate alternative.' *Oh* did indeed carry such a semantic reading in the two cases where it was used by a child, in each of which it prefaced the answer to a question.

(21)

(Five years)

Adult: Who's in the boat?
Child: *Oh . . . we're just playing.*
Adult: But what kind of people are they supposed to be — pirates?
Child: *Oh . . . we're just playing any ole thing.*
(No response)

Notice that the use of *oh* in this way also implies a certain reluctance on the part of the speaker to answer his interlocutor's question.

In addition to the *uh* found within a turn and given in exchange (2) above, the following example was recorded as a preface to the answer to a question, where it carried a different semantic interpretation from that associated with *oh*:

(22)

(Five years)

Adult: What do you call it when something is colored like its surroundings?
Child: *Uh . . . . .*
Adult: You say it's camouflaged.
Child: Yeh! Camouflaged!
(Adult continues to address the group as a whole)

The hesitation marker, in this case, did not reveal to the adult that the child knew the answer to the question and was hesitating to choose between the more than one appropriate responses, but rather that the child, at the time, was attending to the problem of finding *the* answer to the question (see the discussion of the semantic function of *uh* in James 1973).

The third type of hesitation marker, *um*, is similar in semantic function to *uh*, as can be seen in the following exchange (the only one found in the present study):

(23)

(Five years)

(Child raises his hand, looking at the teacher)
Adult: Eric?
Child: *Um . . . I forgot.*
Adult: OK. You sit down and try to remember what it was.

As in the examples with *oh* (21) and *uh* (22), the person who uses the hesitation marker has been designated next speaker by the current speaker, and clearly is under obligation to take a turn at talk. For one reason or another, he chooses to prolong the true beginning of his turn at talk, filling the pause with a hesitation marker. At the same time, he signals to his interlocutor that he is aware of his obligation to talk, and that he intends to take a turn when this becomes possible (for example, in example (23), when the child finally remembers what it was he had in mind when he raised his hand to be recognized).

In 1959, Maclay and Osgood put forth the hypothesis that hesitation fillers such as those found in the present study fulfill a turn-holding function. They wrote:

Let us assume that the speaker is motivated to keep control of the conversational 'ball' until he has achieved some sense of completion. He has learned that un-filled intervals of sufficient length are the points at which he has usually lost this control — someone else has leapt into his gap. Therefore, if he pauses long enough to receive the cue of his own silence he will produce some kind of signal ([m, r], or perhaps a repetition of the immediately preceding unit) which says, in effect, 'I'm still in control — don't interrupt me'(41).

This hypothesis has been criticized by several authors. Boomer (1965: 154–155), for example, found that 72% of the hesitation markers which he studied were preceded by no pause and a further 11% were preceded by pauses which were shorter than the subject's mean pause length, with only 17% of the markers in his study being preceded by longer than average pauses. The error in the work of both Maclay/ Osgood and their critics is that the turn-holding function of hesitation markers is seen to hinge upon only one variable — time. But, as much of the conversational analysis accomplished in recent years has shown, time itself is important only in relation to other turn-taking variables in spontaneous conversation. The length of time judged to be critical for the holding of a conversational turn will be different if the turn-taker is self-selecting for a turn or whether, as in our examples, he has been selected by the current speaker. It will likewise vary depending on whether the current speaker hesitates at turn-transition relevance points, rather than between, where listeners might be ready to self-select. Thus, counting the length of the speaker's pauses will not necessarily tell you the pressure which he feels in terms of signalling to his listeners that he plans to begin or continue his turn in due course. We can only conclude, at this point, that a turn-holding function for hesitation markers appears, from introspection and consideration of the turn-taking rules of spontaneous conversation, a likely prospect. In order to disprove such a hypothesis, one would have to produce evidence that the hesitation markers occurred randomly in relation to the critical interaction units of conversation. To my knowledge, this has not been done. In any case, in the present study, six out of seven hesitation markers were actually followed by a turn by the hesitator.

3.   SUMMARY AND CONCLUSION

Summarizing the data presented in Section 2, we find that prestarts were more prominent in the conversations of the five-year-olds than in those of the three- or even the four-year-old children. Of the four types of prestarts examined in this paper, only the connectives — in some ways the simplest and most straightforward of the prestarts — were fairly well established in the conversations of the youngest children. *Well* was employed with some regularity as a hedging device, but not as a signal of topical change.

The major changes which occurred between the ages of three and four years with respect to conversational prestarts were (1) an increase in the variety and frequency of occurrence of the connectives; (2) the first appearance of the topic-shifting function of prestart *well*; (3) the beginning of children's use of affirmatives or acknowledgments as prestarts for a continuation of Alter's talk; (4) an increase in the rate at which the children interpreted an adult's affirmative or acknowledgment as a prestart for a continuation of his (the child's) talk; and (5) the introduction of prestarts as a means of retroactively interpreting a lack of response on the part of an interlocutor as a zero signifier.

Several significant changes took place between four and five years of age: (1) The frequency of use of *well* increased dramatically, and the topic-shifting function, especially as found in children's arguments, took on greater importance. (2) Hesitation markers made their first appearance, but primarily as prestarts of turns by a child who has been assigned the floor by an adult current speaker. (3) Affirmatives or acknowledgments used as prestarts to a self-selected turn by a child were found for the first time at this age. (4) There was an increase in the rate at which the child responded to an interlocutor's (adult or child) acknowledgment or affirmative as a prestart to a continuation of his own (the child's) turn.

The semantic and pragmatic (turn-taking) functions of the four prestarts are, as noted above, interdependent, so that the age-related increase in children's reliance on them no doubt reflects a growing awareness of the subtle transformation of utterance meanings which they make possible as well as of their perlocutionary force. That the data presented here do indicate an increment in the child's sensitivity to the conversational rule of avoiding gaps is seen by the fact that, for example, affirmation or acknowledgment of the statement of a co-participant's turn is usually expressed as a presupposition of a self-selected turn made in response to it. The addition of an affirmative or acknowledgment prestart is thus, semantically speaking, redundant, and the most plausible reason for its presence in the conversation is its contribution to the smooth, uninterrupted allocation of turns among conversationalists. More or less the same situation applies to the other three types of prestarts.

Perhaps the most convincing proof of an increase in the preschool child's ability to read and manipulate silences in ways similar to those employed by adults is the alteration in the range of prestart turn-taking functions between the ages of three and five. For the three-year-old, prestarts were principally a means of being the first to self-select for a turn and thus for obtaining a turn for oneself. The effect of the use of prestarts at that age was to facilitate smooth turn allocation, but the impetus was an egocentric one, the aim a single turn at talk.

By five years of age, however, one finds prestarts as signs which reinterpret preceding silences, as, for example, those of the speaker, in the employment of hesitation markers prior to a delayed taking of an Alter-selected turn at talk, or those of a listener, for example when a preturn connective analyzes a lack of response to Ego's turn as conversationally meaningful. Equally significant is the use, by age five, of prestarts as a way of projecting an interpretation onto possible future silences, as, for example, when a participant holds a turn for a co-participant with a prestart affirmative or acknowledgment, or, on the contrary, for himself, as with an intra-turn hesitation marker. Another form of projective interpretation is when *well* is used to indicate an impending change of topic, for in such cases the prestart interjection indicates to listeners either that the speaker is about to have the last word about a topic, and the silence of the listeners immediately following the *well* means that they do not object to the closing down of the topic and are willing to self-select at the conclusion of the turn in order to introduce a new one (if they do not, it would mean that talk as a whole might be closed), or that he is about to select the next speaker as the person who is to have the last word, in which case, if that person does not take a turn, the silence will be read as belonging to him. By age five, in other words, the preschool child not only avoids gaps in conversation by taking his own turn as quickly as possible at a turn-transition relevance point, either as a self-selector or someone appointed by current speaker, but by creating conversational situations in which co-participants would be more or less obliged to assign a restricted set of meanings to silences, and these interpretations influence his conversational partners in the direction of producing precisely timed turns of their own. These preschool advances in the control of conversational turn-taking testify to the importance for language acquisition studies of the investigation of what goes on between turns — both the signs of silence and silent signs, as distinguished from simply nonverbal signifiers and signifieds — for the child is as intent on developing adultlike expertise in this area as in those available directly to the senses.

NOTES

1. The following is a brief summary of the discussion of conversational sequencing rules by Sacks, Schegloff and Jefferson (1974): Current speaker may select next speaker and, if he has not done so by the completion of the construction unit of his turn, listener may self-select, with earliest starter generally taking the floor. If there is no self-selection, current speaker may or may not continue speaking, and, if so, rule one regarding current speaker selecting next speaker again becomes operative, and so forth.
2. On verbal *'signes zéros'* or *'Nullzeichen'*, see especially Jakobson (1971b: 211–222), and on verbal and nonverbal 'zero-signifiers' and 'zero-signifieds' more generally, see Sebeok (1976:118).
3. This paper is based on chapter 6 ('Avoiding Gaps and Overlapping') of Umiker-Sebeok (1976:261–281). Due to space limitations for this paper, I have eliminated discussion of the crucial issue of the effect of different types of interlocutors on preschool prestart behavior. On this question, see Umiker-Sebeok (1976, 1977).
4. Omitted from consideration here are double adjacency-pair first pair-parts when used as turn prestarts and the acknowledgment OK, both of which are discussed separately, in Umiker-Sebeok (in preparation).
5. A question mark between square brackets indicates that a section of a conversational turn was unintelligible to the recorder of the exchange. A series of three periods marks a brief pause, longer pauses being signified by: . . . (pause) . . .
6. On preschool children's hedges, see the discussions below of *well* and hesitation markers.
7. The figures relating to the frequency of use of prestart *well* by three- and four-year-olds

reflect an adjustment which takes into account the overproduction of this form by certain individuals.

8. Hedge verbs are in some cases prestarts to conversational turns, although they are not as easily 'deletable' as the forms discussed in this paper. With the exception of *to know* (e.g. the *I know* included in this paper as an affirmative prestart), hedge verbs were not a common element in the preschool conversations in the present study. Only one or two examples of *I think* or *I guess* were recorded, being used by the oldest children.

9. While *yeh* and *yes* were both used as both prestart/back-channel signals and answers to questions, by far the most common pattern of usage was *yeh* as a prestart/back-channel signal, *yes* as a reply to a question.

PART V

Theoretical Approaches to Human Interaction

ALBERT SZENT-GYÖRGYI

Dionysians and Apollonians[1]

Wilhelm Ostwald (1909)[2] divided scientists into the classical and the romantic. One could call them also systematic and intuitive. John R. Platt (personal communication) calls them Apollonian and Dionysian. These classifications reflect extremes of two different attitudes of the mind that can be found equally in art, painting, sculpture, music, or dance. One could probably discover them in other alleys of life. In science the Apollonian tends to develop established lines to perfection, while the Dionysian rather relies on intuition and is more likely to open new, unexpected alleys for research. Nobody knows what 'intuition' really is. My guess is that it is a sort of subconscious reasoning, only the end result of which becomes conscious.

These are not merely academic problems. They have most important corollaries and consequences. The future of mankind depends on the progress of science, and the progress of science depends on the support it can find. Support mostly takes the form of grants, and the present methods of distributing grants unduly favor the Apollonian. Applying for a grant begins with writing a project. The Apollonian clearly sees the future lines of his research and has no difficulty writing a clear project. Not so the Dionysian, who knows only the direction in which he wants to go out into the unknown; he has no idea what he is going to find there and how he is going to find it. Defining the unknown or writing down the subconscious is a contradiction in absurdum. In his work, the Dionysian relies, to a great extent, on accidental observation. His observations are not completely 'accidental', because they involve not merely seeing things but also grasping their possible meaning. A great deal of conscious or subconscious thinking must precede a Dionysian's observations. There is an old saying that a discovery is an accident finding a prepared mind. The Dionysian is often not only unable to tell what he is going to find, he may even be at a loss to tell how he made his discovery.

Being myself Dionysian, writing projects was always an agony for me, as I described not long ago in *Perspectives of Biology and Medicine*

(Szent-Györgyi 1971). I always tried to live up to Leo Szilard's (personal communication) commandment, 'don't lie if you don't have to'. I had to. I filled up pages with words and plans I knew I would not follow. When I go home from my laboratory in the late afternoon, I often do not know what I am going to do the next day. I expect to think that up during the night. How could I tell then, what I would do a year hence? It is only lately that I can see somewhat ahead (which may be a sign of senescence) and write a realistic proposal, but the queer fact is that, while earlier all my fake projects were always accepted, since I can write down honestly what I think I will do my applications have been invariably rejected. This seems quite logical to me; sitting in an easy chair I can cook up any time a project which must seem quite attractive, clear, and logical. But if I go out into nature, into the unknown, to the fringes of knowledge, everything seems mixed up and contradictory, illogical, and incoherent. This is what research does; it smooths out contradiction and makes things simple, logical, and coherent. So when I bring reality into my projects, they become hazy and are rejected. The reviewer, feeling responsible for 'the taxpayer's money', justly hesitates to give money for research, the lines of which are not clear to the applicant himself.

A discovery must be, by definition, at variance with existing knowledge. During my lifetime, I made two. Both were rejected offhand by the popes of the field. Had I predicted these discoveries in my applications, and had these authorities been my judges, it is evident what their decisions would have been.

These difficulties could perhaps, be solved to some extent, by taking into account the applicant's early work. Or, if the applicant is young and has had no chance to prove himself, the vouching of an elder researcher acquainted with the applicant's ability may be considered. The problem is a most important one, especially now, as science grapples with one of nature's mysteries, cancer, which may demand entirely new approaches.

NOTES

1. Reprinted from *Science* 176 (June 2, 1972): 966.
2. Ostwald (1909), *Grosse Männer*. Leipzig, Akademische Verlagsgesellchaft GMBH.

ARNOLD M. ZWICKY

The Analogy of Linguistics with Chemistry[1]

The Substance Theory of Semantic Primes, as I have already pointed out, is analogous to Boyle's requirement, in the 'Sceptical Chymist' of 1661, that chemical elements be isolable substances and not abstract principles. We have also seen Katz's comparison of semantic structure to chemical structure. Here I will press this analogy further, with the intention of using the chemical case to suggest useful lines of inquiry in the linguistic case. That is, I will be claiming that the parallels between chemical structure and semantic structure are deep ones. This is not to say, of course, that the two subfields of the different disciplines are isomorphic in every detail. I do not anticipate the discovery of a set of deep principles from which the properties of chemical structure and those of semantic structure will both be derivable. Indeed, there are aspects of each subfield which are without obvious analogs in the other; for instance, there is nothing in the chemical case that is a natural correspondent of the phonological identity that unites the two senses of *persuade* (CAUSE-INCHOATIVE-INTEND and CAUSE-INCHOATIVE-BELIEVE) or the distinct senses (each a separate lexical unit) of many other words.

The initial analogy is of language to matter. The strategy of the disciplines, linguistics and chemistry, respectively, is to analyze heterogeneous physical material (speech, materials) into its parts (words, substances) and then to treat these parts as either elemental substances (semantic primes, elements) or compounds of such elemental substances. These analytic preliminaries require the identification and removal of various kinds of intrusive factors.

The central part of the analogy, then, is an occurrence of a semantic prime in some language, on the one hand, and an atom of some chemical element, on the other. Corresponding to lexical entries are molecules.[2] Certain molecules, hydrogen molecules for instance, are composed of only one sort of atom. In the same way, certain lexical entries, the entry for *cause* for instance, are composed of only one sort of prime. Other molecules, the sulfuric acid molecule for one, possess an internal structure in which more than one sort of atom (hydrogen, sulfur, oxygen) occurs. Just so, some lexical entries, the entry for *kill* among them, possess an internal structure with more than one sort of prime (CAUSE, INCHOATIVE, NOT, ALIVE).

In both linguistics and chemistry, the great majority of the known substances (or words) are complex. In each field, the number of actually occurring substances is quite large, and the number of possible substances is infinite in principle, though limited in fact by external factors (the physical instability of the molecules, the psychological complexity of the words).

Also, in both linguistics and chemistry, there are molecular properties which are 'emergent', in the sense that they are not predictable by known principles from the character of the constituents of the molecule. Broad (1925) writes of a familiar chemical example:

Oxygen has certain properties and Hydrogen has certain other properties. They combine to form water, and the proportions in which they do this are fixed. Nothing that we know about Oxygen itself or in combination with anything but Hydrogen could give us the least reason to suppose that it could combine with Hydrogen at all . . . And most of the chemical and physical properties of water have no known connexion, either quantitative or qualitative, with those of Oxygen and Hydrogen. Here we have a clear instance where, so far as we can tell, the properties of a whole composed of two constituents could not have been predicted from a knowledge of these properties taken separately, or from this combined with a knowledge of the properties of other wholes which contain these constituents (62–63).

The linguistic analog is the apparent impossibility of predicting the full range of syntactic properties of a lexical item given its decomposition into primes. From what semantic analysis of the verb *question* could one predict that it can be used performatively when its direct object is a simple NP (as in *I question that statement*) or a *whether*-clause (as in *I question whether we should do this*) but not when it is any other sort of *wh*-clause (**I question where he lives*) or a *that*-clause (**I question that he was responsible*) or an *if*-clause (**I question if we should do this*)?

In the quantitative atomic theory proposed by Dalton, it is assumed that the atoms of the same element are identical, in the sense that they have identical masses, and that atoms of different elements have different masses. The corresponding assumptions in semantics are that instances of the same semantic prime are associated with the same cognitive meaning (that is, that the cognitive meaning of a semantic prime is invariant across languages) and that different semantic primes have different meanings.

The tasks of chemistry are partly analytical (to devise methods for isolating and identifying substances), partly descriptive (to say what sorts of substances occur and what their properties are), and partly explanatory (to give an account of chemical structure from which the observed phenomena could be predicted). The analytical and descriptive aspects of elemental theory are summarized well in Weeks (1968), from which I conclude that semantics is a few hundred years behind chemistry simply in the matter of listing elements, not to mention explaining their properties. It is as if we were really sure of only a dozen or so chemical elements. Semantics has had no Mendeleev to organize the elements in a periodic table according to their salient common properties; and the linguistic analog of the Bohr atom, from which the groupings in the periodic table could be predicted, is scarcely imaginable.

If the structural analogy between chemistry and semantics is deep, what sorts of developments can we expect in semantics? Three, at least: the discovery of isotopes, a theory of valence, and the hypothesis of subatomic structure. I believe that there are indications that all three of these expectations are met.

First, there is the matter of isotopes. The discovery of different atoms of the 'same' element with different masses (and even of atoms of 'different' elements with the same mass) is an obvious embarrassment for a theory which takes an invariant mass to be criterial for a given element. The existence of isotopes, especially those which (like light and heavy hydrogen) have quite distinct properties, makes the study of subatomic structure inevitable. What are the semantic analogs of isotopes? They are occurrences of the 'same' semantic prime with different meanings. Just this sort of situation is exhibited by lexical items which are 'denotatively' distinct but do not differ in any independently motivated semantic feature; these are terms for correlative species, for example *rose, chrysanthemum,* and *pansy*, or *snap, crackle, thud*, and *rumble*. (The latter set of cases is from the discussion in Leech (1969: 85–89). It is natural to say that these two sets of items represent only two semantic primes — (SPECIFIC) FLOWER and MAKE A (SPECIFIC) NOISE — and that the individual lexical items differ subatomically.

Next, we turn to a theory of valence, a set of combinatory principles for semantic primes. Among these principles in semantics are conditions stating that a certain predicate 'takes' so many arguments, of such and such a type; these conditions have been much studied by Fillmore (1970, for example), among others. Also relevant here are conditions governing the embedding of one S in another — the deep structure constraints of Perlmutter (1971), restrictions on the occurrence of special classes of predicates, such as the stative and activity predicates, constraints against certain predicates embedding themselves (*TRY *to* TRY, *INTEND *to* INTEND), and the like.

Finally, there is subatomic structure. This is already called for by the isotope cases and might serve to explain the valence phenomena. It could also provide an account of the way in which primes fall into subclasses having properties in common (a set of connectives, like AND and OR, a set of modal elements, like NECESSARY and POSSIBLE, and so on). There are in addition a number of relationships among primes that might be accounted for by means of subatomic structure — the duality relation of NECESSARY–POSSIBLE, REQUIRE–PERMIT, AND–OR, and SOME–EVERY, for instance, or the relation between nonepistemic BE FREE TO and epistemic POSSIBLE (both realized as English *can*) and between nonepistemic HAVE TO and epistemic NECESSARY (both realized as English *must*). In his treatment of semantic primes, Grosu (1970) adopts a theory of subatomic structure without comment by deciding 'to represent them as bundles of semantic and syntactic properties' (41): he includes (84–89) a tentative list of such properties (of types already mentioned) for seven putative primes — CAUSE, IN-CHOATIVE, TRY, INTEND, BE ABLE TO, BE FREE TO, and HAVE TO.

In his discussion of the sort of emergence illustrated earlier in this section, Nagel (1961: 366–374) observes that emergence is relative to a particular theory, so that as theories change, it may become possible to predict properties that were inexplicable within a previous theory. He notes that a change of this sort has occurred in chemistry, where properties of substances which were formerly thought to be emergent now can be predicted from an electronic theory of atomic composition. It is even possible to imagine that all properties of interest to chemists and still considered emergent might be predictable. The rather breathtaking linguistic analog is that there might turn out to be no syntactic exceptions, that the behavior of every lexical item with respect to syntactic rules and constraints might be predictable in some way from its semantic structure.[3]

ANALOGY AND METAPHOR

I have claimed that the parallel between chemical structure and semantic structure is systematic enough to merit study, hence, that it is like the parallel between water waves and electromagnetic phenomena, which is treated at length by Hesse (1966) in her very interesting work on models and analogies. She draws a distinction between metaphors, which are suggestive but not productive, and material analogies, which function to provide models for inquiry.

Merely metaphoric are such names as Ross's 'Post Office Principle' and the 'Free Ride Principle' (1966[1969]), as well as his 'tree-pruning' and 'Pied Piping' (1967: Section 4.3). More information about the way the post office operates is not likely to further the study of the requirement that transformations preserve meaning,[4] and arboricultural research will not elucidate problems of derived constituent structure.

To round out this discussion, I will contrast some instances of merely metaphorical writing with examples of more illuminating analogies, choosing now nontransformational illustrations.

For the unsatisfying cases, I have selected ideas of two of the most original and inspiring traditional grammarians, Noreen and Jespersen. Lotz (1966) summarizes Noreen's theory of the structure of grammar as follows:

Thus, grammar should have three branches, each of which should view the entire speech phenomenon from a special angle: *phonology*, which should treat the articulated sound; *semology*, which should deal with the linguistically formed psychological content; and *morphology*, which should account for the way in which the sound material is formed to express the semantic content. He attempted to elucidate these distinctions by analogies, e.g. a certain object can be regarded as a piece of bone (material), having the shape of a cube (content), and serving as a dice (form); or, as a building composed of bricks (material), in Moorish style (content), and serving as a café (form). But these analogies are rather far-fetched and not very illuminating (58–59).

And McCawley (1970) attacks Jespersen's poetic attempts in *Analytic Syntax* (1937[1969]: 120–121) to distinguish the notions 'nexus' and 'junction':

In *AS*, his characterizations of nexus and junction rest heavily on analogies which I find unenlightening (447).

Compare the corresponding analogies in Jespersen (1924):

Comparisons, of course, are always to some extent inadequate, still as these things are very hard to express in a completely logical or scientific way, we may be allowed to say that the way in which the adjunct is joined to its primary is like the way in which the nose and ears are fixed on the head, while an adnex rests on its primary as the head on the trunk or a door on the wall. A junction is here like a picture, a nexus like a process or drama (116).

In the same work, Jespersen strives to account for the relationships of modifiers by means of an analogy less striking than he had hoped it would be:

. . . it is really most natural that a less special term is used in order further to specialize what is already to some extent special: the method of attaining a high degree of specialization is analogous to that of reaching the roof of a building by means of ladders: if one ladder will not do, you first take the tallest ladder you have and tie the second tallest to the top of it, and if that is not enough, you tie on the next length, etc. In the same way, if *widow* is not special enough, you add *poor*, which is less special than *widow*, and yet, if it is added, enables you to reach farther in specialization; if that does not suffice, you add the subjunct *very*, which in itself is much more general than *poor* (108).

For an instance of a more productive analogy, consider the parallel between replacement of vocabulary items in a language over time and the decay of radioactive elements, a parallel first emphasized by Swadesh and discussed clearly by Lees (1953):

The members of the chosen subset may be likened to the (indistinguishable) atoms in a given mass of a radioactive element. Since the rate of disintegration is predictable at any time during observation of the sample, the mass (or number of remaining atoms) of the element remaining among the decay products at any time in the sample is a measure of how long the sample has been decaying. The analysis of decay products in mineral samples permits the calculation of the age of the earth's crust. Similarly, analyses of morpheme decay products should provide an absolute chronology for lexical history (113–114).

This analogy turns out to have several faults: morpheme decay probably does not proceed at a constant rate, and, even if it did, the resulting estimates of absolute chronologies would normally not be exact enough for ordinary linguistic purposes. Nevertheless, the analogy is close enough to have inspired some important research, and in special cases glottochronological methods are still useful.

Analogies of many kinds were a fancy of nineteenth-century writers on language. In the following passage, Whitney (1867) spoke more truly than he could have known:[5]

There is a yet closer parallelism between the life of language and that of the animal kingdom in general. The speech of each person is, as it were, an individual of a species, with its general inherited conformity to the specific type, but also with its individual peculiarities, its tendency to variation and the formation of a new species. The dialects, languages, groups, families, stocks, set up by the linguistic student, correspond with the varieties, species, genera, and so on, of the zoölogist. And the questions which the students of nature are so excitedly discussing at the present day — the nature of specific distinctions, the derivation of species by individual variation and natural selection, the unity of origin of animal life — all are closely akin with those which the linguistic student has constant occasion to treat. We need not here dwell further upon the comparison: it is so naturally suggested, and so fruitful of interesting and instructive analogies, that it has been repeatedly drawn out and employed, by students both of nature and of language (46–47).

Whitney cites Lyell and Schleicher as additional proponents of the proportion

species : variety = language dialect

and of the related parallels between genetic classification in linguistics and biological taxonomy, although Whitney nevertheless castigates Schleicher for attempting 'to prove by [this proportion's] aid the truth of the Darwinian theory, overlooking the fact that the relation between the two classes of phenomena is one of analogy only, not of essential agreement' (47).

In fact, the analogy is a deep one. There is a population of individuals, who vary in a number of characteristics (linguistic or morphological). The individuals form themselves into a number of groups on the basis of their similarities. There is also an ability for certain pairs of individuals to interact in a special way, if they are brought together. (Their speech is mutually intelligible, in the linguistic case, or they can (inter)breed, in the biological case.) The interactive ability is then used scientifically as a necessary and sufficient test for determining groups within the population. (In the linguistic case, mutual intelligibility is used as a stringent criterion for a *language*, and in the biological case, ability to interbreed is used as a stringent criterion for a *species*.)

Several developments of these notions can be predicted. First, it will frequently not be possible to bring together the appropriate pairs in order to test relationships. Thus, biological specimens may be dead, or geographically separated, or ecologically separated; languages may be defunct or far-flung. In both fields, the consequence is the development of an independent notion of relationship, one based solely on the characteristics. In the case of biology, this is the 'morphological' species, as opposed to the 'biological' species (see, *inter alia*, Cain 1954[1960]). In the case of linguistics, this is the Stammbaum principle of genetic classification, as opposed to a sociolinguistic classification. The new, or 'strict', theory is easily seen to be unsatisfactory because the characteristics will show a considerable degree of independence, hence, a

Wellentheorie in linguistics and a theory of diffusion of characters through gene pools in biology.

Another, less predictable characteristic of the systems we are considering is that the stringent criterion turns out not to characterize a transitive relation. That is, evidence will arise indicating that the criterion is not necessary but merely sufficient. In the case of biology, we have animal chains in which each animal can breed with the animals in the adjoining territory, although the animals at the extremes cannot interbreed (a readable exposition occurs in Dobzhansky [1955: Chapter 8]): in the case of a 'species' of gulls surrounding the North Pole, the extremes happen to occur in the same area and cannot interbreed. The linguistic analogies are well-known cases where groups of speakers find their dialect mutually intelligible with their neighbors' but the extreme dialects are not mutually intelligible. Indeed, knowing the case of the gulls, we might have been able to predict the existence of problematical dialect chains.

The analogy between linguistic and biological classification is a systematic one: in most respects, there is a point-to-point correspondence between the two fields. The claim made in this paper is that the correspondence between semantic and chemical structure is of the same sort.

NOTES

1. This excerpt is from the last part of an article (Sections 3.2. and 3.3.) 'Linguistics as Chemistry: the Substance Theory of Semantic Primes', in (1973), *A Festschrift for Morris Halle*, edited by Stephen R. Anderson and Paul Kiparsky, 467–485. New York, Holt, Rinehart and Winston. Used by permission.
2. This much of the parallel is echoed by Postal (1970: 100–101), who speaks of 'semantic atoms' and 'semantic molecules' but does not take the terms to be more than simple metaphors.
3. Substituted revised footnote: Green (1974) has explored in some detail 'the position that all differences in syntactic properties between two lexical items must be assumed to be based on semantic properties' (66). [A.M.Z.]
4. Although I cannot resist pointing out that structures in violation of derivational constraints are the analogs of pieces of mail returned to the sender.
5. The passage is sandwiched between an analogy relating linguistic history and organic growth and one associating earlier stages of a language with geological strata.

F. T. CLOAK, JR.

Why Electromagnetism Is the Only Causal 'Spook' Required to Explain Completely Any Human Behavior or Institution[1]

In *Chance and Necessity* (1971), Jacques Monod has successfully demonstrated, I think, that ontogenesis — the process by which the ontogeny of an organism occurs — is merely an extension of the process by which atoms unite into simple molecules and simple molecules unite into more complex molecules. This is the process of formation of electron bonds, covalent and noncovalent; its outcome in each case is determined by two things: (1) the structures and spatiotemporal relations of the material structures that went into it, and (2) the mysterious universal causal force or fundamental principle called Electromagnetism. My purpose here is to show that all human behaviors and institutions, too, are determined entirely by (1) entering material structures and relations and (2) Electromagnetism.

SPOOKS

Before I go on discussing ontogenesis, let me digress for a moment to discuss mysterious universal causal forces and fundamental principles or, to use a good old American term in a way borrowed from Wes Jackson (personal communication), 'spooks'. Physicists today generally recognize four spooks; namely, Gravitation, Electromagnetism, and the Strong and Weak Interactions in the atomic nucleus.[2] Reducing the number of spooks is a main goal of physics. In the last century, Maxwell showed that electricity and magnetism can be reduced to one spook, Electromagnetism. Early in this century, Einstein reduced inertia and gravitation to Gravitation alone, and he died trying to unite Electromagnetism and Gravitation under his unified field theory. Today, some theoretical physicists are attempting to reduce the Weak Interaction and Electromagnetism to a single spook; they are encouraged by the fact that these two forces have about the same strength, whereas Gravitation is much much weaker, and the Strong Interaction much much stronger, than they.

To anticipate a bit: the characteristics of any living thing or any product of a living thing — including a behavior, an artifact, or a social organization — are entirely the outcomes of two sequences of events that happen to that thing and/or product — its ontogeny and its phylogeny. Very roughly, its ontogeny is the sequence of events through which the thing develops from seed, and its phylogeny is the sequence of events through which the seed acquired its characteristic ontogeny in the first place. What I aim to show in this essay is that both the ontogeny and the phylogeny of any thing or product can be completely explained without reference to any spook other than those now recognized by physics. In fact, of those four we can make do practically all the time with Electromagnetism alone. There are no special spook principles that apply to organic life — I think Monod shows that — and there are no special spook principles that apply to human affairs; no Duality Principle, no Principle of Equivalence of Siblings, no Principle of Least Effort, no Principle of Logico-Aesthetic Integration, no Principle of Adaptation or Anticipation; we don't need them to explain human affairs scientifically, so to invoke them is to violate the rule of science that entities must not be multiplied beyond necessity: Occam's razor.

EXPLANATION

To the extent that they are valid as empirical generalizations, some of these 'principles' may be useful in scientific activities, and in practical affairs, as mnemonic devices. But the purpose of science is to *explain* events and their relations, not merely to generalize relations between classes of events, although such generalizations may be useful steps in the enterprise of developing explanation. For example, I think we *explain* the movement of the dial on a 'pressure' gauge, of a certain closed cylinder of gas which is being heated, by means of the kinetic theory, i.e. by Electromagnetism. We describe (among other things) the changes in state and activity of the gas molecules in that very cylinder, and show how the gas molecules strike the piston or diaphragm of the gauge with increasing velocity and frequency. We do not explain the event, the movement of the dial, by deduction from Charles' Law; indeed, we do not introduce terms like 'temperature' or 'pressure' into our explanatory discourse at all. Charles' Law, which states the relationship between the temperature and pressure of an enclosed gas, is not an explanatory principle; it is, rather, a general proposition based, first, on generalization and extrapolation from a number of specific experimental instances and, second, on its predictability from the kinetic theory; it does not, however, enter into the *explanation* of specific experimental instances. From the point of view of the history or evolution of science, of course, Charles' Law was very important; its discovery and confirmation led others to work out the kinetic theory. And, of course, it could be very useful in designing, say, a boiler.

I think that microtheories (such as the kinetic theory) are often slow to be accepted because they are contrary to our habits of thought. Confronted by a macroevent, such as the movement of a dial, we prefer to invent, and to cling to, a spook like 'pressure' — something that will give us a macroexplanation. As the Reverend Mr. Hale says, in Arthur Miller's *The Crucible*, 'Man, we must look to the cause proportionate.' A recurring example of this practice, in evolutionary studies, is the 'argument from Design'. But the ubiquity of the inverse square law suggests to me that *all* macroevents have microexplanations. If that is true, we are wasting our time when we look for correlations between classes of macroevents without simultaneously seeking microexplanations to provide the causal links; heating the cylinder was a determinant of the moving of the dial not because 'heating an enclosed gas always increases its pressure', but because we have a series of microexplanatory links between the heating and the moving.

ONTOGENESIS

For purposes of this article, ontogenesis is not the same thing as ontogeny. The word 'ontogeny' refers to a specific sequence of events in a specific organism, from conception to adulthood and conception again; then on to senescence and death. (The ontogeny of a bacterium, I suppose, begins with cell division and ends with the next cell division.) An initial characterization of 'ontogenesis', on the other hand, would be 'the underlying process by which ontogeny takes place'. But that characterization would be a very bad definition, or really no definition at all; the 'by which' part spoils it, turning it into nothing but a label covering ignorance; as soon say 'lithogenesis is the underlying process by which lithogeny (rock-formation) takes place'. By studying the ontogenies of organisms of various kinds, however, we begin to get an idea of what ontogenesis *is*, and not just what it does. We see the same things, the same variants of the ontogenetic process, occurring again and again.[3]

As one variant, we see two or more structures that have drifted close together suddenly aligning themselves in a certain relationship and bonding together to form a larger structure; we see this repeated again and again — when two structures similar to those meet they align and form a similar larger structure. We see this in the assembly of the protein coat of a tobacco mosaic virus, where the initial structures are all the same kind of protein and they form a cylinder by bonding together in a tight helix. We see it also in the spontaneous linking up of the disparate parts of a T-4 bacteriophage, and ribosomes may be formed from protein molecules and RNA nucleotides by this automatic 'self-assembling' process.

A second variant of the ontogenetic process occurs when a relatively large structure unites temporarily with a small structure, as in the first variant; but this time a bond within the small structure is broken, and then the two components of the small structure are released separately, leaving the large structure in its previous form; in other words the large structure, an enzyme molecule, breaks the small structure down into two of its constituents. Examples include a chlorophyll molecule breaking a water molecule down into hydrogen and oxygen ions, and a digestive enzyme breaking a starch down into a sugar and a something else.

A third variant is an opposite of the second. An enzyme forms a temporary structure with *two* small structures which bond together while attached to the enzyme and are released as a single new structure, again leaving the enzyme as before. A series of such reactions, each involving a different enzyme and two structures constructed by previous enzymes in the series, builds up quite large structures — structures with as much as one percent of the mass of the enzyme itself. Indeed, structures constructed this way include *components* of enzymes and other proteins; namely, amino acid molecules. They also include nucleic acid molecules, vitamins, sugars, fatty acids — in fact, any 'middle-sized' molecule. Each enzyme, of course, is different in structure from any other enzyme and, according to its structure, ordinarily enters into just one constructive reaction with just two specific small structures.

A fourth variant is as follows. DNA nucleotides in a strand bond to free nucleotides of DNA or RNA and then release the latter as a complementary strand, forming a gene or gene-partner, an RNA messenger, or perhaps the RNA component of a ribosome or amino-acid transfer unit.

A fifth variant is really a sequenced combination of all of the first four. One end of an RNA messenger-strand bonds to a ribosome, then its first codon bonds to the anti-codon of a transfer unit. The messenger then moves one codon-length into the ribosome, its second codon bonds to another transfer unit, and the amino acid bonded to the first transfer unit bonds to that carried by the second. As this process is repeated over and over, the messenger ratchets through the ribosome, the transfer units unbond from their amino acids, and a strand of 100 to 300 amino acids, a polypeptide, emerges from the ribosome.

A sixth variant, practically the same as the first, is the automatic folding of the polypeptide into its characteristic globular, protein form, as various free bonding-sites on its constituent amino acids form bonds with each other.

A seventh variant is the temporary bonding of a gene or protein by a small molecule which prevents, or permits, or alters, its formation of other bonds. The latter may include those bonds entered into in the sixth variant; thus the temporary bonding or the subsequent unbonding may change the gross shape of a protein.

An eighth variant is alteration in any of the above reactions by an increase or decrease in the activity of atoms in the entering structures, caused by electromagnetic radiation from other, near or distant structures — as when sunlight activates chlorophyll in a green plant or stimulates enzymes to form vitamin D in an animal.

There may be other variants that I haven't remembered to mention. It seems clear, however, that all the microprocesses of ontogenesis are based on the formation and de-formation of chemical bonds between material structures of various kinds and of various submicroscopic and microscopic sizes: The only spook involved is that which causes bonding to take place — Electromagnetism.

It is not difficult, moreover, to imagine how an ordered sequence of such microprocesses, in series and parallel, can result in an ordered sequence of macroevents, producing a structure as complicated as a virus or a cell, stocking it with substructures of various kinds, and even endowing it with what for it is gross behavior. And, of course, the ontogenetic process of mitosis, or cell division, is well understood and, again, it is not difficult to imagine several, or even several dozen, cells remaining bonded together, membrane-protein to membrane-protein, after division. To get a true multicellular organism, then, we need only have a mechanism to control the ontogeny of individual cells — to stop and start it and to produce cells of different sorts from the same identical set of genes. The details of this mechanism are not at all understood yet, although it seems clear that at every differentiation point in the ontogenetic process some form of positional cueing of genes is involved. In other words, every gene for every kind of cell is included in every individual cell, but the sequential order of microevents varies according to the cell's relationship to events occurring in other cells and in the rest of its surroundings; these events 'disturb' the cueing of its genes, that is to say they determine or prevent the bonding — and hence inactivation — of some genes, through the seventh variant of the ontogenetic process. Many genes, as a result, never participate in the fifth variant of the process at all in certain cells so that, for example, a liver cell lacks enzymes and even larger structures that a neuron has, and *vice-versa*.

THE SPECIAL ROLE OF THE GENES

Biologists are fond of saying that '(only) the genes contain all the information' for the ontogeny of a particular organism. I think that abstract biological expression can be dissected into the following: In any ordered set of ontogenetic processes, some variables are controlled by processes of the set and some are not; specifically, some structures entering into reactions in the set are the products of preceding reactions and some must be found in the surroundings. The latter, of course, must be found in *full sufficiency* or the ontogenetic process will not run its full course. Among the former, the structures produced by preceding reactions, genes have a sort of existential priority: An ontogenetic process can be completely reconstituted in the total absence of structures of one specific kind or even of several specific kinds *except for genes*; if enzymes of one kind are completely absent, for instance, they will be assembled, in the necessary quantity, through the fifth variant of the process; if amino acids of one kind are completely absent, enzymes will synthesize them through the third variant; and so forth. But if *genes* of one specific kind are completely absent they *can't* be synthesized, so the enzyme or protein they code for can never be replaced as it is used up or worn out, and so the ontogenetic process cannot run its full course and may very well abort completely or even run wild. So, in a sense, genes are like those structures that must be found in the surroundings; unlike those structures, however, they need not be found in full sufficiency, because they (and they alone) have the ability to *replicate themselves* through the fourth variant of the ontogenetic process. Theoretically, at least, just one gene of each kind is sufficient for the construction of a trillion-celled organism or, indeed, a whole population of such.

So we are prepared to make two assertions:

First, any microevent in the ontogeny of any organism can be explained by two things: (1) the structure of the structures that entered that event, in particular the spatial relationships of bonding-sites on their 'surfaces' and the electrical charge at each bonding-site, and (2) the great spook of Electromagnetism.

Second, any macroevent in the ontogeny of an organism is nothing but an outcome of an ordered sequence of such microevents — in fact, the ontogeny as a whole is such a macroevent.

From these two assertions it follows that given a complete set of genes, a 'starter-set' of amino-acids, enzymes, ribosomes, etc., an adequate supply of certain small and middle-sized molecules and a certain range of levels of energy of different frequencies in the surroundings, and the great spook of Electromagnetism, each step in the ontogeny of a bacterium or a rat, from fertilized egg to adult and fertilized egg, is inevitable.

Aha, one might say. Such a process might result in an adult rat, but it wouldn't be a normal adult rat; it would be a stupid, incompetent, psychologically maimed adult rat, because it wouldn't have had the *experience* a rat needs to grow up properly. And, of course, that is right; indeed, it wouldn't be a proper rat at all.

But let's look again and see what ontogenesis can do besides constructing bacteria and the psychologically empty husks of rats; perhaps, given the necessary material structures and relations, it can account for all behavior, even learned behavior, even culturally acquired behavior and its products.

BEHAVIOR

First, let's consider an act of (unlearned) gross behavior on the part of a simple metazoan.[4] Such a macroevent is the outcome of an ordered sequence of microevents, some occurring in parallel, some in series, all of them examples of the ontogenetic process. First, a molecule, a change in electromagnetic radiation, or some other disturbance in the organism's surroundings releases activity of an enzyme in a peripheral cell. That activity, in turn, results in the release of packets of acetylcholine or other neurotransmitter molecule into a synaptic cleft. The latter acts on proteins in the membrane of the following nerve cell (neuron), depolarizing that membrane in a chain reaction, the action-potential, which results in the dumping of neurotransmitters into the next synaptic cleft, and so on, until finally, in a motor-cell, some enzyme-manufactured small molecules bond to protein molecules in the cell-membrane causing the protein molecules, and thus the membrane, the tissue, and the organ (muscle), to contract.[5] That's ontogenesis, all right. We probably wouldn't want to call it 'ontogeny', however, because it doesn't have a (semi)permanent effect; that is, in a few moments the muscle relaxes again. The sequence is *based* on ontogeny, of course: an ontogenic sequence made the sensory cells, the interneurons, the motor cells, and all the supporting cells and tissues, and stocked each cell with the enzymes, neurotransmitters, and so forth, so that it took only a cue from the environment to set the whole thing off. So a behavioral event is contingent upon *two* sequences of ontogenetic processes: There is the sequence of processes through which the behavior is released but, first, there is the sequence of processes which constructed the microstructures which enable those releasing processes, i.e. which constructed the macrostructure which can do the behavior.

INSTRUCTIONS

An *instruction*, a structure which can do a certain behavior, is like any other material structure except that it has this peculiar ability to behave on cue and then return to its pre-behavior state and hence, to behave again on cue. One can say that the instruction *is* the structure which can do behavior: or, metaphorically, that the structure *carries* the instruction; or that a pre-existing structure is *programmed* with the instruction by the modification of its fine structure.

The act of gross behavior described above was performed by an instruction consisting of cells, enzymes, and so forth. But when we described the microevents that underlay it, we described a sequence of, again, behavioral acts, each performed by a different microstructure. So each neuron is an instruction, in fact each enzyme molecule and membrane-protein molecule is an instruction — components, at various levels of inclusion, of the gross-behavior instruction; the ontogenetic processes in the second sequence, through which the behavior is released, are behaviors of those instructions, the results of one behavior being the cue for the next. And the ontogenetic processes in the first sequence, which constructed the gross instruction-structure (indeed, the whole organism) in the first place, are also behaviors of instructions; those instructions include not only enzymes and other proteins, of course, but also genes, RNA messengers, ribosomes, and transfer units; they, too, are cued either by variations in the surroundings of the developing organism or by the behavioral results or products of other instructions in the series.

To recapitulate, a gross behavior is contingent upon two sequences of ontogenetic processes. Via the first sequence, instructions construct an organism and program it with instructions; in other words, ontogeny takes place. Via the second sequence, those instructions release the gross behavior, and each returns to its respective *status quo ante*.

It would appear that ontogeny does not take place via the second sequence, since no (semi)permanent structure results; there appears to be no durable thing that we can speak of the ontogeny *of*, as we could speak of the ontogeny of an organism or instruction occurring via the first sequence. In fact, however, gross behaviors of organisms do sometimes result in (semi)permanent structures, of two kinds. A structure of the first kind is an artifact, a material structure such as a spider's web, a bird's nest, a clay pot, or a house. There is no incongruity in speaking of the ontogeny of an artifact, referring to the sequence of behaviors of instructions — including, now, gross-behavior instructions — by which it is constructed.

SOCIAL INSTRUCTIONS

A structure of the second kind is a *social* structure or group or organization, constructed and maintained as follows: Some of the gross behavior instructions of an organism are (1) cued by the results of gross behavior by a conspecific (an organism of the same species); or (2) 'directed toward' a conspecific, e.g. when they behave, they move the behaver along a vector determined by the location of the conspecific or they cue another instruction carried by the conspecific; or (3) both. Among these *social instructions* are many whose principal or even sole behavioral outcome is the bringing or keeping of organisms into certain spatial relationships (usually, but not always, including proximity). An ordered sequence of such *sociogenic* instructions, acting in series and in parallel, constructs and maintains a social organization in a manner quite precisely analogous to the way in which genes, messengers, enzymes, etc., construct and maintain an organism. As with artifacts, there is no incongruity in speaking of the ontogeny of a social organization or in asserting that that ontogeny is ontogenetic, i.e. based entirely on chemical bonding processes, hence on Electromagnetism.

While a social organization is maintained, of course, it has effects on the behaviors of individual organisms, both members and nonmembers. These effects fall into two categories: In the short term, group-behaviors release or cue an instruction carried by one or more individual organisms; the resultant behavior may itself be sociogenic, as when a group-member, cued by being in the group situation, directs some sanctioning behavior toward another member cueing, in turn, some conformist behavior on his/her part — social control, in a phrase. In the longer term, the social organization and its behaviors make up a salient part of the environment controlling the subsequent *evolution* (phylogeny) of the instructional *repertory* of the population — again including sociogenic and other social instructions. I will return to this evolutionary/environmental role of social organizations later.

As implied above, not all social instructions are sociogenic; not all participate in the *ontogeny* of a social organization. Many participate in the gross behavior of the social organization instead (or in addition). In other words, just as there are two sequences of ontogenetic processes — behaviors of microscopic instructions — in the organism, so there are two sequences of ontogenetic processes — behaviors of gross organismic instructions — in the organization.

For example, the greeting and allo-grooming instructions of *ants* and the instructions that bring them home after foraging behave in the first sequence, being ontogenetic of the ant society; the instructions that build the nest (an artifact, n.b.), swarm out to attack predators, cooperate to feed the queen and larvae, etc., behave in the second sequence. The latter instructions are thus components of the gross-behavior instructions of the society.[6] The ontogeny of the ant society and the social behaviors of both kinds, like the ontogenies and behaviors of the individual ants, are composed entirely of variants of the single ontogenetic process (summarized above), and Electromagnetism is the only spook involved.

LEARNING

The information I have presented so far to back my arguments is quite certain, but now I must leave the certain for the plausible. In the above discussion I remarked that 'an ontogenic sequence (first sequence of ontogenetic processes) made the sensory cells, the interneurons, the motor cells, and all the supporting cells and tissues, and stocked each cell with the enzymes, neurotransmitters, and so forth, so that it took only a simple cue from the environment to set the whole thing off (following the second sequence of ontogenetic processes)'. Now, that description will do for a gross behavior instruction which is (entirely) genetically programmed. What I think happens in learning, or environmental modification of behavior, is this: There are a great many possible, incomplete sets of neurons which, if complete, would compose a gross behavior instruction; which, that is, would comprise a complete *neural routeway* and thus could enable a sequence of ontogenetic processes of the second, or behavior releasing, kind. But each of these neural routeways is incomplete because one or more of its constituent interneurons lacks a certain enzyme; the enzyme, for instance, that does an essential step in the assembly of neurotransmitter molecules, or of the molecule that controls the release of neurotransmitter into a following synaptic cleft. Anyway, because of the lack of the enzyme, an action potential (behavior) of that neuron does not cue the following neuron(s). Learning, then, involves 'activation' or 'programming' of a set of neurons through cueing the production of the lacking enzyme in each. Since every neuron, like every other cell, contains a complete set of genes, each neuron in question contains the gene that codes an RNA messenger to produce that enzyme, but the action of that gene is blocked because it is bonded by a molecule — let's call it molecule X. Molecule X was produced, I suppose, by an enzyme process early in ontogeny, a process which has since been permanently inactivated. (So to say that a neural routeway is 'genetically programmed' is really to say that, by positional cueing, molecule X was never produced in any of the neurons in that routeway.) So, if this neuron is to be able to cue the other neurons that synapse upon it, we need only get molecule X to let go of the gene. A simple way to do that is to introduce into the cell another molecule for which molecule X has a greater affinity than it has for the gene, much as iron ore is reduced by attracting its oxygen atom away with a carbon atom. Now, how do we introduce this molecule — let's call it Y — into a neuron? Since the neuron is deep in the nervous system, and since we must address it very precisely, the only way I can think of is through a neural routeway.

In short, I propose that a completely programmed ('standard') routeway and an incomplete routeway run close together for part of their lengths. Suppose that the standard routeway is responding to cue C, each of its constituent neurons firing in sequence and a certain gross behavior occurring. When it fires, each neuron of the standard routeway releases molecule Y into its immediate vicinity. Suppose, next, that in that vicinity is a nontransmitting neuron N cued, via a partially complete neural routeway, by cue C'. Because C' is occurring (as well as C), N is firing, and *only because it is firing* it absorbs the Y, from a nearby standard routeway neuron, through osmosis.[7] Y then bonds to X, un-blocking the gene, which proceeds to code RNA messengers, which construct the enzyme which produces neurotransmitter. N thereby becomes a *transmitting* neuron; whenever it fires, thereafter, it cues the neurons which synapse upon it. A few milliseconds later, one of those following neurons is programmed by the same process, which is repeated over and over again until a new routeway is completed. So, with serial and parallel repetitions of this process, an environmental cue, to which the existing standard routeway responds, directs the programming of a *new* routeway which responds to a different environmental cue, the one that was firing the neurons in the new routeway as it was programmed; and the change is permanent for the life of the organism. The organism is carrying a new gross behavior instruction.

Needless to say, this description is vastly oversimplified, both as to the quantity and quality of activity that must take place in the environmental programming of a single gross behavior instruction, and as to the variety of results.[8] But it explains or at least accounts for a couple of phenomena; namely, the increase in RNA that has been observed to take place in neurons during intensive learning, and the ramification or diffusion of similar experience-acquired instructions throughout large portions of the brain — since each experience-acquired routeway can serve as a *standard* routeway for subsequent events of learning, when C and C' are the same as well as when they are different. Also, since one must begin with genetically programmed routeways (albeit perhaps a very large and variegated endowment thereof), it also accounts for the fact that learning is species-specific; e.g. rats learn mazes easily but can't be trained to copulate for a food reward, and certain birds that navigate by the sun easily learn to look for grain at different times of day in what they calculate is a certain direction (say, east), but find it difficult to learn to look for grain simply in the direction of the sun.

More important, from my point of view, this account describes processes both ontogenetic (chemical) and ontogenic (helping produce normal adult animals). It can easily be integrated with the account of the ontogeny and gross behavior of social organizations, as well, since the environmental cue for existing and for learned routeways may be a conspecific's behavior, and the behavioral outcome of either routeway (or both) may be 'directed toward' conspecifics; in other words, social instructions may be acquired this way just as well as other gross behavior instructions.

So it seems plausible, to reiterate, that, 'given a complete set of genes, a 'starter-set' of amino-acids, enzymes, ribosomes, etc., an adequate supply of certain small and middle-sized molecules . . . a certain range of levels of energy of different frequencies, *and an adequate supply of sufficiently variegated sensory cues* in the surroundings, and the great spook of Electromagnetism, each step in the ontogeny of a bacterium or a *healthy* rat *and even a healthy rat society* is inevitable' (repeated from above, emphasized portions added). Learning, in short, is another outcome of the ontogenetic process.

CULTURAL ACQUISITION

All we need to add, in order to substitute 'human' for 'rat', in the above, is a means for transmitting an extragenetic tradition, or behavioral heritage. If my ontogenetic model of learning is plausible, one can easily imagine an expanded learning brain in which events like these take place: A certain genetically programmed routeway is fired by a cue consisting of (light rays reflected from) a conspecific *animal who has just completed a behavioral act*. The *result* of that behavioral act is also, simultaneously, cueing a neural routeway, but one which is heretofore incomplete. Hence the first, genetically controlled, routeway completes the programming of the second routeway. Subsequently, the second routeway, the one which responds to the behavioral *result*, serves as a standard routeway for ordinary learning. Thus the observing animal's behavior is shaped to approximate that of the demonstrator; i.e. he carries a set of neural instructions analogous to a set carried by the demonstrator. He has learned from observation. With repetition of such learning, genetically identical animals of different populations can come to carry different gross behavior instructions, with a high amount of variation between populations and a low amount of variation within populations.

This observational learning capacity goes to a sort of limit in a brain large enough (enough free neurons) that the observer records the results of the demonstrator's behavior at a rate varying around about ten per second. At this rate, each behavioral result is 'recorded' as the cue which released the behavior which led to the next behavioral result, so observational learning in such an animal is very smooth, very swift, and very accurate.

— Social groups of such animals develop and maintain extragenetic traditions or behavioral heritages or cultures, consisting of instructions programmed as above. Being sort of traditional myself, I call neural instructions so programmed 'cultural instructions'.

—Some sets of such cultural instructions are in ontogenic pathways leading to the construction of artifacts (e.g. a tool, a pot) and social organizations (e.g. a hunting party, a university).

— All elements in that cultural process are variants of ontogenesis.

But in this animal, we have a new requirement for the ontogeny of a healthy animal and society, besides the ones we arrived at immediately preceding. In a sense, this is a special case of any learning species' requirement for 'an adequate supply of sufficiently variegated sensory cues in the surroundings', but in the cultural case, those 'cues' do more than stimulate a lot of self-programming in the animal — they 'contain all (or nearly all) the information' that the learning animal thereby acquires. If that sounds familiar, it should. Ontogenically, cultural instructions are precisely analogous to genes. In a preceding section, 'The Special Role of the Genes', I dissected the statement that 'the genes contain all the information'; to paraphrase that dissection, this time including cultural instructions: 'In any ordered set of ontogenetic processes, some variables are controlled by processes of the set and some are not; specifically, some structures entering into reactions in the set are the products of preceding reactions and some must be found in the surroundings. The latter, of course, must be found in full sufficiency or the ontogenetic process will not run its full course. Among the former, genes *and cultural instructions* have a sort of existential priority: An ontogenetic process can be completely reconstituted in the total absence of structures of one specific kind or even of several specific kinds, *except for* genes and *cultural instructions*; if social groups of one kind or tools of one kind are completely absent, for instance, they will be assembled, in the necessary quantity, by (carriers of) the appropriate cultural in-structions. But if *cultural instructions* of one specific kind are completely absent (e.g. those for tying the blade of the tool to its shaft) they can't simply be made up, so the tool or social group they help construct can never be replaced as it wears out or breaks up, and so the ontogenetic process cannot run its full course and may very well abort completely or even run wild. So, in a sense, cultural instructions are like those cues that must be found in the surroundings; unlike those cues, however, they need not be found in full sufficiency because they (and they alone, among such cues) have the ability to replicate themselves, through the learning process just described. Theoretically, at least, just one cultural instruction of each kind is sufficient for the construction and main-tenance of a complete functioning human society of millions of people.'

So genes and cultural instructions have important characteristics in common: they are behaving structures which, when appropriately cued, enter into ontogenetic processes, often ontogenic processes. Because they are the only structures capable of replicating themselves, they play a role in those processes fundamentally different from that played by other structures; metaphorically, only they 'contain all the information' necessary for constructing the complete set of routeways. Finally, their components, although these are instructions (e.g. nucleotides for genes, activated neurons for cultural instructions), are not capable of replicating themselves; so genes and cultural instructions are *elementary self-replicating instructions* (SRI's, for short). Given complete sets of both, and the necessary environmental stuff with which to get started and keep going, each step in the ontogeny of a total human society, including its personnel, its institutions, and its traditions, is inevitable.

NATURAL SELECTION, THE ONTOGENETIC PROCESS OF GENETIC AND CULTURAL CONTINUITY AND EVOLUTION

To finish my task of presenting a method of 'explain(ing) completely any human behavior or institution', promised in the title of this article, there remains only to sketch out the process by which a set of SRI's — of elementary self-replicating genetic and cultural instructions — is com-piled and maintained; the process, in other words, which underlies the phylogeny and continuity of a population's genetic and cultural repertory. This process, too, will be found to be entirely ontogenetic, i.e. chemical, the only spook involved being Electromagnetism.

As SRI's, genes and cultural instructions have certain characteristics which determine their role in the phylogenetic process. A gene is a string of roughly 300 to 900 DNA nucleotides (of which there are four different kinds) which codes a messenger (fourth variant of ontogenetic process), which codes a protein (fifth variant). Of all the astronomical number of possible DNA-strings of that length, only a tiny fraction are genes (the others don't code protein). Of all the huge number of genes, only a tiny fraction are equivalent; i.e. only a tiny fraction code for the same protein. So the *a priori* probability that any given gene (or its equivalent) will be part of even a large set of SRI's is vanishingly small. Yet at least a tenth of all DNA nucleotides found in strings in nature are elements of genes, and those genes that are found together in sets are, most improbably, the very genes that interact in ontogenetic processes that produce elaborate and intricate organic, social, and artifactual structures — structures superbly adapted to survive, endure, and prevail, in the peculiar particular environmental situations in which they are found. How are these genes 'selected' from the total universe of actual genes, theoretically possible genes, and nonsense DNA- strings?

A cultural SRI is a set of activated neurons synapsing on one another to form a reticulated set of strings through a primate brain, linking a huge number of sensory fibers to a huge number of motor fibers. There is a practically infinite number of such sets possible in any brain. Of these, only a tiny fraction are actually cultural SRI's, because only that tiny fraction, cued by some coherent sensory stimulus, in turn cue some coherent motor activity. Of all the huge number of cultural SRI's, only a tiny fraction are equivalent; i.e. only a tiny fraction respond to the same cue and produce the same behavior. So the *a priori* probability that any given cultural SRI (or its equivalent) will be part of even a large set of SRI's is vanishingly small. We have no way of estimating what proportion of the programmed neurons in a human brain are components of cultural instructions, but it's clearly substantial; and those cultural SRI's that are found together in sets are, most improbably, the very cultural SRI's that interact with each other and with genes in ontogenetic processes that produce elaborate and intricate behavioral, social, and artifactual structures — structures superbly adapted to survive, endure, and prevail, in the peculiar particular environmental situations in which they are found. How are these cultural SRI's selected from the total universe of actual cultural SRI's, theoretically possible cultural SRI's, and nonsense networks of activated neurons?

To begin, it might be well to recall that SRI's are themselves very intricate and fragile material structures. SRI's of both kinds, and their components, are highly vulnerable to electromagnetic radiation of various frequencies, to dismemberment by chemical agents of various kinds, to desiccation, to mechanical damage, and so forth. In other words, they can exist only at locations in space/time where certain very narrowly defined conditions obtain — where the value of each of a large number of physicochemical variables falls within a very narrow range. And — it seems obvious to say it — SRI's can exist only at locations where all their components not only *and* occur but *do in fact* occur.

Now, let's perform a thought-experiment. Prevent the SRI's on the planet Earth from behaving for a few days or a week, until all ontogenetic activity ceases. Then try to find a location, anywhere on Earth, where the conditions of existence of an SRI are met. There will be very few, if any, such locations. That's strange; a week ago there were billions of such locations. How could that have been? The answer seems obvious: as a rule, SRI's can *exist* on this planet only when the *behaviors* of SRI's, through ontogenetic processes, have met the conditions of their existence.

We must keep in mind, however, that there are many different sorts of locations on the planet, in terms of the exact values of the different essential variables at each. And the behavior of an SRI, and hence its effect in ontogenesis, is highly specific, and is a strict function of its fine structure. So for any given spatiotemporal location, certain *specific* SRI's must occur and behave 'nearby' if the conditions of SRI existence are to be met at that location. Then, and only then, can SRI's replicate themselves into that location or survive there; in general, because of sheer proximity, these will include the same SRI's that behaved and met the conditions there. In general, also, they will remain there only so long as they, or their ontogenetic products, continue to help meet the conditions there.

ENS: THE EVENT-SET OF NATURAL SELECTION

Each time a certain SRI occurs in a location, and occurs there only because it has behaved in a nearby location, I call that an ENS, an *event-set of natural selection*, of the SRI. An ENS includes, then, (a) a set of ontogenetic events, including the SRI's behavior, through which an SRI helps meet (or maintain) a condition of its existence at some location, and (b) an occurrence of that SRI at that location, i.e. the meeting of all the rest of its conditions of existence there.

I'll give a couple of homely examples of ENS's. First: C1 is a cultural SRI, whose behavior, a carpentry technique, results in a certain feature of building contruction. C1 helps build a house in a certain location, the carpenter lives in that house, and he survives a bad winter. Without the behavior of C1, the house would have collapsed and the carpenter perished, and C1 would have perished along with him. C1 has ENSed. Second: C2, again a carpentry SRI, helps build a house. A passerby admires the house, and hires the carpenter to build him a boat. He would not have admired the house if C2 had not behaved. With the added income and work to do, the carpenter takes on a new helper. The helper, watching the carpenter at work, is programmed with C2. C2 has ENSed. These two examples, and a comparison between them, illustrate a number of points:

1. In neither case does the carpentry SRI build a house and ENS all by itself. It *cooperates* in an elaborate ontogenetic process with other Carpentry SRI's, with the genetic SRI's that built the carpenter, with SRI's that built his tools, and so on, to build the house. I say these SRI's cooperate because (a) they all go into the house-building ontogenetic process and (b) they all ENS through that process; both (a) and (b) are necessary for cooperation, properly speaking, to take place.[9]

2. In the first example, ENS of C1 occurred through survival of the carrying organism. C1 helped build a house for *its* 'house', the carpenter, thus meeting a condition of its existence by altering the value(s) of some variable(s) of the so-called 'natural' or 'physical' environment. That is to say, the initial values of these variables were set by 'nature'. C1 might ENS that way in a wide variety of locations in, say, the so-called temperate zone. It would not ENS that way in, say, the arctic zone, because the house would collapse in spite of C1's behavior and the carpenter and C1 would perish. It would not ENS that way in, say, the tropics, either, because the house would *stand*, and the carpenter and C1 would survive, even if C1 *didn't* behave.

3. In the second example, ENS took place through a different ontogenetic pathway. Here, the behavior of C2 cued certain other cultural SRI's, carried by the passerby; the passerby's SRI's then helped meet certain conditions of existence of C2 at an otherwise 'unreachable' spatiotemporal location; to wit, the brain of the man who became the carpenter's helper. In this ENS, C2 has *exploited* those SRI's carried by the passerby; thus this ENS could have occurred only in a location where someone was carrying those cultural SRI's or, metaphorically, only in a certain 'cultural environment'.

4. If, however, hiring the C2-carrying-and-exhibiting carpenter actually makes the passerby's boat more durable than it would have been had he hired someone else; and if the boat therefore enables the passerby and his SRI's to survive, they too have ENSed, and the relation between C2 and the passerby's instructions is cooperation, not one-way exploitation.

5. An ENS does not an evolution make. Either of the above event-sets could happen just once, or maybe a few times, with C1 (or C2, as the

case might be) soon being lost. Or, on the contrary, C1 could already be well established in the cultural repertory of the carpenter's population; in that case, those ENSes would be commonplace, merely *maintaining* C1's frequency.

6. On the other hand, it might be that C1 (or C2) was novel to that population's repertory, having been just recently invented or acquired through observational learning from an alien. Then, if it ENSed more than a few times (along either or both pathways) it would *become* established in the repertory — it would be added to the complete set of SRI's, genetic and cultural, that construct that population and endow it with its traditions and institutions, through the ontogenetic pathways. An event would have occurred in the *phylogeny* of that society. *Evolution* has taken place.

7. Practically any SRI has its effect on the world, and it ENSes, through a cooperative ontogenetic process; the behavioral result of almost any SRI, therefore, is determined not only by its own behavior but also by the behaviors of other instructions entering the process. The behavior of an SRI 'borrowed' from one system by another may thus have a quite unexpected result in the borrowing system; one can *ascertain* the SRI's behavioral result in either system, of course, but one can't *predict* its result, or whether it will ENS, from one system to another.

8. When it helps meet a condition of its own existence (e.g. the survival of the carpenter), an SRI generally helps meet that same condition for other SRI's in its vicinity. At the same time, if a situation of *competition* prevails, it may *unmeet* that (or another) existence condition for still other SRI's (e.g. SRI's carried by the carpenter who would have been hired to build the passerby's boat had C2 not got the job for the carpenter carrying it).

Once established in the repertory, therefore, an SRI, by its behavioral results, alters the *environment* (both 'physical' and 'cultural'), and thus helps to determine whether, and under what conditions, other SRI's — both novel and established — will ENS; and thus helps determine changes in *their* relative and absolute frequencies. So a complete set of SRI's is more than just a collection, it is a complex system of behaving structures in a dynamic balance, the behavior of each having a determining effect on the frequency of many of the others.

SOCIOLOGY

Suppose, now, that some individual acquires a certain cultural SRI novel to his/her population. Suppose, further, that that SRI, S1, is sociogenic;

i.e. its behavior enters into an ontogenetic process constructing/maintaining a group, organization, or institution G, so its behavioral result is some modification in the structure of G. *If* S1 ENSes repeatedly, and thus becomes established in the population's repertory, that modification will be present in the structure of many or all groups like G.

For each such ENS, however, (a) S1's behavioral result must meet some condition of its existence at a location, and (b) the rest of those conditions must also be met there. And behaviors of already established SRI's entering the G-making process are surely important determinants of both (a) S1's behavioral result (point (7)) and (b) the meeting of the rest of the conditions of S1's (and their own) existence (point (8)). In short, the existing sociogenic instructions, process, and outcome — the group itself — determines in large part which novel sociogenic instructions will succeed (ENS) and which will fail, and thus the group (organization, institution) exercises environmental control over the repertories of SRI's of its members and, thereby, over its own evolution.[10]

COOPERATION, PARASITISM, DOMESTICATION

SRI's are not, of course, *inherently* cooperative; ENS refers, with iron necessity, to the ontogenetic process by which an SRI enables its *own* occurrence. To be sure, on this planet the initial environment (the one in the thought experiment) varies through space from somewhat hostile to SRI's to extremely hostile to SRI's to totally unliveable by SRI's. SRI's have progressively occupied more and more hostile territories by cooperating in ever greater numbers and building ever more elaborate organisms, artifacts, and social structures through (of course) the ontogenetic process. So for a couple of reasons, we find mainly 'cooperative' SRI's when we look around. One reason is that they are statistically vastly overrepresented in hostile territory because they ENS there. Another reason is that we detect and know SRI's by their works, and more cooperative SRI's build bigger and fancier works; the solitary parasitic freeloaders among SRI's are hard to detect. And if a parasitic freeloader SRI should mutate and start having some detectable behavioral result, that behavioral result will probably not be neutral. It will either ENS — and that will almost certainly be by cooperating with an existing system — or else it will 'anti-ENS' i.e. be lethal, prevent its own occurrence in a location where it otherwise *would* have occurred, if it hadn't behaved.

But *systems* of SRI's often become actively parasitic on other systems, preying on them, exploiting them, even domesticating them. With genetic systems this is difficult to accomplish and easy to see, because each system constructs and occupies a different organism. With systems of cultural SRI's, on the other hand, exploitation is easier to accomplish and more difficult to see, because elements of several systems occupy the same brains, and elements of the same system occupy different brains. Consider, for example, the cultural SRI (or set thereof) — call it 'FC' — that makes its carrier say 'A man's gotta fight for his country' and act upon that aphorism (McDermott 1967). Carried by young American working-class males, FC is an element of the sociogenic system that constructs and maintains the so-called Military–Industrial Complex. Its function in that system is literally to recruit its carriers and ensure their willing participation in the complex's activities. When FC performs its function, behaviors of 'working-class SRI's' — the cultural SRI's that construct and maintain working-class families and neighborhoods and the genetic SRI's that construct and maintain working-class people — result not in occurrences of those working-class SRI's (ENS, in a word) but in occurrences of Military–Industrial Complex SRI's, including FC. In wartime, moreover, because of FC's behavior the behaviors of those working-class SRI's sometimes result in *non*-occurrences of their carriers and of themselves (and of FC). FC, and through it the Military–Industrial Complex, is indeed a parasite on the working class.

But if FC is at best an exploiter of working-class SRIs, and at worst a lethal, why doesn't it become extinct? How is it maintained in the cultural repertory of the working-class population? The answer, I think, is that the Military–Industrial Complex is not merely a parasite on the working-class system. Rather, it is part of a much larger political and economic system which exercises control over the *environment* of the working-class sytem to the general effect that only workers who carry FC, and other SRI's which build or maintain that political economy, have been able to demonstrate their cultural SRI's to the young; in that environment, noncarriers of FC have usually ended up in breadlines or in prison. In an almost classic sense, the working-class sytem has been taken over and *domesticated* by the political economy, its repertory of SRI's systematically altered to the latter's service.

The structures and relations and behaviors that human scientists are interested in are determined by ontogenetic processes which are in turn controlled by the behaviors of SRI's. Each change in the composition of the set of SRI's that enters into a given ontogenetic process is determined in part by the outcomes of that ontogenetic process and in part by the 'environment' — which always includes the outcomes of other ontogenetic processes. All ontogenetic processes consist, in the final analysis, of the formation and breaking of chemical bonds; so unless human scientists want to get involved with questions of cosmogeny, geogeny, meteorology, etc., they can do their work of scientific explanation secure in the knowledge that they need consider only one spook: Electromagnetism.

NOTES

1. This is a revised version of a paper, of similar title, delivered in May, 1973, at the conference *Son of Fringe: New Directions in Theoretical Anthropology (II)*, Carleton University, Ottawa, Ontario.
2. The *behavior* of these scientific spooks is quite well known, of course, and has been described in the form of laws and constants. What remains mysterious (spooky) about them is *why* they exist and/or behave so.
3. The information on variants of the ontogenetic process presented here is now part of the basic repertory of biological science. I acquired it mainly from Monod (1971) and from *Scientific American* offprints: Crick (1954, 1966), Horowitz (1956), Hurwitz and Furth (1962), Penrose (1959), Wood and Edgar (1967).
4. This information, too, is basic biology; I acquired it partly from Eccles (1965) and Kandel (1970).
5. The words 'and so on' here hardly do justice to the elaborate squence of neuronal processes actually involved in any but the very simplest behavior. Most importantly, an observed gross behavior of an organism is practically always the outcome of a whole *series* of behaviors such as are described here, the series functioning to obtain, maintain, or avoid a certain perception and thereby a certain state of affairs in the organism, in its environment, or in the relation between them. Peripheral (sensory) cells thus play two roles in a behavior: (1) they recognize the cue that releases the behavior and (2) they feed information back to the neural system which keeps the behavior going until they inform it that the perceptual situation it controls for is now the case. How such control systems operate, and how they are themselves organized into hierarchies, has been worked out in considerable detail by Powers (1973).
6. To give an example involving *culturally*-programmed instructions (which follow below), instructions of the first sociogenic ontogenetic sequence bring and/or keep a group of men together in a social group we would call a 'hunting party'; instructions of the second, social gross behavior ontogenetic sequence search for, stalk, wound, track, fix, and kill a large mammal and bring home the meat.
7. This process requires a synapse of a special kind, different from those through which transfer of neurotransmitter takes place, lest the standard routeway be cueing, as well as programming, the incomplete routeway.
8. The programming of a control system routeway (note 5, and Powers (1973)) takes places as follows, if my conjecture is correct: An existing control system operates until perception P (say, a sweet taste) is obtained. At the moment that P is obtained, or a fraction of a second before, perception P′ (say color-and shape of a ripe berry of a certain species) happens to be obtained also. The simultaneous firings of the P-recognition routeway and of neurons cued by P′ chemically program the latter into a control system that, even after, operates until P′ is obtained.

9. The *function* of an SRI, its behavior, or the result thereof, is its contribution to a cooperative ENS. Thus an SRI ENSes and is propagated/maintained in the population only because it performs its function in a *system* of cooperating instructions. For a discussion of how cultural features are shaped to their function, see Cloak (1975: 169–170).

10. This sort of 'downward causation' (Campbell 1974) is precisely analogous to the control exercised by an existing organism — genotype, ontogenic process, and/or phenotype — over its subsequent evolution; since it often results in elimination of a novel SRI, I think it is the material basis of Wilson's (1975) proposed spook, 'phylogenetic inertia'.

11. For a more general and theoretical treatment of these matters, see Cloak (1976).

Bibliography

JOURNAL

Cycles: official bulletin of the Foundation for the Study of Cycles (Pittsburgh, Pennsylvania).

AUTHORS

Abbott, Edwin Abbott [sic] (1884 [1963]), *Flatland: A Romance of Many Dimensions*. New York, Barnes and Noble.

Adamson, Lauren. *See* Brazelton, T. Berry, S. Dixon, E. Tronick, M. Yogman.

Aldis, Owen (1975), *Play Fighting*. New York, Academic Press.

Alexander, Samuel (1927), *Space, Time and Deity*, Vol. 1. New York, Macmillan.

Allen, Donald E. and Rebecca F. Guy (1974), *Conversation Analysis. The Sociology of Talk*. The Hague, Mouton.

Als, Heidelise. *See* Brazelton, T. Berry, S. Dixon, E. Tronick, M. Yogman.

Andrews, Lynnwood. *See* Shilkret, Robert.

Argyle, Michael (1972), 'Non-verbal communication in human social interaction', in *Non-Verbal Communication*, ed. by R. A. Hinde, 243–269. Cambridge University Press.

— (1975), *Bodily Communication*. London, Methuen.

Argyle, Michael. *See* Graham, Jean Ann.

Argyle, Michael and Janet Dean (1965), 'Eye contact, distance, and affiliation', *Sociometry* 28(3): 289–304.

Argyle, Michael and Adam Kendon (1972), 'The experimental analysis of social performance', in *Communication in Face-to-Face Interaction*, ed. by John Laver and Sandy Hutcheson, 19–63. Harmondsworth, Middlesex, Penguin.

Ashby, W. Ross (1960), *Design for a Brain: the Origin of Adaptive Behavior*, 2nd ed. revised. New York, John Wiley and Sons.

Ashcraft, Norman and Albert E. Scheflen (1976), *People Space: The Making and Breaking of Human Boundaries*. New York, Anchor Books.

Ashley Montagu, M. F. (1971), *Touching: The Human Significance of the Skin.* New York, Columbia University Press.

Austin, Gilbert (1806 [1966]), *Chironomia: Or a Treatise on Rhetorical Delivery: Comprehending Many Precepts, Both Ancient and Modern, for the Proper Regulation of the Voice, the Countenance and Gesture: Together with an Investigation of the Elements of Gesture, and a New Method for the Notation Thereof: Illustrated by Many Figures.* London. Reprinted by Southern Illinois University Press.

Austin, J. L. (1962), *How to Do Things with Words.* Cambridge, Mass., Harvard University Press.

Bacon, Albert M. (1875), *A Manual of Gesture: Embracing a Complete System of Notation, Together with the Principles of Interpretation and Selections for Practice.* Chicago, S. C. Griggs and Company.

Baer, Donald M. *See* Gewirtz, Jacob L.

Bahr, Donald, and J. Richard Haefer (1978), 'Song in Piman curing', *Ethnomusicology* 22(1): 89–122.

Baker, Charlotte (1976), 'What's not on the other hand in American sign language'. Paper presented at the 12th Regional Meeting of the Chicago Linguistic Society, University of Chicago.

Bally, Charles (1921), *Traité de Stylistique* I–II. Heidelberg, Winter; Paris, Klincksieck.

— 1932 [1965], *Linguistique Générale et Linguistique française.* Bern, Francke.

Bateson, Gregory. *See* McQuown, Norman A.

Battro, Antonio M. *See* Fridman, Ruth.

Baxter, James C., Elaine P. Winter and Robert E. Hammer (1968), 'Gestural behavior during a brief interview as a function of cognitive variables', *Journal of Personality and Social Psychology* 8(3): 303–307.

Beattie, G. *See* Butterworth, B.

Beavin, Janet H. *See* Watzlawick, Paul.

Ben Debba, M. *See* Garvey, Catherine.

Benjamin, A. Cornelius (1966), 'Ideas of time in the history of philosophy', in *The Voices of Time*, ed. by J. T. Fraser, 3–30. New York, George Braziller.

Bennett, Joanne (1974), 'Usage of verbal connectives by children in relation to age and contextual variation'. Unpublished M.A. Thesis, Clark University.

Benveniste, Emile (1973), *Indo-European Language and Society.* Coral Gables, Florida, University of Miami Press.

Bergson, Henri L. (1911), *Matter and Memory.* London, Allen and Unwin.

— (1946), *The Creative Mind.* New York, Philosophical Library.

Bernstein, Basil B., (1971), *Class, Codes and Control*, Vol. 1, *Theoretical Studies towards a Sociology of Language.* London, Routledge and Kegan Paul.

Bertalanffy, Ludwig von (1955), 'An essay on the relativity of categories', *Philosophy of Science* 22(4): 243–263.

— (1968), *General System Theory: Foundations, Development, Applications.* New York, George Braziller.

Birdwhistell, Ray L. (1970a), *Kinesics and Context.* Pittsburgh, University of Pennsylvania Press.

— (1970b), 'A kinesic-linguistic exercise: the cigarette scene', in *Kinesics and Context*, 227–250. Pittsburgh, University of Pennsylvania Press.

Birdwhistell, Ray L. *See* McQuown, Norman A.

Bishop, Yvonne M. M., S. E. Fienberg and P. W. Holland (1975), *Discrete Multivariate Analysis: Theory and Practice*. Cambridge, Mass., MIT Press.

Black, Mary B. (1973), 'Ojibwa questioning etiquette and use of ambiguity', *Studies in Linguistics* 23: 13–29.

Blass, Thomas, N. Freedman and I. Steingart (1974), 'Body movement and verbal encoding in the congenitally blind', *Perceptual and Motor Skills* 39: 272–293.

Bloomfield, Leonard (1939 [1962]), 'Linguistic aspects of science', in *International Encyclopedia of Unified Science* 1(4). Chicago, University of Chicago Press.

Blount, Ben G. *See* Sanches, Mary.

Blount, Ben G. and E. J. Padgug (1977), 'Prosodic, paralinguistic, and interactional features in parent–child speech: English and Spanish', *Journal of Child Language* 4(1): (February): 67–86.

Blumberg, Steven R. (1971), 'The response of children from elaborated and restricted code background to face and word in communication'. Unpublished M. A. Thesis, Clark University.

Bolinger, Dwight (1965), 'The atomization of meaning', *Language* 41:555–573.

— (1975), *Aspects of Language*, 2nd ed. New York, Harcourt Brace Jovanovich.

— (1977), 'Intonation and "nature"'. Paper presented at *Fundamentals of Symbolism,* Burg Wartenstein Symposium No. 74, New York.

— (1978), 'Intonation across languages' in *Universals of Human Language*, ed. by Joseph Greenberg, 471–524. Stanford, California, Stanford University Press.

Boomer, Donald S. (1965), 'Hesitation and grammatical encoding', *Language and Speech* 8: 148–158.

Boumendil-Lucot, A. (1977), 'Enquête sociolinguistique effectuée auprès de sujets parisiens'. Ph.D. Thesis, University of Paris III.

Bower, T. G. R., M. K. Broughton and K. Moore (1970), 'The coordination of visual and tactual input on infants', *Perception and Psychophysics* 8: 51–53.

Boyes-Braem, P. *See* Rosch, E.

Brandon, Samuel G. F. (1970), 'The deification of time', *Studium Generale* 23: 485–497. Reprinted (1972), in *The Study of Time*, ed. by J. T. Fraser et al., 370–380. New York, Springer.

Brandt, Linda. *See* Brooks, Robert.

Brazelton, T. Berry, B. Koslowski and M. Maine (1974), 'The origins of reciprocity: the early mother–infant interaction', in *The Effect of the Infant on Its Caregiver*, ed. by M. Lewis and L. Rosenblum. New York, Wiley-Intersciences.

Brazelton, T. Berry, Edward Tronick, Lauren Adamson, Heidelise Als and Susan Wise (1975), 'Early mother–infant reciprocity', in *Parent–Infant Relationship*, Ciba Foundation Symposium 33, ed. by M. A. Hofer, 137–154. New York, Elsevier, Excerpta Medica, North Holland.

Brazelton, T. Berry. *See* Dixon, S., E. Tronick, M. Yogman

Bregman, Albert S. *See* Moeser, Shannon D.

Broad, Charlie Dunbar (1925), *The Mind and Its Place in Nature*. London, Routledge and Kegan Paul.

Bromley, M. (1967), 'The linguistic relationship of Grand Valley Dani: a lexico-statistical classification', *Oceania* 37(4).

— (1973), 'Ethnic groups in Irian Jaya', *Irian* 3: 1–37.

Brooks, Robert, Linda Brandt and Morton Wiener (1969), 'Differential response to two communication channels: socioeconomic class differences in response to verbal reinforcers communicated with and without tonal inflection', *Child Development* 40(2): 453–470.

Brosin, Henry W., William S. Condon and William D. Ogston (1970), 'Film recording of normal and pathological behavior', in *Hope: Psychiatry's Commitment*, ed. by A. W. R. Sipe, 137–150. New York, Brunner/Mazel.

Brosin, Henry W. *See* Condon, William S. and Norman A. McQuown.

Broughton, M. K. *See* Bower, T. G. R.

Brown, J. F. and A. C. Voth (1937), 'The path of seen movement as a function of the vector-field', *American Journal of Psychology* 49: 543–563.

Brown, Roger (1958), *Words and Things*. Glencoe, Ill., The Free Press.

— (1973), *A First Language: The Early Stages*. Cambridge, Mass., Harvard University Press.

— (1976), 'Reference: in memorial tribute to Eric Lenneberg', *Cognition* 4: 125–153.

Bruneau, Thomas J. (1973), 'Communicative silences: forms and functions', *Journal of Communication* 23(1): 17–46.

— (1974), 'Time and nonverbal communication', *Journal of Popular Culture* 8(3): 658–666.

— (1976), 'Silence, mind-time relativity, and interpersonal communication'. Third Conference, International Society for the Study of Time, Alpbach, Austria, July 1–10, 1976.

—(1977), 'Chronemics: the study of time in human interaction (with a glossary of chronemic terminology)' *Communication, Journal of the Communication Association of the Pacific* 6, University of Hawaii: 1–30.

— (in preparation), 'Modes of tension in the mental present'.

Bruner, J. (1971), 'The growth and structure of skill', in *Motor Skills,* ed. by K. J. Connolly. London, Academic Press.

— (1975), 'The ontogenesis of speech acts', *Journal of Child Language* 2: 1–19.

Buffery, A. W. H. and J. A. Gray (1972), 'Sex differences in the development of spatial and linguistic skills', in *Gender Differences: Their Ontogeny and Significance*, ed. by C. Ounsted and D. C. Taylor. Edinburgh, Churchill Livingstone.

Bullowa, Margaret (1970), 'The start of the language process', in *Actes du Xe Congrès International des Linguistes, Bucarest, 1967,* 191–200. Editions de l'Académie de la République Socialiste de Roumanie.

— (1976), 'From non-verbal communication to language', *International Journal of Psycholinguistics* (Mouton Publishers) 6: 5–14.

Burton, Michael. *See* Kirk, Lorraine.

Butterworth, B. and G. Beattie (1976), 'Gesture and silence as indicators of planning in speech'. Presented at the Conference on the Psychology of Language, University of Stirling.

Cain, Arthur James (1954 [1960]), *Animal Species and Their Evolution*. London, Hutchinson. Reprinted by Harper Torchbooks.

Campbell, Donald T. (1966), 'Ostensive instances and entitativity in language learning and linguistic relativism'. Paper presented at The Center for Advanced Study in the Behavioral Sciences, Palo Alto, Cal.

— (1974), '"Downward causation" in hierarchically organized biological systems', in *Studies in the Philosophy of Biology*, ed. by Francisco J. Ayala and Theodosius Dobzhansky. London, Macmillan.

Carpenter, Edmund (1972), *Oh, What a Blow That Phantom Gave Me!* New York, Holt, Rinehart and Winston.

Carpenter, G. (1974), 'Visual regard of moving and stationary faces early in infancy', *Merrill Palmer Quarterly* 20: 181-194.

Carroll, J. B. and M. N. White (1973), Age-of-acquisition norms for 220 picturable nouns', *Journal of Verbal Learning and Verbal Behavior* 12: 563-576.

Cassirer, Ernst (1953), *The Philosophy of Symbolic Forms*, Vol. 1, *Language*. New Haven, Conn., Yale University Press.

— (1955), *The Philosophy of Symbolic Forms*, Vol. 2, *Mythical Thought*. New Haven, Conn., Yale University Press.

— (1957), *The Philosophy of Symbolic Forms*, Vol. 3, *The Phenomenology of Knowledge*. New Haven, Conn., Yale University Press.

Cattell, Raymond B. (1957), *Personality and Motivation Structure and Measurement*. New York, Harcourt, Brace and World.

— (1965), *The Scientific Analysis of Personality*. Harmondsworth, Middlesex, Penguin.

Chafe, Wallace L. (1970), *Meaning and the Structure of Language*. Chicago, University of Chicago Press.

Chapple, Eliot D. (1970), *Culture and Biological Man*. New York, Holt, Rinehart and Winston.

— (1971), 'Toward a mathematical model of interaction: some preliminary considerations', in *Explorations in Mathematical Anthropology*, ed. by Paul Kay. Cambridge, Mass., MIT Press.

Chase, W. G. and H. H. Clark (1972), 'Mental operations in the comparison of sentences and pictures', in *Cognition in Learning and Memory*, ed. by L. W. Gregg. New York, Wiley.

Chomsky, Noam (1959 [1964]), Review of Skinner, *Verbal Behavior, Language 35*: (January-March): 26–57. Reprinted as No. A-34 in the reprint series on the behavioral sciences by Bobbs-Merrill, Inc. Reprinted also in *The Structure of Language*, ed. by J. J. Katz and J. A. Fodor. New York, Prentice-Hall.

— (1962), 'Explanatory models in linguistics', in *Logic, Methodology and Philosophy of Science, Proceedings of the 1960 International Congress*, ed. by Nagel, Suppes, Tarski, 528–550. Stanford University Press.

— (1965), *Aspects of the Theory of Syntax*. Cambridge, Mass., MIT Press.

— (1968 [1972]), *Language and Mind*, extended edition. New York, Harcourt Brace and World.

— (1975), *Reflections on Language*. New York, Pantheon.

— (1976), 'On the biological basis of language capacities', in *The Neuropsychology of Language*, ed. by R. W. Rieber. New York, Plenum Press. (Lenneberg Memorial Symposium, Cornell University).

— (in press), 'Introduction: linguistic and psycholinguistic background', (with Edward Walker) in *Explorations in the Biology of Language*, ed. by Edward Walker. Bradford Books.

Cicourel, Aaron V. (1973), *Cognitive Sociology. Language and Meaning in Social Interaction*. Harmondsworth, Middlesex, Penguin.

Clark, H. H. and P. Lucy (1975), 'Understanding what is meant from what is said. A study in conversationally conveyed request', *Journal of Verbal Learning and Verbal Behavior* 14: 56–72.

Clark, H. H. *See* Chase, W. G.

Classe, André (1939), *The Rhythm of English Prose*. Oxford, Blackwells.

Cloak, F. T., Jr. (1975), 'Is a cultural ethology possible?', *Human Ecology* 3: 161–182.

— (1976), 'The evolutionary success of altruism and urban social order', *Zygon* 11: 219–240.

Cohen, A. A. and R. P. Harrison (1973), 'Intentionality in the use of hand illustrators in face-to-face communication situations', *Journal of Personality and Social Psychology* 28: 276–279.

Cohen, A. and J. 't Hart (1970), 'Comparison of Dutch and English intonation contours in spoken news bulletins'. *IPO Annual Progress Report* 5: 78–82. University of Utrecht.

Cohen, John (1966), 'Subjective time', in *The Voices of Time*, ed. by J. T. Fraser, 257–275. New York, George Braziller.

— (1967), *Psychological Time in Health and Disease*. Springfield, III., Charles C. Thomas.

Condon, William S. (1963a), 'Lexical-kinesic correlation'. Paper presented at Western Psychiatric Institute, Pittsburgh, Pa.

— (1963b), 'Synchrony units and the communicational hierarchy'. Paper presented at Western Psychiatric Institute, Pittsburgh, Pa.

— (1964), 'Process in communication'. Paper presented at Western Psychiatric Institute, Pittsburgh, Pa.

— (1968), 'Linguistic-kinesic research and dance therapy', *American Dance Therapy Association Proceedings:* 21–44.

— (1970), 'Method of micro-analysis of sound films of behavior', *Behavioral Research Methods and Instrumentation* 2(2): 51–54.

— (1971), 'Report on linguistic-kinesic analysis of a retarded child'. Butler, Pennsylvania, Irene Stacy Mental Health Center.

— (1973), 'Communication and order: the micro-rhythm hierarchy of speaker behavior'. Paper presented at school psychologists' convention, New York.

— (1974a), 'How neonate body movements synchronize with adult speech', *Contemporary Ob/Gyn* 4: 97–100.

— (1974b), 'Multiple response to sound in autistic-like children', *National Society for Autistic Children Conference Proceedings*.

— (1974c), 'Speech makes babies move', *New Scientist* 62(901) (June): 624–627.

— (1975a), 'Dysfunctional children: dysfunctional organization', *New England Kindergarten Conference Proceedings* (Conference held December 1974).

— (1975b), 'Multiple response to sound in dysfunctional children', *Journal of Autism and Childhood Schizophrenia* 5(1): 37–56.

— (1976), 'An analysis of behavioral organization', *Sign Language Studies* 13 (Winter): 285–318.

— (1977), 'A primary phase in the organization of infant responding behavior', in *Studies in Mother–Infant Interaction*, ed. by H. R. Schaffer. New York, Academic Press.

Condon, William S. and Henry W. Brosin (1969), 'Micro linguistic-kinesic events in schizophrenic behavior', in *Schizophrenia: Current Concepts and Research*, ed. by D. V. Siva Sankar, 812–837.

Condon, William S., Henry W. Brosin and William D. Ogston (1970), 'Film recording of normal and pathological behavior', in *Hope: Psychiatry's Commitment*, ed. by A. W. R. Sipe. New York, Brunner/Mazel.

Condon, William S. and William D. Ogston (1966), 'Sound film analysis of normal and pathological behavior patterns', *Journal of Nervous and Mental Disease* 143(4): 338–347.

— (1967a), 'A method of studying animal behavior', *Journal of Auditory Research* 7: 359–365.

— (1967b), 'A segmentation of behavior', *Journal of Psychiatric Research* 5: 221–235.

— (1971), 'Speech and body motion synchrony of the speaker–hearer', in *Perception of Language*, ed. by D. L. Horton and J. J. Jenkins, 150–173. Columbus, Ohio, Charles E. Merrill.

Condon, William S., William D. Ogston and Larry V. Pacoe (1969), 'Three faces of Eve revisited: a study of transient microstrabismus', *Journal of Abnormal Psychology* 74(5): 618–620.

Condon, William S. and Louis W. Sander (1974a), 'Neonate movement is synchronized with adult speech: interactional participation and language acquisition', *Science* 183 (4120): 99–101.

— (1974b), 'Synchrony demonstrated between movements of the neonate and adult speech', *Child Development* 45: 456–462.

Cormier, Judith (1975), 'Comprehension of a descriptive passage and pre-experimental familiarity with the referent events'. Unpublished M.A. Thesis, Clark University.

Cranach, Mario von (1971), 'Die nichtverbale Kommunikation im Kontext des kommunikativen Verhaltens', *Jahrbuch der Max-Planck Gesellschaft zur Förderung der Wissenschaften e. V.*: 104–148.

Cranach, Mario von and Ian Vine, eds. (1973), *Social Communication and Movement: Studies of Interaction and Expression in Man and Chimpanzee*. New York, Academic Press.

Crick, F. H. C. (1954), 'The structure of the hereditary material', *Scientific American* (October) (reprint no. 5).
— (1966), 'The genetic code: III', *Scientific American* (October) (reprint no. 1052).
Crile, George W. (1915 [1970]), *The Origin and Nature of the Emotions*. Philadelphia. Reprinted College Park, Maryland, McGrath.
Critchley, Macdonald (1961), 'The nature of animal communication and its relation to language in man'. New York, *Mount Sinai Hospital Journal* 28(3): 252–267.
Cromer, Ward (1970), 'The difference model: a new explanation for some reading difficulties', *Journal of Educational Psychology* 61: 471–483.
Cromer, Ward. *See* Wiener, Morton.
Crystal, David (1974), 'Paralinguistics', in *Current Trends in Linguistics* 12(1): 265–295. The Hague, Mouton.
Crystal, David and Derek Davy (1969), *Investigating English Style*. Bloomington, Ind., Indiana University Press.
Cuçeloĝlu, Dogan M. (1967), 'A cross-cultural study of communication via facial expressions'. Ph.D. dissertation, Urbana, University of Illinois.
Darwin, Charles R. (1872), *The Expression of the Emotions in Man and Animals*. London, John Murphy.
Davis, Flora (1973), *Inside Intuition: What We Know about Non-verbal Communication*. New York, McGraw-Hill.
Davy, Derek. *See* Crystal, David.
Dean, Janet. *See* Argyle, Michael.
De Laguna, Grace (1927), *Speech: Its Function and Development*. New Haven, Yale University Press.
Delgado, José M. R. (1969), *Physical Control of the Mind: Toward a Psychocivilized Society*. New York, Harper and Row.
Dell, Cecily (1970), *A Primer for Movement Description Using Effort-Shape and Supplementary Concepts*. New York, Dance Notation Bureau.
DeLong, Alton J. (1974), 'Kinesic signals at utterance boundaries in pre-school children', *Semiotica* 11(1): 43–73.
De Silva, M. W. Sugathapala (1976), 'Verbal aspects of politeness expression in Sinhalese with reference to asking, telling, requesting and ordering', *Anthropological Linguistics* 18(8): 360–370.
Deutsch, Robert D. (1977), 'Spatial structurings in everyday face-to-face behavior: a neurocybernetic model'. Association for the Study of Man–Environment Relations. Orangeburg, New York.
Devoe, Shannon. *See* Jancovic, Merry Ann, Owen Robbins and Morton Wiener.
Dewey, Edward R., with Og Mandino (1971), *Cycles: The Mysterious Forces that Trigger Events*. New York, Hawthorne Books.
Dillon, Wilton S. *See* Eisenberg, J. F.
Dixon, S. Yogman, M., Edward Tronick, L. Adamson, Heidelise Als and T. Berry Brazelton (1976), 'Early social interaction of infants with parents and strangers'. Paper presented to American Academy of Pediatrics, Chicago.
Dixon, S. *See* Yogman, M.

Dobrogaev, S. M. (1931), 'The study of reflex in problems of linguistics', in *Lazykovedenie i Materializm* [Linguistics and Materialism], Vol. II, ed. by W. A. Marr, 105-173. Moscow and Leningrad, State Social Economic Publishing House.

Dobson, E. J. (1957), *English Pronunciation 1500-1700*, I-II. Oxford, Blackwell.

Dobzhansky, T. (1955), *Evolution, Genetics, and Man.* New York, Wiley.

Doob, Leonard W. (1971), *Patterning of Time.* New Haven, Yale University Press.

Dubois, J. et al. (1970), *Rhétorique générale.* Paris, Larousse.

Duncan, Starkey D., Jr. (1972), 'Some signals and rules for taking speaking turns in conversations', *Journal of Personality and Social Psychology* 23(2): 283-292. Reprinted in *Nonverbal Conversation*, ed. by Shirley Weitz, 298-311. Oxford University Press.

— (1974), 'On the structure of speaker-auditor interaction during speaking turns', *Language in Society* 3(2): 161-180.

— (1975), 'Interaction units during speaking turns in dyadic, face-to-face conversations', in *Organization of Behavior in Face-to-Face Interaction*, ed. by A. Kendon, R. M. Harris, and M. R. Key, 197-213. The Hague, Mouton.

— (in press), 'Working the other side of the sequence: studying interaction strategy', in *Nonverbal communication: Readings with commentary*, ed. by Shirley Weitz. New York, Oxford University Press.

— (in press), 'Face-to-face interaction', in *Psycholinguistic research*, ed. by R. W. Rieber and D. Aaronson. Hillsdale, N. J., Erlbaum.

Duncan, Starkey D., Jr. and Donald W. Fiske (1977), *Face-to-Face Interaction: Research, Methods, and Theory.* Hillsdale, N. J., Erlbaum.

Duncan, Starkey D., Jr. and George Niederehe (1974), 'On signalling that it's your turn to speak', *Journal of Experimental Social Psychology* 10: 234-247.

Du Noüy, P. Lecomte (1937), *Biological Time.* New York, Macmillan.

Eccles, Sir John (1965), 'The synapse', *Scientific American* (January) (reprint no. 1001).

Edgar, R. S. *See* Wood, William B.

Efron, David (1941 [1972]), *Gesture and Environment.* New York, King's Crown Press. Reprinted as *Gesture, Race and Culture.* Approaches to Semiotics No. 9. The Hague, Mouton.

Eibl-Eibesfeldt, Irenäus (1969), *Grundriss der vergleichenden Verhaltensforschung.* Munich, Piper.

— (1970a), *Ethology: The Biology of Behavior.* New York, Holt, Rinehart and Winston.

— (1970b), *Liebe und Hass: Zur Naturgeschichte elementarer Verhaltensweisen.* Munich, Piper.

— (1971), 'Eine ethnologische Interpretation des Palmfrucht-festes der Waika-Indianer (Yanoama) nebst Bemerkungen über bindende Funktion von Zwiege sprächen', *Anthropos* 66: 767-778.

— (1972a), *Die Iko-Buschmanngesellschaft. Gruppenbindung und Aggressionskontrolle bei einem Jäger- und Sammlervolk.* Munich, Piper.

— (1972b), 'Similarities and differences between cultures in expressive movements', in *Non-verbal Communication*, ed. by R. A. Hinde, 297–312. Cambridge University Press.

— (1973), *Der vorprogrammierte Mensch. Das Ererbte als bestimmender Faktor in menschlichen Verhalten*. Vienna, Molden.

— (1976), *Menschenforschung auf neuen Wegen. Die naturwissenschaftliche Betrachtung kultureller Verhaltensweisen*. Vienna, Molden.

Eibl-Eibesfeldt, Irenäus. *See* Pitcairn, T.K.

Eiseley, Loren (1975), *All the Strange Hours: The Excavation of a Life*. New York, Charles Scribner's Sons.

Eisenberg, J. F. and Wilton S. Dillon, eds. (1971), *Man and Beast: Comparative Social Behavior*. Washington, D.C., Smithsonian Institution.

Ekman, Paul and Wallace V. Friesen (1969), 'The repertoire of nonverbal behavior: categories, origins, usage, and coding', *Semiotica* 1(1):49–98.

— (1972), 'Hand movements', *Journal of Communication* 22: 353–374.

Eliot, Thomas S. (1934), 'The love song of J. Alfred Prufrock', *Collected Poems*, 1909–1935. New York, Harcourt, Brace.

Elzinga, R. A. (1978), 'Temporal aspects of Australian and Japanese conversation'. Unpublished Ph.D. Thesis, Australian National University.

Empson, W. (1930 [1953]), *Seven Types of Ambiguity*. London, Chatto.

Engel, Walburga von Raffler (1964), *Il Prelinguaggio Infantile*. Brescia, Paideia Editrice.

— (1972), 'The relationship of intonation to the first vowel articulation in infants', *Acta Universitatis Carolinea-Philologica* 1: 197–202.

Erickson, Frederick (1971), 'Chicano and black mask'. Unpublished manuscript.

— (1975), 'One function of proxemic shifts in face-to-face interaction', in *Organization of Behavior in Face-to-Face Interaction*, ed. by A. Kendon, R. M. Harris, and M. R. Key, 175–187. The Hague, Mouton.

Erikson, Erik (1964), *Insight and Responsibility*. New York, W. W. Norton.

Ervin-Tripp, Susan (1970), 'Discourse agreement: how children answer questions', in *Cognition and Language Learning*, ed. by Richard Hayes, 79–107. New York, Wiley.

— (1972), 'On sociolinguistic rules: alternation and co-occurrence', in *Directions in Sociolinguistics*, ed. by John J. Gumperz and Dell Hymes, 213–250. New York, Holt, Rinehart and Winston.

— (1976), 'Is Sybil there? The structure of some American English directives', *Language in Society* 5: 25–66.

Ervin-Tripp, Susan and Wick Miller (1977), 'Early discourse: some questions about questions', in *Interaction, Conversation, and the Development of Language*, ed. by Michael Lewis and Leonard A. Rosenblum, 9–25. New York, Wiley.

Estienne, H. (1578 [1885]), *Deux Dialogues du Nouveau français Italianisé* I–II, ed. by P. Ristelhuber. Paris.

Eucken, R. (1880), *Ueber die Bilder und Gleichnisse in der Philosophie*. Leipzig, Veit und Co.

Fant, C. G. *See* Jakobson, Roman.
Faulconer, B. A. *See* Potter, M. C.
Feldman, Heidi. *See* Goldin-Meadow, Susan.
Ferenczi, S. (1927-1939), *Bausteine der Psychoanalyse* I-IV. Leipzig, Vienna, Zürich, Hans Huber.
Ferenczi, S. *See* Hollos, I.
Ferguson, Charles A. (1976), 'Structure and use of politeness formulas', *Language and Society* 5: 137-151.
Ferris, David C. (1977), 'Scoring jargon', *Verbatim* 4(2): 3-4.
Fienberg, S. E. *See* Bishop, Yvonne M. M.
Fillmore, Charles J. (1968), 'The case for case', in *Universals in Linguistic Theory*, ed. by Emmon Bach and Robert T. Harms, 1-88. New York, Holt, Rinehart and Winston.
— (1970), 'The grammar of hitting and breaking', in *Readings in English Transformational Grammar*, ed. by R. A. Jacobs and P. S. Rosenbaum, 120-133. Waltham, Mass., Ginn.
Fischer, Roland (1966), 'Biological time', in *The Voices of Time*, ed. by J. T. Fraser, 357-382. New York, George Braziller.
— (1967), 'The biological fabric of time', in *Interdisciplinary Perspectives of Time*, ed. by Roland Fischer, 440-488. *Annals of the New York Academy of Sciences*, Vol. 138, Art. 2.
— (1971a), 'A cartography of the ecstatic and meditative states', *Science* 174: 897-904.
— (1971b), 'Time: a biocybernetic and psychopharmological approach', in *Time in Science and Philosophy*, ed. by Jiri Zeman, 165-178. Prague, Czechoslovak Academy of Sciences.
— (1974), 'Visions, hallucination, consciousness, hemispheres, symbols', *Journal of Altered States of Consciousness* 1: 145-151.
— (1975), 'Cartography of inner space', in *Hallucinations: Behavior, Experience and Theory*, ed. by R. K. Siegel and L. J. West, 197-239. New York, Wiley.
Fischer, Roland and John Rhead (1974), 'Nature, nurture and cerebral laterality', *Confinia Psychiatrica* 17: 192-202.
Fishman, Joshua A. (1972), 'Domains and the relationship between micro- and macrolinguistics', in *Directions in Sociolinguistics*, ed. by John J. Gumperz and Dell Hymes, 435-453. New York, Holt, Rinehart, and Winston.
Fiske, Donald W. *See* Duncan, Starkey D., Jr.
Fodor, J. A. (1965), 'Could meaning be an r_m?', *Journal of Verbal Learning and Verbal Behavior* 4: 73-81.
Fodor, J. and M. Garrett (1966), 'Some reflections on competence and performance', in *Psycholinguistics Papers*, ed. by John Lyons and R. J. Wales, 135-179. Edinburgh University Press.
Fónagy, Ivan (1956), 'Uber den Verlauf des Lautwandels', *Acta Linguistica Academiae Scientiarum Hungaricae* 6: 173-278.
— (1962), 'Mimik auf glottaler Ebene', *Phonetica* 8: 209-219.
— (1963), *Die Metaphern in der Phonetik*. The Hague, Mouton.
— (1964), 'L'Information du style verbal', *Linguistics* 4 (March): 19-47.

— (1965), 'Form and function in poetic language', *Diogenes* 51: 72–110.
— (1970), 'Les bases pulsionnelles de la phonation I, Les sons', *Revue française de Psychanalyse* 34: 101–136.
— (1971a), 'Double coding in speech', *Semiotica* 3(3): 189–222.
— (1971b), 'Les bases pulsionnelles de la phonation II, La prosodie', *Revue française de Psychanalyse* 35: 543–591.
— (1971c), 'Synthèse de l'ironie', *Phonetica* 23: 42–51.
— (1975a), 'Prélangage et regressions syntaxiques', *Langue* 36: 163–208.
— (1975b), 'Structure sémantique des constructions possessives,' in *Langue, Discours, Société*, ed. by Emile Benveniste. Paris, Seuil.
— (1975c), 'The simile', *Encyclopedia of World Literature* IV, 259–272. Budapest, Akadémiai Kiado.
— (1976), 'La mimique buccale. Aspect radiologique de la vive voix', *Phonetica* 33: 31–44.
Fónagy, Ivan and Judith Fónagy (1976), 'Prosodie professionnelle et changements prosodiques', *Le Français Moderne* 44(3): 193–228.
Fónagy, Ivan, H. Han and P. Simon (in preparation), 'Analyse ciné-radiographique de l'expression des émotions'.
Fónagy, Judith. *See* Fónagy, Ivan.
Fraisse, Paul (1963), *The Psychology of Time*. New York, Harper and Row.
— (1973), 'Temporal isolation, activity rhythms, and time estimation', in *Man in Isolation and Confinement*, ed. by John E. Rasmussen, 85–97. Chicago, Aldine.
Frake, Charles O. (1975), 'How to enter a Yakan house', in *Sociocultural Dimensions of Language Use*, ed. by Mary Sanches and Ben G. Blount, 25–40. New York, Academic Press.
Fraser, Julius T., ed. (1966), *The Voices of Time*. New York, George Braziller.
— (1975), *Of Time, Passion, and Knowledge: Reflections on the Strategy of Existence*. New York, George Braziller.
Freedman, Norbert (1972), 'The analysis of movement behavior during the clinical interview', in *Studies in Dyadic Communication*, ed. by A. Seigman and B. Pope, 153–175. Elmsford, New York, Pergamon Press.
Freedman, Norbert. *See* Blass, Thomas.
French, Patrice L., (1977), 'Nonverbal measurement of affect: the graphic differential', *Journal of Psycholinguistic Research* 6: 337–347.
Freud, S. (1940–1946), *Gesammelte Werke*, I–XVIII. London, Imago.
Fridman, Ruth (1971), 'The evolutive development of the sonorous expression of the baby and its relation with music'. Paper read at the II International Seminar of Musical Education (ISME), Buenos Aires.
— (1973), 'The first cry of the newborn: basis for the child's future musical development', *Journal of Research in Music Education* 21: 264–269.
— (1974a [1976], 'Affective communication through the baby's sonorous expression in relation to mental health and future musical activity'. Paper read at the XI International Conference of the International Society for Music Education, Perth, Australia and published by the Department of Music, University of Western Australia, in *Challenges in Music Education*, 94–97.

— (1974b), *Los Comienzos de la Conducta Musical* [a documentary record accompanies the book]. Buenos Aires, Editorial Paidós.

— (1974c), 'Proto-rhythms of musical and articulated languages'. Paper read at the 1st Congress of Music and Communication and IV International Seminar on Musical Research organized by ISME (International Society of Music Educators), Mexico City.

— (1975), 'Early responses to music', *Journal of Speech Therapy*, New Zealand (November): 12–16.

— (in preparation) 'Proto-rhythms'.

Fridman, Ruth and Antonio M. Battro (1977), 'Vocal rhythms in the newborn: the first day of life', *Estudos Cognitivos* 2(1) (June) — San Pablo, Brazil: 25–30.

Friedman, Lynn A. (1976), 'Phonology of a soundless language: phonological structure of American sign language'. Unpublished Ph.D. dissertation, University of California, Berkeley.

— (1977), *On the Other Hand, New Perspectives in American Sign Language*, ed. by Lynn A. Friedman. New York, Academic Press.

Fries, Charles Carpenter (1952), *The Structure of English*. New York, Harcourt, Brace.and World.

Friesen, Wallace V. *See* Ekman, Paul.

Fromkin, Victoria A. (1971), 'The non-anomalous nature of anomalous utterances', *Language* 47(1): 27–52.

Fry, D. B. (1966), 'The development of the phonological system in the normal and the deaf child', in *The Genesis of Language,* ed. by Frank Smith and George A. Miller, 187–206. Cambridge, Mass., MIT Press.

Furth, J. J. *See* Hurwitz, Jerard.

Gale, Richard M. (1968), *The Language of Time*. London, Routledge and Kegan Paul.

Garrett, M. *See* Fodor, J.

Garvey, Catherine (1977a), *Play*. Cambridge, Mass., Harvard University Press.

— (1977b), 'The contingent query: a dependent act in conversation', in *Interaction, Conversation, and the Development of Language*, ed. by Michael Lewis and Leonard A. Rosenblum, 63–93. New York, Wiley.

Garvey, Catherine and M. Ben Debba (1974), 'Effects of age, sex, and partner on children's dyadic speech', *Child Development* 45: 1159–1161.

Garvey, Catherine and Ronald Hogan (1973), 'Social speech and social interaction: egocentrism revisited', *Child Development* 44: 562–568.

Geller, Jesse. *See* Wiener, Morton.

Gelman, Rachel and Marilyn Shatz (1977), 'Appropriate speech adjustments: the operation of conversational constraints on talk to two-year-olds', in *Interaction, Conversation, and the Development of Language*, ed. by Michael Lewis and Leonard A. Rosenblum, 27–61. New York, Wiley.

Gelman, Rachel. *See* Shatz, Marilyn.

Gewirtz, Jacob L. and Donald M. Baer (1958), 'The effect of brief social deprivation on behaviors for social reinforcers', *Journal of Abnormal and Social Psychology* 56: 49–56.

Gibson, J. J. (1966), *The Senses Considered as Perceptual Systems*. Boston, Houghton-Mifflin.

Gillo, M. W. (1972), 'MAID, a Honeywell 600 program for an automized survey analysis', *Behavioral Science* 17: 251-252.

Gioscia, Victor (1971), 'On social time', in *The Future of Time*, ed. by Henri Yaker et al., 73-141. New York, Doubleday.

Gladwin, Thomas (1964), 'Culture and logical process', in *Explorations in Cultural Anthropology*, ed. by Ward H. Goodenough, 167-177. New York, McGraw-Hill.

— (1970), *East is a Big Bird: Navigation and Logic on Puluwat Atoll*. Cambridge, Harvard University Press.

Goffman, Erving (1963), *Behavior in Public Places: Notes on the Social Organization of Gatherings*. Glencoe, Ill., Free Press.

— (1971), *Relations in Public*. New York, Basic Books.

— (1972), 'Replies and responses', *Language and Society* 5: 257-313.

— (1974), *Frame Analysis*. New York, Harper and Row.

Goldin-Meadow, Susan (in press), 'Structure in a manual communication system developed without a conventional language model: language without a helping hand', in *Studies in Neurolinguistics*, Vol. 4, ed. by H. Whitaker and H. A. Whitaker. New York, Academic Press.

Goldin-Meadow, Susan and Heidi Feldman (1977), 'The development of language-like communication without a language model', *Science* 197: 401-403.

Gonseth, Ferdinand (1972), *Time and Method: An Essay on the Methodology of Research*. Springield, Ill., Charles C. Thomas.

Goodman, L. A. and W. H. Kruskal (1954), 'Measures of association for cross-classifications', *Journal of the American Statistical Association* 49: 732-764.

Graham, Jean Ann and Michael Argyle (1975), 'A cross-cultural study of the communication of extraverbal meaning by gestures', *International Journal of Psychology* 10(1): 57-67.

Gray, J. A. *See* Buffery, A. W. H.

Gray, W. *See* Rosch, E.

Green, Georgia M. (1974), *Semantics and Syntactic Regularity*. Bloomington, Indiana, Indiana University Press.

Grinker, Roy R., ed. (1956), *Toward a Unified Theory of Human Behavior*. New York, Basic Books.

Grosu, A. (1970), 'On coreferentiality constraints and EQUI-NP-DELETION in English'. Unpublished Master's thesis, Ohio State University.

Gruber, Jeffrey S. (1965), 'Studies in lexical relations'. Unpublished Ph.D. dissertation, MIT, reproduced by the Indiana University Linguistics Circle, mimeo.

Gumperz, John J. (1972), 'Sociolinguistics and communication in small groups', in *Sociolinguistics*, ed. by J. B. Pride and J. Holmes, 203-324. Harmondsworth, Middlesex, Penguin.

Gumperz, J. J. and Dell Hymes, eds. (1972), *Directions in Sociolinguistics: The Ethnography of Communication*. New York, Holt, Rinehart and Winston.

Guy, Rebecca F. *See* Allen, Donald E.

Guyton, A. C. (1971), *Textbook of Medical Physiology*, 4th ed. Philadelphia, Saunders.

Habermas, J. (1969), *Knowledge and Human Interests*. Boston, Boston Press.

Haefer, J. Richard. *See* Bahr, Donald.

Hall, Edward T. (1963), 'A system for the notation of proxemic behavior', *American Anthropologist* 65(5): 1003-1026.

— (1966), *The Hidden Dimension*. New York, Doubleday.

— (1974), 'Proxemics', in *Nonverbal Communication*, ed. by Shirley Weitz, 205-229. Oxford University Press.

— (1977), *Beyond Culture*. New York, Anchor Books.

Hall, Robert A., Jr. (1964), *Introductory Linguistics*. New York, Chilton Books.

Halle, Morris. *See* Jakobson, Roman.

Halliday, Michael A. K. (1973), *Explorations in the Functions of Language*. London, Arnold.

— (1975a), 'Language as social semiotic: towards a general sociolinguistic theory', in *The First LACUS Forum 1974*, ed. by Adam Makkai and Valerie Becker Makkai, 17-46. Columbia, South Carolina, Hornbeam Press.

— (1975b), *Learning How to Mean: Explorations in the Development of Language*, Explorations in Language Study Series, ed. by Peter Doughty and Geoffrey Thornton. London, Edward Arnold.

Hamilton, William D. (1971), 'Selection of selfish and altruistic behavior in some extreme models', in *Man and Beast: Comparative Social Behavior*, ed. by J. F. Eisenberg and Wilton S. Dillon, 57-91. Washington, D.C., Smithsonian Institution.

Hammer, Robert E. *See* Baxter, James C.

Han, H. *See* Fónagy, Ivan.

Handelman, Don (1973), 'Gossip in encounters: the transmission of information in a bounded social setting', *Man* 8(2): 210-227.

Harris, Richard M. *See* Kendon, Adam.

Harrison, R. + *See* Cohen, A. A.

Hart, J. 't. *See* Cohen, A.

Hartmann, D. (1973), 'Begrüszungen und Begrüszungsrituale', *Zeitschrift für germanistische Linguistik* 1: 133-162.

Hastorf, Albert H. *See* Ono, Hiroshi.

Hastorf, Albert H., Charles E. Osgood and Hiroshi Ono (1966), 'The semantics of facial expressions and the prediction of the meanings of stereoscopically fused facial expressions', *Scandinavian Journal of Psychology* 7: 179-188.

Haudricourt, A. G. and A. G. Juilland (1949), *Essai pour une Histoire Structurale du Phonétisme français*. Paris.

Hayek, F. A. (1955), 'Degrees of explanation', *British Journal for the Philosophy of Science* 6: 209-225.

— (1960), *The Constitution of Liberty*. Chicago, University of Chicago Press.

Hebb, D. O. (1949), *The Organization of Behavior: A Neuro-physiological Theory*. New York, Wiley.

Heeschen, V. (1975), 'Grammatik der Eipo-Sprache'. Unpublished manuscript.
— (1977a), 'Überlegungen zum Begriff "sprachliches Handeln"', Zeitschrift für germanistische Linguistik 4: 273–301.
— (1977b), Review of Voorhoeve, Languages of Irian Jaya, Anthropos 3/4: 649–651.
Heider, K. G. (1970), The Dugum Dani. A Papuan Culture in the Highlands of West New Guinea. Chicago, Aldine.
Henderson, Harold G. (1958), An Introduction to Haiku. Garden City, New York, Doubleday.
Herczog, E. (1913), Historische Sprachlehre des Neufranzösischen I, Lautlehre. Heidelberg, Winter.
Herzog, George (1976), 'Drum-signaling in a West African Tribe', in Speech Surrogates: Drum and Whistle Systems, ed. by Thomas A. Sebeok and Donna Jean Umiker-Sebeok, 553–573. The Hague, Mouton.
Hesse, M. B. (1966), Models and Analogies in Science. Notre Dame, University of Notre Dame Press.
Hewes, Gordon W. (1973a), 'An explicit formulation of the relationship between tool-using, tool-making, and the emergence of language', Visible Language 7(2): 101–127.
— (1973b), 'Primate communication and the gestural origin of language', Current Anthropology 14(1–2): 5–24.
Hill, Jane H. (1974), 'Possible continuity theories of language', Language 50(1) (March): 134–150.
Hinde, Robert A., ed. (1972), Nonverbal Communication. Cambridge University Press.
Hindret, J. (1687), L'art de bien prononcer et de bien parler la langue française. Paris.
Hobbes, Thomas (1651 [1950]), LEVIATHAN: the Matter, Form, and Power of a Commonwealth: Ecclesiastical and Civil. New York, E. P. Dutton.
Hockett, Charles F. See McQuown, Norman A.
Hogan, Ronald. See Garvey, Catherine.
Holland, P. W. See Bishop, Yvonne M. M.
Hollos, I. and S. Ferenczi (1922), Zur Psychoanalyse der paralytischen Geistesstörungen. Leipzig, Vienna, Zürich, Internationaler Psychoanalytischer Verlag.
Holmes, J. See Pride, J. B.
Hoosain, Rumjahn (1977), 'The processing of negative or incongruent perceptual and combined perceptual/linguistic stimuli', British Journal of Psychology 68: 245–252.
Hoosain, R. See Osgood, Charles E.
Horwitz, Norman H. (1956), 'The gene', Scientific American (October) (reprint no. 17).
Houdebine, A. M. (1977), 'La prononciation du français contemporain au seuil du Poitou'. Unpublished PhD. thesis, University of Paris V.
Hull, C. L. (1930), 'Knowledge and purpose as habit mechanisms', Psychological Review 37: 511–525.

— (1943), *Principles of Behavior: An Introduction to Behavior Theory*. New York, Appleton-Century-Crofts.

Hurwitz, Jerard and J. J. Furth (1962), 'Messenger RNA', *Scientific American* (February) (reprint no. 119).

Husserl, E. (1922), *Logische Untersuchungen* II. Halle.

Hutcheson, Sandy. *See* Laver, John.

Huttenlocher, Janellen (1975), 'Encoding information in sign language', in *The Role of Speech in Language*, ed. by J. F. Kavanagh and J. E. Cutting, 229-240. Cambridge, Mass., MIT Press.

Hyman, Larry M. (1975), 'On the nature of linguistic stress'. Preprint.

Hymes, Dell (1972), 'Models of the interaction of language and social life', in *Directions in Sociolinguistics,* ed. by John J. Gumperz and Dell Hymes, 35-71. New York, Holt, Rinehart and Winston.

Hymes, Dell. *See* Gumperz, John J.

Ingram, D. (1975), 'Motor asymmetries in young children', *Neuropsychologia* 13: 95-102.

Jackson, Don D. *See* Watzlawick, Paul.

Jakobson, Roman (1941 [1968]), *Child Language, Aphasia and Phonological Universals*. The Hague, Mouton.

— (1970), 'Linguistics', in *Main Trends of Research in the Social and Human Sciences*, 419-463. The Hague, Mouton.

— (1971a), *Selected Writings,* I. *Phonological Studies*. The Hague, Mouton.

— (1971b), *Selected Writings*, II. *Word and Language*. The Hague, Mouton.

— (1972), 'The editor interviews Roman Jakobson', *Modern Occasions* 2(1) (Winter): 14-20.

Jakobson, Roman, C. G. Fant and Morris Halle (1951 [1963]), *Preliminaries to Speech Analysis*. Cambridge, Mass., MIT Press.

James, Deborah (1973), 'The syntax and semantics of some English interjections', Ph.D. dissertation, University of Michigan.

Jancovic, Merry Ann, Shannon Devoe and Morton Wiener (1975), 'Age-related changes in hand and arm movements as nonverbal communication: some conceptualizations and an empirical exploration', *Child Development* 46: 922-928.

Jefferson, Gail (1972), 'Side sequences', in *Studies in Social Interaction*, ed. by David Sudnow, 294-338. New York, Free Press.

— (1973), 'A case of precision timing in ordinary conversation: overlapped tag-positioned address terms in closing sequences', *Semiotica* 9(1): 47-96.

Jefferson, Gail. *See* Sacks, Harvey.

Jespersen, Otto (1924 [1968]) *Philosophy of Grammar*. London, George Allen and Unwin.

— (1937 [1969]), *Analytic Syntax*. New York, Holt, Rinehart and Winston.

Johnson, D. *See* Rosch, E.

Johnson-Laird, Philip N. *See* Miller, George A.

Joos, Martin (1962), 'The five clocks', *International Journal of American Linguistics* 28(2) Part V: 1-62.

Jorio, Andrea de (1832), *Mimica Degli Antichi Investigata nel Gestire Napoletano*. Naples, Stamperia del Fibreno.

Juilland, A. G. *See* Haudricourt, A. G.

Kandel, Eric R. (1970), 'Nerve cells and behavior', *Scientific American* (July) : (reprint no. 1182).

Kapferer, B., cd. (1976), *Transaction and Meaning. Directions in the Anthropology of Exchange and Symbolic Behavior*. Philadelphia, Inst. Study Hum. Iss.

Kaplan, Bernard. *See* Werner, Heinz.

Karwoski, Theodore F., H. S. Odbert and Charles E. Osgood (1942), 'Studies in synesthetic thinking, II: the roles of form in visual responses to music', *Journal of General Psychology* 26: 199–222.

Katz, Jerrold J. (1966), *The Philosophy of Language*. New York, Harper and Row.

Kaye, Alan S. (1977), Review of Mary Ritchie Key, *Paralanguage and Kinesics, Lingua* 43: 394–397.

Kaye, K. (in press), 'The maternal role in developing communication and language', in *Before Speech: The Beginnings of Human Communication*, ed. by M. Bullowa. Cambridge, Cambridge University Press.

Kempton, Willett M. (1975), 'The use of micro-kinesic signals in speech understanding', *The Journal of Auditory Research* 15: 81–86.

Kendon, Adam (1970), 'Movement coordination in social interaction', *Acta Psychologica* 32(2): 100–125.

— (1972), 'Some relationships between body motion and speech: an analysis of an example', in *Studies in Dyadic Communication*, ed. by A. Siegman and B. Pope, 177–210. New York, Pergamon Press.

— (1975), 'Gesticulation, speech and the gesture theory of language origins', *Sign Language Studies* 9: 349–373.

— (1976), 'Differential perception and attentional frame in face-to-face interaction: two problems for investigation'. Paper read at the 75th meeting of the American Anthropological Association, Washington, D.C.

— (1977), *Studies in the Behavior of Face-to-Face Interaction*. Lisse, Peter de Ridder Press.

Kendon, Adam. *See* Argyle, Michael.

Kendon, Adam, Richard M. Harris and Mary Ritchie Key, eds. (1975), *Organization of Behavior in Face-to-Face Interaction*. The Hague, Mouton.

Key, Mary Ritchie (1962 [1964]), 'Gestures and responses: a preliminary study among some Indian tribes of Bolivia', *Studies in Linguistics* 16(3–4): 92–99. Reprinted in *Practical Anthropology* 11 (March): 71–76.

— (1970), 'Preliminary remarks on paralanguage and kinesics in human communication', *La Linguistique* 6(2): 17–36.

— (1971 [1974]), 'Differences between written and spoken language'. Paper read at the American Dialect Society, Chicago. Abstract printed in *Claremont Reading Conference 38th Yearbook*, Claremont Graduate School: 94–96.

— (1974a), Review of *Sign Language Among North American Indians* by Garrick Mallery, *Linguistics* 132 (July 15): 116–123.

— (1974b), 'The relationship of verbal and non-verbal communication',

Proceedings of the Eleventh International Congress of Linguists, August 1972, Vol. II, 103–110. Bologna.
— (1974c), 'U.S.A. — Nonverbal Communication', *VS: Quaderni di Studi Semiotici* 8/9, Special Issue, 'Bibliographia Semiotica' (May-December): 248–280.
— (1975a), *Male/Female Language*, especially Chapter XI 'Non-verbal, extra-linguistic messages'. Metuchen, New Jersey, Scarecrow Press.
— (1975b), *Paralanguage and Kinesics (Nonverbal Communication): With a Bibliography*. Metuchen, New Jersey, Scarecrow Press. Review by Shozo Usami, Radio and Television Cultures Research Institute, Japan Broadcasting Corporation, Tokyo, Japan.
— (1975c), Review of *Gesture, Race and Culture* by David Efron, *Linguistics* 163: 70–77.
— (1977a), *Nonverbal Communication: A Research Guide and Bibliography*. Metuchen, New Jersey, Scarecrow Press.
— (1977b), Commentary on 'Spatial structurings in everyday face-to-face behavior' by Robert D. Deutsch, 53–55. Association for the Study of Man-Environment Relations, Orangeburg, New York.
— (1978), Brief notice of *Speech Surrogates* by Thomas A. Sebeok and D. J. Umiker-Sebeok, *Language* 54(1): 252–253.
— (in press), 'Development of paralinguistic and kinesic expression of roles', *Proceedings of Conference on Language, Children, and Society*. Ohio State University, Pergamon Press.
Key, Mary Ritchie. *See* Kendon, Adam.
Kimura, D. (1976), 'The neural basis of language *qua* gesture', in *Studies in Neurolinguistics*, Vol. II, ed. by H. A. Whitaker and H. Whitaker. New York, Academic Press.
Kingdon, Roger (1958), *The Groundwork of English Intonation*. London, Longman.
Kirk, Lorraine and Michael Burton (1977), 'Maternal kinesic behavior and cognitive development in the child', *Annals of the New York Academy of Sciences*, Vol. 285 (March 18): 389–407.
Kleitmann, Nathaniel (1963), *Sleep and Wakefulness*. Chicago, University of Chicago Press.
Koch, G. (1977), 'Die Eipo. Anatomie einer Steinzeitkultur', *Bild der Wissenschaft* 9: 44–59.
Kock, M. A. de (1912), 'Eenige ethnologische en anthropologische gegevens omtrent een dwergstam in het bergland van Zuid Nieuw Guinea', *Tijdschrift van het Koninklijk Nederlandsch Aardrijkskundig Genootschap* 29: 387–400.
Kortland, A. (1940), 'Eine Uebersicht über die angeborenen Verhaltensweisen des mitteleuropäischen Kormorans', *Arch. neerl. Zool.* 4: 401–442.
Korzybski, Alfred (1966), *Time-Binding: The General Theory*, 2nd ed. Lancaster, Pa., International Non-Aristotelian Library.
Koslowski, B. *See* Brazelton, T. B.
Krippner, Stanley (1970), 'Psychedelic experience and the language processes',

in *Communication: General Semantics Perspectives*, ed. by Lee Thayer, 95–115. New York, Spartan Books.

Kruskal, W. H. *See* Goodman, L. A.

Kuschel, Rolf (1973), 'The silent inventor: the creation of a sign language by the only deaf mute on a Polynesian island', *Sign Language Studies* 3: 1–27.

Labov, William (1972), *Sociolinguistic Patterns*. Philadelphia, University of Pennsylvania Press.

Laing, R. D. (1969), *Self and Others*, 2nd revised ed. New York, Pantheon Books.

Lakoff, George (1972), 'Hedges: a study in meaning criteria and the logic of fuzzy concepts', *Papers from the Eighth Regional Meeting of the Chicago Linguistic Society*, 183–228. Chicago, Linguistics Department, University of Chicago.

Lakoff, Robin (1973), 'Questionable answers and answerable questions', in *Papers in Honor of Henry and Renée Kahane*, ed. by Braj B. Kachru et al., 453–467. Urbana, University of Illinois Press.

Langer, Susanne K. (1971), 'The great shift: instinct to intuition', in *Man and Beast: Comparative Social Behavior*, ed. by J. F. Eisenberg and Wilton S. Dillon, 315–322. Washington, D.C., Smithsonian Institution Press.

Lashley, Karl S. (1951 [1967, 1960, 1961]), 'The problem of serial order in behavior', in *Cerebral Mechanisms in Behavior*, ed. by Lloyd A. Jeffress, 112–136. New York, Wiley. Reprinted, New York, Hafner: 112–146; also in Frank A. Beach, Donald O. Hebb, and Clifford T. Morgan, *The Neuropsychology of Lashley*, 506–528. New York, McGraw-Hill; and Sol Saporta, ed., *Psycholinguistics*, 180–198. New York, Holt, Rinehart and Winston.

Latz, E. *See* Stechler, G.

Lausberg, J. (1960), *Handbuch der Literarischen Rhetorik* I–II. Munich, Max Hueber.

Laver, John (1975), 'Communicative functions of phatic communion', in *Organization of Behavior in Face-to-Face Interaction*, ed. by A. Kendon, R. M. Harris and M. R. Key, 215–238. The Hague, Mouton.

— (1976), 'Language and nonverbal communication', in *Handbook of Perception*, Vol. 7, ed. by E. C. Carterette and M. P. Friedman, 345–361. New York, Academic Press.

Laver, John and Sandy Hutcheson, eds. (1972), *Communication in Face-to-Face Interaction*. Harmondsworth, Middlesex, Penguin.

Lawrence, D. H. (1949), 'Acquired distinctiveness of cues: I. transfer between discriminations on the basis of familiarity with the stimulus', *Journal of Experimental Psychology* 39: 770–784.

— (1950), 'Acquired distinctiveness of cues: II. selective associations in a constant stimulus situation', *Journal of Experimental Psychology* 40: 175–188.

Leech, Geoffrey (1969), *Towards a Semantic Description of English*. Bloomington, Indiana University Press.

— (1974), *Semantics*. Harmondsworth, Middlesex, Penguin.

Lees, Robert B. (1953), 'The basis of glottochronology', *Language* 29: 113–127.

— (1960), 'The grammar of English nominalizations', *International Journal of American Linguistics* 26(3): 1–205.

Lehiste, Ilse (1970), *Suprasegmentals*. Cambridge, Mass., MIT Press.

— (1977), 'Isochrony reconsidered', *Journal of Phonetics* 5: 253–263.

Lenneberg, Eric H. (1967), *Biological Foundations of Language*. New York, John Wiley and Sons.

Léon, P. (1971), 'Etudes de phonostylistique', *Studia Phonetica* 4. Montréal, Dider.

Levin, Samuel R. (1962), *Linguistic Structure in Poetry*. The Hague, Mouton.

— (1964), 'Poetry and grammaticalness', *Proceedings of the Ninth International Congress of Linguists*, 308–314. The Hague, Mouton.

— (1965), 'Statistische und determinierte Abweichungen in poetischer Sprache', in *Mathematik und Dichtung*, ed. by H. Kreutzer and R. Gunzenhäuser. Munich, Nymphenburger.

Lévi-Strauss, Claude (1944–1957 [1963]), *Structural Anthropology*. New York, Basic Books.

— (1966), *The Savage Mind*. Paris. Reprinted, University of Chicago Press.

Lewis, Michael and Leonard A. Rosenblum, eds. (1977), *Interaction, Conversation, and the Development of Language*. New York, Wiley.

Lilly, John C. (1972a), *Programming and Metaprogramming in the Human Biocomputer*. New York, Julian Press.

— (1972b), *The Center of the Cyclone*. New York, Julian Press.

List, George (1963), 'The boundaries of speech and song', *Ethnomusicology* 7(1): 1–16.

Lomax, Alan (1977), 'Appeal for cultural equity', *Journal of Communication*, Spring.

Lorenz, Konrad (1973), Quoted in *Newsweek* (August 6): 58.

Lotz, J. (1966), 'Plan and publication of Noreen's *Vårt Språk*', in *Portraits of Linguists*, Vol. 2, ed. by T. A. Sebeok. Bloomington, Indiana University Press. Originally published in *Studia Linguistica* 8: 82–91.

Louis, P. (1945), *La Métaphore de Platon*. Paris.

Luce, Gay Gaer (1971), *Body Time: Physiological Rhythms and Social Stress*. New York, Pantheon Books.

Lucy, P. *See* Clark, H. H.

Luhmann, N. (1972), 'Einfache Sozialsysteme', *Zeitschrift für Soziologie* 1: 51–65.

Lyall, Archibald (1956), 'The Italian sign language', *Twentieth Century* 159: 600–604.

McCawley, James D. (1970), Review of Jespersen (1937), *Language* 46(2): 442–449.

McCormack, William C. and Stephen A. Wurm, eds. (1976), *Language and Man. Anthropological Issues*. The Hague, Mouton.

McDermott, John (1967), 'Thoughts on the movement: who does the movement move?', *Viet-Report* (September-October).

Maclay, Howard (1971), Overview for Part II, 'Linguistics', in *Semantics: an Interdisciplinary Reader in Philosophy, Linguistics and Psychology,* ed. by

D. D. Steinberg and L. A. Jakobovits, 157-182. Cambridge, Cambridge University Press.

Maclay, Howard and Charles E. Osgood (1959), 'Hesitation phenomena in spontaneous English speech', *Word* 15(1): 19-44.

McLuhan, Marshall (1962), *The Gutenberg Galaxy*. University of Toronto Press.

— (1964), *Understanding Media: The Extensions of Man*. New York, New American Library.

McNeill, David (1966), 'Developmental psycholinguistics', in *The Genesis of Language*, ed. by Frank Smith and George A. Miller, 15-84. Cambridge, Mass., MIT Press.

— (1977), 'On the origin of language'. Paper presented at the Werner Riemer Stiftung Conference on Human Ethology, Bad Homburg.

McQuown, Norman A., Gregory Bateson, Ray L. Birdwhistell, Henry W. Brosin and Charles F. Hockett, eds. (1971), *The Natural History of an Interview*, microfilm Collection of Manuscripts on Cultural Anthropology, 15. Chicago, The University of Chicago, Dept. of Photoduplication.

McRoberts, R. *See* Rosenfeld, Howard M.

Maine, M. *See* Brazelton, T. Berry.

Malinowski, B. (1923 [1956]), 'The problem of meaning in primitive languages', suppl. I. of C. K. Ogden and I. A. Richards, *The Meaning of Meaning*, 296-326. London, Routledge.

Mandino, Og. *See* Dewey, Edward R.

Marslen-Wilson, William (1973), 'Linguistic structure and speech shadowing at very short latencies', *Nature* 244(5417): 522-523.

Marshall, John C. (1970a), 'The biology of communication in man and animals', in *New Horizons in Linguistics*, ed. by John Lyons, 229-241. Harmondsworth, Middlesex, Penguin.

— (1970b), 'Can humans talk?', in *Biological and Social Factors in Psycholinguistics*, ed. by John Morton, 2-52. Urbana, III., University of Illinois Press.

Marshall, Lorna (1961 [1968]), 'Sharing, talking, and giving: relief of social tensions among !Kung bushmen', *Africa* 31: 231-249. Reprinted in *Readings in the Sociology of Language*, ed. by Joshua A. Fishman, 179-184. The Hague, Mouton.

Martin, James G. (1972), 'Rhythmic (hierarchical) versus serial structure in speech and other behavior', *Psychological Review* 79(6): 487-509.

Martinet, André (1955), *Économie des Changements Phonétiques*. Bern, A. Francke.

Martirena, Ana María (1976), 'A study of interaction markers in conversational Spanish', in *Language and Man. Anthropological Issues*, ed. by William C. McCormack and Stephen A. Wurm, 269-286. The Hague, Mouton.

Masland, Richard L. (1972), 'Some neurological processes underlying language', in *Perspectives on Human Evolution*, No. 2, ed. by S. L. Washburn and Phyllis Dolhinow, 421-437. Berkeley, University of California Press.

Mathiot, Madeleine (1979), 'Toward a frame of reference for the analysis of face-to-face interaction', *Semiotica* 24(3/4): 199–220. (Special issue Face-to-Face Interaction, ed. by M. Mathiot.)

Mauron, Charles (1950), *Introduction à la Psychanalyse de Mallarmé*. Neuchâtel, La Baconnière.

Mauss, M. (1950), *Essai sur le Don*. Paris, Presses Universitaires de France.

May, W. H. *See* Osgood, Charles E.

Mead, George H. (1934), *Mind, Self and Society*. Chicago, University of Chicago Press.

Mehrabian, Albert (1972), *Nonverbal Communication*. Chicago, Aldine and Atherton.

Mehrabian, Albert. *See* Wiener, Morton.

Mervis, C. B. *See* Rosch, E.

Metzler, S. and R. Shepard (1974), 'Transformational studies of the internal representation of three-dimensional objects', in *Theories in Cognitive Psychology*, ed. by R. Soho. New York, Lawrence Erlbaum Associates.

Michel, Paul (1973), 'The optimum development of musical abilities in the first years of life', *Psychology of Music* 1 (June): 14–20.

Miles, Walter R. (1931), 'Movement interpretation of the silhouette of a revolving fan', *American Journal of Psychology* 43: 392–405.

Miller, George A. and Philip N. Johnson-Laird (1976), *Language and Perception*, 558–582. Cambridge, Harvard University Press.

Miller, George A. *See* Smith, Frank.

Miller, Wick. *See* Ervin-Tripp, Susan.

Minkowski, Eugène (1970), *Lived Time*. Evanston, Ill., Northwestern University Press.

Miron, M. S. *See* Osgood, Charles E.

Moeser, Shannon D. and Albert S. Bregman (1972), 'The role of reference in the acquisition of a miniature artificial language', *Journal of Verbal Learning and Verbal Behavior* 11: 759–769.

Moeser, Shannon D. and A. Joyce Olson (1974), 'The role of reference in children's acquisition of a miniature artificial language', *Journal of Experimental Child Psychology* 17: 204–218.

Møller, A. (1958), 'Intra-aural muscle contraction in man, examined by measuring acoustic impedance of the ear', *Laryngoscope* 68: 48–62.

Monod, Jacques (1971), *Chance and Necessity: an Essay on the Natural Philosophy of Modern Biology,* transl. from the French by Austryn Wainhouse. New York, Alfred A. Knopf.

Montagner, H. et al. (1973), 'Les activités ludiques du jeune enfant. Jeu ou ontogenèse?', *Vers l'Éducation Nouvelle*, Bordeaux: 1–32.

Moore, K. *See* Bower, T. G. R.

Morgan, Jerry L. (1975), 'Some interactions of syntax and pragmatics', in *Syntax and Semantics*, Vol. 3, ed. by Peter Cole and J. L. Morgan. New York, Academic Press.

Morton, John, ed. (1970), *Biological and Social Factors in Psycholinguistics*. Urbana, Ill., University of Illinois Press.

Mosher, Joseph A. (1916), *The Essentials of Effective Gesture*. New York, Macmillan.

Mumford, Lewis (1934), *Technics and Civilization*. New York, Harcourt, Brace and World.

— (1952), *Art and Technics*. New York, Columbia University Press.

Nagel, E. (1961), *The Structure of Science*. New York, Harcourt, Brace, Jovanovich.

Nathanson, Susan N. *See* Stark, Rachel E.

Niederehe, George. *See* Duncan, Starkey D., Jr.

Nilsson, Martin P. (1920), *Primitive Time-Reckoning*. Lund, CWK Gleerup.

Noyes, Pierre (1974a), 'Human unity'. Stanford Linear Accelerator Center, Pub-1506.

— (1974b), 'A scientific retrodiction of our past'. Stanford Linear Accelerator Center, Pub-1380.

— (1975), 'The abandonment of simultaneity', *Theoria to Theory* 9: 23–32.

Odbert, H. S. *See* Karwoski, Theodore F.

Ogston, William D. *See* Condon, William S.

Olson, A. Joyce. *See* Moeser, Shannon D.

Ono, Hiroshi. *See* Hastorf, Albert H.

Ono, Hiroshi, Albert H. Hastorf and Charles E. Osgood (1966), 'Binocular rivalry as a function of incongruity in meaning', *Scandinavian Journal of Psychology* 7(4): 225–233.

Opačić, G. (1973), 'Natural order in cognizing and clause order in the sentencing of conjoined expressions'. Unpublished Ph.D. dissertation, Urbana, University of Illinois.

Ornstein, Robert E. (1972), *The Psychology of Consciousness*. San Francisco, W. H. Freeman.

Osgood, Charles E. (1953), *Method and Theory in Experimental Psychology*. New York, Oxford University Press.

— (1960), 'The cross-cultural generality of visual–verbal synesthetic tendencies', *Behavioral Science* 5: 146–169.

— (1966), 'Dimensionality of the semantic space for communication via facial expressions', *Scandinavian Journal of Psychology* 7(1): 1–30.

— (1971), 'Where do sentences come from?', in *Semantics: An Interdisciplinary Reader in Philosophy, Linguistics and Psychology*, ed. by Danny D. Steinberg and Leon A. Jakobovits, 497–529. London, Cambridge University Press.

— (i.p.), 'What is a language?', in *Psycholinguistic Research: Past, Present and Future*, ed. by D. Aaronson and R. Rieber. Hillsdale, New Jersey, Erlbaum.

— (in preparation), *Toward an Abstract Performance Grammar: A Neobehavioral Theory of Cognizing and Sentencing*.

Osgood, Charles E. *See* Hastorf, Albert H., T. F. Karwoski, Howard Maclay, and Hiroshi Ono.

Osgood, Charles E. and Rumjahn Hoosain (1974), 'Salience of the word as a unit in the perception of language', *Perception and Psychophysics* 15: 168–192.

Osgood, Charles E., W. H. May and M. S. Miron (1975), *Cross-cultural Universals of Affective Meaning*. Urbana, Illinois, University of Illinois Press.

Osgood, Charles E., George J. Suci and P. H. Tannenbaum (1957), *The Measurement of Meaning*. Urbana, Illinois, University of Illinois Press.

Osgood, Charles E. and C. Tanz (1977), 'Will the real direct object in bitransitive sentences please stand up?', in *Linguistic Studies in Honor of Joseph Greenberg*, ed. by A. Juilland. Saratoga, California, Anima Libri.

Oshiro, Marian M. (1976), 'Eye contact: an annotated bibliography', *Man-Environment Systems* 6(4): 187–200.

Ostrow, Ronald J. (1977), 'Leaks and retaliation', *Los Angeles Times* (November 7): 1.

Ostwald, Peter (1972), 'The sounds of infancy', *Developmental Medicine and Child Neurology* 14: 350–361.

Ott, Edward Amherst (1892), *How to Gesture*. New York, Hinds, Noble and Eldridge.

Ott, John N. (1973), *Health and Light; the Effects of Natural and Artificial Light on Man and Other Living Things*. Old Greenwich, Conn., Devin-Adair.

Ounsted, Christopher and David C. Taylor (1972), *Gender Differences: Their Ontogeny and Significance*. London, Churchill Livingstone.

Pacoe, Larry V. *See* Condon, William S.

Padgug, E. J. *See* Blount, Ben G.

Palmer, John D. (1976), *An Introduction to Biological Rhythms*. New York, Academic Press.

Papousek, Hanus (1976), 'Food and psychological development', reprinted from *Food, Man and Society* by Dwain N. Walcher, Norman Kretchmer and Henry L. Barnett, 244–254. New York, Plenum.

Pear, Tom Hatherley (1931). *Voice and Personality*. London, Chapman and Hall.

Penfield, Wilder (1958), *The Excitable Cortex in Conscious Man*. The Sherrington Lectures. Liverpool, Liverpool University Press.

— (1966), 'Speech, perception and the uncommitted cortex', in *Brain and Conscious Experience*, ed. by John C. Eccles, 229–235. New York, Springer.

Penfield, Wilder and Th. Rasmussen (1950), *The Cerebral Cortex of Man*. New York, Macmillan.

Penfield, Wilder, and Lamar Roberts (1959), *Speech and Brain-Mechanisms*. Princeton, N.J., Princeton University Press.

Penrose, L. S. (1959), 'Self-reproducing machines', *Scientific American* (June) (reprint no. 74).

Perlmutter, David M. (1971), *Deep and Surface Structure Constraints in Syntax*. New York, Holt, Rinehart and Winston.

Petchenik, Barbara Bartz. *See* Robinson, Arthur H.

Piaget, Jean (1955), *The Language and Thought of the Child*. Cleveland, Meridian.

Pike, Kenneth L. (1945), *The Intonation of American English*. Ann Arbor, Mich., University of Michigan Press.

— (1954–1960 [1967]), *Language: in Relation to a Unified Theory of the Structure of Human Behavior*, 2nd revised ed. The Hague, Mouton.

— (1966), 'Etic and emic standpoints for the description of behavior', in

Communication and Culture: Readings in the Codes of Human Interaction,
ed. by Alfred G. Smith, 152–163. New York, Holt, Rinehart and Winston.

Pilbeam, D. (1972), *The Ascent of Man*. New York, Macmillan.

Pillot, J. (1550), Gallicae linguae instituo. Paris.

Pinchon, J. *See* Wagner, R. L.

Pitcairn, T. K. and Irenäus Eibl-Eibesfeldt (1976), 'Concerning the evolution of
nonverbal communication in man', in *Communicative Behavior and
Evolution*, ed. by M. E. Hahn and E. C. Simmel, 81–113. New York,
Academic Press.

Pittenger, Robert E. and Henry Lee Smith, Jr. (1957), 'A basis for some contributions of linguistics to psychiatry', *Psychiatry* 20(1): 61–78.

Postal, Paul M. (1970 [1971]), 'On the surface verb "remind"', *Linguistic
Inquiry* 1(1): 37–120. Reprinted in *Studies in Linguistic Semantics*, ed. by C.
J. Fillmore and D. T. Langendoen. New York, Holt, Rinehart and Winston.

Potter, M. C. (1975), 'Meaning in visual search', *Science* 187: 965–966.

Potter, M. C. and B. A. Faulconer (1975), 'Time to understand pictures and
words', *Nature* 253: 437–438.

Potter, M. C., V. V. Valian and B. A. Faulconer (1977), 'Representation of a
sentence and its pragmatic implications: verbal, imagistic, or abstract',
Journal of Verbal Learning and Verbal Behavior 16: 1–12.

Powers, William T. (1973), *Behavior: The Control of Perception*. Chicago,
Aldine.

Poyatos, Fernando (1972), 'The communication system of the speaker–actor and
his culture: a preliminary investigation', *Linguistics* 83 (May): 64–86.

Preziosi, Donald (1976), 'The non-dichotomy of sensory and grammatical
relationships', in *The Second LACUS Forum 1975*, 627–636. Columbia,
South Carolina, Hornbeam Press.

— (1977), 'Toward a relational theory of culture', in *The Third LACUS
Forum 1976*, 278–286. Columbia, South Carolina, Hornbeam Press.

— (1978), 'Language and perception', in *The Fourth LACUS Forum 1977*,
51–60. Columbia, South Carolina, Hornbeam Press.

— (1979a), 'Hierarchies of signs in nonverbal semiosis', in *The Fifth LACUS
Forum 1978*. Columbia, South Carolina, Hornbeam Press.

— (1979b), *Architecture, Language and Meaning*. The Hague, Mouton.

— (1979c), *The Semiotics of the Built Environment*. Bloomington, Indiana,
Indiana University Press.

Pride, J. B. and J. Holmes, eds. (1972), *Sociolinguistics*. Harmondsworth,
Middlesex, Penguin.

Quine, W. (1952 [1962]), *Methods of Logic*. London, Routledge and Kegan
Paul.

Reichstein, R. (1960), 'Etudes des variations sociales et géographiques des faits
linguistiques', *Word* 16: 55–59.

Reitz, H. (1937), *Impressionistische und Expressionistische Stilmittel bei
Rimbaud*. Munich.

Rhead, John. *See* Fischer, Roland.

Richter, E. (n.d.), 'Das psychische Geschehen und die Artikulation'. *Archives de Phonétique Expérimentale* 13.

Rips, L. J. *See* Smith, E. E.

Robbins, Owen, Shannon Devoe and Morton Wiener (1976), 'The regulation of speakers in a communication exchange by middle-class and working-class subjects'. Manuscript.

Robert, F. (1977), 'Analyse spectrographique des voyelles du français moderne'. Unpublished Ph.D. thesis, University of Paris III.

Roberts, Lamar. *See* Penfield, Wilder.

Robinson, Arthur H. and Barbara Bartz Petchenik (1976), *The Nature of Maps: Essays Toward Understanding Maps and Mapping*. University of Chicago Press.

Robinson, W. P. (1972), *Language and Social Behavior*. Harmondsworth, Middlesex, Penguin.

Rogers, Sinclair, ed. (1975), *Children and Language: Readings in Early Language and Socialization*. London, Oxford University Press.

Róheim, Géza (1955), *Magic and Schizophrenia*. New York.

Rosch, E., C. B. Mervis, W. Gray, D. Johnson and P. Boyes-Braem (1976), 'Basic objects in natural categories', *Cognitive Psychology* 8: 382–439.

Rosenberg, Bruce (1970), *The Art of the American Folk Preacher*. New York, Oxford University Press.

Rosenberg, S. and H. Simon (1977), 'Modeling semantic memory: effects of presenting semantic information in different modalities', *Cognitive Psychology* 9: 293–325.

Rosenblum, Leonard A. *See* Lewis, Michael.

Rosenfeld, Howard M. (1965), 'Effect of an approval-seeking induction in interpersonal proximity', *Psychological Reports* 17: 120–122.

— (1966), 'Instrumental affiliative functions of facial and gestural expressions', *Journal of Personality and Social Psychology* 4(1): 65–72.

— (1978), 'Conversational control functions of nonverbal behavior', *Nonverbal Behavior and Communication*, ed. by A. Siegman and S. Feldstein, 291–328. Hillsdale, N. J., Lawrence Erlbaum Associates.

Rosenfeld, Howard M. and R. McRoberts (1977), 'Effects of topographical features and nonverbal context on ratings of teacher head nods'. Unpublished manuscript, University of Kansas.

Ross, John R. (1966 [1969]), 'A proposed rule of tree-pruning', in Report NSF-17, Harvard Computation Laboratory, Section IV. Reprinted in *Modern Studies in English*, ed. by D. A. Reibel and S. A. Schane, 288–299. Englewood Cliffs, N.J., Prentice-Hall.

— (1967), 'Constraints on variables in syntax'. Unpublished Ph.D. dissertation, M.I.T.

Rossi-Landi, Ferruccio (1975), *Linguistics and Economics*. The Hague, Mouton.

Rubano, Maureen V. (1974), 'The assessment of linguistic complexity in terms of discrimination of relations'. Unpublished M.A. Thesis, Clark University.

Rubinow, Stuart (1974), 'Conceptual criteria for encoded communications applied to two-hand gestures'. Unpublished Ph.D. dissertation, Clark University.

Rubinow, Stuart. *See* Wiener, Morton.

Russell, Bertrand (1915), 'On the experience of time', *The Monist* 25: 212–233.

Russett, Cynthia Eagle (1966 [1968]), *The Concept of Equilibrium in American Social Thought.* New Haven, Yale University Press.

Ryan, J. (1974), 'Early language development: towards a communicational analysis', in *Integration of the Child into a Social World*, ed. by P. M. Richards. Cambridge University Press.

Sacks, Harvey (1975), 'Everyone has to lie', in *Sociocultural Dimensions of Language Use*, ed. by Mary Sanches and Ben G. Blount, 57–79. New York, Academic Press.

Sacks, Harvey. *See* Schegloff, Emanuel A.

Sacks, Harvey, Emanuel A. Schegloff and Gail Jefferson (1974), 'A simplest systematics for the organization of turn-taking for conversation', *Language* 50: 696–735.

Sadock, Jerrold M. *See* Zwicky, Arnold M.

Sanches, Mary and Ben G. Blount, eds. (1975), *Sociocultural Dimensions of Language Use*. New York, Academic Press.

Sander, Louis W. *See* Condon, William S.

Sankoff, G. (1974), 'A quantitative paradigm for the study of communicative competence', in *Explorations in the Ethnography of Speaking*, ed. by R. Bauman and J. Sherzer, 18–49. London, Cambridge University Press.

Sapir, Edward (1929), 'The status of linguistics as a science', *Language* 5: 207–214.

Saussure, Ferdinand de (1915 [1976]), *Cours de Linguistique Générale*, édition critique, ed. by T. de Mauro. Paris, Payot.

Schatzman, Leonard and Anselm Strauss (1955), 'Social class and modes of communication', *American Journal of Sociology* 60: 329–338.

Scheflen, Albert E. (1964 [1972]), 'The significance of posture in communication systems', *Psychiatry* 27(4): 316–331. Reprinted in *Communication in Face-to-face Interaction*, ed. by John Laver and Sandy Hutcheson, 225–246. Harmondsworth, Middlesex, Penguin.

— (1965 [1973]), *Stream and Structure of Communicational Behavior: Context Analysis of a Psychotherapy Session*. Behavioral Studies Monograph # 1, Eastern Pennsylvania Psychiatric Institute. Reprinted as *Communicational Structure: Analysis of a Psychotherapy Transaction*. Bloomington, Ind., Indiana University Press.

— (1966), 'Systems and psychosomatics: an introduction to psychosomatic manifestations of rapport in psychotherapy', *Psychosomatic Medicine* 28(4), (Part I): 297–304.

— (1973), *How Behavior Means*. New York, Gordon and Breach, Science Publishers Inc.

Scheflen, Albert E. *See* Ashcraft, Norman.

Schegloff, Emanuel A., (1968 [1972]), 'Sequencing in conversational openings', *American Anthropologist* 70(6): 1075–1095. Reprinted in *Directions in Sociolinguistics*, ed. by John J. Gumperz and Dell Hymes, 346–380. New York, Holt, Rinehart and Winston.

Schegloff, Emanuel A. *See* Sacks, Harvey.
Schegloff, Emanuel and Harvey Sacks (1973), 'Opening up closings', *Semiotica* 8: 289-327.
Schiefenhövel, Wulf (1976), 'Die Eipo-Leute des Berglands von Indonesisch-Neu-Guinea', *Homo* 26: 263-275.
Searles, H. F. (1965), *Collected papers on Schizophrenia and Related Subjects.* London, Hogarth Press.
Sebeok, Thomas A. (1976), *Contributions to the Doctrine of Signs.* Lisse, Peter de Ridder Press.
Sebeok, Thomas A. *See* Umiker-Sebeok, D. Jean.
Sechehaye, M. A. (1969), *Journal d'une Schizophrène.* Genève.
Sharpe, Ella Freeman (1940), 'Psycho-physical problems revealed in language: an examination of metaphor', *International Journal of Psychoanalysis* 21: 201-213.
Shatz, Marilyn. *See* Gelman, Rachel.
Shatz, Marilyn and Rachel Gelman (1973), 'The development of communication skills: modifications in the speech of young children as a function of listener', *Monographs of the Society of Research in Child Development* 38, serial no. 152: 1-37.
— (1977), 'Beyond syntax: the influence of conversational constraints on speech modifications', in *Talking to Children. Language Input and Acquisition*, ed. by Catherine E. Snow and Charles A. Ferguson, 189-198. London, Cambridge University Press.
Sheinkopf, Sylvia (1970), 'A comparative study of the affective judgments made by anomic aphasics and normals on a nonverbal task'. Unpublished Ph.D. dissertation, Boston University.
Shepard R. *See* Metzler, S.
Sherrington, Charles S. (1951), *Man on His Nature.* Cambridge, Cambridge University Press.
Shibles, W. A. (1971), *Metaphor. An annoted bibliography.* Whitewater, Wisc., The Language Press.
Shilkret, Robert B. *See* Wiener, Morton.
Shilkret, Robert B., Lynnwood Andrews and Morton Wiener (1976), 'Adults speak to children: adult modification of speech to children as a function of experience with them', in Final Report to the National Institute of Education for Grant Project No. 4-470, 'Complexity in Auditory and Graphic Language', co-principal investigators Morton Wiener and Robert Shilkret, Clark University.
Shilkret, Robert B., Marian Viets and Morton Wiener (1977), 'Effects of redundancy and intonational stress in facilitating children's comprehension of temporally ordered events', in Final Report to the National Institute of Education for Grant Project No. 4-470, 'Complexity in Auditory and Graphic Language', co-principal investigators Morton Wiener and Robert Shilkret, Clark University.
Shilkret, Robert B. and Morton Wiener (1972), 'The contribution of syntactic and parasyntactic cues in the comprehension of spoken and written language'.

U.S. Office of Education Research Grant, Final Report, February.

Shoben, E. J. *See* Smith, E. E.

Simon, H. *See* Rosenberg, S.

Simon, P. *See* Fónagy, Ivan.

Singer, Jerome L. (1966), *Daydreaming*. New York, Random House.

Smith, E. E., E. J. Shoben and L. J. Rips (1974), 'Structure and process in semantic memory: a feature model for semantic decisions', *Psychological Review* 81: 214-241.

Smith, Frank and George A. Miller (1966), *The Genesis of Language*. Cambridge, Mass., MIT Press. Introductory remarks include comments by Chomsky, 1-13.

Smith, Henry Lee, Jr. *See* Pittenger, Robert E.

Spitzer, Leo (1926), *Stilstudien* I-II. Munich, Max Hueber.

Stanjek, Klaus (1978), 'Das Ueberreichen von Gaben: Funktion und Entwicklung in den ersten Lebensjahren', *Zeitschrift für Entw. Psych. und Pädag. Psych.* 2.

Stark, Rachel E. and Susan N. Nathanson (1974), 'Spontaneous cry in the newborn infant; sounds and facial gestures', in *Fourth Symposium on Oral Sensation and Perception: Development in the Fetus and Infant*, ed. by J. F. Bosma, 323-352. Bethesda, Maryland, U.S. Government Printing Press.

Stechler, G. and E. Latz (1966), 'Some observations on attention and arousal in the human infant', *Journal of the Academy of Child Psychiatry* 5: 517-527.

Steingart, I. *See* Blass, Thomas.

Stewart, Ann Harleman (1976), *Graphic Representation of Models in Linguistic Theory*. Bloomington, Indiana, Indiana University Press.

Stokoe, William C. (1960), 'Sign language structure: an outline of the visual communication systems of the American deaf', *Studies in Linguistics*, Occasional Papers, no. 8.

— (1972), *Semiotics and Human Sign Languages*. The Hague, Mouton.

Strauss, Anselm. *See* Schatzman, Leonard.

Strauss, Leo (1952), *Persecution and the Art of Writing*. Glencoe, Illinois, Free Press.

Sturtevant, Edgar H. (1917), *Linguistic Change*. Chicago, University of Chicago Press.

— (1947), *An Introduction to Linguistic Science*. New Haven, Yale University Press.

Suci, George J. *See* Osgood, Charles E.

Sudnow, David (1972), 'Temporal parameters of interpersonal observation', in *Studies in Social Interaction*, ed. by D. Sudnow, 259-279. New York, Free Press.

Szent-Györgyi, Albert (1972), 'Dionysians and Apollonians', *Science* 176 (June 2): 966.

Tanizaki, Junichiro (1961), *The Key*. New York, Alfred A. Knopf.

Tannenbaum, P. H. *See* Osgood, Charles E.

Tanz, C. *See* Osgood, Charles E.

Taylor, David C. *See* Ounsted, Christopher.

Thom, René (1975), *Structural Stability and Morphogenesis: An Outline of a*

General Theory of Models, trans. by D. H. Fowler. Reading, Mass., W. A. Benjamin.

Thom, René and E. C. Zeeman (1975), 'Catastrophe theory: its present state and future perspectives', in *Dynamical Systems—Warwick 1974: Proceedings,* ed. by Anthony Manning, 366-401. New York, Springer.

Thorne, Barrie and Nancy Henley (1975), *Language and Sex.* Rowley, Mass., Newbury House.

Thurot, Ch. (1881-1883), *De la Prononciation française* I-II. Paris.

Tiger, Lionel (1969), *Men in Groups.* London, Thomas Nelson.

Tinbergen, N. (1940'7, 'Die Uebersprungbewegung', *Zeitschrift für Tierpsychologie* 4: 1-40.

Titon, Jeff Todd (1975), 'Tonal system in the chanted oral sermons of the Rev. C. L. Franklin'. Paper read at the Society for Ethnomusicology, Wesleyan University.

— (1976a), *'Dry Bones in the Valley* from a musical perspective: intonation pattern as a constraint upon diction and syntax in the chanted portions of Reverend C. L. Franklin's extemporaneous sermons'. Paper read at the American Folklore Society, Philadelphia, Pennsylvania.

— (1976b), 'Son House: two narratives' [with plastic soundsheet], *Alcheringa: Ethnopoetics* 2(1): 2-26.

— (1977), 'Talking about music: analysis, synthesis, and song-producing models', *Essays in Arts and Sciences* 6(1): 53-57.

Tolman, E. C. (1938), 'Determiners of behavior at a choice-point', *Psychological Review* 45: 1-41.

— (1948), 'Cognitive maps in rats and men', *Psychological Review* 55: 189-208.

Tonkova-Yampol'skaya, R. V. (1973), 'Development of speech intonation in infants during the first two years of life', in *Studies of Child Language Development,* ed. by C. A. Ferguson and Dan I. Slobin, 128-138. New York, Holt, Rinehart and Winston.

Trevarthen, C. (1977), 'Descriptive analyses of infant communicative behavior', in *Studies in Mother–Infant Interaction,* ed. by H. R. Shaffer. London, Academic Press.

Trojan, F. (1952), *Der Ausdruck der Sprechstimme.* Vienna, Dusseldorf, Maudrich.

Tronick, Edward, Heidelise Als and Lauren Adamson (in press), 'The communicative structure of face-to-face interaction', in *Before Speech: The Beginnings of Human Communication,* ed. by M. Bullowa. Cambridge, Cambridge University Press.

Tronick, Edward, Heidelise Als, Lauren Adamson, Susan Wise and T. Berry Brazelton (1978), 'The infant's response to entrapment between contradictory messages in face-to-face interaction', *Journal of the American Academy of Child Psychiatry* 17(1): 1-13.

Tronick, Edward, Heidelise Als and T. Berry Brazelton (1977a), 'The monadic phase manual'. Unpublished manuscript.

— (1977b), 'Mutuality in mother–infant interaction', *Journal of Communication* (Spring): 74-79.

— (in press), 'Monadic phases: a structural descriptive analysis of infant–mother face-to-face interaction', *Merril Palmer Quarterly*.

Tronick, Edward and T. Berry Brazelton (in press), 'The joint regulation of infant–adult interaction', *Cybernetic Forum*.

Tronick, Edward. *See* Brazelton, T. Berry, S. Dixon and M. Yogman.

Turner, Ernest Sackville (1954), *A History of Courting*. England, Gresham Press.

Tversky, A. (1977), 'Features of similarity', *Psychological Review* 84: 327–352.

Uexküll, Jakob von (1934 [1957]), 'A stroll through the worlds of animals and men', in *Instinctive Behavior*, ed. by Claire H. Schiller, 5–80. Introduction by Karl S. Lashley. New York, International Universities Press.

Umiker-Sebeok, D. Jean (1976), 'The conversational skills of preschool children'. Unpublished Ph.D. dissertation, Indiana University, Bloomington.

— (1977), 'Signs of growing up: learning the art of conversation'. Paper read at the symposium on Semiotic Perspectives in Human Relations, Meeting of the Central States Anthropological Association, Cincinnati, March.

— (in press), 'Preschool children's intraconversational narratives', *Journal of Child Language* 5.

— (in preparation), 'Single and double adjacency pairs in preschool conversation'.

Umiker-Sebeok, D. Jean and Thomas A. Sebeok (1977), 'Aboriginal sign "languages" from a semiotic point of view', *Ars Semeiotica* 1(4): 69–97.

Valian, V. V. *See* Potter, M. C.

Varga, László (1975), *A Contrastive Analysis of English and Hungarian Sentence Prosody*. Budapest, Linguistics Institute of the Hungarian Academy of Sciences and Center for Applied Linguistics.

Viets, Marian. *See* Shilkret, Robert B.

Vine, Ian. *See* Cranach, Mario von.

Voegelin, C. F. and F. M., A. Y. and F. Y. Yamamoto (1977), 'Presuppositional culture spaces', *Anthropological Linguistics* 19(7): 320–353.

Voorhoeve, C. L. (1975), *Languages of Irian Jaya. Checklist, Preliminary Classification, Language Maps, Wordlists*. Pac. Ling. B 31, ANU, Canberra.

Voth, A. C. *See* Brown, J. F.

Wagner, R. L. and J. Pinchon (1962), *Grammaire du français*. Paris, Hachette.

Ward, Ritchie R. (1971), *The Living Clocks*. New York, Alfred A. Knopf.

Watson, O. Michael (1974a), 'Conflicts and directions in proxemic research', in *Nonverbal Communication*, ed. by Shirley Weitz, 230–241. Oxford University Press.

— (1974b), 'Proxemics', *Current Trends in Linguistics* 12: 311–344.

Watt, W. C. (1970), 'On two hypotheses concerning psycholinguistics' in *Cognition and the Development of Language*, ed. by J. R. Hayes. New York, Wiley.

Watzlawick, Paul, Janet H. Beaven and Don D. Jackson (1967), *Pragmatics of Human Communication*. New York, W. W. Norton.

Weber, Max (1956), *Wirtschaft und Gesellschaft. Grundriss der Verstehenden Soziologie*, 4th ed., ed. by J. Winckelmann. Tübingen, Mohr.

Weeks, M. E. (1968), *Discovery of the Elements,* 7th ed. rev. and expanded by Henry M. Leicester. Easton, Pa., *Journal of Chemical Education.*

Weinrich, Harald (1966), *Linguistik der Lüge.* Heidelberg, Lambert Schneider. Translated, 'Per una linguistica dalla menzogna', *Lingue e Stile* 1: 7-22.

Weir, Ruth H. (1966), 'Some questions on the child's learning of phonology', in *The Genesis of Language,* ed. by Frank Smith and George A. Miller, 153-168. Cambridge, Mass., MIT Press.

Weiss, E. (1922), 'Psychoanalyse eines Falles von nervösem Asthma', *Internationale Zeitschrift für Psychoanalyse* 8.

Weitz, Shirley, ed. (1974), *Nonverbal Communication.* Oxford University Press.

Werner, Heinz (1940), *Comparative Psychology of Mental Development,* Chapter 6, 'Primitive notions of time'. New York, Harper.

— (1953), *Einführung in die Entwicklungspsychologie.* Munich.

Werner, Heinz and Bernard Kaplan (1963), *Symbol Formation.* New York, John Wiley.

Weyl, Hermann (1952), *Symmetry.* Princeton, N.J., Princeton University Press.

White, M. N. *See* Carroll, J. B.

White, Sheila J. (1977), 'Are LASSes (language acquisition socialization systems) better than LADs (language acquisition services)?'. Paper presented at the New York Academy of Sciences, April.

Whitehead, Alfred North (1929), *Process and Reality.* New York, Humanities Press.

Whitney, W. D. (1867), *Language and the Study of Language.* New York, Scribner.

Wiener, Morton and Ward Cromer (1967), 'Reading and reading difficulties: a conceptual analysis', *Harvard Educational Review* 37: 620-643.

Wiener, Morton and Shannon Devoe (1977a), 'Channels and regulators in communication disruption'. Progress Report, NIMH Grant No. 25775.

— (1977b), 'Ontogenesis of nonverbal communication patterns'. Grant proposal.

Wiener, Morton, Shannon Devoe, Stuart Rubinow and Jesse Geller (1972), 'Nonverbal behavior and nonverbal communication', *Psychological Review* 79(3): 185-214.

Wiener, Morton and Albert Mehrabian (1968), *Language within Language.* New York, Appleton-Century-Crofts.

Wiener, Morton and Robert B. Shilkret (1977), 'Complexity in auditory and graphic language'. U.S. Department of Health, Education, and Welfare, National Institute of Education, Project 4-470, Final Report.

Wiener, Morton. *See* Brooks, Robert, Merry Ann Jancovic, Owen Robbins and Robert B. Shilkret.

Wiener, Norbert (1948 [1961]), *Cybernetics: Or Control and Communication in the Animal and the Machine.* Cambridge, Mass., MIT Press.

Wilson, Edward O. (1975), *Sociobiology: The New Synthesis.* Cambridge, Mass., Belknap Press of Harvard University Press.

Winter, Elaine P. *See* Baxter, James C.

Wise, Susan. *See* Brazelton, T. Berry and Edward Tronick.

Wittgenstein, Ludwig (1961), *Tractatus Logico-Philosophicus*. London, Routledge and Kegan Paul.

Wood, William B. and R. S. Edgar (1967), 'Building a bacterial virus', *Scientific American* (July) (reprint no. 1079).

Woodbridge, Frederick J. E. (1940), *An Essay on Nature*. New York, Collumbia University Press.

Wright, Lawrence (1968), *Clockwork Man*. New York, Horizon Press.

Wurm, S. A. *See* McCormack, W. C.

Yamamoto, A. Y. and F. Y. *See* Voegelin, C. F. and F. M.

Yau, S. C. (1977), 'Constraints on basic sign order and word order universals'. Unpublished manuscript, Centre National de la Recherche Scientifique, Paris.

Yngve, V. H. (1970), 'On getting a word in edgewise', in *Papers from the Sixth Regional Meeting, Chicago Linguistic Society*, ed. by M. A. Campbell et al., 567–578. Chicago, University of Chicago, Department of Linguistics.

Yogman, M., S. Dixon, Edward Tronick, L. Adamson, Heidelise Als and T. Berry Brazelton (1976), 'Development of infant social interaction with fathers'. Paper presented at Eastern Psychological Association Meeting, New York.

Yogman, M. *See* Dixon, S.

Young, John Zachary (1960), *Doubt and Certainty in Science: a Biologist's Reflections on the Brain*. Oxford, Oxford University Press.

— (1971), *An Introduction to the Study of Man*. Oxford, Clarendon Press.

Yule, G. U. (1900), 'On the association of attributes in statistics', *Philosophical Transactions, Series A,* 194: 257–319.

Zeeman, E. C. *See* Thom, René.

Zipf, George Kingsley (1935 [1968]), *The Psycho-Biology of Language*. Cambridge, Mass., MIT Press.

Zwicky, Arnold M. and Jerrold M. Sadock (1975), 'Ambiguity tests and how to fail them', in *Syntax and Semantics*, Vol. 4, 1–36. New York, Academic Press.

Index